12   Helbling, Robert
14

first-year GERMAN

Goslar

Wolfenbüttel

first-year GERMAN

ROBERT E. HELBLING

University of Utah

WOLF GEWEHR

Pädagogische Hochschule Münster

WOLFF A. VON SCHMIDT

University of Utah

HOLT, RINEHART AND WINSTON

New York   San Francisco   Toronto   London

Rothenburg

Illustration credits appear on page 504.

Library of Congress Cataloging in Publication Data

Helbling, Robert E.
  First-Year German.

  Includes index.
  1. German language—Grammar—1950–   I. Gewehr,
Wolf, joint author.   II. Von Schmidt, Wolff A., joint
author.   III. Title.
PF3112.H4   438'.2'421   74-26929
ISBN 0-03-012101-9

Foreign Language Department / 5643 Paradise Drive / Corte Madera, California 94925

Printed in the United States of America

5 6 7 8 9 0   032   9 8 7 6 5 4 3 2 1

Contents

Tiroler

Wien

Penzberg

Inntal

Hamburg

München

Introduction

Purpose

FIRST-YEAR GERMAN is the result of a comprehensive, nationwide survey conducted among instructors and professors of German in junior colleges, colleges, and universities, which clearly indicated that preferences lie with flexibility of approach rather than purity of method and an emphasis on the student rather than on the method. Thus, FIRST-YEAR GERMAN combines the oral and analytic approaches to language learning—not merely eclectically but coherently in a concern for pedagogic effectiveness—and simultaneously develops the four language skills—listening, speaking, reading, and writing.

The text contains twenty-two chapters, each of which follows a carefully planned development from seeing and hearing, through understanding of grammatical principles, to speaking, reading, and writing the language. This progression from correct speaking to correct writing enables the students to use the less complex forms and smaller vocabulary of the spoken language and better prepares them to read formal narratives and to express themselves in writing. The vocabulary development follows a similar progression: the vocabulary of the oral practice stays largely within the limits of the model sentences, the conversation, and that used in previous chapters; the reading passage enlarges the range and stimulates associative thinking.

The presentation of certain grammatical points, such as the use of the subjunctive and indirect discourse, illustrates the language in flux and is based on the latest surveys of actual usage available to us from the Pädagogische Hochschule in Münster, Westphalia.

Organization

Each chapter includes the following listening/speaking sections, in order.

Useful Phrases. Several everyday German phrases, with English equivalents, listed at the beginning of the chapter help initiate and facilitate simple exchanges in German between students and instructor, and among students.

Model Sentences. German sentences with English equivalents introduce new grammar through the use of boldface so that students can readily see and study the elements in context.

Grammar Explanations. No more than three grammar topics are presented within each chapter, and the grammatical and structural principles are explained straight-forwardly in English. The grammar explanations are presented prior to the exercise material since, without some intellectual grasp of the underlying grammatical prin-ciples of the target language, the linguistic code of the students' native language interferes too strongly to be expunged simply through repetition of pattern phrases. The explanation of each grammar topic is followed by a series of *Check Your Com-prehension* exercises, allowing students to test their understanding before proceeding to the next topic.

Conversation. Students see, hear, and read illustrations of the new grammar within the context of a natural German conversation. The topic of conversation centers on some aspect of contemporary daily life in one of the German-speaking countries— West and East Germany, Austria, or Switzerland. The English equivalent of the conversation is included in the appendix.

Oral Practice. A series of diverse exercises is based essentially on the vocabulary of the model sentences and conversation and the vocabulary presented in previous chapters. Each exercise concentrates on one particular structural or grammatical operation. Although these exercises are intended for oral practice, they may also be done in writing.

Guided Conversation. Topics for conversation are suggested to enable students to personalize and utilize familiar vocabulary and structures through natural, spon-taneous conversation. The topics are either similar or peripheral to the conversation, or they encourage the use of the chapter vocabulary and grammar. Sometimes additional vocabulary items are given as a further aid.

Then, each chapter includes the following reading/writing sections, in order.

Reading. The reading passage illustrates the use of the new grammatical elements within the context of the written language, which is more formal and explicit than the spoken language (as illustrated in the conversation). The reading topic is different from that of the conversation, but it still focuses on some aspects of contemporary life in the German-speaking countries. *Questions* on the reading, to be answered orally or in writing, provide an opportunity to practice the new vocabulary and structures in context; *Vocabulary Exercises* after the reading help students incorporate words and expressions from the conversation and reading in a slightly altered context.

Review Exercises. Another series of exercises reinforces all the principles presented within the chapter. These exercises may be done orally or in writing.

Guided Composition. Topics for composition are suggested to enable students to personalize the chapter material by developing short, written compositions. They are similar or peripheral to the reading, and they encourage use of the chapter vocabulary and structures.

Special Features

Other features of the student text are the following.

Chapter Vocabulary. A list of all vocabulary presented for the first time is included in Chapters 1 through 5.

End Vocabulary. A complete German-English vocabulary combines all vocabulary items and idiomatic expressions used throughout the book. It is arranged in dictionary style for easy accessibility and use. An English-German vocabulary includes words and phrases from exercise material only.

Chapter 22: Review. A general overview of the year's work is presented in the final chapter, which summarizes the major grammatical topics: tense system of weak and strong verbs; case system of nouns and adjectives; word order; and mood and style (passive voice, subjunctive II, and indirect discourse). Brief explanations, contextual examples, and comprehensive exercises are provided. It summarizes important aspects of the first-year's work and prepares the student for second-year studies. The chapter is designed for classroom use or for independent review.

Appendix. The appendix includes English equivalents for all conversations; a list of strong and irregular weak verbs; and a list of common weights and measures in both the American and German system and their equivalents.

Index. A thorough index to the grammatical points covered concludes the book.

Supplementary Materials

The FIRST-YEAR GERMAN program includes the following supplementary materials.

Laboratory Manual and Tapes. Each chapter corresponds to the respective chapter in the student text and consists of oral exercises slightly modified from those contained in the text, the conversation presented at normal speed in a natural atmosphere by native speakers, a set of multiple-choice questions based on the conversation, and a dictation of modified sentences from the conversation. (The dictated sentences are given at the end of the manual for self-checking.) An introductory chapter on pronunciation is followed by additional drills in each of the first eleven chapters.

The manual and tapes are designed for classroom or independent use, and the two components may be used together or separately.

Instructor's Manual. An introduction to the instructor's manual explains the methodology and suggests a general plan for treating chapter material. Then, on a chapter-by-chapter basis, useful hints, refinements in the language, and further, more advanced explanations of grammatical concepts are presented. Suggestions are also provided for effective integration of the student text and supplementary materials.

Readers. The program includes two readers: CURRENT ISSUES, focusing on contemporary life—social and economic problems, life styles, entertainment, feelings, attitudes, and so on—in the German-speaking countries; and ARTS AND LETTERS, concentrating on the contemporary arts—literary, performing, and visual—in these countries. The reading selections are short and have marginal annotations to facilitate comprehension. Questions on content and topics to generate classroom discussion follow each selection. Either reader or both may be used starting midway through the course to stimulate student interest in language and culture and to encourage and develop reading comprehension skills.

Acknowledgments

We gratefully acknowledge our appreciation to the panel of specialists teaching at various institutions throughout the country who offered valuable advice and closely monitored the progress and development of this program.

Robert E. Helbling
Wolf Gewehr
Wolff A. von Schmidt

first-year GERMAN

Chapter 1

Kassel

Useful Phrases

Learn the following everyday German phrases. They will be useful in conversation.

Guten Tag! — Hello.

Auf Wiedersehen! — Good-bye.

Wie heißen Sie, bitte? — What is your name, please?

Ich heiße Judy Miller. — My name is Judy Miller.

Ich heiße { Herr / Frau / Fräulein } Miller. — My name is { Mr. / Mrs. Miller. / Miss }

Danke! — Thank you.

Bitte! — You're welcome; please.

Viel Glück! — Good luck.

MODEL SENTENCES

Read and study the following sentences carefully. Note the words in boldface in each set of sentences and try to determine why and how these words are used, how they are alike, and how they differ from each other.

I

Ich suche das Deutsch-Institut. — I'm looking for the German institute.

Es ist gleich da drüben. — It's right over there.

Sie studieren Deutsch? — Are you studying German?

II

Wie **heißen** Sie? — What is your name?

Und wie **heißt** du? — And what is your name?

Sie **findet** das Deutsch-Institut. — She finds the German institute.

Sie **sind** aus Amerika? — Are you from America [the U.S.A.]?

Ja, ich **bin** aus Buffalo, New York. — Yes, I'm from Buffalo, New York.

Das **ist** interessant. — That's interesting.

Der Katalog ist da drüben.	The card catalogue is over there.
Hier ist **ein** Buch von Kafka.	Here is a book by Kafka.
Es heißt „Amerika".	It's called *Amerika*.
Das Buch ist interessant.	The book is interesting.

Grammar Explanations

Although the science of grammar, like any other science, does operate with a technical jargon of its own, we will try to keep our use of a specialized grammatical language to a minimum. At times, of course, the terms for basic concepts must be properly defined to understand the structure and idiosyncrasies of a language, and we will provide working definitions of key terms as they occur in our discussions.

I. PERSONAL PRONOUNS: NOMINATIVE CASE

Each part of a sentence performs a certain function. The *subject* of a sentence answers the question "who" or "what"; it denotes anyone, anything, or even any abstract concept that acts or is acted upon or of which something is said. The subject is always a noun or a pronoun. (A pronoun replaces a noun: *pro*noun = *for* a noun.)

Judy (she)	studies German.
The card catalogue (it)	is over there.
German (it)	is a modern language.

The subject of a sentence is in the *nominative case*. The *case* of a noun or pronoun indicates its function and its relationship to other elements of the sentence—that is, whether it is the subject or object of the verb or the object of a preposition, for example. In addition to the nominative case, there are three other cases in German which will be discussed later.

Grammar distinguishes pronouns by three "persons."

	Singular	Plural
1st person (the writer or speaker)	I	we
2nd person (the person addressed)	you	you
3rd person (the person or thing spoken of but not the speaker or the person addressed)	he she it	they

A noun, unless it is a person addressed, is replaced by a third-person pronoun.

the girl	she
Mr. Keller	he
the card catalogue	it
Judy and Mr. Keller	they

The German personal pronouns follow the same pattern as the English.

Personal Pronouns: Nominative Case

	Singular		Plural	
1st pers.	ich	I	wir	we
2nd pers. (fam.)	du	you	ihr	you
3rd pers.	er	he	sie	they
	sie	she		
	es	it		
2nd pers. (pol.)	Sie	you	Sie	you

But there are some differences.

1. The first-person singular, **ich,** is not capitalized in German.
2. The second-person singular and plural have two forms in German, the *familiar* and the *polite*. Use the familiar form to address relatives, close friends, pets, and children: use **du** to address one person; use **ihr** to address more than one. Use the polite form, **Sie,** to address most other people, especially people you meet for the first time. **Sie** is identical in the singular and plural forms.
3. The polite form of the second person, both singular and plural, **Sie,** is capitalized.

Familiar Form

2nd pers. sing.:	Peter, **du** bist da.
	(Peter, you are there.)
2nd pers. pl.:	Peter und Doris, **ihr** seid da.
	(Peter and Doris, you are there.)

Polite Form

2nd pers. sing.:	Fräulein Miller, **Sie** studieren Deutsch?
	(Miss Miller, are you studying German?)
2nd pers. pl.:	Herr und Frau Miller, **Sie** leben in Amerika?
	(Mr. and Mrs. Miller, do you live in America?)

Check Your Comprehension

Complete the sentence with the required personal pronoun.

1. _____ suchen das Englisch-Institut. (we)
2. _____ bist da. (you, *fam. sing.*)
3. _____ heißt Peter. (he)
4. _____ heißt Maria. (she)
5. _____ studiere hier Deutsch. (I)
6. _____ studiert Englisch, Peter und Maria? (you, *fam. pl.*)
7. _____ ist ein Problem. (it)
8. _____ sind Herr und Frau Miller? (you, *pol. pl.*)
9. Ja, und _____ sind Herr Meyer? (you, *pol. sing.*)

II. PRESENT TENSE

The infinitive indicates the meaning of a verb but not person or number. The infinitive is the basic form of the verb and is given in vocabulary lists or dictionaries.

In English, the infinitive usually consists of the preposition **to** and a form of a verb that is most often the same as the first-person singular: **to go, I go.** In German, no preposition is needed and, with very few exceptions, the infinitive ends in **–en.**

hoff **en**	to hope
studier **en**	to study
such **en**	to look for

The present tense of most German verbs is formed by dropping the infinitive ending **–en,** leaving the verb *stem*, and adding a set of personal endings.

Present Tense: Personal Endings

	Singular	Plural
1st pers.	**-e**	**-en**
2nd pers. (fam.)	**-st**	**-t**
3rd pers.	**-t**	**-en**
2nd pers. (pol.)	**-en**	**-en**

Thus, the present tense of a regular German verb is as follows.

Present Tense: **hoffen** (to hope)

	Singular			Plural	
1st pers.	ich hoff **e**	I hope		wir hoff **en**	we hope
2nd pers. (fam.)	du hoff **st**	you hope		ihr hoff **t**	you hope
3rd pers.	er sie es hoff **t**	he she it hopes		sie hoff **en**	they hope
2nd pers. (pol.)	Sie hoff **en**	you hope		Sie hoff **en**	you hope

If the verb stem ends in **–s, –ss, –ß, –x, –z,** or **–tz** (as in **heiß–en,** to be called), add only **–t** and not **–st** to the stem of the **du**-form.

du heiß**t**	you are called

The result is that the **du** and **er** forms are identical.

2nd pers. sing. (fam.):	du heißt
3rd pers. sing.:	er sie es heißt

If the stem of the verb ends in **–t** or **–d** (as in **arbeit–en**, to work, or **find–en**, to find), insert an **–e–** between the stem and the endings **–st** and **–t**. This makes it easier to hear and to pronounce the endings.

2nd pers. sing. (fam.):	du arbeit **e** st	du find **e** st
2nd pers. pl. (fam.):	ihr arbeit **e** t	ihr find **e** t

3rd pers. sing.: er / sie / es } arbeit **e** t   er / sie / it } find **e** t

Also insert an **–e–** before these endings when the stem ends in **–m** or **–n** when it is preceded by a consonant other than **l** or **r**, as in **öffnen** (to open).

du öffn **e** st
ihr öffn **e** t
er / sie / es } öffn **e** t

Note that there is no tense form in German equivalent to the English progressive (I am hoping) or emphatic (I do hope).

ich hoffe { I hope / I am hoping / I do hope

In English the simple present expresses (1) a timeless fact, as in "Water freezes at 32° Fahrenheit" or (2) some habitual action, attitude, or capacity, as in "He works hard" (He's a hard worker) and "He plays the piano well" (He's a good piano player). The progressive form, however, stresses the idea of something going on at the moment of speaking, as in "He's working hard" and "He's playing well." In German, the sentence "Er arbeitet hart" can mean both "He works hard" and "He's working hard."

The emphatic form in English, indicated by a form of the verb **do** plus the infinitive ("He does work hard") can be expressed in German only with the aid of an adverb, as in "Er arbeitet *wirklich* hart" or through intonation, as in "Ja, er arbeitet hart′."

The present tense can also express an action projected into the future, especially in connection with a time phrase, such as **heute abend** (this evening) and **gleich** (right away, shortly), when it suggests the relatively near future.

In this case, the present tense in German has the meaning of the English "I am going to" or "I'll."

Ich **komme** heute abend.	I'll come this evening.
Er **geht** gleich.	He will be going right away.

The verb **sein**, as its equivalent **to be** in English, is the most frequently used verb in German, and each form must be carefully memorized because it follows a different pattern from most other verbs. **Sein** is often used as an *auxiliary* verb. (Auxiliary verbs will be discussed later.)

Present Tense: **sein** (to be)

	Singular		*Plural*	
1st pers.	ich **bin** I am		wir **sind** we are	
2nd pers. (fam.)	du **bist** you are		ihr **seid** you are	
3rd pers.	er sie } **ist** she } is es it		sie **sind** they are	
2nd pers. (pol.)	Sie **sind** you are		Sie **sind** you are	

In a sentence using the verb **sein**, the predicate noun as well as the subject of the verb is in the *nominative* case.

Nominative		*Nominative*	
„Amerika"	ist	**ein Buch**	von Kafka.
(*Amerika*	is	a book	by Kafka.)

Check Your Comprehension

A. *Supply the appropriate present tense form of* **suchen** (to look for).

1. wir _____   4. ihr _____
2. sie (*fem. sing.*) _____   5. du _____
3. Sie _____   6. ich _____

B. *Supply the appropriate present tense form of* **arbeiten** (to work).

1. er _____   4. ihr _____
2. ich _____   5. sie (*pl.*) _____
3. du _____   6. wir _____

C. *Supply the appropriate present tense form of* **sein.**

1. Du _____ da.   4. Ich _____ da.
2. Wir _____ da.   5. Ihr _____ da.
3. Fräulein Miller _____ da. 6. Herr und Frau Miller _____ da.

III. ARTICLE, GENDER, AND NUMBER OF NOUNS

German nouns are *always* capitalized, no matter where they appear in a sentence or in a title.

Das **B**uch ist hier.
Hier ist das **B**uch.

Nouns in German as in English have both a *definite* and an *indefinite* article: the definite article refers to a specific entity; the indefinite article to any one of a class of objects.

Definite		*Indefinite*	
das Buch	**the** book	**ein** Buch	**a** book

The article in German indicates the grammatical *gender* of a noun, "gender" being a linguistic term rather than a biological one. Thus, all German nouns have a gender—either *masculine*, *feminine*, or *neuter*.

	Definite			*Indefinite*		
masc.:	**der** Mann		man	**ein** Mann		man
fem.:	**die** Frau	the	woman	**eine** Frau	a	woman
neut.:	**das** Kind		child	**ein** Kind		child

Note that sometimes biological and linguistic gender are the same (as in **der Mann** and **die Frau**), but there is most often no biological way of telling what linguistic gender a noun will be (as in **das Kind** and **das Buch**). Since gender is so important to the structure of the German language, it is essential that you *memorize the gender of the noun with the noun.* You do this by memorizing the definite article with each noun.

der Katalog (*masc.*)	the card catalogue
ein	a
die Auskunft (*fem.*)	the information
eine	a (piece of)
das Institut (*neut.*)	the institute
ein	a(n)

Although English does not differentiate between gender in the use of definite and indefinite articles with nouns, it does show gender in the third-person singular of the pronouns, where it usually indicates the biological gender of the noun it replaces. In German, however, the gender of the pronoun must agree with the grammatical gender of the noun it replaces.

der Katalog		the card catalogue
	er	he (*lit.*)
die Sprache		the language
	sie	she (*lit.*)
das Mädchen		the girl
	es	it (*lit.*)

As is also true in English, the definite article in the *plural* has only *one* form in German: **die.**

Singular		*Plural*
der Mann		⌈ Männer
die Frau	**die**	⟨ Frauen
das Buch		⌊ Bücher

The *pronoun* that replaces the plural noun in all three genders is **sie** (they).

The indefinite article is dropped in the plural. Note that the numeral *one* is the same as the indefinite article **ein** or **eine** when it is used as an adjective.

	Singular		*Plural*	
indef.:	ein Buch	a book	— Bücher	— books
	eine Frau	a woman	— Frauen	— women
numeral:	**ein** Buch	*one* book		
	eine Frau	*one* woman		

Definite and Indefinite Articles: Nominative Case

	Definite Article	Indefinite Article	Third-Person Pronouns
Singular			
masc.	der	ein	er
fem.	die	eine	sie
neut.	das	ein	es
Plural			
all gend.	die	—	sie

Nouns are almost always preceded by the definite or indefinite article in all cases. The following are two exceptions.

1. When the noun indicates a nationality or an occupation.

<blockquote>
Er ist Amerikaner. He's an American.
Ich bin Student. I'm a student.
</blockquote>

2. When the noun is the name of a city, country, or continent (for exceptions, see footnote, p. 23).

<blockquote>
West-Berlin ist in Europa. West Berlin is in Europe.
Ich studiere in Deutschland. I'm studying in Germany.
</blockquote>

If you look closely at the examples of the plural forms of the German nouns, you will see that there are many different plural endings, whereas almost all English nouns take the plural ending **–s**. Again there is often no way to determine what the plural form is to be, and thus you must *memorize the plural of German nouns along with the gender.* You will find the plural forms indicated with every noun in the chapter vocabulary list as well as in the end vocabulary, and they are indicated in the following way.

<blockquote>
das Buch, ⸚er book
die Sprache, -n language
der Tag, -e day
</blockquote>

Thus, the plural forms are: die **Bücher,** die **Sprachen,** die **Tage.** A detailed discussion on aspects of German nouns is given in Chapter 17.

A. *Substitute the appropriate personal pronoun for the noun.*

1. Das Institut ist da drüben.
2. Der Katalog ist da drüben.
3. Die Johannisstraße ist da drüben.
4. Das Fräulein ist da drüben.
5. Die Auskunft ist interessant.
6. Das Programm ist interessant.

B. *Substitute the indefinite article for the definite article.*

1. das Institut
2. die Sprache
3. der Mann
4. das Programm
5. die Frau
6. der Katalog
7. das Pamphlet
8. die Auskunft

C. *Substitute the definite article for the indefinite article.*

1. ein Buch
2. eine Sprache
3. ein Pamphlet
4. ein Katalog
5. eine Straße
6. ein Mann
7. eine Frau
8. ein Institut

D. *Change the noun from plural to singular form and use the appropriate definite article.*

1. die Bücher
2. die Sprachen
3. die Tage
4. die Männer
5. die Frauen
6. die Institute

E. *Change the noun from plural to singular form and use the appropriate indefinite article.*

1. Bücher
2. Sprachen
3. Tage
4. Männer
5. Frauen
6. Institute

CONVERSATION

Read the following conversation several times, both silently and aloud, and in the process try to commit to memory the new words, phrases, and structures.

Eine Auskunft

Judy is an American student who has a scholarship to study at a German university. She stops at the information desk of the library to inquire about the location of the German department. There she talks with Mr. Keller.

JUDY	Guten Tag! Ich suche das „Institut für Deutsche Sprache und Literatur".
HERR KELLER	Johannisstraße eins. Es ist gleich da drüben.—Sie sind aus Amerika?
JUDY	Ja, ich bin aus Buffalo, New York. Ich heiße Judy Miller. 5
HERR KELLER	Und Sie studieren jetzt hier in Deutschland?
JUDY	Ja. Ich studiere Deutsch und Soziologie.
HERR KELLER	Das ist interessant.
JUDY	Ich suche übrigens gerade ein Buch von Kafka. Es heißt „Amerika". Ich hoffe, es ist da. 10
HERR KELLER	Ich bin nicht sicher. Der Katalog ist gleich da drüben. Viel Glück!
JUDY	Danke für die Auskunft. Auf Wiedersehen!
HERR KELLER	Auf Wiedersehen, Fräulein Miller!

ORAL PRACTICE

A. *Supply the appropriate personal pronoun.*

EXAMPLE   _____ sind aus Amerika. (*1st pers. pl.*)
                  Wir sind aus Amerika.

1. _____ bin aus Amerika.
2. _____ ist aus Amerika. (die Frau)
3. _____ bist aus Amerika.
4. _____ seid aus Amerika.
5. _____ sind aus Amerika. (*3rd pers. pl.*)
6. _____ ist da drüben. (der Katalog)
7. _____ heiße Paul.
8. _____ bist gleich da.
9. _____ ist da. (das Buch)
10. _____ studiert Deutsch. (Judy)

B. *Supply the appropriate present tense form of* **sein.**

EXAMPLE   Ich _____ nicht sicher.
                  Ich **bin** nicht sicher.

1. Wir _____ nicht sicher.
2. Ihr _____ nicht sicher.
3. Du _____ nicht sicher.
4. Sie _____ nicht sicher. (*3rd pers. sing.*)
5. Sie _____ nicht sicher. (*3rd pers. pl.*)
6. Das Institut _____ in Deutschland.
7. Herr und Frau Meyer _____ interessant.
8. Judy, du _____ aus Amerika?
9. Er _____ jetzt in Deutschland.
10. Herr und Frau Miller _____ in Buffalo, New York.

C. *Supply the appropriate present tense of the verb in parentheses.*

> EXAMPLE   Wir _____ in Amerika. (arbeiten)
> Wir **arbeiten** in Amerika.

1. Judy _____ das Institut. (suchen)
2. Ich _____, das Buch ist da. (hoffen)
3. Du _____ Soziologie? (studieren)
4. Er _____ Paul Klein. (heißen)
5. Ihr _____ in Berlin. (leben)
6. Herr Miller _____ die Tür. (öffnen)

D. *Substitute the indefinite article for the definite article.*

> EXAMPLE   Das Institut ist da drüben.
> **Ein** Institut ist da drüben.

1. Der Tag ist lang.
2. Das Buch ist von Kafka.
3. Die Auskunft ist interessant.
4. Deutsch ist die Sprache.
5. Da drüben ist der Katalog.
6. Das Fräulein ist aus Deutschland.
7. Der Mann heißt Franz Keller.
8. Die Straße ist lang.
9. Das Kind ist aus Berlin.
10. Das Programm ist gut.

E. *Substitute the appropriate personal pronoun for the noun.*

> EXAMPLE   Das Institut ist da drüben.
> **Es** ist da drüben.

1. Hier ist der Katalog.
2. Die Auskunft ist interessant.
3. Die Johannisstraße ist gleich da drüben.
4. Das Programm ist wirklich gut.
5. Der Mann heißt Herr Miller.
6. Das Pamphlet ist nicht lang.

F. *Substitute the definite article for the indefinite article.*

1. „Amerika" ist ein Buch von Kafka.
2. Ein Programm ist da drüben.

3. Hier ist ein Katalog.

4. Da drüben ist ein Institut.

G. *Change the noun from plural to singular and make the necessary change in the verb.*

1. Die Bücher sind interessant.
2. Die Sprachen sind modern.
3. Die Tage sind lang.
4. Die Männer sind hier.
5. Die Frauen sind da drüben.

H. *Change the noun from plural to singular, making the necessary verb change and using the indefinite article.*

1. Bücher sind interessant.
2. Sprachen sind modern.
3. Tage sind lang.
4. Männer sind hier.
5. Da drüben sind Frauen.

I. *Substitute or add each phrase as it is introduced into the previous sentence.*

EXAMPLE

Judy und Paul sind aus Texas.   Judy und Paul sind aus Texas.

Wir _____   **Wir**   sind aus Texas.

_____ in Berlin.   Wir sind   **in Berlin.**

Judy lebt   in Deutschland.

_____ studiert _____ _____

_____ das Buch.

_____ sucht _____

_____ das Institut.

_____ in Berlin.

GUIDED CONVERSATION

The following are some suggestions for carrying on a conversation in German, but you need not follow this pattern exactly. Use your own ideas, applying any of the expressions, vocabulary, and constructions you have learned so far. Your conversation should be as natural and free-flowing as possible. In later chapters, more than one conversational topic may be suggested from which to choose.

Begin a conversation with the person sitting next to you. You might exchange all or some of the following: greetings, your names, where you are from, what you are studying, how you find the course (**interessant**), your instructor's name, the names of some of the other students in your class, good-bye, good luck.

You may use either the familiar or the polite form of addressing a person, but be sure to use the same form throughout your conversation. For additional practice, carry on a second conversation with someone else and use the form of address you did not use in your first conversation.

READING

Read the following passage and, as in the conversation, note all new words, phrases, and structures. As in English, written language is more formal and explicit than the spoken language because the writer cannot rely on gestures and intonation to make his meaning clear. After you have finished reading the passage and fully understand what it says, answer the questions that follow it.

Das Deutsch-Institut

Judy Miller findet die Johannisstraße 1. Es ist das Deutsch-Institut. Sie öffnet die Tür. Da steht ein Student. Er verteilt ein Pamphlet. Es ist ein Programm. Es heißt:

informieren

diskutieren 5

verändern

Judy studiert das Programm. Sie findet es wirklich sehr interessant.

Der Student informiert Judy über das Studentenparlament. Sie diskutieren über Politik in Deutschland und Amerika. Verändern: ja oder nein? Was und wie? Sie diskutieren fast eine Stunde. 10

Judy sucht jetzt das Buch von Kafka. Sie findet es in Raum 9 unter „Literatur". Sie öffnet das Buch und arbeitet fast eine Stunde. Sie findet Kafka wirklich interessant.

QUESTIONS

1. Was findet Judy Miller?
2. Wie heißt die Straße?
3. Wer öffnet die Tür?
4. Wer verteilt ein Pamphlet?
5. Was ist ein Pamphlet?
6. Wie heißt das Programm?
7. Was studiert Judy?
8. Wie findet sie das Programm?
9. Über was informiert der Student Judy?
10. Über was diskutieren sie?
11. Was sucht Judy?
12. Wo findet Judy das Buch?
13. Wie findet Judy Kafka?

VOCABULARY EXERCISES

A. *Supply the appropriate word from the list on the right.*

1. Das _____ ist von Kafka.
2. Die _____ sind lang.
3. Das _____ studiert das Programm.
4. Die _____ ist Deutsch.
5. Der _____ heißt Herr Meyer.
6. Ich suche ein _____.
7. Judy und der Student diskutieren eine _____.

a. Sprache
b. Institut
c. Mann
d. Stunde
e. Buch
f. Tage
g. Fräulein

B. *Give the German equivalent for the English phrase.*

1. Thank you.
2. You're welcome.
3. Good-bye.
4. Hello.
5. What's your name?
6. My name is _____.
7. Good luck!
8. His name is _____.

Review Exercises

A. *Supply the correct personal pronoun.*

1. _____ ist da drüben. (*fem.*)
2. _____ sind in Deutschland. (*1st pers.*)
3. _____ bin da.
4. _____ arbeitest eine Stunde.
5. _____ bist aus Amerika?
6. _____ seid interessant.
7. _____ hofft, er ist gleich da. (*2nd pers.*)
8. _____ studiert Deutsch. (*masc.*)
9. _____ heißt Peter. (*2nd pers.*)

10. _____ heißt Judy. (*3rd pers.*)
11. _____ suchen das Buch. (*1st pers.*)
12. _____ arbeiten da drüben. (*3rd pers.*)

B. *Supply the appropriate present tense form of the verb in parentheses.*

1. Ich _____ Judy. (heißen)
2. Es _____ da drüben. (sein)
3. Herr Miller _____ in New York. (arbeiten)
4. Du _____ Peter? (sein)
5. Wir _____ ein Buch. (suchen)
6. Sie _____ das Institut. (finden, *3rd pers. sing.*)
7. Ihr _____ da drüben. (sein)
8. Das Pamphlet _____. (informieren)
9. Judy _____ Deutsch. (studieren)
10. Wir _____ die Tür. (öffnen)
11. Ihr _____ das Programm. (verändern)
12. Er _____ Peter. (heißen)
13. Sie _____ in Amerika. (sein, *pl.*)
14. Er _____ Judy. (informieren)
15. Herr Miller, Sie _____ fast eine Stunde. (diskutieren)
16. Sie _____ das Institut. (finden, *3rd pers. pl.*)

C. *Substitute the appropriate personal pronoun for the noun.*

1. Das Pamphlet ist hier.
2. Das Fräulein ist da.
3. Der Katalog ist da drüben.
4. Das Buch ist interessant.
5. Der Student steht da drüben.
6. Die Auskunft ist nicht interessant.
7. Die Straße ist in Berlin.
8. Der Mann und die Frau sind da.

D. *Substitute the indefinite article for the definite article.*

1. Die Frau ist da drüben.
2. Das Pamphlet ist interessant.

3. Der Mann heißt Herr Keller.
4. Die Sprache ist interessant.
5. Das Buch ist von Kafka.
6. Der Student studiert in New York.
7. Der Katalog ist modern.

E. *Substitute the definite article for the indefinite article.*

1. Ein Mann ist aus Amerika.
2. Ein Programm ist interessant.
3. Eine Sprache ist Deutsch.
4. Ein Fräulein heißt Judy.
5. Da ist eine Frau.
6. Da drüben ist ein Katalog.

F. *Change the subject of the sentence from plural to singular, making all other necessary alterations.*

1. Die Bücher sind da drüben.
2. Die Männer arbeiten in Amerika.
3. Die Kinder suchen ein Buch.
4. Die Programme sind lang.
5. Die Mädchen sind aus Berlin.
6. Die Frauen finden das Institut interessant.
7. Die Stunden sind lang.
8. Die Tage sind lang.

GUIDED COMPOSITION

The following are some suggestions for writing a composition in German. You may choose either A or B, but you need not follow the suggestions exactly; rather, use your own ideas and apply whatever vocabulary and grammar constructions you have learned so far. Your composition should be as clear and concise as possible.

A. Write a very brief paragraph about yourself, stating your name, where you are from, and what you are studying.

B. Are you presently reading an interesting book? Write a very brief paragraph stating the title of the book, who it is written by, and that you find it interesting.

Chapter Vocabulary

(das)* **Amerika** America
der **Amerikaner, -** American
    arbeiten to work
    aus from
die **Auskunft, ∸e** (piece of)
    information

    bitte please; you're
    welcome
das **Buch, ∸er** book

    da there
       da drüben over
       there
    danke thank you
    das that
(das) **Deutsch** German (*noun:*
    language; subject)
    deutsch German
    (*adjective/adverb:* mode)
(das) **Deutcshland** Germany
    diskutieren to discuss

    ein(s) [numeral] one
(das) **Englisch** English (*noun:*
    language; subject)
    englisch English
    (*adjective/adverb:* mode)
    entweder either

    fast almost
    finden to find
die **Frau, -en** woman
    Frau Miller Mrs.
    Miller
das **Fräulein, -** young lady
    Fräulein Miller
    Miss Miller
der **Freund, -e** (male) friend
    für for

    gehen to go

    gerade just (now)
    gleich right; right away
das **Glück** happiness, luck,
    fortune
    gut good

    hart hard
    heißen to be called
der **Herr, -en** man; gentle-
    man
       Herr Miller Mr.
       Miller
    heute abend this even-
    ing
    hier here
    hoffen to hope

    in in
    informieren to inform
das **Institut, -e** institute
    interessant interesting

    ja yes
    jetzt now

der **Katalog, -e** (card)
    catalogue
das **Kind, -er** child
    kommen to come

    lang long
    leben to live, reside
die **Literatur, -en** literature

das **Mädchen, -** girl
der **Mann, ∸er** man
    modern modern

    nein no
    nicht not

    oder or
    öffnen to open

das **Pamphlet, -e** pamphlet
die **Politik** politics
das **Programm, -e** program

der **Raum, ∸e** space, room

    sehr very
    sein to be
    sicher sure
die **Soziologie** sociology
die **Sprache, -n** language
    stehen to stand
die **Straße, -n** street
der **Student, -en** student
    (male)
das **Studentenparlament, -e**
    student senate
    studieren to study
die **Stunde, -n** hour
    suchen to look for

der **Tag, -e** day
die **Tür, -en** door

    über about (concerning);
    over
    übrigens by the way
    und and
    unter under

    verändern to change
    verteilen to distribute
    viel much
    von by; from

    was what
    wer who
    wie how
das **Wiedersehen, -** reunion
    wirklich really
    wo where

---

* With some exceptions (die Schweiz, die Tschechoslowakei, die Türkei, die Vereinigten Staaten), the names of countries do not require an article. In the vocabulary listing we have inserted the article in parentheses for use in replacing the noun by a pronoun.

Chapter 2

Dom in Köln

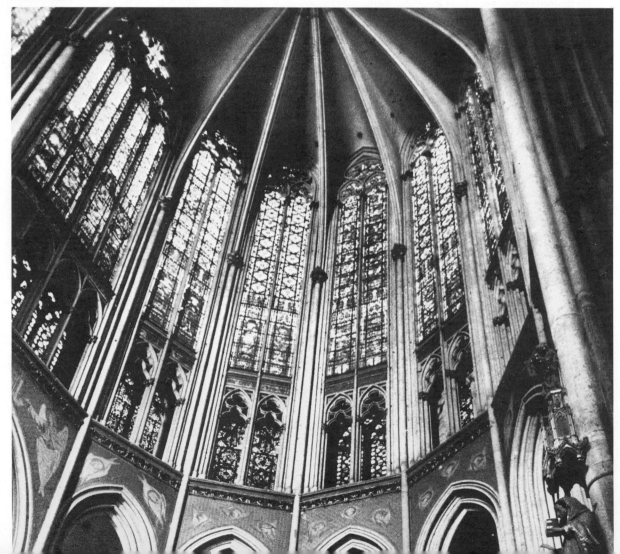

Useful Phrases

Wirklich?	Really?
Mensch, toll!	Man, (that's) great!
Prima!	Great! Wonderful!
Tschüß!	So long.
Bis gleich!	See you later.
Verzeihung!	Pardon me.
Klar!	Certainly. (That's) clear.
zum Beispiel	for example

MODEL SENTENCES

I

Ich suche **den** Katalog.	I'm looking for the card catalogue.
Monika hat **einen** Freund.	Monika has a friend.
Ich habe **eine** Platte.	I have a record.
Wir haben **kein** Tonbandgerät.	We don't have a tape recorder.

II

Du **hast** Jazz-Platten.	You have jazz records.
Ihr **habt** eine Stereo-Anlage.	You have a stereo set.
Sie **hat** ein Tonbandgerät.	She has a tape recorder.

III

Hier ist Monika.	Here is Monika.
Den Klang finde ich gut.	I think the sound is good. [I find the sound good.]
Neu ist die Platte nicht.	The record isn't new.
Kennst du die Platte von Neil Young?	Do you know the record by Neil Young?
Nein. **Ist** die Platte neu?	No. Is the record new?
Was hast du von Dave Brubeck?	What do you have by Dave Brubeck?

Grammar Explanations

I. DEFINITE AND INDEFINITE ARTICLES: ACCUSATIVE CASE

Another basic part of almost every sentence, the *direct object*, is directly affected by the action or situation expressed in the verb. It answers the question "whom" or "what." Thus it can be said that the direct object is the immediate "receiver" of the action, and it may be a person, a thing, or an abstract concept. The direct object is in the *accusative case*.

Nominative		*Accusative*
Monika	has	a friend.
Monika	finds	a record.
Monika	studies	a language.

In German, the forms of the definite and indefinite articles in the *accusative* case are almost the same as in the nominative, with few exceptions. The masculine singular for both the definite and indefinite articles has special forms in the accusative case.

def. art.:	**den**
indef. art.:	**einen**

In all other instances, however—feminine singular, neuter singular, and plural of all genders of the definite article—the accusative forms of the definite and indefinite articles are the same as in the nominative. And the indefinite article in the accusative, as in the nominative case, has no plural form.

Definite and Indefinite Articles: Accusative Case

	Definite Article	Indefinite Article
Singular		
masc.	**den**	**einen**
fem.	die	eine
neut.	das	ein
Plural		
all gend.	die	—

Definite and Indefinite Articles:
Nominative and Accusative Cases

	Nominative	*Accusative*
Singular		
masc.	der Katalog	**den** Katalog
	ein	**einen**
fem.	die Zigarette	die Zigarette
	eine	eine
neut.	das Tonbandgerät	das Tonbandgerät
	ein	ein
Plural		
all gend.	die { Kataloge / Zigaretten / Tonbandgeräte	die { Kataloge / Zigaretten / Tonbandgeräte

The adjective **kein,** meaning "no," "not a," or "not any," is used to negate nouns and takes the same endings as the indefinite article.

Ich bin **kein** Student.	I'm not a student.
Judy hat **keinen** Freund.	Judy has no friend.
Ich rauche **keine** Zigaretten.	I don't smoke any cigarettes.

kein: Nominative and Accusative Cases

	Nominative	*Accusative*
Singular		
masc.	kein	**keinen**
fem.	keine	keine
neut.	kein	kein
Plural		
all gend.	**keine**	**keine**

Notice that in contrast to **ein, kein** *does* have a plural form in both the nominative and accusative cases: **keine** Zigaretten.

Check Your Comprehensión

A. *Change the definite article to the indefinite article in the accusative case.*

1. Wir suchen die Stereo-Anlage.
2. Ihr sucht den Plattenspieler.
3. Ich suche das Buch.
4. Er sucht das Fräulein.
5. Sie suchen den Katalog.
6. Du suchst die Zigaretten.

B. *Supply the appropriate form of the definite article in the accusative case.*

1. Herr Klein findet _____ Klang fantastisch.
2. Ich finde _____ Programm fantastisch.
3. Judy findet _____ Bücher fantastisch.
4. Jürgen findet _____ Platte fantastisch.
5. Er findet _____ Fräulein fantastisch.
6. Wir finden _____ Pamphlet fantastisch.

C. *Supply the appropriate form of* **kein.**

1. Jürgen ist _____ Student.
2. Das Pamphlet ist _____ Programm.
3. Das ist _____ Platte.
4. Er hat _____ Plattenspieler.
5. Ich habe _____ Tonbandgerät.
6. Monika hat _____ Zigaretten.

II. PRESENT TENSE OF <u>haben</u> (to have)

After the verb **sein** (to be), the most frequently occurring verb in German is **haben** (to have). Carefully note and memorize its forms.

Present Tense: **haben** (to have)

	Singular	Plural
1st pers.	ich **habe**	wir **haben**
2nd pers. (fam.)	du **hast**	ihr **habt**
3rd pers.	er sie } **hat** es	sie **haben**
2nd pers. (pol.)	Sie **haben**	Sie **haben**

Check Your Comprehension

Supply the appropriate form of **haben.**

1. Wir _____ ein Buch.
2. Sie _____ cin Buch. (*fem. sing.*)
3. Ich _____ ein Buch.
4. Du _____ ein Buch.
5. Der Mann _____ ein Buch.
6. Sie _____ ein Buch. (*2nd pers. pol.*)
7. Ihr _____ ein Buch.

III. WORD ORDER

An important aspect of studying a language is learning the pattern of word order, for each language has developed its own conventions. At times, these conventions are the same in any given two languages; at other times, they differ widely. In German there are three basic patterns of word order: "normal," "inverted," and that used in questions.

A. Normal Word Order

Just as in English, the normal order of the major parts of speech in a German sentence is the following.

Subject	Verb	Direct Object
Der Mann	hat	einen Plattenspieler.
(The man	has	a record player.)

Note that in German the adverb in a sentence with normal word order is placed between the verb and the direct object; whereas in English it is often placed between the subject and the verb, thus changing the normal subject-verb pattern.

Subject	Verb	Adverb	Direct Object
Der Mann	hat	wirklich	einen Plattenspieler.
The man	actually → has		a record player.

B. Inverted Word Order

For various reasons—meaning, emphasis, and stylistic balance, for example—many German sentences begin with an element *other* than the subject. In this case, the subject is placed directly *behind* the verb. The word order is thus "inverted."

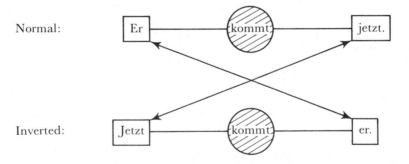

Normal: Er — kommt — jetzt.

Inverted: Jetzt — kommt — er.

In this instance, German differs radically from English. In English you simply cannot say "Now is coming he" instead of "Now he is coming"; it would be considered unacceptable or even gibberish. On the other hand, the German feels exactly the same way about the sentence "Jetzt er kommt"; his innate feeling for his native tongue will automatically make him say "Jetzt kommt er." This important distinction in the conventions governing word order in the two languages cannot be overemphasized.

The following sentences also illustrate the fact that no matter which element is in the beginning, or front position, of a sentence—for instance the subject, direct object, adverb, or question word—the *verb remains in the second position*.

Er **findet** den Plattenspieler gut. ⎫
Den Plattenspieler **findet** er gut. ⎬ He likes the record player.
Gut **findet** er den Plattenspieler. ⎭
Wo **findet** er den Plattenspieler?   Where does he find the record player?

When the following expressions occur at the beginning of a sentence, normal word order prevails: exclamations (**ach, aha**); the name of the person you are speaking to (**Fräulein Miller**); some conjunctions, such as **und, aber,** and **oder;** and **bitte, ja,** and **nein.**

Fräulein Miller, ich **finde** den Plattenspieler   Miss Miller, I like the record player.
   gut.
Aber er **findet** den Plattenspieler gut.   But he likes the record player.
Ja, er **findet** den Plattenspieler gut.   Yes, he likes the record player.

In the following illustrations, the symbol ⊘ is used to denote the fixed position of the verb and the symbol ☐ is used to illustrate the other parts of speech, such as the subject, object, and adverb, that may change their position within a sentence.

1. For purposes of emphasis or style the *direct object* may be in the first position.

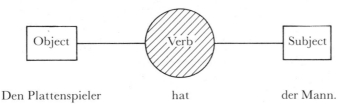

Den Plattenspieler   hat   der Mann.

2. Quite frequently an *adverb* or an adverbial phrase may occupy the first position in a sentence.

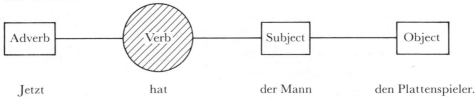

Jetzt   hat   der Mann   den Plattenspieler.

3. *Question words*, such as, "wo," "wie," and "warum," that introduce a question always stand in the first position.

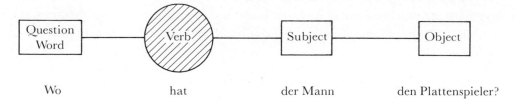

| Wo | hat | der Mann | den Plattenspieler? |

C. Word Order in Questions

In example *3* above, the question includes a "question word," but there may be questions that require a "yes" or "no" answer and, therefore, do not contain a question word. In this case, the verb is in the first position but is still followed by the subject; that is, the sentence is still in the inverted word order.

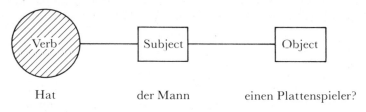

| Hat | der Mann | einen Plattenspieler? |

(Does the man have a record player?)

Never use the German verb **tun** (to do) for formulating questions that are not introduced by question words. "Do you have" is rendered in German by "hast du."

Check Your Comprehension

A. *Change the sentence word order by placing the direct object in the first position.*

1. Er findet den Plattenspieler.
2. Wir suchen einen Katalog.
3. Du hast eine Platte.
4. Sie arbeiten eine Stunde.
5. Ihr habt ein Tonbandgerät.
6. Sie verteilt ein Programm.

B. *Change the word order by placing the adverb in the first position.*

1. Er kommt jetzt.
2. Der Katalog ist gleich da drüben.
3. Ich habe leider keine Zigaretten.
4. Du hast vielleicht eine Platte.
5. Er hat wirklich keine Bücher.

C. *Convert the sentence into a question by using the question word in parentheses and make the necessary changes in word order.*

1. Monika hat einen Plattenspieler. (Was)
2. Monika arbeitet in Berlin. (Wo)
3. Monika findet das Buch gut. (Wie)
4. Monika verteilt Programme. (Wer)
5. Monika studiert Deutsch. (Was)

D. *Convert the sentence into a question that requires the answer* **ja** *or* **nein.**

1. Die Platte ist von Dave Brubeck.
2. Ihr kommt gleich.
3. Du suchst ein Buch.
4. Er findet das Buch.
5. Du kommst.
6. Sie raucht eine Zigarette.

CONVERSATION

Ein Telefongespräch

Monika calls her friend Jürgen on the phone and invites him to her house to listen to some records.

MONIKA   Du, Jürgen, hier ist Monika. Ich hoffe, du hast gerade einen
Moment Zeit.

JÜRGEN	Hm. Warum?
MONIKA	Wir haben nämlich jetzt eine Stereo-Anlage mit Tonbandgerät und Plattenspieler. Sie ist ganz neu.
JÜRGEN	Wirklich? Mensch, toll! Habt ihr eine Stereo-Anlage von Grundig?
MONIKA	Nein, ich glaube, sie ist von Sony. Den Klang finde ich ganz fantastisch. Hast du vielleicht eine Platte von Dave Brubeck?
JÜRGEN	Von Brubeck habe ich leider keine Platte, aber ich habe ein paar Jazz-Platten, zum Beispiel von Louis Armstrong und . . .
MONIKA	Toll! Kennst du übrigens die Platte „Down by the River" von Neil Young?
JÜRGEN	Nein, ist sie neu?
MONIKA	Neu ist sie nicht, aber ich finde die Platte wirklich gut.
JÜRGEN	Prima! Ich komme gleich. Tschüß, Monika!
MONIKA	Tschüß, Jürgen! Bis gleich!

ORAL PRACTICE

A. *Change the definite article to an indefinite article.*

1. Wir haben die Stereo-Anlage von Sony.
2. Ich finde den Plattenspieler fantastisch.
3. Jürgen sucht das Buch.
4. Er studiert den Katalog.
5. Sie raucht die Zigarette.

B. *Supply the appropriate form of the definite article.*

1. Ich finde _____ Klang fantastisch.
2. Herr Klein studiert _____ Programm.
3. Judy sucht _____ Bücher.
4. Jürgen kennt _____ Platte von Dave Brubeck.
5. Wir suchen _____ Tür.
6. Ich kenne _____ Mann.

C. *Substitute the item in parentheses for the word in boldface, supplying the appropriate form of the indefinite article.*

1. Wir suchen **ein Buch.** (Katalog)
2. Der Mann findet **eine Frau.** (Institut)
3. Ich habe **ein Tonbandgerät.** (Plattenspieler)
4. Sie kennen **eine Stereo-Anlage** von Sony. (Tonbandgerät)
5. Hast du **einen Moment Zeit?** (Buch von Kafka)
6. **Den Klang** finde ich wirklich gut. (Programm)

D. *Supply the appropriate form of* **kein.**

1. Wir haben _____ Zeit.
2. Er hat _____ Plattenspieler.
3. Jürgen ist _____ Student.
4. Monika raucht _____ Zigaretten.
5. Ich habe _____ Platte von Johann Strauß.
6. Die Frau hat _____ Mann.

E. *Supply the appropriate form of* **haben.**

1. Ihr _____ keine Platten.
2. Ich _____ ein Buch von Thomas Mann.
3. Wir _____ einen Moment Zeit.
4. Du _____ ein Tonbandgerät.
5. _____ Sie keine Zeit, Herr Miller?
6. Er _____ ein Programm.

F. *Form a sentence in normal word order from the elements in parentheses.*

EXAMPLE   _____ hast _____. (eine Platte / du)
   Du hast eine Platte.

1. _____ sucht _____. (das Buch / die Frau)
2. _____ finden _____ _____. (den Katalog / Sie / da drüben)
3. _____ arbeiten _____. (in Berlin / wir)
4. _____ kennt _____. (das Buch / das Fräulein)

G. *Place the word in parentheses at the beginning of the sentence and change the word order accordingly.*

1. Ich habe keine Platte. (leider)
2. Er findet das Buch wirklich gut. (eigentlich)
3. Wir kommen. (gleich)
4. Monika studiert in Deutschland. (jetzt)

H. *Place the subject at the beginning of the sentence and change the word order accordingly.*

1. Übrigens suche ich eine Platte.
2. In Deutschland studiert sie Deutsch.
3. Da drüben ist der Plattenspieler.
4. Jetzt bin ich sicher.
5. Vielleicht haben wir das Buch von Kafka.

I. *Convert the sentence into a question using the question word in parentheses.*

1. Monika hat einen Plattenspieler. (Was)
2. Herr Meyer arbeitet in Berlin. (Wo)
3. Sie heißt Judy Miller. (Wie)
4. Der Student verteilt Pamphlete. (Wer)
5. Judy studiert Deutsch in Deutschland. (Was)

J. *Convert the sentence into a question that requires the answer* **ja** *or* **nein.**

   1. Die Stereo-Anlage ist von Sony.
   2. Du hast eine Platte von Dave Brubeck.
   3. Sie kommen gleich.
   4. Sie hat einen Moment Zeit.
   5. Jürgen studiert das Programm.

K. *Substitute or add each phrase as it is introduced into the previous sentence and make any necessary alterations in verb ending or word order.*

Den Plattenspieler findet der Mann gut.
Das Tonbandgerät _____
_____ Jürgen _____
_____ fantastisch.
Die Jazz-Platten _____
_____ wir _____

GUIDED CONVERSATION

A. Begin a conversation with two or three persons sitting near you. Discuss the music equipment you have, including some or all of the following: whether you have a stereo set, tape recorder, or record player; what brand the record player, tape recorder, or stereo set is; whether you have records; the names of some of your records and the names of the recording artists; which records you do not have but find especially good.

B. Ask two or three members of your class if they are acquainted with the works **(die Werke)** of Thomas Mann (or some other author you particularly like); if they find Mann interesting, or even fantastic; if they have a book by Mann, and if so, what the book is called and if they believe it is good.

Whether you choose A or B, practice using the familiar forms of address. Use the plural form when addressing the group as a whole and the singular form when directing a question to one person in particular.

Das Problem

Verzeihung! Haben Sie eigentlich auch eine Schwäche? Ich meine:[1] Trinken Sie, essen Sie oder rauchen Sie zuviel? Natürlich ist das ungesund. Klar! Aber ich glaube, wir alle haben eine Schwäche, oder nicht?

Ich zum Beispiel habe ein Problem. Nein, nein, ich trinke nicht. Wirklich, ich trinke fast keinen Alkohol. Aber ich rauche zuviel. Das ist das Problem. 5 Ich rauche keine Zigarren,[2] nein, ich rauche Zigaretten. Ich rauche „Camels."

Viele Zigaretten haben einen Filter und viele haben keinen Filter. Die „Camel" ist zum Beispiel eine Zigarette ohne Filter, die „Camel ohne". In Deutschland finden Sie ein Plakat, es hat die Aufschrift „The Camels are coming!". Das Plakat kommt aus Amerika, die Zigaretten auch. 10

Sie in Amerika haben einen Vorteil. Die Zigarettenpackung hat dort eine Warnung. Sie heißt: „The surgeon general has determined that cigarette smoking is dangerous to your health." In Deutschland haben wir keine Warnung. Natürlich sind Zigaretten ungesund. Das ist klar. Aber leider haben fast alle Menschen eine Schwäche! 15

---

[1] German uses a colon to introduce indirect or direct statements or thoughts.
[2] A comma is often used where English would use a period or a semicolon.

QUESTIONS

1. Haben Sie eine Schwäche?
2. Trinken Sie zuviel Alkohol?
3. Essen Sie zuviel?
4. Rauchen Sie zuviel?
5. Rauchen Sie Zigarren?
6. Was ist ungesund?
7. Was hat die Zigarettenpackung in Amerika?
8. Was haben viele Zigaretten?
9. Was haben viele Zigaretten nicht?

VOCABULARY EXERCISES

A. *Supply the appropriate word from the list on the right.*

1. Haben Sie auch eine _____?
2. Die Zigarettenpackung hat eine _____.
3. Die _____ ist von Grundig.
4. Die _____ ist von Dave Brubeck.
5. Wir haben einen _____.
6. Habt ihr ein _____?
7. Sic hat keine _____.
8. Den _____ finde ich wirklich gut.

a. Zeit
b. Klang
c. Tonbandgerät
d. Warnung
e. Stereo-Anlage
f. Plattenspieler
g. Platte
h. Schwäche

B. *Give the German equivalent for the English phrase.*

1. So long!
2. See you later.
3. Great!
4. Really?
5. Pardon me!
6. Certainly.

Review Exercises

A. *Substitute the item in parentheses for the words in boldface and supply the appropriate form of the definite or indefinite article or* **kein.**

1. Wir alle haben **eine Schwäche.** (Problem)
2. Sie raucht zum Beispiel **keine Zigarren.** (Zigarette)
3. In Amerika haben Sie **einen Vorteil.** (Warnung)
4. In Deutschland hat die Zigarettenpackung **keine Warnung.** (Aufschrift)
5. Wie finden Sie **die Aufschrift** von „Camel"? (Plakat)

B. *Convert the sentence into normal word order.*

1. Vielleicht trinken Sie zuviel Alkohol.
2. Eigentlich rauche ich keine Zigarren.

3. Natürlich ist das ungesund.
4. Einen Filter haben viele Zigaretten.
5. In Deutschland finden Sie ein Plakat von „Camel".
6. Das Plakat finde ich sehr interessant.

C. *Place the word in boldface at the beginning of the sentence and change the word order accordingly.*

1. Wir haben **leider** keine Zigaretten.
2. Sie haben **eigentlich** keine Zeit.
3. Ich rauche **jetzt** zuviel.
4. Ihr findet **in Deutschland** ein Plakat von „Camel".
5. Das Plakat kommt **aus Amerika.**
6. Ich habe **vielleicht** eine Zigarette.
7. Du trinkst **zum Beispiel** zuviel.

D. *Convert the sentence to a question that requires the answer* **ja** *or* **nein.**

1. Die Zigarette hat einen Filter.
2. Das ist klar.
3. Die Zigarettenpackung hat eine Warnung.
4. Sie trinkt wirklich fast keinen Alkohol.
5. Wir essen zuviel.
6. Das Plakat kommt aus Amerika.
7. Zigaretten sind ungesund.
8. Sie haben eine Zigarette.
9. Du hast wirklich keine Schwäche.
10. Ihr habt zum Beispiel ein Problem.

GUIDED COMPOSITION

A. **Wir alle haben eine Schwäche.** Write a brief composition regarding your particular weakness or weaknesses. Which of the most common vices do you share with millions of other people? Which do you not share? If you smoke cigarettes, which brand do you smoke? Does this brand have a filter? If you drink, what do you drink? Is your weakness a problem? Is it unhealthy?

B. Write a brief composition regarding your record player, tape recorder, or stereo set. Is it new? Does it have good sound? Which company makes (manufactures) it? What are some of your favorite records? Is there a particular record you are looking for? What is it? Which artist does it feature?

Whether you choose A or B, you may write your composition in the second or third person, singular or plural, or the first-person plural, if you wish, rather than the first-person singular as suggested.

For additional practice, write your composition a second time and change the emphasis of certain sentences by changing the word order.

Chapter Vocabulary

aber but
der **Alkohol, –ika** alcohol
alle all
auch also
die **Aufschrift, –en** inscription

das **Beispiel, –e** example
bis until; to; up to

eigentlich actually
ein paar a few
essen to eat

fantastisch fantastic
der **Filter, –** filter

ganz quite; completely
der **Geburtstag, –e** birthday
das **Gespräch, –e** conversation
glauben to believe, think

haben to have

die **Jazz-Platte, –n** jazz record

kein no; not a; not any

kennen to know, be acquainted with
der **Klang, ¨e** sound

leider unfortunately

meinen to mean
der **Mensch, –en** man
mit with
der **Moment, –e** moment
nämlich namely; because
natürlich naturally
neu new
noch still; yet

ohne without

das **Paar, –e** pair, couple
das **Plakat, –e** poster
die **Platte, –n** record
der **Plattenspieler, –** record player
das **Problem, –e** problem

rauchen to smoke

die **Schwäche, –n** weakness; vice

die **Stereo-Anlage, –n** stereo set

das **Telefon, –e** telephone
das **Tonbandgerät, –e** tape recorder
trinken to drink
tun to do

übrigens by the way; moreover
ungesund unhealthy

die **Verzeihung,** pardon
viele many
vielleicht perhaps
der **Vorteil, –e** advantage

die **Warnung, –en** warning
warum why

die **Zeit, –en** time
die **Zigarette, –n** cigarette
die **Zigarettenpackung, –en** cigarette package
die **Zigarre, –n** cigar
zuviel too much

Chapter 3

West-Berlin

Useful Phrases

Tag!	Hi!
Stimmt's?	(Is that) right?
Ach so!	I see. So that's it.
heute abend	tonight; this evening
Moment mal!	Just a moment.
Schade!	(That's) too bad.
Vielen Dank!	Thank you very much.

MODEL SENTENCES

I

Er **nimmt** den Bus.	He's taking the bus.
Siehst du das Taxi?	Do you see the cab?
Sie **fährt** nach Hannover.	She's driving to Hannover.

II

Steigen Sie bitte **ein!**	Step in, please.
Kommen Sie bitte **her!**	Come here, please.
Der Taxifahrer **hält an.**	The cab driver stops.
Wo **fährst** du heute abend **hin?**	Where are you going tonight?

III

Komm, Peter!	Come, Peter.
Kommt, Peter und Monika!	Come, Peter and Monika.
Kommen Sie, Herr Meyer!	Come, Mr. Meyer.

Grammar Explanations

I. PRESENT TENSE: STEM-VOWEL CHANGES

The stem vowel **e, a,** or **au** of many common verbs in German undergoes a change *in the second and third persons singular of the present tense,* known as "vowel variation."

> **e** changes to **i** or **ie**
> **a** changes to **ä** (Umlaut)
> **au** changes to **äu** (Umlaut)

Present Tense: Stem-Vowel Changes of Strong Verbs

	nehmen (to take)	**sehen** (to see)	**fahren** (to drive)	**laufen** (to run)
Singular				
1st pers.	ich nehme	ich sehe	ich fahre	ich laufe
2nd pers. (fam.)	du **nimm**st	du **sieh**st	du **fähr**st	du **läuf**st
3rd pers.	er **nimm**t	er **sieh**t	er **fähr**t	er **läuf**t
Plural				
1st pers.	wir nehmen	wir sehen	wir fahren	wir laufen
2nd pers. (fam.)	ihr nehmt	ihr seht	ihr fahrt	ihr lauft
3rd pers.	sie nehmen	sie sehen	sie fahren	sie laufen
Singular/Plural				
2nd pers. (pol.)	Sie nehmen	Sie sehen	Sie fahren	Sie laufen

Notice that **nehmen** changes form completely, except for the personal endings: du **nimmst** and er **nimmt**.

Some other common verbs with vowel variation include the following.

Infinitive	2nd Person Singular	3rd Person Singular
essen (to eat)	du ißt	er ißt
fallen (to fall)	du fällst	er fällt
geben (to give)	du gibst	er gibt
halten (to stop)	du hältst	er hält
lassen (to let)	du läßt*	er läßt
lesen (to read)	du liest	er liest
sprechen (to speak)	du sprichst	er spricht
tragen (to carry)	du trägst	er trägt
vergessen (to forget)	du vergißt	er vergißt
verlassen (to leave)	du verläßt*	er verläßt

Note that, as is true for regular verbs (*see* Chapter 1), if the stem of the verb ends in **–s, –ss, –ß, –x, –z,** or **–tz,** the ending of the **du**-form is only **–t** (not **–st**).

ich les e	verlass e	schließ e
du lies **t**	verläß **t**	schließ **t**
er		
sie } lies t	verläß t	schließ t
es		

An important verb with a stem ending in **–ss** is **wissen** (to know). Memorize its special conjugation as you have done for **sein** and **haben**.

Present Tense: **wissen** (to know)

	Singular	Plural
1st pers.	ich **weiß**	wir **wissen**
2nd pers. (fam.)	du **weißt**	ihr **wißt**
3rd pers.	er sie } **weiß** es	sie **wissen**
2nd pers. (pol.)	Sie **wissen**	Sie **wissen**

---

* The **–ss–** changes to **–ß–** (1) if the preceding vowel is long, (2) before a **–t,** and (3) at the end of a verb. There is no difference in its pronunciation.

Complete the sentence with the correct form of the verb in parentheses.

1. Er _____. (nehmen)
2. Sie (*2nd pers. sing. pol.*) _____. (geben)
3. _____ du? (lesen)
4. Er _____. (sprechen)
5. Ihr _____. (fallen)
6. Du _____. (vergessen)
7. _____ sie? (sprechen)
8. _____ du? (sehen)

II. PRESENT TENSE: VERBS WITH SEPARABLE PREFIXES

Many German verbs consist of the verb itself and a particle known as a prefix, usually an adverb or a preposition that can stand alone as a word. This particle is placed directly in front of the infinitive (*pre* = in front of) and attached to it to form a unit: for example, **einsteigen** (to step in, that is, into a vehicle).

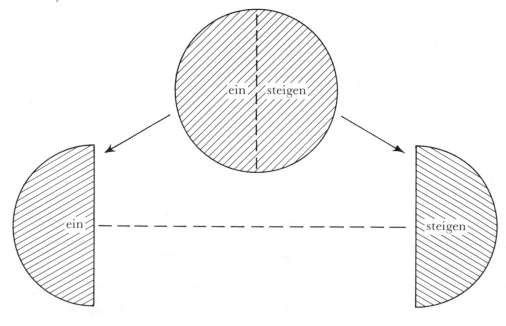

This attachment occurs in the infinitive form and in all tenses but the present and past. In the present tense (or in the simple past, to be discussed later), some prefixes become detached from the verb and move behind it, to the very end of the clause. These detachable prefixes are known as *separable prefixes*.

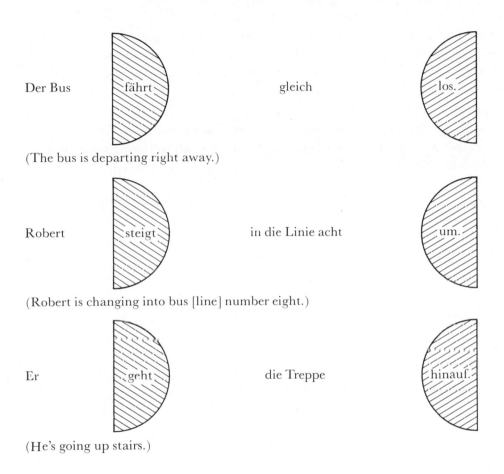

Der Bus   fährt   gleich   los.

(The bus is departing right away.)

Robert   steigt   in die Linie acht   um.

(Robert is changing into bus [line] number eight.)

Er   geht   die Treppe   hinauf.

(He's going up stairs.)

The prefix, when separated, is always placed at the end of the sentence or clause.

Note that the separable prefix remains affixed to its infinitive if the latter is dependent on another (inflected) verb.

	Principal Verb		*Dependent Infinitive*
Er	**sieht**	Rauch und Flammen	**aufsteigen.**
(He	sees	smoke and flames	rise up.)

Some of the most frequent separable prefixes include the following.

ab	ein	hinein	vorbei
an	heran	hinunter	weiter
auf	hin	los	zu
aus	hinauf	um	zurück

There are quite a few more. In the vocabularies contained in the book the separable prefix will be indicated by a dot · as in **ein·steigen.** This lexicographical device will alert you to the presence of a separable prefix. Remember, however, that the dot is not part of the spelling; it is only an aid to you.

These verbs with separable prefixes must be studied for their meanings, since these meanings change with the prefix. Sometimes related concepts are indicated, and sometimes the meaning is changed altogether. Be sure to look at the end of each German sentence to understand the verb correctly.

Er kommt aus Amerika.	He comes from America.
Er kommt in Deutschland **an.**	He arrives in Germany.
Er kommt die Treppe **herauf.**	He comes up the stairs.
Er kommt in das Haus **herein.**	He enters the house.

English also has many particles that occur in conjunction with a verb and very often change its meaning substantially. In many instances, however, the particle is placed *after* the verb.

to carry a burden
but to carry **on** a conversation

to look surprised
but to look **at** a picture
to look **after** a child
to look the lesson **over again**

In other situations, the particle is a genuine prefix and always remains attached to the verb, as in **to upstage, to offset,** and **to overcome.**

In German, some common verbs with separable prefixes include the following.

ab·fahren (to depart)	an·kommen (to arrive)
an·halten (to stop)	an·rufen (to telephone)

auf·schließen (to unlock)

auf·steigen (to rise)

aus·rufen (to announce)

aus·steigen (to get out)

ein·steigen (to step in)

heran·kommen (to approach)

hin·fahren (to drive there)

hinauf·gehen (to go up)

hinein·lassen (to let in)

hinunter·gehen (to go down)

los·fahren (to depart)

um·steigen (to change)

weiter·gehen (to go on)

zu·machen (to close)

zurück·laufen (to run back)

Note that you accent the prefix in pronouncing these verbs.

As you might have noticed, some of the above examples are constructed with the separable prefixes **hin** (or **hinauf, hinein, hinunter,** and so forth) suggesting a movement *away from* the position of the speaker, and **her** (or **heran, herein, herunter,** and so forth) suggesting a movement *toward* the speaker.

Away *from the speaker*	**Toward** *the speaker*
hin·fahren (to drive there)	her·kommen (to come here)
hinauf·gehen (to go up there)	heran·kommen (to approach)
hinein·lassen (to let in there)	herein·kommen (to come in here)
hinunter·gehen (to go down there)	herunter·kommen (to come down here)

Hin and **her** should not be confused with **hier** and **dort,** which indicate fixed position only and not movement.

Check Your Comprehension

Complete the sentence with the correct form of the verb in parentheses.

1. Ich _____ gleich _____. (losfahren)
2. Wir _____ in die Linie acht _____. (umsteigen)
3. Sie (*2nd pers. sing. pol.*) _____ das Zimmer _____. (aufschließen)
4. Der Bus _____ nach Hannover _____. (weiterfahren)
5. Ihr _____ in Berlin _____. (ankommen)
6. Flammen _____ _____. (aufsteigen)
7. Er _____ schnell _____. (zurücklaufen)
8. _____ Sie den Mann _____? (hineinlassen)

III. THE IMPERATIVE

The imperative form of the verb is used to give a command or make a suggestion. German distinguishes between three forms of direct address in the imperative: the **Sie–, du–,** and **ihr**-forms.

In the polite, or **Sie**-form, the imperative is identical to the second-person polite present-tense form, except that the pronoun follows the verb (inverted word order).

> **Kommen Sie,** bitte! Come (on), please.
> **Gehen Sie,** bitte! Please, go.

The command form of the second-person plural (familiar), the **ihr**-form, is identical to the present-tense form, except that the pronoun is dropped.

> **Kommt,** bitte! Please, come.
> **Geht,** bitte! Please, go.

The command form of the second-person singular (familiar), the **du**-form, is like the present-tense form, except that it drops the personal ending **–st** as well as the pronoun.

Present Tense	Imperative
du komm st	komm!
du geh st	geh!
du sprich st	sprich!
du nimm st	nimm!
du fähr st	fahr!
du läß t	laß!

Note that verbs with the vowel variation a > ä or au > äu do not carry the Umlaut into the singular imperative.

In all three forms of the imperative, the separable prefixes always follow the imperative forms or move to the end of the imperative clause.

du-form:	**Geh** bitte **weiter!**
ihr-form:	**Geht** bitte **weiter!**
Sie-form:	**Gehen** Sie bitte **weiter!**

Move on, please. [Go on, please.]

The verb **sein** (to be) has the following irregular imperative forms, which must be memorized.

du-form:	**Sei** gut!	
ihr-form:	**Seid** gut!	Be good!
Sie-form:	**Seien** Sie gut!	

Notice that the imperative forms in German are always followed by an exclamation mark.

The infinitive may be used as an "impersonal" imperative form to give instructions to the public. A bus driver, for instance, might call out the following.

Bitte, **einsteigen!**	Please, step in.
Weitergehen, bitte!	Please, move on.
Bitte, **aussteigen!**	(Everybody) out, please.

Check Your Comprehension

Give the three imperative forms of the verbs.

1. nehmen
2. kommen
3. gehen
4. weitergehen

5. sprechen
6. losfahren
7. tragen
8. zurücklaufen

CONVERSATION

Eine Busfahrt

Flugplatz Berlin-Tempelhof. Robert kommt gerade aus Hannover in West-Berlin an. Er nimmt das Gepäck und verläßt die Halle. Draußen warten Taxis. Er fragt einen Taxifahrer um Auskunft.

ROBERT	Verzeihung! Fährt ein Bus von hier nach Schöneberg[1]?	
TAXIFAHRER	Na, kommen Sie! Steigen Sie ein! Ich fahre Sie hin.	5
ROBERT	Nein danke. Wissen Sie: Ich bin Student. Ich habe leider nicht genug Geld für ein Taxi.	

TAXIFAHRER   Schade!—Sehen Sie die Bus-Haltestelle da drüben? Nehmen
Sie die Linie fünfzehn!

Robert sieht einen Bus kommen.   10

BUSFAHRER   Schnell, schnell! Bitte, einsteigen! Wir fahren sofort los.
Steigen Sie ein und stellen Sie das Gepäck dort in die Ecke!
ROBERT   Sie fahren schon los? Fahren Sie direkt nach Schöneberg?
BUSFAHRER   Nee, nee, wissen Sie: Wir fahren in die Stadtmitte, wo das
Europa-Center ist und der Kurfürstendamm.   15
ROBERT   Ach, dann ist das nicht die Linie fünfzehn? Was mache ich
denn² jetzt?
BUSFAHRER   Kaiser-Wilhelm-Straße umsteigen! Linie acht.
ROBERT   Ach so! Dann bitte einen Fahrschein bis Schöneberg.
BUSFAHRER   Eins vierzig, bitte.   20

Der Busfahrer ruft die Kaiser-Wilhelm-Straße aus. Robert steigt in die Linie
acht um. Der Bus ist sehr voll.

BUSFAHRER   Gehen Sie weiter! Bitte, weitergehen!
ROBERT   Rathaus Schöneberg, bitte. Wie weit ist das von hier?
BUSFAHRER   Vier Haltestellen. Ich rufe es gleich aus.   25
ROBERT   Vielen Dank!

---

¹ Schöneberg is a district in West Berlin.
² The word **denn** may occur in *questions* for purposes of emphasis. It does not alter the content
of the statement and cannot be directly translated.

ORAL PRACTICE

A. *Substitute each word in parentheses for the subject of the sentence, making any other
necessary alterations.*

1. Ich nehme den Bus Linie acht.
   (Robert / du / Sie / sie [*3rd pers. sing.*] / ihr / die Studenten / wir)
2. Fährt er nach Berlin?
   (ihr / Sie / du / wir / ihr / der Student aus Amerika)
3. Wissen Sie das wirklich?
   (der Taxifahrer / du / sie [*3rd pers. sing.*] / wir / Robert und
   Margret / ihr / sie [*3rd pers. pl.*])

B. *Substitute the appropriate form of each verb in parentheses for the verb in the sentence.*

1. Er nimmt den Bus.
   (sehen / verlassen / anhalten / fahren)
2. Du fährst sehr schnell.
   (laufen / sprechen / lesen / essen)
3. Fahren Sie bitte los!
   (einsteigen / aufschließen / weitergehen / herkommen)

C. *Convert the sentence into the imperative form.*

> EXAMPLE   Sie steigen aus.
> **Steigen Sie aus!**

1. Sie halten an.
2. Du verläßt den Raum.
3. Ihr fahrt schnell ab.
4. Ihr steigt hier ein.
5. Sie sind ein Mann.
6. Du sprichst Deutsch.
7. Ihr geht die Treppe hinauf.
8. Du nimmst den Fahrschein.
9. Ihr fahrt nach Schöneberg.
10. Sie sprechen Deutsch, Herr Miller.
11. Du läßt den Mann herein.
12. Du vergißt das Gepäck nicht.

D. *Substitute or add each phrase as it is introduced into the previous sentence and make any necessary structural changes.*

1. Sehen Sie die Bus-Haltestelle dort?
   _____ du _____?
   _____ den Flugplatz _____?
   _____ Sie _____?
   _____ das Gepäck _____?
   _____ ihr _____?
   _____ den Mercedes _____?
   _____ er _____?

2. Fahrt ihr oder lauft ihr nach Schöneberg?
   _____ du _____ du _____?
   _____ wir _____ wir _____?
   _____ Maria _____ sie _____?
   _____ Sie _____ Sie _____?
   _____ ich _____ ich _____?
   _____ Klaus _____ er _____?

E. *Supply the appropriate form of the verb in parentheses.*

1. Wann _____ du heute abend _____? (ankommen)
2. Wir _____ gleich _____. (aussteigen)
3. _____ ihr bitte die Tür _____! (zumachen)
4. Margret _____ Robert nicht _____. (hineinlassen)
5. Sie (*3rd pers. sing.*) _____ gerade die Treppe _____. (hinuntergehen)
6. Der Bus _____ in zehn Minuten _____. (abfahren)
7. _____ Sie bitte sofort _____! (herkommen)
8. Ich sehe, du _____ die Tür _____. (aufschließen)
9. _____ (du-*form*) noch zweihundert Meter _____! (weitergehen)
10. Der Busfahrer _____ die Haltestelle gleich _____. (ausrufen)

GUIDED CONVERSATION

A. As an exercise in using the command forms, exchange commands with someone in your class. Take turns giving commands, and continue the exchange until one of you misses or cannot think of a command that has not already been given. Practice using the **Sie–, du–,** and **ihr–**forms, and use **bitte** with each command.

B. Begin a conversation with the person sitting next to you. After exchanging greetings, you might comment on some of the following topics: the languages you speak (**Englisch, Deutsch, Französisch, Russisch, Spanisch**); the languages you are studying; whether you take a bus or a taxi, and if you take a bus, which line; whether you read books; whether you read a newspaper and, if so, what the name of it is.

READING

Feuer!

Robert verläßt das Hotel „Adler" und macht einen Spaziergang. Plötzlich hört er eine Sirene und sieht einen Feuerwehrwagen herankommen. Alle Autos fahren nach rechts und halten an. Robert sieht Rauch und Flammen aufsteigen. „Moment mal!", denkt er. „Ist das möglich? Ist das nicht das Hotel Adler?" 5

Er läuft schnell zurück, aber die Feuerwehr läßt Robert nicht hinein. Er protestiert vergeblich. Nach ungefähr zehn Minuten geht er die Treppe hinauf. Überall nichts als Rauch!

Robert schließt Zimmer „dreizehn" auf. Da liegt das Gepäck. Es ist ganz naß. Robert macht das Fenster zu. —„Besser naß als verbrannt!", denkt er. 10 Er geht in die Hotel-Bar hinunter und bestellt einen Whisky.

QUESTIONS

1. Was macht Robert gerade?
2. Was hört er plötzlich?
3. Was sieht er?
4. Was machen die Autofahrer?
5. Was steigt auf?
6. Läßt die Feuerwehr Robert hinein?
7. Wohin geht Robert nach ungefähr zehn Minuten?
8. Was findet er in Zimmer „dreizehn"?
9. Wohin geht Robert dann und was bestellt er?

VOCABULARY EXERCISES

Supply the appropriate word from the list on the right.

1. _____ warten Taxis.   a. Ecke
2. Robert fragt einen Busfahrer _____.   b. überall

3. Er hat _____ nicht genug Geld für ein Taxi.
4. Ich stelle das Gepäck in die _____.
5. Sie _____ nicht, wieviel das kostet.
6. Er hat einen _____ bis Schöneberg.
7. Du läufst _____ zehn Minuten.
8. _____ ist nichts als Rauch.
9. Sie machen einen _____.
10. Das Gepäck ist naß, aber nicht _____.

c. weiß
d. Fahrschein
e. draußen
f. um Auskunft
g. verbrannt
h. ungefähr
i. leider
j. Spaziergang

Review Exercises

A. *Substitute the correct form of the verb in parentheses for the word in boldface.*

1. Robert **verläßt** das Hotel „Adler". (sehen)
2. Ich **fahre** einen Volkswagen. (anhalten)
3. Wir **gehen** die Treppe **hinunter.** (heraufkommen)
4. Du **fährst** immer sehr schnell. (laufen)
5. Bitte, **steigen** Sie **ein!** (weitergehen)
6. **Mach** bitte die Tür **zu!** (aufschließen)
7. Wo **geht** ihr **hin?** (herkommen)
8. Sie **sieht** die Zeitung. (lesen)
9. **Lesen** Sie deutsch? (sprechen)
10. Warum **studiert** ihr nicht? (protestieren)

B. *Convert the sentence into a command.*

1. Robert verläßt das Hotel „Adler".
2. Herr Meyer, Sie fahren schnell.
3. Du gehst sofort die Treppe hinauf.
4. Ihr schließt das Fenster.
5. Robert und Margret essen heute abend.
6. Herr und Frau Meyer kommen her.

C. *Complete the sentence by using the correct form of the verb in parentheses.*

1. Richard, _____ in das Zimmer _____! (hinaufgehen)
2. Margret, _____ bitte das Fenster _____! (zumachen)
3. Bitte, Herr Meyer, _____ Sie _____! (weitergehen)
4. _____ Sie heute abend das Hotel _____? (anrufen)
5. Er _____ das Gepäck _____. (hineintragen)
6. Monika, _____ bitte die Zeitung _____! (herbringen)
7. Was _____ du? (meinen)
8. Hier, _____ die Warnung! (lesen, *sing. fam.*)
9. Sie _____ gleich _____. (losfahren, *3rd pers. sing.*)
10. Herr Meyer, bitte, _____ Sie nicht so schnell! (laufen)
11. Robert, _____ bitte das Gepäck! (nehmen)
12. Monika, _____ nicht, den Mann um Auskunft zu fragen! (vergessen)

GUIDED COMPOSITION

A. Do you use a local bus service? Write a brief description of one of your regular bus routes. Make your composition action-oriented by using as many verbs with separable prefixes as possible.

B. Write a brief eyewitness report of a fire, as if you were right there on the scene. Use some of the vocabulary contained in the reading passage.

Chapter Vocabulary

der **Abend, –e** evening
ab·fahren to depart, drive off
acht eight
als than
an·halten to stop
an·kommen to arrive (at a place)
an·rufen to call, telephone
auf·schließen to unlock
auf·steigen to rise
aus·rufen to announce
aus·steigen to get out

das **Auto, –s** car, automobile
der **Autofahrer, –** (car) driver, motorist

die **Bar, –s** bar
besser better
bestellen to order
der **Brief, –e** letter
der **Bus, –se** bus
der **Busfahrer, –** bus driver

der **Dank** thanks, gratitude
dann then
denken to think
direkt directly

dort there
draußen outside
dreizehn thirteen

die **Ecke, –n** corner
ein·steigen to step in

fahren to drive; go (by vehicle)
der **Fahrschein, –e** ticket
fallen to fall
das **Fenster, –** window
das **Feuer, –** fire
die **Feuerwehr, –en** fire brigade

der **Feuerwehrwagen,–** fire truck
die **Flamme, –n** flame
der **Flugplatz, ¨e** airport
fragen to ask
fünfzehn fifteen

geben to give
das **Geld, –er** money
genug enough
das **Gepäck** luggage

die **Halle, –n** hall; room
halten to stop
die **Haltestelle, –n** (bus or train) stop
hart heavily; hard
heran·kommen to approach
herauf·kommen to come up (here)
her·bringen to bring (here)
herein·kommen to come in (here)
herein·lassen to let in (here)
her·kommen to come (here)
herunter·kommen to come down (here)
heute today
hinauf·gehen to go up (there)
hinaus·gehen to go out (there)
hinein·lassen to let in (there)
hinein·tragen to carry in (there)
hin·fahren to drive (there)
hinunter·gehen to go down (there)
hören to hear
das **Hotel, –s** hotel

kosten to cost

lassen to leave, go; permit

laufen to run; go (by foot)
lesen to read
liegen to lie, rest, be situated
die **Linie, –n** line
los·fahren to drive off, depart

machen to do; make
mal just
meinen to mean; have an opinion
der **Mercedes, –** Mercedes-Benz (automobile)
das **Meter, –** meter [approx. 1 yard]
die **Minute, –n** minute
möglich possible

nach to; after
naß wet
nehmen to take
nichts nothing
nichts als nothing but

plötzlich suddenly
protestieren to protest

das **Rathaus, ¨er** city hall
der **Rauch** smoke
rechts right (hand)
nach rechts to the right

schließen to lock; close
schnell quickly, fast
schon already
sehen to see
die **Sirene, –n** siren
sofort right away, at once
der **Spaziergang, ¨e** walk
einen Spaziergang machen to take a walk
sprechen to speak
die **Stadtmitte, –n** city center
stellen to put, place

das **Taxi, –s** cab
der **Taxifahrer, –** cab driver
tragen to carry
die **Treppe, –n** stairs

über about; over
überall everywhere
der **Umlaut, –e** *modification of a vowel*
um·steigen to change (buses, trains)
ungefähr about, approximately

verbrannt burnt up
vergeblich in vain
vergessen to forget
verlassen to leave (behind)
vier four
vierzig forty
der **Volkswagen, –** Volkswagen (automobile)
voll full, packed
von from
von ... nach from ... to

wann when
warten wait
weit far
weiter·fahren to drive (further) on
weiter·gehen to go on, move on
wieviel how much
wissen to know (a fact)
wohin where (to)

zehn ten
die **Zeitung, –en** newspaper
das **Zimmer, –** room
zu·machen to close
zurück·laufen to run back
zweihundert two hundred

Chapter 4

Weingut

Useful Phrases

Bitte sehr?	May I help you?
immer wieder	again and again
zu Fuß gehen	to go by foot
nach Hause gehen	to go home
zu Hause sein	to be (at) home
Nun (ja)!	Well.

MODEL SENTENCES

I

Ich gebe **dem Mann** die Adresse.	I give the man the address.
Er schickt **einer Frau** ein Formular.	He sends a form to a woman.
Sie bezahlt **dem Studenten** das Geld.	She pays the student the money.

II

Ich komme gerade **aus der Küche.**	I'm just coming out of the kitchen.
Wir gehen **zur Bus-Haltestelle.**	We're going to the bus stop.
Sie fahren **mit dem Auto** nach Hause.	They're going home by car.
Heute abend bin ich **zu Hause.**	I will be home tonight.

III

Gehst du heute **zum Architekten?**	Are you going to the architect today?
Hier wohnen zwei **Studentinnen.**	Two (female) students live here.
Gib **dem Herrn** die Adresse!	Give the address to the gentleman.

Grammar Explanations

I. DATIVE CASE

Another important part of a sentence is the *indirect object*, which answers the question "to whom" or "for whom" something is done. The indirect object is in the *dative case*—"dative" derived from the Latin word for "to give." In the act of giving there is a giver (subject), a thing given (direct object), and a receiver of that thing (indirect object).

Subject		*Direct Object*	*Indirect Object*
Tom	gibt	das Geld	dem Mann(e).
(Tom	gives	the money	to the man.)

In English, the indirect object is recognized by the preposition "to" or "for" which may be expressed or silently understood. In German, the indirect object occurs without a preposition and is indicated by special forms of the definite and indefinite articles and the negative **kein.**

Jürgen bezahlt $\begin{cases} \textbf{dem} \\ \textbf{einem} \\ \textbf{keinem} \end{cases}$ Hausbesitzer das Geld.

Jürgen bezahlt $\begin{cases} \textbf{der} \\ \textbf{einer} \\ \textbf{keiner} \end{cases}$ Hausbesitzerin das Geld.

Jürgen bezahlt $\begin{cases} \textbf{dem} \\ \textbf{einem} \\ \textbf{keinem} \end{cases}$ Mädchen das Geld.

Definite and Indefinite Articles, **kein:** Dative Case

	Definite Article	*Indefinite Article*	**kein**
Singular			
masc.	de**m** Mann(e)	ein**em** Mann(e)	kein**em** Mann(e)
fem.	de**r** Frau	ein**er** Frau	kein**er** Frau
neut.	de**m** Kind(e)	ein**em** Kind(e)	kein**em** Kind(e)
Plural			
masc.			
fem.	**den** ⎰Männern / Frauen / Kindern⎱	—	**keinen** ⎰Männern / Frauen / Kindern⎱
neut.			

Note that monosyllabic masculine and neuter nouns *may* add an **–e** in the dative. Additionally, in the plural of the dative, all nouns must add an **–n** if they do not already end in **–n**.

Nominative Plural	*Dative Plural*
die Männer	**den** Männer**n**
die Kinder	**den** Kinder**n**
die Hausbesitzer	**den** Hausbesitzer**n**
die Studentinnen	**den** Studentinnen

One exception is that foreign words ending in **–s** in the plural (*see* Chapter 17) do not end in **–n**.

nom. sing.:	das Auto
nom. pl.:	die Auto**s**
dat. pl.:	den Auto**s**

Thus a sample sentence with the dative plural is the following.

Jürgen bezahlt ⎰ **den** / **keinen** ⎱ Hausbesitzer**n** das Geld.

Normally in German the dative precedes the accusative if the two objects are nouns.

Jürgen bezahlt dem Hausbesitzer das Geld.　　Jürgen pays the house owner the money.

(If the two objects are a noun and a pronoun or if both of them are pronouns, *see* Chapter 5 for word order.)

A summary of the definite and indefinite articles and **kein** in the three cases learned so far is presented in the following table.

Definite and Indefinite Articles, **kein:**
Nominative, Accusative, and Dative Cases

	Nominative	*Accusative*	*Dative*
Singular			
masc.	der	den	dem
	ein	einen	einem
	kein	keinen	keinem
fem.	die	die	der
	eine	eine	einer
	keine	keine	keiner
neut.	das	das	dem
	ein	ein	einem
	kein	kein	keinem
Plural			
all gend.	die	die	den
	—	—	—
	keine	keine	keinen

Check Your Comprehension

A. *Form the dative case of the noun with the definite article in the singular or plural as indicated by the article.*

1. das Fenster
2. die Garage
3. der Architekt
4. das Fräulein
5. das Auto
6. der Kamin

7. das Zimmer	13. die Studenten
8. das Kind	14. die Busse
9. das Bild	15. die Formulare
10. die Fenster	16. die Zimmer
11. die Garagen	17. die Kinder
12. die Architekten	18. die Bilder

B. *Form the dative singular of the noun with the indefinite article.*

1. ein Zimmer	6. ein Kind
2. ein Bild	7. ein Architekt
3. ein Fenster	8. eine Kasse
4. ein Auto	9. ein Mann
5. ein Fräulein	10. ein Student

II. PREPOSITIONS WITH THE DATIVE

A *preposition* is a structural component of a phrase that indicates the relation of a noun to a verb, pronoun, or another noun. The prepositional phrase is completed by the object of the preposition.

In German, each preposition governs a specific case, generally the accusative or dative—for example, the preposition **mit** "takes" the dative case.

The following is a list of prepositions that are *always* completed by the dative case. Memorize them, for they occur frequently. Note that the English translations are general and flexible, primarily because in any two given languages, prepositions are used in widely divergent ways, depending on the context of the entire sentence.

> aus (out of; from)
> außer (besides; except)
> bei (with; near)
> gegenüber (opposite)
> mit (with; by means of)
> nach (after; to; according to)
> seit (since; for *in reference to time*)
> von (from; by; of)
> zu (to)

The prepositions **bei, zu,** and **von** are usually contracted with the definite article.

bei	dem	=	**beim**
von	dem	=	**vom**
zu	dem	=	**zum**
zu	der	=	**zur**

Some of the above prepositions **require special attention.**

zu (to, referring to persons and public buildings)

Ich gehe **zu** den Kindern.	I'm going to the children.
Sie geht gerade **zur** Post.	She's going to the post office.

nach (to, referring to cities and countries)

Wir fahren morgen **nach** Köln.	We're going to Cologne tomorrow.

aus (from, indicating origin in a certain city or country)

Jürgen kommt **aus** Köln.	Jürgen comes from Cologne.

(*or* out of, indicating location)

Die Hausfrau kommt **aus** der Küche.	The housewife is coming out of the kitchen.

von (from, indicating from one point to another)

Jürgen fährt **von** Köln nach Düsseldorf.	Jürgen drives from Cologne to Düsseldorf.

bei (at or with, indicating someone's house or home)

Heinz wohnt **bei** Frau Becker.	Heinz lives at Mrs. Becker's place.
Sie wohnt **bei** uns.	She lives with us.

Two phrases using prepositions governing the dative case have special meanings: **zu Hause** indicates a fixed position, *at home*; **nach Hause** indicates a movement *toward home*.

Zu Hause habe ich einen Hund.	At home I have a dog.
Wir gehen jetzt **nach Hause.**	Now we're going home.

A. *Complete the prepositional phrase by using the noun in parentheses.*

1. aus _____ (das Fenster)
2. gegenüber _____ (der Kamin)
3. mit _____ (die Kinder)
4. außer _____ (ein Buch)
5. zu _____ (keine Frau)

6. seit _____ (ein Tag)
7. von _____ (der Freund)
8. nach _____ (die USA, *pl.*)
9. aus _____ (ein Wagen)
10. mit _____ (keine Küche)

B. *Complete the sentence by using the appropriate phrase, either* **zu Hause** *or* **nach Hause.**

1. Wir gehen gleich _____ .
2. Ich bin heute abend _____ .
3. Der Student lebt seit einem Jahr _____ .
4. Der Hund läuft _____ .
5. _____ ist der Hund nicht so wild.

III. SPECIAL NOUN DECLENSIONS

Although most nouns do not add any endings in the nominative, accusative, and dative singular, there are certain masculine nouns of non-Germanic origin, such as **der Student, der Philosoph,** and **der Architekt,** that add **–en** to all cases *except* the nominative. These nouns maintain the **–en** ending throughout the plural. The noun **der Mensch** (person, human being) also belongs to this declension.

Declensions: Certain Masculine Nouns

	No Ending	**–en** *Ending*	
Singular			
nom.	der Hausbesitzer	der Student	der Mensch
acc	den Hausbesitzer	den Student**en**	den Mensch**en**
dat.	dem Hausbesitzer	dem Student**en**	dem Mensch**en**
Plural			
nom.	die Hausbesitzer	die Student**en**	die Mensch**en**
acc.	die Hausbesitzer	die Student**en**	die Mensch**en**
dat.	den Hausbesitzer**n**	den Student**en**	den Mensch**en**

The frequently occurring noun **der Herr** (gentleman *or, without the article*, Mr.) deviates slightly from this special declension; it adds **–n** in the accusative and dative singular and **–en** in all plural forms.

Declension: **der Herr**

	Singular	*Plural*
nom.	der Herr	die Herr**en**
acc.	den Herr**n**	die Herr**en**
dat.	dem Herr**n**	den Herr**en**

Most nouns that designate a male form their feminine counterparts by adding **–in.**

Masculine	*Feminine*
der Freund	die Freund**in**
der Student	die Student**in**
der Partner	die Partner**in**
der Autofahrer	die Autofahrer**in**
der Hausbesitzer	die Hausbesitzer**in**

As is true of most feminine nouns in German, nouns ending in **–in** have no case endings in the singular. They have an **–en** ending throughout the plural, yet for phonological reasons they double the final **–n** of the stem.

sing.: die Freundin   pl.: die Freundin**n**en

Declension: **die Freundin**

	Singular	Plural
nom.	die Freundin	die Freundinnen
acc.	die Freundin	die Freundinnen
dat.	der Freundin	den Freundinnen

Check Your Comprehension

Put the noun into the case as indicated.

1. der Architekt (*dat. sing.*)
2. der Student (*acc. pl.*)
3. der Herr (*dat. sing.*)
4. der Hausbesitzer (*dat. pl.*)
5. die Partnerin (*nom. pl.*)
6. die Taxifahrerin (*dat. sing.*)
7. der Herr (*acc. pl.*)

CONVERSATION

Das Studentenzimmer

Heinz ist Student in Marburg. Er sucht ein Zimmer. Er geht zum Vermitt-lungsbüro und spricht mit Fräulein Schell.

FRL.[1] SCHELL	Guten Morgen! Bitte sehr?
HEINZ	Ich bin Student hier in Marburg und suche ein Zimmer.
FRL. SCHELL	Was für ein Zimmer möchten Sie denn? Ich meine, für wieviel?
HEINZ	Für ungefähr zweihundert Mark monatlich.
FRL. SCHELL	Moment bitte! Wie ist es mit einem Zimmer direkt bei der Universität? Es kostet zweihundertvierzig Mark mit Heizung.

HEINZ	Hm! Das ist nicht gerade billig! Ist das mit einer Kochgelegen-heit?	10
FRL. SCHELL	Ja, ich bin sicher.	
HEINZ	Hat das Zimmer auch Dusche oder Bad?	
FRL. SCHELL	Nein, aber eine Waschgelegenheit.	
HEINZ	Und wie ist es mit der Toilette?	15
FRL. SCHELL	Sie ist direkt gegenüber dem Zimmer.	
HEINZ	Und wie weit ist es zur Bus-Haltestelle?	
FRL. SCHELL	Ungefähr fünf Minuten zu Fuß.	
HEINZ	Nicht schlecht! Wie ist die Adresse, bitte?	
FRL. SCHELL	Frau Becker, Lindenstraße fünf.—Beim Hindenburgplatz.	20
HEINZ	Danke! Was kostet das?	
FRL. SCHELL	Acht Mark. Unterschreiben Sie bitte das Formular und geben Sie es Frau Becker.	
HEINZ	Und wo bezahle ich die acht Mark?	
FRL. SCHELL	Gehen Sie bitte da drüben zur Kasse!	25
HEINZ	Ja, vielen Dank! Auf Wiedersehen!	

---

[1] **Frl.** is the abbreviation for **Fräulein.**

ORAL PRACTICE

A. *Substitute the items in parentheses for the noun in boldface and make the necessary changes. Note that some substitutions are singular and some plural.*

1. Bringt ihr **der Dame** den Brief?
   (Fräulein / Professor / Hausbesitzer / Eltern / Mädchen / Studenten / Frau / Mann)
2. Glaubst du **dem Architekten?**
   (Busfahrer / Kinder / Frau Becker / Freund / Menschen / Mädchen / Dame)
3. Wir geben **einem Studenten** immer einen Platz.
   (Mädchen / Autofahrer / Freund / Frauen / Hausbesitzer / Kind / Freundin)

B. *Substitute the noun in parentheses for the noun in boldface and make the necessary changes.*

1. Er bezahlt **dem Hausbesitzer** das Geld. (Hausbesitzerin)
2. Das Mädchen schickt **dem Freund** einen Brief. (Freundin)
3. Der Busfahrer gibt **dem Studenten** einen Fahrschein. (Studentin)
4. Der Hund bringt **dem Mann** die Zeitung. (Herr)
5. Der Taxifahrer gibt **der Dame** eine Auskunft. (Fräulein)

C. *Substitute the items in parentheses for the noun in boldface and make the necessary changes.*

1. Monika kommt aus **der Universität.**
   (Badezimmer / Küche / die Rocky Mountains / Bus / Toilette / Hotel / Garage)
2. Sie bekommt monatlich einen Brief von **einem Taxifahrer.**
   (Freundin / Professor / Mädchen / Kind / Dame / Busfahrer / Freund)
3. Gegenüber **dem Kamin** hängt das Bild von Picasso.
   (Sofa / Küche / Heizung / Radio / Dusche / Fenster / Toilette / Tür)
4. Wir geben **dem Herrn** die Bilder.
   (Student / Damen / Kinder / Mensch / Freund / Professorin / Studenten)

D. *Substitute the noun in parentheses for the noun in boldface and make the necessary changes.*

1. Außer **der Zeitung** bringt er Paul einen Brief. (das Geld)
2. Ich gehe selten **zur Post.** (Flugplatz)
3. Der Freund fährt mit **einem Bus.** (Auto)
4. Er kommt aus **der Wohnung.** (Zimmer)
5. Sie wohnt bei **einem Freund.** (keine Studentinnen)

E. *Supply the appropriate expression, either* **zu Hause** *or* **nach Hause.**

1. Heute abend sind wir _____.
2. Kommt ihr bald _____?
3. Fahren wir jetzt _____?
4. Der Hund ist _____.
5. Die Eltern sind heute nicht _____.

F. *Substitute or add each phrase as it is introduced into the previous sentence and make any necessary structural changes.*

Geben Sie bitte der Dame   den Brief!
_____ Herr _____!
_____ eine Auskunft!
_____ Student_____!
Gib _____!
_____ die Zeitung!
Bringt _____!
_____ Architekt _____!

GUIDED CONVERSATION

Begin a conversation with someone in your class. After exchanging greetings, ask where he/she lives. Ask if his/her apartment or room has a bathroom, shower, toilet, garage, cooking facilities, heating. You might also ask if the apartment or room is cheap, near the university, not far from a bus stop. Describe your own room or apartment; or, if you are looking for one, explain what type you want.

Eine Autofahrt

Jürgen fährt den Wagen aus der Garage und schaltet das Licht an. Es ist schon spät. Er fährt ungefähr zwei Stunden bis Köln.

Unterwegs denkt er: Was geschieht mit der Wohnung? Wann ist sie fertig? Der Architekt sagt in zwei Wochen. Wie ist es möglich, die Küche und das Badezimmer so schnell fertig zu haben? Das glaube ich einfach nicht. 5

Wo stellen wir eigentlich das Sofa hin? Links von der Tür? Oder vielleicht besser rechts vom Fenster? Wo hängen wir denn das Bild von Picasso hin? Vielleicht gegenüber dem Kamin? Wann bekommen wir denn Telefon?

Warum bezahlen wir dem Hausbesitzer eigentlich soviel Geld für die Wohnung? Nun, das Öl ist jetzt wirklich nicht billig. Immer wieder Öl-Krisen! 10

Bald sieht Jürgen die Rheinbrücke. Er schaltet das Radio an und hört Nachrichten. Man[1] spricht von der Öl-Krise . . .

---

[1] The word **man** is an indefinite personal pronoun, usually denoting the generalization "one," "a person," "you," "they," "anyone," or "everyone": "**Man** spricht von einer Öl-Krise" is expressed in English as "**They** speak about an oil crisis."

QUESTIONS

1. Wohin fährt Jürgen?
2. Wie lange fährt er bis Köln?
3. Wann, sagt der Architekt, ist die Wohnung fertig?
4. Glaubt Jürgen dem Architekten?
5. Wo ist der Platz für das Sofa?
6. Wo ist der Platz für das Bild von Picasso?
7. Warum ist das Öl jetzt nicht billig?
8. Wem bezahlt Jürgen soviel Geld?
9. Jürgen schaltet das Radio an. Was hört er?

VOCABULARY EXERCISES

A. *Supply the appropriate word from the list on the right.*

1. Heinz sucht ein _____.	a. Formular
2. Er geht zu einem _____.	b. Heizung
3. Er bezahlt 240 Mark für das Zimmer mit _____.	c. Vermittlungsbüro
4. Das Zimmer hat kein _____.	d. Toilette
5. Es hat aber eine _____.	e. Bad
6. Die _____ ist direkt gegenüber dem Zimmer.	f. Waschgelegenheit
7. Heinz unterschreibt das _____.	g. Zimmer

B. *Do the same with the following sentences.*

1. Jürgen _____ das Licht _____.	a. bekommt
2. Er denkt: Was _____ mit der Wohnung?	b. hängt . . . hin
3. Wo _____ er das Sofa _____?	c. schaltet . . . an
4. Wo _____ er das Bild von Picasso _____?	d. bezahlt
5. Wann _____ er Telefon?	e. geschieht
6. Warum _____ er dem Hausbesitzer soviel Geld?	f. stellt . . . hin

Review Exercises

A. *Complete the sentence by using the dative form of the noun in parentheses.*

1. Geben Sie bitte _____ den Brief! (der Architekt)
2. Bitte, gib _____ kein „Wiener Schnitzel"! (ein Hund)
3. Gibst du _____ fünf Mark? (das Fräulein)
4. Ich gebe _____ eine Rose. (eine Dame)
5. Barbara schickt _____ eine Postkarte. (die Eltern)
6. Geben Sie _____ nicht zuviel Geld! (die Frau)
7. Gib _____ die Hand, Emil! (das Mädchen)
8. Bringen Sie _____ ein Glas Wasser! (der Professor)
9. UNICEF hilft _____ in Afrika. (Kinder)
10. Bringst du _____ die Zeitung? (die Freundin)

B. *Do the same with the following sentences.*

1. Ich wohne bei _____. (die Eltern)
2. Das Sofa steht gegenüber _____. (der Kamin)
3. Außer zwei _____ bekommt er heute fünf Postkarten. (Briefe)
4. Monika wohnt bei _____. (eine Freundin)
5. Heute bekommt sie einen Brief von _____. (ein Taxifahrer)
6. Heute abend gehen wir zu . (der Architekt)
7. Er fliegt nach _____ in Afrika. (ein Land)
8. Fährst du mit _____ nach Köln? (der Bus)
9. Fahrt ihr sofort zu _____? (der Flugplatz)
10. Ich komme gerade aus _____. (das Badezimmer)

C. *Supply the appropriate case of the noun in parentheses.*

1. Das Mädchen gibt _____ die Hand. (der Herr)
2. Er bezahlt _____ viel Geld. (der Hausbesitzer)
3. In den USA sieht man mehr _____ als in Deutschland. (Taxifahrerin, *pl.*)
4. In Deutschland rauchen _____ mehr Zigaretten als die Studenten. (die Studentin, *pl.*)
5. Heute abend sehe ich wahrscheinlich _____. (der Architekt)

GUIDED COMPOSITION

A. Write a brief composition regarding where you live. You might begin by stating your address, then explaining your location in terms of what is opposite, near, and not far away. You might also mention in whose place you live or with whom you live. Try to use as many of the prepositional phrases you have learned in this chapter as possible.

B. Using the expressions **Ich bin . . .** and **Ich bin kein(e) . . .** , write a brief composition regarding who you are and who you are not. Among others, you might include the following: **Student(in), Hausbesitzer(in), Taxifahrer(in), Amerikaner(in).** Use as many other terms as you can think of.

Chapter Vocabulary

die **Adresse, –n** address
(das) **Afrika** Africa
an · schalten to switch on, turn on
der **Architekt, –en** architect
die **Autofahrerin, –nen** (female) auto driver
die **Autofahrt, –en** ride, drive

das **Bad, ̈er** bath (room)
das **Badezimmer, –** bathroom
bald soon
bekommen to get, receive
bezahlen to pay
das **Bild, –er** picture
billig cheap
bringen to bring; take to
die **Brücke, –n** bridge

die **Dame, –n** lady
der **Dollar, –** *unit of American currency*
die **Dusche, –n** shower

einfach simply
die **Eltern** (*pl.*) parents

fertig ready
das **Formular, –e** form (sheet)
die **Freundin, –nen** (female) friend
fünf five
der **Fuß, ̈e** foot

die **Garage, –n** garage
geschehen to happen
das **Glas, ̈er** glass

die **Hand, ̈e** hand
hängen to hang
das **Haus, ̈er** house
der **Hausbesitzer, –** house *or* property owner
die **Hausbesitzerin, –nen** (female) house *or* property owner
die **Heizung, –en** heating system
die **Herrin, –nen** lady
hin · hängen to hang (there)
hin · stellen to put (there)
der **Hund, –e** dog

immer always

das **Jahr, –e** year

der **Kamin, –e** fireplace
die **Kasse, –n** cashier's desk
die **Kochgelegenheit, –en** cooking facilities
die **Krise, –n** crisis
die **Küche, –n** kitchen

das **Land, ̈er** country
das **Licht, –er** light
links left (side)
nach links to the left

man someone
die **Mark** *unit of German currency*
mehr more
mehr als more than
monatlich monthly

die **Nachrichten** (*pl.*) news
nie never

das **Öl, –e** oil

der **Partner, –** partner
die **Partnerin, –nen** female partner

der **Philosoph, –en** philosopher

der **Platz, ⸚e** place

die **Post** post office; mail

die **Postkarte, –n** postcard

der **Professor, –en** professor

das **Radio, –s** radio

die **Rheinbrücke, –n** bridge over the Rhine

die **Rose, –n** rose

schicken to send

schlecht bad

selten seldom

sicher certain

das **Sofa, –s** sofa

soviel so much

spät late

die **Studentin, –nen** (female) student

die **Taxifahrerin, –nen** (female) cab driver

die **Toilette, –n** toilet

die **Universität, –en** university

unterschreiben to sign

unterwegs on the way

die **USA** (*pl.*) United States

das **Vermittlungsbüro, –s** rental agency

der **Wagen, –** vehicle

wahrscheinlich probably

die **Waschgelegenheit, –en** washing facilities

das **Wasser, –** water

wem to whom

wild wild

die **Woche, –n** week

wohnen to live

die **Wohnung, –en** apartment

zu • hören to listen to

Chapter 5

Bonn

Useful Phrases

Ach!	Oh!
Aha!	I see.
So!	I see.
Liebe Elke, . . .	Dear Elke, . . .
Lieber Wolfgang, . . .	Dear Wolfgang, . . .
Wie bitte?	What did you say?
Wie geht's?	How are you? [How's it going?]
Danke, gut.	Fine, thank you.
Wie geht es dir?	How are you?
Danke, (mir geht es) gut.	I'm fine, thanks.

MODEL SENTENCES

I

Ich **habe** Coca-Cola **getrunken**.	I drank a coke.
Du **hast** alles **vergessen**.	You forgot everything.
Sie **hat** Wodka **hineingemischt**.	She mixed in some Vodka.
Wir **sind** in Frankfurt **gelandet**.	We landed in Frankfurt.
Er **ist** sehr schnell **gerannt**.	He ran very fast.
Bei uns **ist** allerhand **passiert**.	Quite a lot happened with us.
Ich **wohne seit** drei Jahren hier.	I have been living here for three years.

II

Hast du **ihn** vergessen?	Did you forget him?
Ich liebe **dich**.	I love you.
Gib **mir** eine Antwort!	Give me an answer.
Antworten Sie **ihm**!	Answer him.

Ich kenne ihn **nicht.**	I don't know him.
Ich habe ihn wirklich **nicht** gekannt.	I really didn't know him.
Er ist **nicht** gesund.	He isn't well.
Sie ist **nicht** zu Hause.	She isn't at home.

Grammar Explanations

I. PRESENT PERFECT TENSE

As previously explained, German has only one present-tense form to express present time. To denote *past time*, however, German, like English, makes use of several tenses: present perfect, past, and past perfect. The formation and the differing uses of these past tenses need careful study.

A. Usage

In German the *present perfect tense* is most commonly used in the spoken language or in an informal type of writing, such as a letter to a friend, to indicate an action that occurred in the past and ended in the past, before the moment of speaking or writing. This use of the present perfect in German is often termed the "conversational past." In this case, the present perfect tense genuinely expresses *past time*; in English, the simple past tense is used in such instances.

Ich **habe** eine Party **besucht.**	I went to a party.
Ich **habe** den Baum nicht **gesehen.**	I did not see the tree.
Wie **ist** das **passiert?**	How did it happen?
Ich **bin** schnell nach links **gefahren.**	I quickly turned left.

In German, the present perfect tense may also indicate a "stretch" of time—referring to an action that occurred in the past and ended in the *recent* past or in the present. In this instance, the present perfect is often used with an expression such as **schon** or **gerade.** In this case, it corresponds to English usage, and it occurs in both conversational and literary style.

Ich **habe** es schon **gemacht.**	I have already done it. [I no longer have to do it.]
Haben Sie es schon **vergessen?**	Have you already forgotten it? [I no longer can forget it since I already have forgotten it.]
Kürzlich **ist** bei uns viel **passiert.**	A lot has happened to us recently. [But no longer.]

An important distinction between German and English is that when an action or state of being *starts at some point in the past and continues through the present into the future*, German uses the present tense, often in conjunction with the preposition **seit,** whereas English adheres to the present perfect tense.

Ich **wohne seit** drei Jahren hier.	I have lived here for three years. [Understood: "...and still do."]
Seit Montag **arbeitet** er wieder.	He has been back at work since Monday. [Understood: "...and is still working."]

As is true of the present tense in German, the present perfect tense covers a wide range of meanings in the corresponding English translation, including the progressive and emphatic forms.

	He visited us.
	He has visited us.
Er hat uns besucht.	He was visiting us.
	He did visit us.

The simple past tense is preferred as the formal, literary tense (*see* Chapter 6) for a point of time in the past; the past perfect tense indicates an action that began in the past and ended in the *late* past (*see* Chapter 12).

Note the following contrastive analysis of expressing past actions in German and English.

Past Time: Contrastive Analysis

Time Action Occurred		German	English
"Point" of time in the past	Present	Present Perfect (conversational style)	Past
●		Wie **ist** das **passiert?**	How **did** that happen?
"Stretch" of time extending from past to the present	Present	Present Perfect (with **schon**)	Present Perfect
●——————→		**Haben** Sie es schon **vergessen?**	**Have** you already **forgotten** it?
"Stretch" of time extending from past through present into future	Present	Present (with **seit**)	Present Perfect
●——————→		Seit Montag **arbeitet** er wieder.	He **has been** back at work since Monday.

B. Formation

The present perfect is at times called a "compound" tense because it consists of two entities: (1) the present tense of the auxiliary verb, either **haben** or **sein,** and (2) the past participle of the principal verb.

Infinitive	Auxiliary	Past Participle
besuchen (to visit)	Ich habe . . .	besucht.
trinken (to drink)	Er hat . . .	getrunken.
gehen (to go)	Wir sind . . .	gegangen.

1. Weak Verbs. Weak verbs form the past participle by placing the unchanged verb stem between the frame **ge——t.**

Infinitive	Stem	Past Participle	
glauben (to believe)	glaub	ge glaub	t
machen (to make)	mach	ge mach	t
merken (to notice)	merk	ge merk	t
sagen (to say)	sag	ge sag	t

If the stem of a weak verb ends in **–d** or **–t,** as in **landen** (to land) and **arbeiten** (to work), or in **–m** or **–n** when preceded by a consonant other than **l** and **r** as in **atmen** (to breathe) and **öffnen** (to open), an **–e–** is inserted between the stem and the **–t** of the participial ending in order to facilitate pronunciation.

geland **e** t
gearbeit **e** t
geatm **e** t
geöffn **e** t

2. Strong Verbs. Strong verbs form their past participles by placing a changed or, in a few cases, the unchanged form of the stem between the frame **ge——en.**

Infinitive	Stem	Past Participle	
fahren (to ride)	fahr	ge fahr	en
kommen (to come)	komm	ge komm	en
schreiben (to write)	schrieb	ge schrieb	en
trinken (to drink)	trunk	ge trunk	en
gehen (to go)	gang	ge gang	en
singen (to sing)	sung	ge sung	en
schwimmen (to swim)	schwomm	ge schwomm	en

Since the stem changes are not predictable, you must memorize the past participle of each verb when you learn the infinitive. In the chapter and end vocabularies, the past participles are indicated if there is a stem change.

Frequently, verbs with cognate forms in English show the same or similar vowel changes.

kommen	gekommen		trinken	getrunken		singen	gesungen
to come	come		to drink	drunk		to sing	sung

3. Irregular Verbs. Irregular weak verbs are *hybrids* that have the frame **ge——t** of the weak verbs but feature a stem vowel change similar to the strong verbs. There are very few of these, some of which are the following.

Infinitive	*Past Participle*		
brennen (to burn)	ge	brann	t
bringen (to bring)	ge	brach	t
denken (to think)	ge	dach	t
kennen (to know)	ge	kann	t
nennen (to name)	ge	nann	t
rennen (to run)	ge	rann	t
senden (to send)	ge	sand	t
wenden (to turn)	ge	wand	t

Four important irregular verbs have special forms for the past participle that follow no pattern and must be memorized individually.

Infinitive	*Past Participle*		
sein (to be)	ge	wes	en
tun (to do)	ge	ta	n
werden (to become)	ge	word	en
wissen (to know)	ge	wuß	t

Verbs with separable prefixes insert the **ge–** of the past participle form *between the separable prefix and the stem.*

an·halten (to stop)	an**ge**halten
um·steigen (to change)	um**ge**stiegen
hinein·mischen (to mix in)	hinein**ge**mischt

One more category of special irregular past participles is verbs with inseparable prefixes. These prefixes always remain attached to the verb, unlike the separable prefixes, which move to the end of the main clause or sentence in the simple tenses (*see* Chapter 3).

Some prefixes that are inseparable are **be–, emp–, ent–, er–, ge–, ver–,** and **zer–.** In pronunciation, accent the verb stem, not the prefix. These verbs do not take a **ge–** prefix, and this means that sometimes the past participle looks like the infinitive.

	Infinitive	*Past Participle*
	bekommen (to get, receive)	bekommen
	vergessen (to forget)	vergessen
	verlassen (to leave)	verlassen
but		
	verstehen (to understand)	verstanden
	verbrennen (to burn)	verbrannt

(Inseparable and separable prefixes will be further discussed in Chapter 15.)

Finally, verbs ending in **–ieren** also do not use the **ge–** prefix in the past participle, and always take the suffix **–t.**

Infinitive	*Past Participle*
studieren (to study)	studiert
telefonieren (to phone)	telefoniert

C. The Auxiliary: <u>sein</u> or <u>haben</u>?

Most verbs use the auxiliary **haben** to form the present perfect tense; however, there are some verbs that use the auxiliary **sein**. To use **sein** as the auxiliary, the verb must: (1) be intransitive—that is, it does not govern the accusative case (there is no direct object) and (2) indicate a change in the position or the condition of the grammatical subject. Some examples of verbs with **sein** as the auxiliary are the following.

Infinitive	*Auxiliary*	*Past Participle*
fahren (to drive)	Er ist . . .	gefahren.
kommen (to come)	Wir sind . . .	gekommen.
gehen (to go)	Ihr seid . . .	gegangen.
werden (to become)	Du bist . . .	geworden.

The auxiliary verb **sein** (to be) itself and the verb **bleiben** (to remain), both intransitive, though not showing motion, are nevertheless conjugated with sein.

Ich bin dort gewesen.	I've been there.
Er ist hier geblieben.	He's stayed here.

To avoid asking oneself constantly whether to use **sein** or **haben,** it is best to memorize the needed auxiliary along with the past participle. In the vocabularies of this book those verbs with the auxiliary **sein** are indicated in the following way: **fahren, ——, <u>ist</u> gefahren**. Verbs that take the auxiliary **haben** carry no special indication in the past participle form: **trinken, ——, getrunken**.

In some cases, a verb of motion may take a direct object, and then it requires the auxiliary **haben.**

Er **ist** nach Berlin **gefahren.**	He drove to Berlin.
Er **hat** *das Auto* **gefahren.**	He drove *the car.*

Sie **sind** mit dem Flugzeug **geflogen.**	You flew (somewhere) with the airplane.
Sie **haben** *das Flugzeug* **geflogen.**	You flew (piloted) the airplane.

D. Word Order

The past participle is always placed at the end of the clause.

Ich habe eine Party **besucht.**	I visited a party.
Sie haben natürlich Orangensaft **getrunken.**	Naturally you drank orange juice.
Wie ist das mit dem Unfall **gewesen?**	How was that with the accident?

Thus, in the present perfect tense, the verb in second position in the sentence (*see* Chapter 2) is the conjugated auxiliary.

Check Your Comprehension

A. *Supply the correct present-perfect-tense form of the indicated verb.*

1. Ich _____ Orangensaft _____. (trinken)
2. Wie _____ das _____? (sein)
3. Was _____ Sie _____? (machen)
4. Wir _____ nach Hause _____. (fahren)
5. Er _____ dort _____. (umsteigen)
6. Der Baum _____ rechts _____. (stehen)

7. Du _____ Wodka _____. (hineinmischen)
8. Ihr _____ ein Radio _____. (haben)
9. Sie (sing.) _____ einen Brief _____. (bekommen)
10. Wir _____ den Mann _____. (kennen)

B. *Change the sentence to the present perfect tense, and be sure to watch the position of the past participle.*

1. Die Polizei macht eine Blutprobe.
2. Ich sehe den Baum.
3. Er mischt Wodka hinein.
4. Ein Porsche kommt von rechts.
5. Wir fahren schnell nach links.

C. *Give the English equivalent of the German sentence.*

1. Ich habe einen Freund besucht.
2. Was ist passiert?
3. Wo sind Sie gewesen?
4. Ich bin in Schöneberg umgestiegen.
5. Wir arbeiten wieder seit zwei Wochen.

II. PERSONAL PRONOUNS: ACCUSATIVE AND DATIVE CASES

The personal pronouns, introduced in the nominative case in Chapter 1, also have accusative and dative case forms.

In the plural first and second persons, the pronouns are the same in the dative and accusative cases. If there are two objects in a sentence, and both of them are pronouns, the word order is accusative before dative.

Jürgen bezahlt es ihm.　　Jürgen pays [it] (to) him.

If one object is a pronoun and the other a noun, the pronoun precedes the noun.

Jürgen bezahlt es dem Hausbesitzer.　　Jürgen pays [it] (to) the house owner.
Jürgen bezahlt ihm das Geld.　　Jürgen pays him the money.

Personal Pronouns: Nominative, Accusative, Dative Cases

	Nominative	Accusative	Dative
Singular			
1st pers.	ich	mich	mir
2nd pers. (fam.)	du	dich	dir
3rd pers.	er	ihn	ihm
	sie	sie	ihr
	es	es	ihm
Plural			
1st pers.	wir	uns	uns
2nd pers. (fam.)	ihr	euch	euch
3rd pers.	sie	sie	ihnen
Singular / Plural			
2nd pers. (pol.)	Sie	Sie	Ihnen

Check Your Comprehension

Supply the appropriate form of the pronoun in parentheses.

1. Er kennt _____. (you, *fam. sing.*)
2. Sie kennt _____. (you, *fam. pl.*)
3. Sie kennen _____. (me)
4. Kennst du _____? (him)
5. Er kennt _____. (us)
6. Sie kennt _____. (you, *pol.*)
7. Er kennt _____. (her)
8. Kennen Sie _____? (them)
9. Kennst du _____? (it)
10. Sie schreibt _____ sehr oft. (to him)
11. Schreiben sie _____ oft? (to you, *pol.*)
12. Schreibst du _____ sehr oft? (to her)

13. Ich schreibe _____. (to you, *fam. sing.*)
14. Ich schreibe _____ oft genug. (to you, *fam. pl.*)
15. Sie schreiben _____ oft. (to us)

III. POSITION OF <u>nicht</u>

The position of **nicht** (not) varies considerably in German. It should be gradually learned through careful observation. The following rules of thumb will, however, provide a few useful guidelines.

    A.   In general, **nicht** is placed *behind the direct and indirect objects*. This means that in the present tense it is at the end of the clause.

Ich kenne ihn	nicht.
Warum schreibst du mir	nicht?
Ich verstehe die Erklärung	nicht.

Nicht must also precede the separable prefix when that prefix falls at the end of a clause.

Er kommt	nicht	an.
Steigen Sie	nicht	ein?
Der Busfahrer ruft die Haltestelle	nicht	aus.

If the verb is in the present perfect tense, however, **nicht** precedes the past participle (because the past participle must always fall at the end of the clause).

Ich habe ihn	nicht	gekannt.
Warum hast du mir	nicht	geschrieben?
Ich habe die Erklärung	nicht	verstanden.
Er ist	nicht	angekommen.

Notice that in the above examples, **nicht** *negates the whole clause.*

B. **Nicht** is inserted between the verb **sein** (to be) and the predicate adjective or predicate noun.

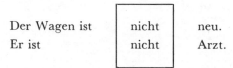

| Der Wagen ist | nicht | neu. |
| Er ist | nicht | Arzt. |

C. With adverbs the position of **nicht** varies. Some adverbs, such as **tatsächlich** (really) and **wahrscheinlich** (probably) that merely add emphasis, precede **nicht.**

| Er kommt tatsächlich | nicht. | |
| Sie fährt wahrscheinlich | nicht | ab. |

Nicht precedes more descriptive adverbs.

| Er spricht | nicht | laut. |
| Sie fährt | nicht | schnell. |

D. **Nicht** is usually placed in front of prepositional phrases.

| Sie geht | nicht | nach Hause. |
| Wir fahren | nicht | in die Stadtmitte. |

Thus, in general, one may say that **nicht** is placed (1) at the end of a sentence when it negates the complete thought or (2) in front of the sentence element that it directly negates. In the sentence "Hans spricht **nicht** laut" **nicht** negates not "spricht" but "laut."

However, in the sentence "Er kommt wahrscheinlich **nicht**" **nicht** does not specifically negate "wahrscheinlich" but, rather, the *whole* action and situation expressed in "Er kommt wahrscheinlich."

In the sentence "Ich kenne ihn **nicht**" **nicht** obviously negates the whole idea expressed in the sentence. But in the sentence "Ich kenne **nicht** *ihn*, sondern *sie*" (I do not know *him*, but [I do know] *her*) **nicht** merely negates "ihn," in contrast to "sie."

Remember that nouns preceded by **ein** are negated by **kein,** not by **nicht** (*see* Chapter 2). In other words, **nicht** plus **ein** becomes **kein.**

Ich bin keine Hausbesitzerin, sagte sie.   I'm not a property owner, she said.

Place **nicht** *in the correct position in the sentence.*

1. Die Polizei hat mich angehalten.
2. Er hat den Baum gesehen.
3. Ich habe die Party besucht.
4. Der Volkswagen hat uns überholt.
5. Kennst du ihn?
6. Sie schreibt mir oft.
7. Trinken Sie wirklich Orangensaft?
8. Bist du tatsächlich krank gewesen?

CONVERSATION

Vor Gericht

STAATSANWALT	Herr Steinhoff, jetzt sagen Sie uns bitte: Wie ist das mit dem Unfall gewesen?
ANGEKLAGTER	Ja, ich habe eine Party bei Freunden besucht.
STAATSANWALT	Aha, Sie haben eine Party besucht! Was haben Sie denn da getrunken?
ANGEKLAGTER	Wir haben Wein, Bier oder Orangensaft getrunken.
STAATSANWALT	So! Und Sie haben natürlich Orangensaft getrunken.
ANGEKLAGTER	Ich glaube, ja.
STAATSANWALT	Wie bitte? Sie glauben? Ich verstehe Sie nicht. Die Polizei

5

	hat Sie unterwegs angehalten und eine Blutprobe gemacht. [10]
	Haben Sie wirklich nur Orangensaft getrunken?
ANGEKLAGTER	Jemand hat mir vielleicht etwas Wodka hineingemischt. Ich bin nicht sicher.
STAATSANWALT	Und das haben Sie natürlich nicht gemerkt!—Oder haben Sie es schon vergessen? Sie haben Staatseigentum be- [15] schädigt!
ANGEKLAGTER	Ach, Sie meinen den Baum? Ja, wie ist das eigentlich passiert? Da ist ein Porsche von rechts gekommen und hat mich überholt. Und dann bin ich schnell nach links gefahren.
STAATSANWALT	Herr Steinhoff, der Baum hat aber rechts gestanden! [20]
ANGEKLAGTER	Nun ja, ich habe ihn wahrscheinlich nicht gesehen, weil . . .
STAATSANWALT	Antworten Sie mir, bitte!
ANGEKLAGTER	Ich weiß nicht . . .
STAATSANWALT	Dann gebe ich Ihnen die Antwort. Die Antwort ist klar: Sie haben leider etwas zuviel Orangensaft im[1] Blut gehabt! [25]

---

[1] im = in dem

ORAL PRACTICE

A. *Substitute the items in parentheses for the pronoun in boldface and make the necessary changes.*

1. **Ich** habe eine Party bei einem Freund besucht.
   (wir / der Staatsanwalt / die Eltern / ihr zwei / du / die Dame / der Angeklagte)
2. **Wir** sind gestern von einem Baum gefallen.
   (du / Herr Steinhoff / ihr / das Mädchen / ich / wir zwei / Sie)

B. *Answer the question with a complete sentence beginning with* **ja** *or* **nein.**

1. Hast du den Professor gekannt?
2. Haben Sie wirklich nur Orangensaft getrunken?
3. Ist das Mädchen wirklich von einem Baum gefallen?
4. Bist du gestern zu Hause geblieben?
5. Hat das Auto rechts vom Baum gestanden?

C. *Supply the correct form of the auxiliary* **haben** *or* **sein,** *as required.*

1. Wie _____ das mit dem Unfall gewesen, Herr Steinhoff?
2. Ich _____ eine Party bei Freunden besucht.
3. Was _____ Sie denn dort getrunken?
4. Wir _____ da Wein, Bier und Orangensaft getrunken.
5. Die Polizei _____ Sie unterwegs angehalten.
6. Sie _____ eine Blutprobe gemacht.
7. Wie bitte? Das _____ Sie nicht gemerkt?
8. Wie _____ das eigentlich passiert?
9. Oder _____ Sie das schon vergessen?
10. Da _____ plötzlich ein Porsche von rechts gekommen und _____ mich überholt.

D. *Substitute the corresponding form of the verb in parentheses for the past participle in boldface.*

1. Du hast zu Hause **studiert.**
   (Wein trinken / nichts sagen / alles verbrennen / nichts merken / einen Brief schreiben / arbeiten / alles vergessen)
2. Ich bin nach Hause **gefahren.**
   (gehen / kommen / laufen / fliegen / schwimmen)

E. *Substitute or add each phrase as it is introduced into the previous sentence and make any necessary structural changes.*

Der Staatsanwalt hat dir   einen Brief geschickt.
Er _____
_____ ihm _____
_____ geschrieben.
Die Polizei _____
Die Freunde _____
_____ euch _____
_____ gesandt.
Wir _____
_____ Ihnen _____

F. *Substitute the word in boldface by the accusative form of the personal pronoun in parentheses.*

1. Ich kenne **sie** seit gestern abend. (du)
2. Wir haben **Sie** wirklich nicht gesehen. (ihr)
3. Hast du **sie** besucht? (er)
4. Sie haben **ihn** tatsächlich eingeladen. (ich)
5. Die Eltern haben **dich** gehört. (sie, *pl.*)
6. Ich liebe **ihn.** (du)
7. Sie kennen **mich** ganz gut. (wir)

G. *Substitute the word in boldface by the dative form of the personal pronoun in parentheses.*

1. Sie dankt **dir** für die Party gestern. (ihr)
2. Die Polizei hat **uns** einen Brief geschickt. (er)
3. Schreibst du **mir** bald wieder? (sie, *pl.*)
4. Gib **uns** bitte die Zeitung! (sie, *sing.*)
5. Bringen Sie **mir** bitte ein Glas Coca-Cola! (wir)
6. Zeigen Sie **ihnen** die Küche! (er)

H. *Substitute a personal pronoun for the noun in boldface.*

1. Die Party ist bei **Freunden** gewesen.
2. Sprechen Sie Deutsch mit **der Dame?**
3. Die Polizei hat **den Gangster** angehalten.
4. Sie meinen **das Badezimmer?**
5. Nein, ich meine **die Küche.**
6. Ich habe **die Eltern** nie gesehen.
7. Sie haben **den Wodka** wirklich nicht gemerkt?

GUIDED CONVERSATION

A. Exchange greetings with someone in your class, and ask if he/she has ever **(einmal)** had an accident. If so, ask what happened: where the accident happened, how it happened, why it happened. You might ask if he/she was driving a Volkswagen, went to a party, had anything to drink; also, if the police came and, if so, if they gave him/her a blood test. You might tell about an accident you had or one that a friend of yours had.

B. After exchanging greetings with your neighbor, ask if he/she is acquainted with (give the names of several persons in your class and also the names of persons you know outside the class and/or the names of famous persons). Each time your neighbor says that he/she is acquainted with a person, ask if he/she writes to that person and if that person writes to him/her.

READING

Ein Brief

Bonn, den 15. Februar

Liebe Elke,

gestern hat es hier endlich aufgehört zu regnen. Ist das Wetter bei Euch[1] auch so schlecht gewesen?

Kürzlich ist bei uns allerhand passiert. Anfang Januar ist Peter zwei Wochen   5
krank gewesen. Er ist beim Skilaufen hingefallen. Resultat: Gehirnerschütterung! Fünf Wochen hat er nicht gearbeitet. Aber seit Montag ist er wieder bei
der Arbeit.

Außerdem hat Gisela die Masern bekommen. So habe ich natürlich allerhand
zu tun gehabt. Ich habe einfach keine Zeit gehabt, Dir zu schreiben. Jetzt   10
geht es uns wieder besser.

Hoffentlich seid Ihr alle gesund geblieben. Hat Karl eigentlich jetzt mit dem
Medizin-Studium begonnen? Es ist sicher nicht einfach, einen Studienplatz zu
bekommen. Ich habe lange nichts von Dir gehört. Schreibst Du mir bald mal
wieder?   15

Sei herzlich gegrüßt
Jutta

P.S.: Grüße auch von Wolfgang.

---

[1] Note that all second-person pronouns in a letter are capitalized.

Frau
Elke Sommer

34 Göttingen
Goethestraße 8

QUESTIONS

1. Wer hat den Brief an Elke geschrieben?
2. Wo hat Jutta den Brief geschrieben?
3. Wie ist das Wetter in Bonn gewesen?
4. Warum war Peter zwei Wochen krank?
5. Was hat Gisela bekommen?
6. Was studiert Karl: Physik, Medizin oder Deutsch?
7. Von wem hat Jutta lange nichts gehört?
8. Was meinen Sie: Wer ist Wolfgang?

VOCABULARY EXERCISES

Supply the appropriate word from the list on the right.

1. Gestern hat es endlich _____ zu regnen.	a. hingefallen
2. Kürzlich ist bei ihnen viel _____.	b. gewesen
3. Peter ist zwei Wochen krank _____.	c. aufgehört
4. Er ist beim Skilaufen _____.	d. bekommen
5. Dann hat Gisela die Masern _____.	e. begonnen
6. Hat Karl jetzt mit dem Medizin-Studium _____?	f. passiert

Bonn, den 15. Februar

Liebe Elke,

gestern hat es hier endlich aufgehört zu
regnen. Ist das Wetter bei euch auch so schlecht
gewesen?

Kürzlich ist bei uns so allerhand passiert.
Anfang Januar ist Peter zwei Wochen krank
gewesen. Er ist beim Schilaufen hingefallen.
Resultat: Gehirnerschütterung! Fünf Wochen hat
er nicht arbeiten können. Aber seit Montag
ist er wieder bei der Arbeit.
Außerdem hat Gisela die Masern bekommen.
So habe ich natürlich allerhand zu tun gehabt.
Ich hatte einfach keine Zeit, Dir zu schreiben.
Jetzt geht es uns wieder besser.
Hoffentlich seid Ihr alle gesund geblieben.
Hat Karl eigentlich jetzt mit dem Medizin-Studium
begonnen? Es ist sicher nicht einfach, einen
Studienplatz zu bekommen. Schreibst Du
mir bald wieder?

Sei herzlich gegrüßt
von
Jutta

P.S.: Grüße auch von Wolfgang.

Review Exercises

A. *Supply the correct verb form in the present perfect tense from the verb in parentheses.*

1. Wie _____ das mit dem Unfall _____, Herr Steinhoff? (sein)
2. Ich _____ eine Party _____. (besuchen)
3. Was _____ Sie dort _____? (trinken)
4. Wir _____ Wein, Bier und Orangensaft _____. (trinken)
5. Die Polizei _____ Sie unterwegs _____. (anhalten)
6. Sie _____ bei Ihnen eine Blutprobe _____. (machen)
7. Wie bitte? Das _____ Sie nicht _____? (merken)
8. Wie _____ das eigentlich _____? (passieren)
9. Oder _____ Sie das schon _____? (vergessen)
10. Da _____ plötzlich ein Porsche von rechts _____. (kommen)

B. *Rewrite the sentence in the present perfect tense.*

1. Es hört endlich auf zu regnen.
2. Ist das Wetter bei Euch auch so schlecht?
3. Bei uns passiert viel seit Anfang Januar.
4. Peter ist krank.
5. Er fällt beim Skilaufen hin.
6. Er arbeitet nicht in Berlin.
7. Dann bekommt Gisela Masern.
8. So habe ich natürlich viel mehr zu tun.
9. Hoffentlich seid Ihr nicht krank!
10. Karl beginnt jetzt mit dem Studium.

C. *Complete the following text by supplying the appropriate personal pronoun in either the accusative or the dative case.*

Herr Steinhoff, jetzt sagen Sie es _____ (wir) endlich! Sie sind bei Freunden gewesen. Was haben Sie bei _____ (sie, *pl.*) gemacht? Den

Willy haben Sie doch gut gekannt. Ist der Wodka vielleicht von _____ (er)? Ist das möglich? Sie kennen _____ (er) besser als wir. Glauben Sie _____ (ich): _____ (Sie) passiert wahrscheinlich nicht viel! Verstehen Sie _____ (ich)? Die Polizei hat _____ (Sie) angehalten und bei _____ (Sie) eine Blutprobe gemacht. Was ist das Resultat? Hier, lesen Sie _____ (es)! Sie sagen: ,,Ein Porsche hat _____ (ich) von rechts überholt.'' Ich sage _____ (Sie): Das ist nicht möglich! Sehen Sie, das ist ein Bild von dem Baum. Kennen Sie den Baum? Natürlich, Herr Steinhoff! Sie haben _____ (er) beschädigt! Und das kostet viel, viel Geld.

GUIDED COMPOSITION

A. Write a short letter to a friend, telling what has happened to you recently. If you had an accident or if you were sick, give some details about your misfortune. If you took a trip, mention where you went and who you visited. If you gave a party, tell who you invited, who came, and who did not come. Mention any other recent news that your friend might find interesting.

Before you write your letter, notice how the form of a German letter differs from that of a letter in English: note how the date is given; note that you address a male friend with **Lieber . . .** and a female friend with **Liebe . . .**; note that the first word in the body of the letter is not capitalized (unless of course that word is a common or proper noun) and that all second-person pronouns (familiar and polite forms, singular and plural) are capitalized.

You might close your letter with one of the following expressions.

> Sei herzlich gegrüßt
> Dein(e) Freund(in)
> Dein(e)
> Viele Grüße

B. The following is part of a report you could expect to fill out if you were to have an accident in Germany. On a separate sheet of paper, supply all the information required in the form and draw a sketch showing how the accident occurred. Use a German-English dictionary to look up unfamiliar words and terms.

FEUERSOZIETÄT

44 Münster, Warendorfer Str. 26/28, Tel. (02 51) 3 00 34, Telex 892 822, Postfach 5965

Vers.-Schein Nr.: KF..   Schaden Nr. 32/5-..

Kasko-Schadensanzeige

des .... in ....
          Name und Beruf des Versicherungsnehmers

Straße: .... Kreis: .... Fernsprech-Nr. ....

Bericht (Genaue Schilderung des Unfallherganges):

Skizze der Unfallstelle (evtl. Straßenbreite, Beschilderung, Standort und Fahrtrichtung der Fahrzeuge)

Chapter Vocabulary

allerhand   quite a lot
der **Anfang, ⸚e**   beginning
der **Angeklagte, –n**   defendant
die **Antwort, –en**   answer
   antworten (*dat.*)   to answer
die **Arbeit, –en**   work
der **Arzt, ⸚e**   physician
   atmen   to breathe
   auf•hören   to stop
   außerdem   besides that
der **Baum, ⸚e**   tree
   beginnen (*pp.*, **begonnen**)
      to begin
   bekommen (*pp.*, **be-
      kommen**)   to get, receive
   beschädigen   to damage
   besser als   better than
   besuchen   to visit
das **Bier, –e**   beer
   bleiben (*pp.*, **ist
      geblieben**)   to stay
das **Blut**   blood
die **Blutprobe, –n**   blood test
   brennen (*pp.*, **gebrannt**)
      to burn
   ein•laden (*pp.*, **ein-
      geladen**)   to invite
   einmal (*or* **mal**)   ever; once
   endlich   finally
die **Erklärung, –en**
      explanation
   fliegen, (*pp.*, **ist** *or* **hat**
      geflogen)   to fly
das **Flugzeug, –e**   airplane
der **Gangster, –**   gangster
   geben (*pp.*, **gegeben**)
      to give
   gehen (*pp.*, **ist gegangen**)
      to go
die **Gehirnerschütterung, –en**
      brain concussion
das **Gericht, –e**   court
   gestern   yesterday
      gestern abend   last
         evening
   gesund   healthy

der **Gruß, ⸚e**   greeting
   grüßen   to greet
   herzlich   cordial(ly)
   hinein•mischen   to mix in
   hin•fallen (*pp.*, **ist hinge-
      fallen**)   to fall (down)
   hoffentlich   hopefully
der **Januar**   January
   jemand   someone
   kennen (*pp.*, **gekannt**)
      to know, recognize
   krank   sick
   kürzlich   recently
   landen (*pp.*, **ist** *or* **hat**
      gelandet)   to land
   lange   for a long time
   laufen (*pp.*, **ist gelaufen**)
      to run
   laut   loud
   lieb   dear
   lieben   to love
die **Masern** (*pl.*)   measles
die **Medizin**   medicine
   merken   to notice
der **Montag, –e**   Monday
   nennen (*pp.*, **genannt**)
      to name, call
   nur   only
der **Orangensaft, ⸚e**   orange
      juice
die **Party, –ies**   party
   passieren (*pp.*, **ist passiert**)
      to happen
die **Physik**   physics
die **Polizei**   police
der **Polizeiwagen, –**   police car
der **Porsche, –**   Porsche (car)
   regnen   to rain
   rennen (*pp.*, **ist gerannt**)
      to run
das **Resultat, –e**   result
   sagen   to say

   schreiben (*pp.*, **ge-
      schrieben**)   to write
   schwimmen (*pp.*, **ist
      geschwommen**)   to swim
   sein (*pp.*, **ist gewesen**)
      to be
   seit   since (temporal); *for*
   senden (*pp.*, **gesandt**)
      to send
   singen (*pp.*, **gesungen**)
      to sing
das **Skilaufen**   skiing
   sprechen (*pp.*, **ge-
      sprochen**)   to speak
der **Staatsanwalt, ⸚e**   district
      attorney
das **Staatseigentum**   state
      property
   stehen (*pp.*, **gestanden**)
      to stand
der **Studienplatz, ⸚e**   place to
      study
das **Studium, –ien**   study
   tatsächlich   indeed, really
   telefonieren   to telephone
   trinken (*pp.*, **getrunken**)
      to drink
   tun (*pp.*, **getan**)   to do
   überholen   to pass
der **Unfall, ⸚e**   accident
   verbrennen (*pp.*, **ver-
      brannt**)   to burn up
   vergessen (*pp.*, **ver-
      gessen**)   to forget
   verlassen (*pp.*, **verlassen**)
      to leave
   verstehen (*pp.*, **ver-
      standen**)   to understand
   viel mehr   much more
der **Wein, –e**   wine
   wenden (*pp.*, **gewandt**)
      to turn, turn to
   werden (*pp.*, **ist
      geworden**)   to become
das **Wetter**   weather
der **Wodka, –s**   Vodka

Chapter 6

Fußball

Useful Phrases

Es tut mir leid!	I'm sorry.
Macht nichts!	(It) doesn't matter.
Nicht so schlimm!	(It's) not so bad.
aus Versehen	by mistake
ein bißchen	a little
ein paar	a few
noch ein	another
Was möchten Sie?	What would you like?
Wohin möchten Sie?	Where would you like to go?
Ich habe Hunger.	I'm hungry.

MODEL SENTENCES

I

Wir **landeten** in Amsterdam.	We landed in Amsterdam.
Klaus **stellte** den Fernseher **an.**	Klaus switched on the television set.
Ich **kannte** ihn nicht.	I didn't know him.
Sie **brachte** den Wein.	She brought the wine.
Du **fuhrst** zu schnell.	You were driving (*or* drove) too fast.
Da **kam** ein Polizist.	A policeman came (on the scene).
Wir **gingen** nach Hause.	We went home.
Er **hatte** eine Verabredung.	He had a date.
Ihr **wart** pünktlich.	You were on time.
Sie **wurden** wieder gesund.	They became well again.

II

Er **will** hier bleiben.	He wants to stay here.
Können Sie Deutsch [verstehen]?	Do you know German?
Ich **möchte** nach Hause [gehen].	I want to go home.
Durften Sie nach Ost-Berlin [fahren]?	Were you allowed to go to East Berlin?
Er **hat** zu Hause **bleiben müssen.**	He had to stay home.
Das **habe** ich nicht **gewollt.**	I didn't want to do that.

Grammar Explanations

I. PAST TENSE

A. Usage

The past tense is used primarily in a literary style, either in writing or in telling a story—that is, in descriptive passages as the "narrative past," when the storyteller enumerates step by step the events that form part of a sequence.

Es **war** gerade drei Uhr.	It was just three o'clock.
Klaus **stellte** den Fernseher **an.**	Klaus turned on the television set.
Es **dauerte** ein paar Sekunden, dann **war** das Bild klar.	It lasted a few seconds, then the picture was clear.

As discussed in Chapter 5, the present perfect tense is generally preferred in conversation; yet the past tense may be used in the spoken language too. This is because often in the midst of a conversation, which is ordinarily a "two-way street," a speaker may turn into a storyteller for a time, which is a "one-way street." So the conversation may contain both tenses: present perfect in the two-way passages and past in the one-way.

Storytelling Past

Ich **fand** eine Parkuhr. . . .	I found a parking meter. . . .
Und da **kam** ein Polizist. . . .	And a policeman came. . . .

Recent Occurrences, Present Perfect

Verzeihung, das **habe** ich nicht **gewollt.**   Pardon me, I didn't want to do that.

Ist etwas **passiert?**   Has anything happened?

In written and spoken German, the past tense indicates action that began and ended at a point in the past and does not relate to the present time.

It is in the *past* tense that the difference in conjugation between the strong and the weak verbs is especially apparent.

B. Formation

1. Weak Verbs. Weak verbs form the past tense by inserting the element –t– between the unchanged stem and a set of personal endings.

Past Tense: **sagen** (to say)

	Stem	Past-forming Element	Personal Ending	Past Tense
Singular				
ich	sag	t	e	ich sagte
du	sag	t	est	du sagtest
er				
sie	sag	t	e	er sagte
es				
Plural				
wir	sag	t	en	wir sagten
ihr	sag	t	et	ihr sagtet
sie	sag	t	en	sie sagten
Singular / Plural				
Sie	sag	t	en	Sie sagten

Note that in English the equivalent of the weak-verb ending is **–ed** as in to play, play**ed.**

In German, since the past-tense-forming element **–t–** must be clearly audible, verbs with a stem ending in **–d** or **–t** insert an **–e–** between the stem and the ending.

> Er land **e** te.   He landed.
> Ich arbeit **e** te.   I worked.

The same is true for verbs with a stem ending in a single **–m** or **–n** preceded by a consonant other than **l** and **r**.

> Ich atm **e** te.   I breathed.
> Du öffn **e** test.   You opened.

All these are the same verbs that use such an **–e–** in the present tense and in the past participle.

2. Strong Verbs. Strong verbs, instead of using the element **–t–**, change their stem vowel in most cases and add to the *changed stem* a different set of personal endings.

Past Tense: **fahren** (to go; drive)

	Past Stem	*Personal Ending*	*Past Tense*
Singular			
ich	fuhr	—	ich fuhr
du	fuhr	st	du fuhrst
er			
sie	fuhr	—	er fuhr
es			
Plural			
wir	fuhr	en	wir fuhren
ihr	fuhr	t	ihr fuhrt
sie	fuhr	en	sie fuhren
Singular/Plural			
Sie	fuhr	en	Sie fuhren

It is important to note that the stem change in the past tense is not necessarily the same as that in the past participle of the present perfect tense.

Infinitive	Past	Present Perfect
fahren	fuhr	ist gefahren
trinken	trank	hat getrunken

And these stem changes are not predictable. So, again, you should memorize the past tense of each verb when you learn the infinitive. In the vocabularies of this book, the past tense is indicated if there is a stem change.

Frequently verbs with cognate forms in English show the same, or similar, vowel changes.

Infinitive	Past	Present Perfect
singen	sang	hat gesungen
(to sing	sang	sung)
trinken	trank	hat getrunken
(to drink	drank	drunk)
kommen	kam	ist gekommen
(to come	came	come)

3. Irregular Verbs. The verbs categorized as "hybrids" in Chapter 5 again change the past stem like strong verbs but take the endings of the weak verbs.

Infinitive	Past	Present Perfect
brennen	brannte	hat gebrannt
kennen	kannte	hat gekannt
nennen	nannte	hat genannt
rennen	rannte	ist gerannt
senden	sandte	hat gesandt
wenden	wandte	hat gewandt

A number of verbs change not only the stem vowel but also the following consonant(s); some of them take the weak, others the strong endings.

	Infinitive	Past	Present Perfect
weak forms:	bringen	brachte	hat gebracht
	denken	dachte	hat gedacht
	wissen	wußte	hat gewußt
strong forms:	gehen	ging	ist gegangen
	stehen	stand	hat gestanden
	tun	tat	hat getan

The two (auxiliary) verbs **haben** and **sein,** as well as the verb **werden** (to become), are also categorized as irregular verbs. Their past forms, as in the present perfect tense, follow no pattern and must be memorized.

Infinitive	Present	Past	Present Perfect
haben	hat	hatte	hat gehabt
sein	ist	war	ist gewesen
werden	wird	wurde	ist geworden

Past and Present Perfect Tenses: **haben, sein, werden**

	Past			Present Perfect		
	haben	**sein**	**werden**	**haben**	**sein**	**werden**
Singular						
ich	hatte	war	wurde	habe gehabt	bin gewesen	bin geworden
du	hattest	warst	wurdest	hast gehabt	bist gewesen	bist geworden
er sie es	hatte	war	wurde	hat gehabt	ist gewesen	ist geworden
Plural						
wir	hatten	waren	wurden	haben gehabt	sind gewesen	sind geworden
ihr	hattet	wart	wurdet	habt gehabt	seid gewesen	seid geworden
sie	hatten	waren	wurden	haben gehabt	sind gewesen	sind geworden
Singular/Plural						
Sie	hatten	waren	wurden	haben gehabt	sind gewesen	sind geworden

Verbs with separable and inseparable prefixes follow the pattern of the simple verb: if it is strong, it changes the stem; if it is weak, it adds **–t–** plus endings.

Infinitive	Past	Present Perfect
kommen	kam	ist gekommen
ankommen	kam an	ist angekommen
bekommen	bekam	hat bekommen

Infinitive, past, and past participle are called the *three principal parts* of the verb. From this point on, you should memorize the three principal parts of strong and irregular verbs and then add the necessary personal endings. As a matter of convention, the past-tense form is indicated by the third-person singular. In verbs with vowel variation in the present tense, the third-person singular will also be listed. The forms of weak verbs, however, need not be memorized individually, since they can easily be derived from the infinitive stem.

In the Appendix, in the back of the book, you will find a list of the most important strong and irregular verbs with all their principal parts.

Check Your Comprehension

A. *Supply the principal parts of the verb: present tense, past tense, and past participle.*

1. vergessen
2. arbeiten
3. geben
4. kommen
5. passieren
6. bringen
7. finden
8. gehen
9. wissen
10. denken
11. haben
12. sein
13. werden
14. vorbeigehen
15. anstoßen

B. *Supply the appropriate past-tense form of the verb in parentheses.*

1. Ich _____ das. (vergessen)
2. Ihr _____ zuviel. (arbeiten)
3. Er _____ mir einen Brief. (geben)
4. Du _____ pünktlich. (kommen)
5. Es _____ da drüben. (passieren)
6. Sie _____ den Kaffee. (bringen)
7. Wir _____ einen Ball. (finden)
8. Sie _____ es schon. (wissen)
9. Ihr _____ richtig. (denken)
10. Erika _____ einen Hund. (haben)
11. Er _____ ein Schäferhund. (sein)
12. Du _____ schnell gesund. (werden)
13. Er _____ ihn _____. (anstoßen)
14. Wir _____ _____. (vorbeigehen)

II. MODALS

In German, as well as in English, certain verbs function as *modal auxiliaries*, describing how an action is viewed. In the sentences "I must go home now" and "You may leave now," for instance, the verbs **must** and **may** show the *mode* or manner in which the speaker feels about going or leaving.

German has six modal auxiliaries: **dürfen, können, mögen/möchten, müssen, sollen,** and **wollen,** expressing permission, ability, desire or possibility, necessity, obligation, and intention. Try to remember their basic meanings rather than any direct word-for-word translations.

The Model Auxiliaries

Modal	Sample Sentence	Approximate Translation	Basic Meaning
dürfen	Du **darfst** dir ein Kleid kaufen. (You may [are allowed to] buy a dress for yourself.)	to be allowed to	permission
können	Ich **kann** Deutsch lesen. (I can read German.)	to be able to, can	ability
mögen/ möchten	Ich **mag** nicht hier bleiben.* (I don't like to stay here.)	to like to	desire, preference
	Ich **möchte** hier bleiben.* (I would like to stay here.)	to want to	
müssen	Ich **muß** nach Hause gehen. (I must [have to] go home.)	to have to, must	necessity, compulsion
sollen	Ich **soll** nach Köln fahren. (I am supposed to go to Cologne.) **Sollen** wir nach München gehen? (Shall we go to Munich?)	to be (supposed) to, to ought to, shall	imposed obligation, (in questions; suggestion)
wollen	Ich **will** hier bleiben. (I want [intend to] stay here.)	to want to	intention, strong wish

Modal auxiliaries take a dependent infinitive without **zu.** The modal is always in the second position of a sentence and is the conjugated verb. If the infinitive does not occur in the sentence, it is usually understood.

---

* **Möchten** is a subjunctive form of **mögen** (*see* Chapter 20) used in the present tense with the meaning "to want to" or "would like to" to make a statement or request more polite.

Ich kann es [tun].	I can do it.
Er wollte es nicht [tun].	He didn't want to do it.
Er wollte es nicht [haben].	He didn't want to have it.
Wir müssen nach Hause [gehen].	We have to go home.

In German, unlike in English, these verbs can be used in all tenses. In the present tense, the modals undergo considerable vowel changes in their conjugation.

Present Tense: Modals

	dürfen	**können**	**mögen/möchten**	**müssen**	**sollen**	**wollen**
ich	darf	kann	mag/möchte	muß	soll	will
du	darfst	kannst	magst/möchtest	mußt	sollst	willst
er sie es	darf	kann	mag/möchte	muß	soll	will
wir	dürfen	können	mögen/möchten	müssen	sollen	wollen
ihr	dürft	könnt	mögt/möchtet	müßt	sollt	wollt
sie	dürfen	können	mögen/möchten	müssen	sollen	wollen
Sie	dürfen	können	mögen/möchten	müssen	sollen	wollen

Notice that, except for **möchten,** the first- and third-persons singular do not add endings.

DIE POLITISCHE KARIKATUR

Professor Kissinger: Strafe muß sein   aus: „Göttinger Tageblatt"

In the past tense, the modals add the **–t–** and the weak verb endings to a slightly changed stem.

Past Tense: Modals

	dürfen	**können**	**mögen**	**müssen**	**sollen**	**wollen**
ich	durfte	konnte	mochte	mußte	sollte	wollte
du	durftest	konntest	mochtest	mußtest	solltest	wolltest
er						
sie	durfte	konnte	mochte	mußte	sollte	wollte
es						
wir	durften	konnten	mochten	mußten	sollten	wollten
ihr	durftet	konntet	mochtet	mußtet	solltet	wolltet
sie	durften	konnten	mochten	mußten	sollten	wollten
Sie	durften	konnten	mochten	mußten	sollten	wollten

Notice that the Umlaut of the infinitive is dropped.

The difference in the use of the present perfect and the past tenses does not apply to **haben, sein,** and the modals. Even in conversational style, the past is preferred over the present perfect to express events that are entirely in the past (as opposed to up-to-now situations).

Ich **wollte** wirklich pünktlich sein.	I really wanted to be on time.
Er **konnte** heute nicht kommen.	He couldn't come today.
Sie **hatten** eine Verabredung.	They had a date.
Sibille **war** in der Kaffee-Bar.	Sibille was in the coffee shop.

In these instances the German use of the past tense obviously corresponds to English usage.

The modals, however, can be used to indicate a stretch of time in the present perfect tense. *When occurring with the infinitive of another verb*, the modals use a participle that is identical to their infinitive forms.

	Dependent Infinitive	*Modal Past Participle*
Er **hat** mir ein Strafmandat	**geben**	**wollen**.
(He wanted to give me a ticket.)		
Ich **habe** nicht nach Bonn	**fahren**	**dürfen**.
(I was not allowed to go to Bonn.)		
Ich **habe** hier	**bleiben**	**müssen**.
(I had to stay here.)		

This is generally termed the *double infinitive construction,* and it also occurs with the verbs **hören, lassen,** and **sehen.** Notice that the conjugated auxiliary is **haben,** even in connection with an intransitive verb: **habe fahren müssen.**

If the infinitive does not occur with the modals, their past participles are regularly formed: **gedurft, gekonnt, gemocht, gemußt, gesollt,** and **gewollt.**

Verzeihung, das habe ich wirklich nicht **gewollt.**	Pardon me, I really didn't want to do that.

Check Your Comprehension

A. *Supply the correct present-tense form of the modal in parentheses.*

1. Ich _____ es tun. (dürfen)
2. Sie (*sing.*) _____ es tun. (können)
3. _____ du es tun? (mögen)
   or _____ du es tun?
4. Er _____ es tun. (müssen)
5. Wir _____ es tun. (sollen)
6. Wer _____ es tun? (wollen)

B. *Supply the correct past-tense form of the modal in parentheses.*

1. Du _____ singen. (dürfen)
2. Wir _____ singen. (können)
3. Ihr _____ singen. (mögen)
4. Ich _____ singen. (müssen)
5. Er _____ singen. (sollen)
6. Sie (*pl.*) _____ singen. (wollen)

C. *Supply the correct present perfect form of the modal in parentheses.*

1. Ich _____ arbeiten _____. (dürfen)
2. Er _____ arbeiten _____. (können)
3. Du _____ arbeiten _____. (mögen)
4. Wir _____ arbeiten _____. (müssen)
5. Ihr _____ arbeiten _____. (sollen)
6. Sie (*pl.*) _____ arbeiten _____. (wollen)

D. *Change the sentence first into the past tense and then into the present perfect tense.*

1. Ich will es.
2. Du kannst es.
3. Wir wollen es.

4. Er darf es.
5. Sie muß es.
6. Ihr möchtet es.

CONVERSATION

Die Kaffee-Bar

Georg und Sibille hatten eine Verabredung für neun Uhr morgens. Der Treffpunkt war eine Kaffee-Bar. Georg kommt fünfzehn Minuten zu spät.

SIBILLE   Da bist du ja endlich! Wo warst du denn?

GEORG   Tag, Sibille! Es tut mir leid! Ich wollte wirklich pünktlich sein. Aber weißt du, ich sollte doch noch ein paar Brötchen mitbringen,   5 und da . . .

SIBILLE   . . . und da konntest du wieder keinen Parkplatz finden! Stimmt's?

GEORG   Nicht ganz. Ich fand eine Parkuhr direkt bei der Bäckerei, aber ich vergaß völlig, einen Groschen einzuwerfen. Und da kam . . .

SIBILLE   . . . natürlich ein Polizist!—Hier ist übrigens der Kaffee für dich.   10 Laß ihn nicht kalt werden! Sahne?

GEORG   Ein bißchen. Genug! Danke!—Nun, da kam ein Polizeiwagen und hielt an. Ein Polizist stieg aus und—was denkst du?—der Mann hat

mir doch tatsächlich ein Strafmandat geben wollen! Zum Glück
konnte ich ihn aber gerade noch rechtzeitig . . .   15

Ein Student wollte gerade an Georg vorbeigehen und stieß ihn aus Versehen an.

STUDENT   Oh, Verzeihung! Das habe ich wirklich nicht gewollt. Ist etwas
passiert?

GEORG   Nicht so schlimm! Ein bißchen Kaffee . . .   20

SIBILLE   Macht nichts! Der Pullover hat schon lange in die Reinigung gemußt. Er ist schon ganz dreckig.

GEORG   Vielleicht können wir ihn gleich da drüben zur Schnell-Reinigung
bringen? Möchtest du noch eine Tasse Kaffee?

SIBILLE   Nein danke! Gehen wir lieber gleich zur Reinigung!   25

ORAL PRACTICE

A. *Change the sentence from the present to the past tense.*

1. Ich trinke oft ein bißchen zuviel.
2. Du hast immer zu wenig Geld.
3. Ihr arbeitet nicht genug.
4. Sie vergißt das oft.
5. Wir wissen das.
6. Ihr geht zur Schule?
7. Sie findet nichts.
8. Die Kinder haben Masern.
9. Wir sind immer pünktlich.
10. Ich bringe ihm den Brief.
11. Sie stößt ihn an.
12. Sie denken zuviel!

B. *Supply the appropriate present tense form of the modal in parentheses.*

1. Ich _____ ein Glas Bier trinken. (dürfen)
2. _____ du hier bleiben? (mögen, *use both forms*)
3. _____ er zu Hause bleiben? (wollen)
4. Sie _____ gut Deutsch sprechen. (können)

5. Wir _____ morgen nach Bonn fahren. (sollen)
6. Ihr _____ jetzt nach Hause gehen. (müssen)

C. *Change the sentence from the present to the past tense.*

1. Wo bist du denn?
2. Ich will wirklich pünktlich sein.
3. Ich soll noch ein paar Brötchen mitbringen.
4. Du kannst keinen Parkplatz finden.
5. Er findet eine Parkuhr.
6. Ein Polizeiwagen kommt.
7. Ein Polizist steigt aus.
8. Er gibt ihm ein Strafmandat.
9. Der Pullover muß schnell zur Reinigung.

D. *Rewrite the sentences above (C) in the present perfect tense.*

E. *Change the sentence from the present perfect to the past tense.*

1. Ich habe viel Zeit gehabt.
2. Wir sind pünktlich gewesen.
3. Er hat ein Glas Bier trinken wollen.
4. Sie hat viel vergessen sollen.
5. Wir haben nichts finden können.
6. Ihr habt nichts sagen mögen.
7. Du hast nicht genug Geld gehabt.
8. Ihr seid krank gewesen.

F. *Change the sentence from the past to the present perfect tense.*

1. Sie konnte nichts finden.
2. Wir wollten nach Berlin fahren.
3. Du hattest viel Zeit.
4. Der Bus war pünktlich.
5. Sie durften singen.
6. Ich wollte dich nicht anstoßen.
7. Ihr brachtet den Hund mit.
8. Ich wußte das nicht.

G. *Change the sentence from the present to the present perfect tense.*

   1. Können Sie Deutsch?

   2. Weißt du das?

   3. Dürft ihr das?

   4. Mögen Sie Wodka mit Orangensaft?

   5. Wir müssen nach Hause.

   6. Ich will das so.

   7. Sie denken zuviel, Herr Meyer!

   8. Ich bringe ihm den Brief.

H. *Substitute or add each phrase as it is introduced into the previous sentence and make any necessary structural changes.*

Er	hat	den Wagen		dort nicht parken dürfen.
____	darf	_____		
____	konnte	_____		
_____	das Auto	____	_____	
Jutta	_____			
____	hat	_____		_____
_____	Frau Meyers Auto	_____		
_____			____ fahren ____	
_____			gemocht.	

GUIDED CONVERSATION

A. Begin a conversation with someone in your class. After exchanging greetings, ask if he/she had a date last night (or recently). Ask with whom (**mit wem**) he/she had the date, where they met, whether he/she was on time, where they went, and so on.

B. Assume that you work as a waiter or waitress in a coffee house, and assume that the person sitting next to you is a customer. Greet the person and ask what he/she would like. If the person wishes coffee, ask if he/she takes sugar, cream, or both with coffee. Ask if he/she would like a roll. Assuming you don't have what the person orders, perhaps you could suggest something else. You might also compliment the person on how well he/she speaks German!

Das Fußballspiel

Das Fußballspiel ist für die Deutschen so wichtig wie für die Amerikaner „basketball" oder „football". Die Amerikaner nennen das Fußballspiel in Deutschland „soccer". Die Kinder lernen das Fußballspiel schon sehr früh und sehen begeistert im Fernsehen den Fußballspielern zu.

Es war gerade drei Uhr. Klaus stellte den Fernseher an. Heute fand das Fußballspiel Deutschland gegen England in Liverpool statt. Klaus war furchtbar aufgeregt. Es dauerte ein paar Sekunden, dann war das Bild klar.

Ein Reporter sagte gerade: „. . . zwei zu eins für England! Noch dreißig Minuten Spielzeit. Die Leute hier im Stadion in Liverpool sind begeistert!" Klaus glaubte, nicht richtig zu hören.

Er griff sofort zum Fernsehprogramm: tatsächlich! Das Fußballspiel hat schon um zwei Uhr begonnen! Klaus war furchtbar ärgerlich. Er hat den Fernseher viel zu spät eingeschaltet.

Die Mannschaften kämpften hart. Zehn Minuten vor Schluß schoß Gerd Müller, ein Fußball-Star aus Deutschland, noch ein Tor. Eine Menge Zuschauer riefen begeistert: „Noch ein Tor! Noch ein Tor!"

Das Publikum aus England feuerte dann die Briten an. Sie waren jetzt fast immer in der Offensive. Plötzlich (Mensch! Wo ist denn der Torwart aus Deutschland?) schießt der Ball durchs Tor. Ein Tor für England! Das Spiel endete mit „drei zu zwei" für die Briten.

Klaus war enttäuscht. Er stellte den Fernseher ab.

QUESTIONS

1. Welcher Sport ist für Deutschland der Nationalsport?
2. Warum stellte Klaus den Fernseher an?
3. War das Bild sofort klar?
4. Wo fand das Fußballspiel statt?
5. Wer spielte gegen wen?
6. Warum war Klaus eigentlich so ärgerlich?
7. Was passierte zehn Minuten vor Schluß?
8. Was riefen die Zuschauer aus Deutschland immer wieder?
9. Was passierte plötzlich?
10. Wie endete das Fußballspiel?
11. Warum war Klaus enttäuscht?

VOCABULARY EXERCISES

Supply the appropriate word from the list on the right.

1. Die zwei Freunde hatten für neun Uhr eine
   _____.
2. Der _____ war eine Kaffee-Bar.
3. Georg wollte ein paar _____ mitbringen.
4. Er konnte keinen _____ finden.
5. Endlich fand er eine _____ fürs Auto.
6. Ein Polizist wollte ihm ein _____ geben.
7. Er bringt den Pullover zur _____.
8. Die Kinder in Deutschland lieben das _____.
9. Klaus liest das _____.
10. Die _____ kämpften hart.
11. Zehn Minuten vor _____ schoß Müller ein Tor.
12. Die _____ aus Deutschland riefen: ,,Noch ein Tor!"

a. Parkuhr
b. Zuschauer
c. Strafmandat
d. Parkplatz
e. Reinigung
f. Treffpunkt
g. Verabredung
h. Fußballspiel
i. Mannschaften
j. Fernsehprogramm
k. Schluß
l. Brötchen

Review Exercises

A. *Change the sentence from the present to the past tense.*

1. Es ist drei Uhr.
2. Klaus stellt den Fernseher an.
3. Es dauert ein paar Sekunden.
4. Klaus greift zum Programm.
5. Das Fußballspiel beginnt um zwei Uhr.
6. Der Star aus Deutschland schießt noch ein Tor.
7. Die Zuschauer rufen: ,,Noch ein Tor!"
8. Klaus ist von dem Spiel enttäuscht.
9. Er denkt: Die Mannschaft aus Deutschland muß noch viel lernen!
10. Klaus hat Hunger.

B. *Rewrite the sentences above (A) in the present perfect tense.*

C. *Supply the appropriate present-tense form of the modal in parentheses.*

1. Ich _____ einen Fernseher kaufen. (dürfen)
2. _____ du telefonieren? (wollen)
3. Sie _____ die Westerns nicht. (mögen)
4. _____ Sie eine Show sehen? (möchten)
5. Du _____ nicht soviel essen, Emil! (sollen)
6. _____ Sie Bridge spielen? (können)
7. Karin _____ schon nach Hause [gehen]. (müssen)
8. Sie _____ schon nach Hause [gehen]. (wollen)

D. *Rewrite the sentences above (C) in the past tense.*

E. *Rewrite the sentences above (C) in the present perfect tense.*

F. *Write the sentence first in the past and then in the present perfect tense.*

1. Ich habe nicht viel Zeit.
2. Er ist sehr ärgerlich.
3. Sie ist sehr aufgeregt.

4. Wir haben Hunger.
5. Sie weiß das alles.

GUIDED COMPOSITION

A. Have you recently watched a sports event on television? Write a brief composition stating some or all of the following facts: what the sports event was, where it took place, who the contestants were, what happened, how the game ended, and whether you were disappointed with the outcome.

Use a German-English dictionary to look up the German term for the sport. If you do not find a German equivalent, use the English term in quotations.

B. Write the basic rules to a simple card game. Make use of the modal auxiliaries to explain what must, should, and/or may be done in order to play the game. Make the rules as clear and concise as possible. The following terms may help you.

| colors | schwarz (black) |
| | rot (red) |

sequence	der Bube, –n (jack)
	die Dame, –n (queen)
	der König, –e (king)
	das As, –se (ace)

suits	das Kreuz (clubs)
	das Pik (spades)
	das Herz (hearts)
	das Karo (diamonds)

mischen (to shuffle)
verteilen (to give; to deal)

die Farbe, –n (suit)
die Karte, –n (card)

If you are stumped as to how to explain a basic rule or step in German, illustrate it instead with a diagram.

Chapter 7

Skigebiet bei Innsbruck

Useful Phrases

Laß mal sehen!	Let's see!
Sag mal!	Say!
Sieh mal!	Look!
Schau mal!	Look!
Warte mal!	Wait a minute!
auf deutsch	in German
auf englisch	in English
schon wieder	once again
Es klappt.	It works.
Das Bild gefällt mir.	I like the picture.
Das Auto gehört dir.	The car belongs to you.
Mir fehlt das Geld.	I lack the money.
Was für (ein Auto) . . . ?	What kind of (car) . . . ?

MODEL SENTENCES

I

Das ist Marias Freund.	That's Maria's friend.
Das ist das Auto **des** Hausbesitzers.	That's the car of the property owner.
Hier ist die Adresse **des** Hauses.	Here's the address of the house.
Das ist das Programm **der** Studenten.	That's the program of the students.
Kennen Sie die Soziologie **der** Sprache?	Do you know the sociology of language?
Statt eines Autos nahmen sie den Zug.	Instead of a car they took the train.
Während der Reise wurde er hungrig.	During the trip he became hungry.

II

Der Zug fährt **durch einen** Tunnel.	The train is going through a tunnel.
Wir gehen **gegen den** Wind.	We're walking against the wind.
Sie geht nie **ohne die** Handtasche aus.	She never goes out without her purse.

Helfen Sie bitte **dem** Mann!	Please help the man.
Ich **vertraue der** Freundin.	I trust my [the] friend.
Das Buch **gefällt mir.**	I like the book.
Wir sind **ihm** gestern **begegnet.**	We met him yesterday.

Grammar Explanations

I. GENITIVE CASE AND PREPOSITIONS

A. Nouns, Definite and Indefinite Articles, and <u>kein</u>

The fourth case in German, the *genitive case*, sometimes is similar to the English possessive in that it denotes the "possessive" relationship of one noun to another.

Wilfrieds Freund heißt Jens.	Wilfried**'s** friend is called Jens.

With proper names, the German genitive is expressed by simply adding an **–s** to the name. Note that in German there is no apostrophe.

Tom**s** Bier	Tom's beer
Frau Meyer**s** Blumen	Mrs. Meyer's flowers

The possessive relationship of the English phrase "the man's dog," however, cannot be shown in German by an **–s** ending added to "der Mann." It must be written as a genitive phrase: "der Hund des Mannes."

Usually, whenever "of" is used in a phrase in English, the genitive case is used in the German equivalent. An exception to the rule occurs with phrases such as "a glass of beer" ("ein Glas Bier") or "a piece of paper" ("ein Stück Papier"). You have already come across some of these phrases in the conversations and readings of previous chapters.

The use of the genitive phrase in German is not limited to possession; it also denotes other relationships, such as the way in which one noun modifies or qualifies another or the relationship of a part to the whole. Whereas in English these genitive relationships are expressed with the preposition *of*, German has special genitive forms for the definite and indefinite articles and **kein**.

Die Qualität **des Bieres** ist gut.	The quality of the beer is good.
Neujahr ist der Beginn **des Jahres**.	New Year's Day is the beginning of the year.

Definite and Indefinite Articles, **kein**: Genitive Case

	Definite Article	Indefinite Article	**kein**
Singular			
masc.	des	eines	keines
fem.	der	einer	keiner
neut.	des	eines	keines
Plural			
all gend.	der	—	keiner

The list of the forms of the definite and indefinite articles and **kein** is now complete.

Declension: Definite and Indefinite Articles, **kein**

	SINGULAR									PLURAL	
	Masculine			Feminine			Neuter			All Genders Pl.	
nom.	der	ein	kein	die	eine	keine	das	ein	kein	die	keine
acc.	den	einen	keinen	die	eine	keine	das	ein	kein	die	keine
dat.	dem	einem	keinem	der	einer	keiner	dem	einem	keinem	den	keinen
gen.	des	eines	keines	der	einer	keiner	des	eines	keines	der	keiner

Certain nouns, in addition to the articles, also have genitive endings in a genitive phrase. If a masculine or neuter noun has more than one syllable and does not end in an "s"-sound (**–s, –ß, –x, –z,** or **–tz**), the genitive-singular ending is usually **–s.**

Nominative	Genitive
der Pullover	des Pullovers
das Publikum	des Publikums

If a masculine or a neuter noun has only one syllable, the genitive singular generally ends in **–es.**

Nominative	Genitive
der Ball	des Ball**es**
das Bier	des Bier**es**

Feminine nouns and plural nouns of all genders do *not* take a special ending in the genitive.

Nominative	Genitive
die Frau	der Frau
die Kinder	der Kinder

Masculine nouns of foreign origin, denoting human beings, such as **der Student** and **der Professor** (and including **der Mensch,** *see* Chapter 4) that form their plurals by adding **–n** or **–en** also take **–en** in the genitive case. They do not add **–s** or **–es.**

Declension: **der Student**

	Singular	Plural
nom.	der Student	die Studenten
acc.	den Studenten	die Studenten
dat.	dem Studenten	den Studenten
gen.	**des** Student**en**	**der** Student**en**

B. Prepositions

As is true in the dative case, certain prepositions require the genitive construction, but these prepositions occur relatively rarely.

außerhalb (outside of)	(an)statt (instead of)
innerhalb (inside of, within)	trotz (in spite of)
diesseits (on this side of)	während (during)
jenseits (on that side of)	wegen (because of; due to)

Statt des Volkswagens wollen sie einen Zug nehmen.

They want to take a train instead of the Volkswagen.

Ist es in Österreich genauso teuer wie **innerhalb Deutschlands,** Urlaub zu machen?

Is it just as expensive to spend one's vacation in Austria as in Germany?

A. *Supply the genitive case of the noun.*

1. das Kleid
2. die Frau
3. der Katalog
4. das Kind
5. der Mann
6. das Mädchen
7. die Literatur
8. das Programm
9. der Tag
10. der Student
11. das Plakat
12. das Problem
13. der Vorteil
14. das Bad
15. das Jahr

B. *Supply the genitive case of the noun in parentheses after the preposition.*

1. außerhalb (Österreich)
2. innerhalb (das Land)
3. statt (der Prospekt)
4. trotz (die Ferien)
5. während (der Skiurlaub)
6. wegen (der Wind)
7. außerhalb (das Hotel)
8. statt (die Dusche)
9. wegen (der Schnee)
10. anstatt (der Architekt)
11. jenseits (der Parkplatz)
12. diesseits (die Rocky Mountains)

II. PREPOSITIONS WITH THE ACCUSATIVE

As is true of the dative case (*see* Chapter 4) and the genitive case (*see* Section I-B, this chapter), the accusative case also frequently governs certain prepositions.

bis (until; as far as)	gegen (against)
durch (through)	ohne (without)
für (for)	um (around; at)

As with **bei, zu,** and **von** in the dative, certain contractions are possible with **durch, für,** and **um.**

durch das = **durchs**   für das = **fürs**   um das = **ums**

The preposition **bis** is used both with an expression of time (until)

Er arbeitet **bis** Samstag.   He works until Saturday.

and with an expression of place (as far as)

Der Zug fährt **bis** Garmisch.   The train goes as far as Garmisch.

The accusative cannot be recognized in these instances since proper names are usually not inflected. The accusative case becomes apparent only by the strong adjective endings, which will be discussed in Chapter 11.

Also notice that the preposition **bis** is often combined with another preposition, such as **nach** or **zu.** When this happens, the final preposition governs the case of the noun.

dat.:   Er fuhr **bis zum** Flugplatz.   He drove as far as the airport.

The preposition **um** is used both with an expression of time and with an expression of place.

Peter kommt **um die** Mitte des Jahres zurück.	Peter will come back around the middle of the year.
Brigitte geht **um den** Zeitungsstand.	Brigitte walks around the newspaper stand.

Check Your Comprehension

Supply the accusative case of the noun after the preposition.

1. durch (der Winter)
2. für (der Skiurlaub)
3. gegen (der Wind)
4. ohne (das Auto)
5. um (die Ecke)
6. durch (das Rheintal)
7. für (ein Sonderzug)
8. gegen (ein Baum)
9. ohne (eine Zeitung)
10. um (ein Zeitungsstand)

III. VERBS REQUIRING THE DATIVE

A number of important German verbs cannot be followed by an accusative object but only by a *dative* object. These must be memorized since there is no pattern or regular rule to follow.

antworten (to answer)	gehören (to belong)
begegnen (to meet)	gelingen (*impers.*, to succeed in)
danken (to thank)	genügen (*impers.*, to suffice)
dienen (to serve)	glauben (to believe)
drohen (to threaten)	glücken (*impers.*, to be fortunate enough)
fehlen (to lack something)	helfen (to help)
folgen (*pp.*, haben) (to obey)	raten (to advise)
folgen (*pp.*, sein) (to follow)	vertrauen (to trust)
gefallen (to please)	

The following sentences illustrate dative case after these verbs.

Wilfried **begegnete dem** Freund.	Wilfried met his friend.
Dem Mann **fehlt** das Geld für das Haus.	The man lacks the money for the house.
Dem Studenten **ist** es **gelungen,** Prospekte zu bekommen.	The student succeeded in getting some brochures.

With most of these verbs English and German usage differs. In the English sentence "I helped the girl," "the girl" is clearly a direct object. But for the native German, the verb **helfen** suggests "to give help *to*" and is therefore followed by the dative: "Ich half dem Mädchen." The English equivalent of **gehören** (to belong *to*), however, includes the preposition "to," which indicates the dative in German: "Das gehört der Frau" (That belongs *to* the woman).

Check Your Comprehension

Supply the correct dative form of the noun or pronoun in parentheses.

1. Ich antworte _____. (der Mann)
2. Wir folgen _____. (ein Auto)
3. Du dankst _____. (das Mädchen)

4. Er drohte _____. (eine Frau)
5. Sie begegneten _____. (ein Hund)
6. Wir helfen _____. (die Kinder)
7. Ich vertraue _____. (der Freund)
8. Sie gefällt _____. (ich)
9. Er rät _____. (sie, *pl.*)
10. Ich danke _____. (du)
11. Die Coca-Cola gehört _____. (er)
12. Das Glas Bier gehört _____. (der Student)

CONVERSATION

Der Skiurlaub

Jens und Wilfried haben Weihnachtsferien und wollen einen Skiurlaub machen. Die Frage ist: Wo? Die Mittelgebirge in Deutschland (zum Beispiel der Harz[1] oder der Schwarzwald) haben während der Weihnachtsferien meistens nicht genug Schnee. Besser sind die Alpen. Mit dem Auto ist es zu weit und zu anstrengend. Statt des Volkswagens wollen sie darum einen Zug nehmen.

JENS	Na, Wilfried, du bist ja schon zurück. Ist es dir gelungen, ein paar Prospekte für den Winterurlaub zu finden?
WILFRIED	Ja, ich war heute früh beim Reisebüro. Du weißt doch, beim „Kaufhof"[2] gleich um die Ecke. Man hat mir geraten, so schnell wie möglich zu buchen. Es ist sehr schwer, noch ein Zimmer zu bekommen. Hier sind übrigens die Prospekte von „Touropa", „Scharnow", „Hummel" und „Tigges".[3]
JENS	Ich sehe, du hast auch einen Prospekt von „Neckermann"[4] mitgebracht. Na, wenn uns das nicht genügt! . . .
WILFRIED	Nun ja, ich habe mal alles mitgebracht—wegen der Preise, weißt du. Man muß ja schließlich vergleichen.
JENS	Klar!—„Tigges." Laß mal sehen!—Hm! Berchtesgaden—herrlich! Und hier Garmisch—auch nicht schlecht! Moment mal— fast vierhundert Mark für einen Skiurlaub von zwei Wochen? Das ist eine Menge Geld!
WILFRIED	Ja, das ist sehr viel! Sag mal, ist es eigentlich in Österreich genauso teuer wie innerhalb Deutschlands, Urlaub zu machen?
JENS	Wahrscheinlich nicht. Mal sehen, was „Neckermann" in Österreich anzubieten hat.—Hier, was hältst du zum Beispiel vom Arlbergpaß in Österreich?
WILFRIED	Als Skigebiet, ideal! Aber was kostet das?
JENS	Warte mal! Hier, vierzehn Tage für dreihundertzwanzig Mark. Das ist mit Dusche, Balkon und Vollpension.
WILFRIED	Das ist billig. Aber warte mal. Schließt das die Bahnfahrt ein?

JENS   Oh ja! Sogar mit einem Sonderzug! Die Sonderzüge einer Reisegesellschaft sind so gut wie die „Intercity"–Züge oder die TEEs.[5]

WILFRIED   Schau mal! Der Zug fährt von Hamburg durch Norddeutschland
und durchs Ruhrgebiet bis Köln. Von dort fährt er durchs
Rheintal und durch den Schwarzwald bis zum Bodensee.   35

JENS   Und dann geht es mit dem Bus weiter bis Arlberg. Die Strecke
kenne ich. Ich schlage vor, wir versuchen, in Arlberg ein Zimmer
zu nehmen. Allerdings möchte ich statt einer Dusche lieber ein
Zimmer mit Bad.

WILFRIED   Mal sehen, was wir so spät noch bekommen können. Ich rufe   40
gleich mal bei „Neckermann" an.

JENS   Hoffentlich klappt es!

---

[1] The following place names occur in this conversation: der **Harz** the Harz mountains;   der
 Schwarzwald the Black Forest; die **Alpen** the Alps; der **Arlbergpaß** mountain pass
  through Arlberg in the Alps; das **Ruhrgebiet** the Ruhr district; das **Rheintal** the Rhine
  valley; der **Bodensee** Lake Constance.
[2] A large department-store chain.
[3] Four well-known German travel agencies.
[4] A large German department store and mail-order business.
[5] Comfortable, first-class express trains. TEE stands for Trans-Europe-Express.

ORAL PRACTICE

A. *Supply the correct genitive endings.*

1. Der Name d_____ Zug_____ ist „Roland".
2. Wilfried_____ Freund heißt Jens.
3. Ich habe den Namen d_____ Reisebüro_____ vergessen.
4. Die Qualität d_____ Bier_____ aus Milwaukee ist gut.
5. Die Spezialität d_____ Haus_____ ist Steak.
6. Der Name d_____ Hund_____ ist Max.
7. Neujahr ist der Beginn d_____ Jahr_____.

B. *Supply the correct genitive endings.*

1. Ich habe während d_____ Tag_____ Hunger bekommen.
2. Du hast statt d_____ Prospekt_____ einen Katalog mitgebracht.
3. Er soll wegen d_____ Buch_____ Deutschland verlassen haben.
4. Innerhalb d_____ Hotel_____ ist es gemütlich.
5. Außerhalb d_____ Flugplatz_____ dürfen wir nicht landen.
6. Statt ein_____ Plattenspieler_____ hat er ein Tonbandgerät.
7. Trotz d_____ Warnung_____ raucht sie zehn Zigaretten täglich.
8. Anstatt ein_____ Student_____ sehen wir eine Studentin.

C. *Supply the correct accusative form.*

1. Gegen d_____ Wind gehen ist anstrengend.
2. Sie sind gut durch d_____ Winter gekommen.
3. Das Reisebüro ist beim „Kaufhof" um d_____ Ecke.
4. Gegen ein_____ Steak hat er nichts.
5. Sie geht um d_____ Zeitungsstand.
6. Er kauft ein Bier für d_____ Freund.
7. Die Kinder sind jetzt ohne d_____ Vater.
8. Wir gehen durch d_____ Hotel.

D. *Supply the correct dative form.*

1. Ein Glas Wodka genügt _____. (ich)
2. Vertraue _____! (der Freund)

3. Das Restaurant gefällt _____. (wir)
4. Du kannst _____ wirklich danken. (die Dame)
5. Ich rate _____, einmal das Pamphlet zu lesen. (Sie)
6. Gehört das Buch _____? (du)
7. Wir helfen _____. (die Kinder)
8. Bist du gestern _____ begegnet? (ein Freund)
9. Kannst du _____ folgen? (er)
10. Antworten Sie _____, bitte! (ich)

E. *Substitute or add each phrase as it is introduced into the previous sentence and make any necessary structural changes.*

Er dankte dem Freund für den Plattenspieler.
_____ Buch.
_____ Freundin _____
Du _____
_____ Zigaretten.
_____ Vater _____
_____ Geld.
Wir _____

GUIDED CONVERSATION

A. Is there a school vacation coming up soon? Discuss your travel plans with someone in your class. Among other things, you might exchange notes on where you plan to go, how you plan to get there, what you plan to do during the vacation, whether you have been to a travel agency, whether the vacation will be cheap or expensive, whether you have the money yet for the trip, and so on. If you have no travel plans, you might discuss a vacation you would like to take.

B. Have you read many books in the last year or so? Discuss the books you have read with someone in your class. During your exchange, you might compare notes on which books you like and which you do not like, why you like or do not like particular books, which books you would like to read. Instead of books, you might prefer to discuss records, films (der Film, –e), or something else.

Der Zeitungsstand

Nach Ankunft des „Donau-Expresses"[1] in München schaut Brigitte aus dem Fenster des Zuges. Sie sieht einen Zeitungsstand. Sie macht eigentlich nie eine Reise ohne ein Buch oder eine Zeitung. Aber heute hat sie wegen des Besuches eines Freundes alles vergessen. Allerdings fehlt ihr oft auch die Geduld, ein Buch ganz zu lesen. Statt eines Buches liest sie dann oft die Zeitung oder einen Kriminalroman.

Brigitte verläßt den Zug für fünf Minuten, natürlich nicht ohne die Handtasche. Sie geht um den Zeitungsstand. Für die Illustrierten zeigt sie wenig Interesse. Die Titelbilder gefallen ihr nicht wegen . . . , nun ja, wegen der Mädchen. Und die Stories bringen fast immer nur Skandale. Wegen der Touristen kann man hier in München auch Zeitschriften aus dem Ausland bekommen.

Brigitte blättert durch eine Zeitschrift aus Amerika. Trotz der fünf Jahre Englisch in der Schule ist es für sie sehr anstrengend, eine Zeitschrift auf

englisch zu lesen. Sie versteht nicht alles, denn sie hat viel vergessen. Schließ- 15
lich kauft sie statt einer Illustrierten eine NEWSWEEK,[2] eine Zeitung und
einen Krimi für die Reise. Das genügt ihr. Sie geht zum Zug zurück.

Sie liest zuerst die Zeitung: „Kanzler dankt der Opposition!" Wirklich?
Das ist neu! Aber für die Politik hatte sie noch nie Interesse. „Metall-Industrie
droht den Arbeitnehmern." Schon wieder Politik! Brigitte legt die Zeitung 20
weg und greift zum Krimi.

---

[1] The following proper names occur in this reading: der **Donau-Express** Danube Express;
München Munich.
[2] Titles of magazines are written in all capital letters.

QUESTIONS

1. Wo hält der Donau-Express gerade?
2. Was tut Brigitte in München?
3. Warum ist Brigitte jetzt ohne ein Buch oder eine Zeitung?
4. Was liest sie oft statt eines Buches?
5. Wie lange verläßt Brigitte den Zug?
6. Für was zeigt sie wenig Interesse?
7. Warum gefallen ihr die Titelbilder nicht?
8. Warum kann man in München auch Zeitungen aus dem Ausland bekommen?
9. Was ist für Brigitte sehr anstrengend?
10. Warum kauft sie eine NEWSWEEK?
11. Was liest sie jetzt während der Reise?
12. Was liest sie bald statt der Zeitung?

VOCABULARY EXERCISES

Supply the appropriate word from the list on the right.

1. _____ Ihnen ein Steak?
2. Wegen der Kalorien _____ sie nicht viel.
3. Glaube mir, es _____ dir!
4. Das sieht wirklich _____ aus.

a. Opposition
b. die Ankunft
c. genügt
d. Touristen

5. _____ des Zuges ist spät.
6. Die Reise war für Brigitte _____.
7. Wegen der _____ kann man auch Zeitschriften aus dem Ausland bekommen.
8. Der Kanzler dankt der _____.
9. Ist das _____ eine Öl-Krise?

e. ißt
f. schon wieder
g. gefällt
h. langweilig
i. gemütlich

Review Exercises

A. *Supply the correct genitive form of each noun in parentheses.*

1. Kennen Sie den Namen _____? (der Hund)
2. Die Adresse _____ weiß ich nicht. (die Freundin)
3. Das Resultat _____ ist drei zu zwei. (das Fußballspiel)
4. Kennen Sie die Wohnung _____? (der Professor)
5. Ist die Qualität _____ gut? (der Volkswagen)
6. Bestellst du für mich die Spezialität _____? (das Haus)
7. Neujahr ist der Beginn _____. (das Jahr)

B. *Rewrite the sentences above (A) using the indefinite article instead of the definite article.*

C. *Indicate possession by using (a) the genitive and (b) the verb* **gehören**.

EXAMPLE   Das ist das Auto **des** Vaters.
           Das Auto gehört **dem** Vater.

1. Das ist das Glas Bier d_____ Freund_____.
   Das Glas Bier gehört d_____ Freund.
2. Der Park ist das Eigentum d_____ Staat_____.
   Der Park gehört d_____ Staat.
3. Das ist das Kleid d_____ Mädchen_____.
   Das Kleid gehört d_____ Mädchen.

4. Das ist der Hund d_____ Professor_____.
   Der Hund gehört d_____ Professor.
5. Das ist die Handtasche d_____ Dame_____.
   Die Handtasche gehört d_____ Dame.

D. *Complete the sentence with the correct form of the noun in parentheses.*

1. Ich bin außerhalb d_____ _____. (Restaurant)
2. Du bist innerhalb d_____ _____. (Zimmer)
3. Er wohnt außerhalb d_____ _____. (Stadt)
4. Wir sind innerhalb d_____ _____. (Halle)
5. Sie liest statt d_____ _____ einen Krimi. (Zeitung)

E. *Rewrite the sentences above (D) using the indefinite article instead of the definite article.*

F. *Complete the sentence with the item in parentheses.*

1. Das Auto fährt durch d_____ _____. (Mittelgebirge)
2. Das Zimmer ist für d_____ _____. (Staatsanwalt)
3. Der Zeitungsstand ist dort drüben um d_____ _____. (Ecke)
4. Sie schaute durch ein_____ _____. (Tür)
5. Das Öl ist für ein_____ _____. (Volkswagen)
6. Der Angeklagte fuhr gegen ein_____ _____. (Baum)

G. *Supply the correct forms of the German equivalent for the English noun or pronoun in parentheses.*

1. Der Angeklagte antwortete d_____ _____. (district attorney)
2. Der Kanzler hat d_____ _____ gedankt. (opposition)
3. Ich muß sagen, Werner, sie gefällt _____. (me)
4. Das Auto gehört d_____ _____. (cab driver)
5. Wir begegneten gestern d_____ _____. (architect)
6. Ich vertraue d_____ _____. (friends)
7. Sie folgten d_____ _____. (street)
8. Habt ihr d_____ _____ geholfen? (parents)
9. Die Coca-Cola gehört ein_____ _____. (student)
10. Das Konzert hat _____ wirklich gut gefallen. (us)

GUIDED COMPOSITION

Write a brief composition outlining your plans for an ideal vacation: when to go, where to go, how to travel, where to stay, what type of accommodation to look for, what to do, whom to meet, and so on. The hotel and resort advertisements here may give you some ideas.

Hotel La Torre: Modernes Hotel in den oberen Etagen eines Hochhauses (15. bis 17. Stock) mit einmalig schönem Blick auf See und Berge, sehr ruhig. Speisesaal mit Panoramablick im 17. Stock. Stadtpark, Freibad und Tennisplätze in der Nähe. 28 Zimmer teilweise mit Dusche/WC oder Bad/WC. Einzelzimmer mit gegenüberliegendem Bad. Auf dem Dach Aufenthaltsraum mit Bar und Sonnenterrasse.
Preiswerteste Tigges-Reise: **DM 447**

Boldt-Hotel-Arcadia: Geschmackvoll eingerichtetes Hotel mit Gartenhaus und vis à vis gelegener Villa am Südhang des Monte Bré, Ortsteil Castagnola. 50 Zimmer teilweise mit Bad/WC, Balkon, Seeblick. Lift. Frühstückszimmer, geräumiger Speisesaal, Halle, TV, Weinstube, Schreibzimmer. Große Terrasse. Beheiztes Schwimmbad mit Liegewiese. Persönliche Atmosphäre; sehr kinderfreundlich.
Preiswerteste Tigges-Reise: **DM 433**

Chapter 8

Volkswagenwerk in Wolfsburg

Useful Phrases

Einen Augenblick!	Just a moment.
In Ordnung!	(It's) all right.
Ganz recht.	Quite right.
erst einmal	first of all
hier oben	up here
da unten	down there
geradeaus	straight ahead

MODEL SENTENCES

Das Auto **steht** in **der** Garage.	The car is [sitting] in the garage.
Er **fährt** das Auto in **die** Garage.	He drives the car into the garage.
Der Vogel **sitzt** auf **dem** Baum.	The bird is [sitting] on the tree.
Der Vogel **fliegt** auf **den** Baum.	The bird is flying onto the tree.
Das Flugzeug **steht** vor **der** TWA-Halle.	The airplane is standing in front of the TWA hall.
Das Flugzeug **rollt** vor **die** TWA-Halle.	The airplane is moving in front of the TWA hall.
Sie **parkt** den Wagen neben **dem** Rathaus.	She parks the car next to the city hall.
Sie **fährt** den Wagen neben **das** Rathaus.	She drives the car next to the city hall.
Wir **gehen** in **dem** Wald **spazieren.**	We walk in the forest.
Wir **gehen** in **den** Wald.	We go into the forest.

Grammar Explanations

PREPOSITIONS WITH ACCUSATIVE OR DATIVE

In addition to the two groups of prepositions that always govern the dative and the accusative cases, there is a group of prepositions that calls for *either* the dative *or* the accusative, which is determined by the situation depicted.

an (at; on; to)	über (over; about)
auf (on; to)	unter (under; among)
hinter (behind)	vor (in front of; before, ago)
in (in; into)	zwischen (between)
neben (beside)	

Use the dative case with these prepositions when the prepositional phrase answers the question "where" (in what place), the *location* in which the action is occurring. Use the accusative case when the prepositional phrase answers the questions "where to"—that is, where there is motion, *direction*, or destination from one place or one condition to another.

acc: Fred geht *in die* Bahnhofshalle.
 (Fred is going into the entrance hall of the station.)

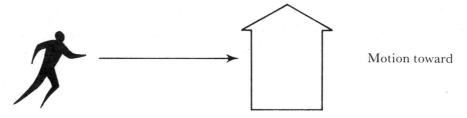

Motion toward

dat: Fred wartet *in der* Bahnhofshalle.
 (Fred is waiting in the entrance hall of the station.)

Position in

dat: Fred geht *in der* Bahnhofshalle auf und ab.
    (Fred is pacing up and down [without "going anywhere"]
    in the entrance hall of the station.)

Motion within

In all three sentences the preposition **in** is used. But the verb in the first sentence denotes a *motion toward* (or into) a place—accusative case; in the second sentence the verb expresses a *position in* a place—dative case; and in the third sentence it depicts a motion, but a *motion within* one place—also dative case. Notice that in the first English sentence "into" is used, but in the second and third English sentences, the equivalent is "in." Thus, to determine whether the accusative or dative case is required, ask the question "Wohin?" or "Wo?"

Wohin geht Fred?   Er geht **in die** Bahnhofshalle.
Wo wartet er?   Er wartet **in der** Bahnhofshalle.
Wo geht er auf und ab?   Er geht **in der** Bahnhofshalle auf und ab.

Wohin fährt das Auto?   Es fährt **in die** Garage.
(Where is the car going?)   (It's going into the garage.)
Wo steht das Auto?   Es steht **in der** Garage.
(Where is the car [sitting]?) (It is [sitting] in the garage.)

There are some verbs that do not express a *physical* motion toward a place but, rather, a kind of outgoing *mental* movement—the verbs of thinking, saying, and hearing, for example. These verbs are often followed by a preposition with the accusative case.

Sie sprechen **über den** Stadtplan.   They are talking about the city map.
Ich denke oft **an das** Mädchen.   I often think of the girl.
Er hört **auf dich.**   He listens to you.
Wir warten **auf den** Zug.   We are waiting for the train.

In these abstract cases it is difficult to give cogent reasons for the use of the accusative. It is best to memorize the proper case with the preposition required by the verb.

Again, some prepositions combine with the definite article to form the following dative and accusative contractions.

Dative			*Accusative*		
an dem	=	**am**	an das	=	**ans**
in dem	=	**im**	auf das	=	**aufs**
			in das	=	**ins**

In conversational German all these prepositional contractions are usually preferred to the full forms.

Check Your Comprehension

A. *Use the preposition in a complete sentence first with the accusative and then with the dative of the noun in parentheses.*

1. an (die Ecke)
2. auf (der Bahnhof)
3. hinter (das Stadttheater)
4. neben (die Aktentasche)
5. über (die Straße)
6. unter (der Arm)
7. vor (die Universität)
8. zwischen (die Adenauer-Allee und der Hauptbahnhof)

B. *Ask the question* **Wo** *or* **Wohin** *to decide which case to supply.*

1. Ich bin in d_____ Halle.
2. Wir fahren in d_____ Stadt.
3. Sie stehen vor d_____ Stadtplan.
4. Die Universität liegt an d_____ Adenauer-Allee.
5. Sie geht neben d_____ Polizisten auf und ab.
6. Der Ball fliegt über d_____ Haus.
7. Der Vogel fliegt auf d_____ Baum.
8. Er hat die Aktentasche unter d_____ Arm.

C. *Use the preposition as a contraction with the article of the noun in parentheses.*

1. an + acc. (das Fenster)
2. an + dat. (der Samstag)
3. auf + acc. (das Sofa)
4. an + dat. (das Sofa)
5. über + acc. (das Haus)
6. in + acc. (das Haus)
7. in + dat. (der Baum)

CONVERSATION

Der Stadtplan

Der Zug aus Frankfurt ist pünktlich. Fred öffnet die Tür und steigt aus dem Zug. Er nimmt die Aktentasche unter den Arm und geht in die Bahnhofshalle. Neben dem Fahrkartenschalter sieht er einen Polizisten. Fred geht zu ihm und bittet ihn um eine Auskunft.

FRED   Verzeihung, wie komme ich von hier zur Universität?   5

POLIZIST   Zur Universität? Ja, das muß ich Ihnen da drüben auf dem Stadtplan zeigen.

Vor dem Stadtplan.

POLIZIST   Sehen Sie, wir sind jetzt hier an dem Pfeil. Da ist der Hauptbahnhof.   10

FRED   Ja. Und wo liegt jetzt die Universität?

POLIZIST   Die Universität liegt hier oben am Karlsplatz. Moment mal! Ach ja, hier.

FRED   Dann muß ich also erst einmal hier über die Straße?

POLIZIST   Ganz recht. Dann kommen Sie da drüben an der Ecke auf die   15 Adenauer-Allee. Gehen Sie da immer geradeaus bis zur Schützenstraße. Das ist zwei, nein, drei Kreuzungen von hier.

FRED   Die Adenauer-Allee ist hier; dann—einen Augenblick—Schützenstraße. Ja, ich habe es.

POLIZIST   Gehen Sie die Schützenstraße bis zum Stadttheater und dann links!   20 Dann immer geradeaus bis zum Karlsplatz.

FRED   Und da, sagten Sie, ist die Universität?
POLIZIST   Ja. Es ist ein Neubau. Zu Fuß etwa fünfzehn Minuten.
FRED   Vielen Dank!
POLIZIST   Bitte sehr!

ORAL PRACTICE

A. *Substitute the item in parentheses for each noun in boldface and make the necessary structural changes.*

1. Wir gehen in die **Stadt.** (Restaurant)
2. Das Auto steht auf dem **Parkplatz.** (Straße)
3. Das Bild ist im **Badezimmer.** (Küche)
4. Der Krimi ist neben dem **Bett.** (Lampe)
5. Er steht vor dem **Stadtplan.** (Halle)
6. Wir steigen in den **Bus.** (Zug)
7. Sie geht ins **Haus.** (Universität)

8. Das Flugzeug fliegt über die **Alpen.** (Mittelgebirge)
9. Das Taxi fährt hinter den **Hauptbahnhof.** (Parkplatz)
10. Das Taxi steht vor dem **Hauptbahnhof.** (Bus)

B. *Substitute the preposition in parentheses for that in boldface and make the necessary changes.*

1. Der Vogel flog **über** den Baum. (auf)
2. Der Junge rannte **ins** Haus. (hinter)
3. Der Baum steht **hinter** der Garage. (neben)
4. Sie fährt den Wagen **neben** die Garage. (in)
5. Wir sitzen **am** Tisch. (auf)
6. Ihr geht **ans** Fenster. (unter)
7. Er parkt den Wagen **vor** dem Haus. (hinter)

C. *Complete the sentence with the appropriate preposition and article. Use a contraction where possible.*

1. Wir gehen _____ Fenster. (an)
2. Er fährt _____ Parkplatz. (auf)
3. Ihr könnt _____ Schnee Skilaufen. (in)
4. Der Ball fiel _____ Tor. (vor)
5. Der Volkswagen steht _____ Garage. (hinter)
6. Der Ball fiel _____ Wasser. (in)
7. Der Vogel sitzt _____ Baum. (auf)

D. *Supply the missing articles after determining the correct case.*

Der Zug aus Frankfurt ist pünktlich. Fred öffnet die Tür und steigt aus _____ Zug. Er nimmt die Aktentasche unter _____ Arm und geht in _____ Bahnhofshalle. Neben _____ Fahrkartenschalter sieht er einen Polizisten. Fred geht zu ihm und bittet ihn um _____ (*indef.*) Auskunft.

E. *Do the same with the following sentences. Use a contraction where possible.*

1. Verzeihung, wie komme ich von hier zu_____ Universität?
2. Das zeige ich Ihnen auf_____ Stadtplan.

3. Wir sind jetzt hier an＿＿＿＿ Pfeil.
4. Die Universität liegt dort an＿＿＿＿ Karlsplatz.
5. Dann muß ich hier über＿＿＿＿ Straße gehen?
6. Ja, dann kommen Sie dort an＿＿＿＿ Ecke auf＿＿＿＿ Adenauer-Allee.

F. *Complete the sentence by supplying the appropriate preposition and article.*

1. Fred bittet den Polizisten ＿＿＿＿ Auskunft. (for an)
2. Ich denke oft ＿＿＿＿ Besuch des Freundes. (of the)
3. Sie sprechen ＿＿＿＿ Buch. (about the)
4. Wir haben viel ＿＿＿＿ gehört, Herr Meyer. (about you)
5. Fred wartet ＿＿＿＿ Gepäck. (for the)

G. *Substitute or add each phrase as it is introduced into the previous sentence and make any necessary structural changes.*

Fred wartet in   der Bahnhofshalle.
＿＿＿＿ steht ＿＿＿＿＿＿＿＿＿＿＿＿＿＿
＿＿＿＿＿＿＿＿ vor ＿＿＿＿＿＿＿＿＿＿
＿＿＿＿＿＿＿＿＿＿＿＿＿＿ Polizisten.
＿＿＿＿＿＿＿＿＿＿＿＿＿＿ Zeitungsstand.
Du ＿＿＿＿＿＿＿＿＿＿＿＿＿＿＿＿＿＿
＿＿＿ gehst ＿＿＿＿＿＿＿＿＿＿＿＿＿ auf und ab.
＿＿＿＿＿＿＿ neben ＿＿＿＿＿＿＿＿＿＿＿＿
＿＿＿＿＿＿＿＿＿＿＿＿ Zug＿＿＿＿＿＿＿＿＿

GUIDED CONVERSATION

A. Imagine that you and one of the students in your class are driving in Germany and are about to enter a German city. Suppose you are just leaving the BAB (Bundesautobahn) and entering the city on the Steinfurter Straße, located in the northwest corner. Using the map provided here, take turns giving directions to the Hauptbahnhof, Dom, Zoo, Schloß, and Universitäts-Kliniken.

For additional practice, give directions on how to get from one place to another within the city—from the Dom to the Schloß, from the Universitäts-Kliniken to the Zoo, and so on.

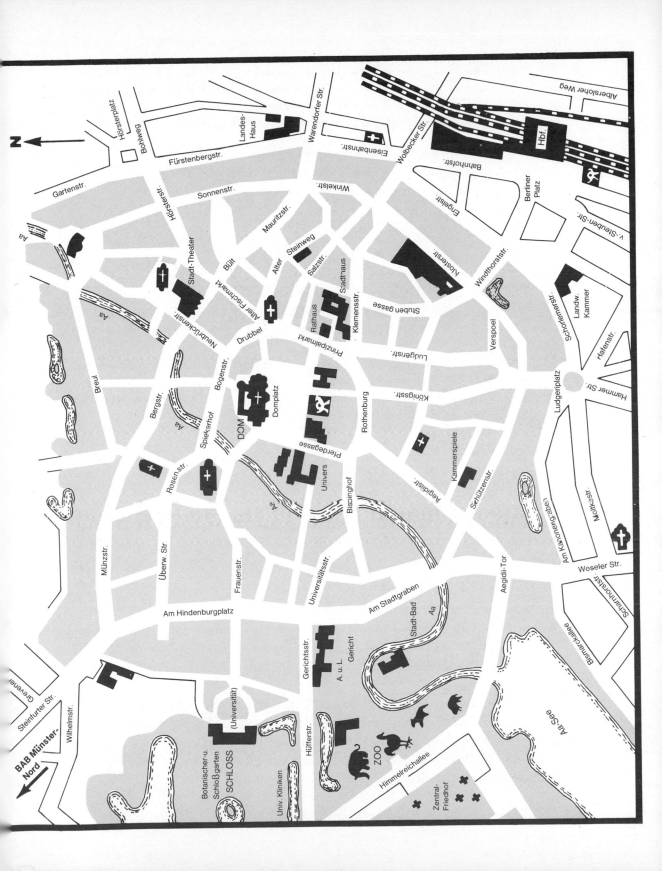

B. Play the following game with two or more persons in your class. Think of an object in the classroom and have the other students guess what it is by asking questions about it. Answer all questions with **ja** or **nein,** repeating the question as an affirmative or negative statement. Give no additional information.

> Ist der Gegenstand (object) unter dem Tisch?
> Nein, der Gegenstand ist nicht unter dem Tisch.
> *or*   Ja, der Gegenstand ist unter dem Tisch.

The following terms may help you.

> der Papierkorb, ⸚e (wastebasket)
> der Stuhl, ⸚e (chair)
> die Tafel, –n (blackboard)
> die Wand, ⸚e (wall)
> das Pult, –e (desk)

A variation of the game is to have someone leave the room while you hide something. Call the person in and answer his/her questions about where you have hidden the object. Again, answer all questions with **ja** or **nein,** repeating the question as an affirmative or negative statement.

READING

Eine Reise nach Deutschland

Alfred studiert Deutsch und Biologie an einer Universität im Staat Wisconsin/USA. Er spricht wirklich schon ganz gut Deutsch. Nur mit der Aussprache hat er noch Schwierigkeiten. Alfred hat ein Stipendium für ein Studium in Deutschland bekommen und will nun ein Jahr in der Stadt Freiburg studieren.   5

Mit einer Boeing 747[1] fliegt er vom O'Hare-Flughafen in Chicago über die Neuengland-Staaten und über den Atlantik nach Frankfurt am Main. Ungefähr zwei Stunden vor der Landung fliegt die Boeing über eine Insel im Atlantik. Es ist Irland. Nach der Auskunft des Flugkapitäns ist das Flugzeug gerade über der Stadt Shannon.   10

Die Stewardess bringt den Passagieren das Frühstück. Bald kann man auf die Küste Belgiens hinuntersehen. Vor der Landung fliegt die Boeing über der Stadt Frankfurt im Kreis. Unten sieht Alfred schon die Landebahn.

Nach der Landung rollt die Maschine vor das Flughafengebäude und stoppt direkt vor der TWA-Halle. Die Passagiere steigen aus dem Flugzeug und gehen ins Flughafengebäude. Alfred muß ein paar Minuten auf das Gepäck warten. An der Paßkontrolle sieht der Beamte nur auf das Bild im Paß. Beim Zoll will Alfred das Gepäck auf den Tisch stellen, aber der Zollbeamte hinter dem Tisch sagt: „In Ordnung! Bitte, weitergehen!"

So einfach ist es heute, von den USA in die Bundesrepublik Deutschland zu reisen!

---

[1] Read: Siebenhundertsiebenundvierzig *or* sieben-vier-sieben.

QUESTIONS

1. Wo studiert Alfred?
2. Was studiert er?
3. Was ist noch eine Schwierigkeit für ihn?
4. Was hat Alfred bekommen?
5. Wo will er jetzt studieren?
6. Wohin fliegt er jetzt?
7. Wie fliegt er nach Frankfurt?
8. Wo ist das Flugzeug ungefähr zwei Stunden vor der Landung?
9. Was bringt die Stewardess den Passagieren?
10. Auf was kann man bald hinuntersehen?
11. Wohin rollt die Boeing gleich nach der Landung?
12. Wo stoppt das Flugzeug?
13. Wohin gehen die Passagiere?
14. Auf was muß Alfred ein paar Minuten warten?

15. Auf was sieht der Beamte an der Paßkontrolle?
16. Wo steht der Zollbeamte?
17. Was ist heute so einfach?

VOCABULARY EXERCISES

Supply the appropriate word from the list on the right.

1. Der Zug aus Frankfurt ist _____.   a. geradeaus
2. Fred _____ aus dem Zug.   b. zu Fuß
3. Neben dem _____ sieht er einen Polizisten.   c. Auskunft
4. Er bittet ihn um eine _____.   d. Fahrkartenschalter
5. Das sind drei _____ von hier.   e. Landung
6. Gehen Sie immer _____!   f. pünktlich
7. _____ ist es etwa fünfzehn Minuten von hier.   g. Kreuzungen
8. Mit der _____ hat Alfred noch Schwie-   h. Bundesrepublik
   rigkeiten.   i. Aussprache
9. Zwei Stunden vor der _____ fliegt die   j. steigt
   Boeing über Irland.
10. Bonn ist die Hauptstadt der _____.

Review Exercises

A. *Complete the sentence by supplying the correct preposition and case.*

1. Alfred studiert _____ Universität in Wisconsin. (at a)
2. _____ Aussprache hat er noch Schwierigkeiten. (with the)
3. Er will _____ Stadt Freiburg wohnen. (in the)
4. Er fliegt _____ Neuengland-Staaten und _____ Atlantik nach
   Frankfurt. (over the / across the)
5. Im Augenblick ist die Boeing gerade _____ Stadt Shannon. (above
   the)

6. _____ Landung rollt die Maschine _____ Flughafengebäude und stoppt direkt _____ TWA-Halle. (after the / up to the / in front of the)

7. Die Passagiere steigen _____ Flugzeug und gehen _____ Flughafengebäude. (out of the / into the)

8. Alfred muß ein paar Minuten _____ Gepäck warten. (for the)

9. Der Beamte sieht nur _____ Bild _____ Paß. (at the / in the)

10. So einfach ist es heute, _____ USA _____ Bundesrepublik Deutschland zu reisen. (from the / into the)

B. *Supply the required prepositions with the necessary articles in the following story.*

Der Name des Hundes _____ (in the) Geschichte ist Max. Ich lag gerade _____ (on the) Sofa und aß eine Bratwurst. Da kam Max _____ (out of the) Küche und nahm mir die Wurst _____ (from the) Teller. Er lief schnell _____ (with the) Wurst _____ (out of the) Haus _____ (into the) Straße. Ich sah Max _____ (behind a) Baum liegen, und die Wurst lag _____ (in front of him). Er sah mich _____ (out of the) Haus kommen. Da lief er schnell _____ (around a) Ecke. Plötzlich stand ich direkt _____ (behind him). Er sah mich und lief schnell wieder _____ (into the) Haus. Schließlich fand ich ihn _____ (in the) Küche _____ (under the) Tisch.

GUIDED COMPOSITION

A. Have you ever lost something and then had to search a long time to find it? Or perhaps you never did find it. Write a brief composition about something you once lost and how you went about looking for it. Mention the many places you looked before the search ended, or before you gave up.

B. Suppose that a friend of yours who lives in another city is coming for a visit. Write a short letter to your friend with directions on how to get to your house from the main highway or freeway. Provide a map or a sketch if you wish.

C. Have you recently taken a trip by plane? Write a brief description of the trip from the point of departure to the point of arrival. You might mention the type of plane you were on; the cities, states, mountains, lakes, or other interesting features you flew over; what you had to eat or drink during the trip; where the plane landed and stopped; and so on.

Chapter 9

Industrie und Gärten bei Ludwigshafen

Useful Phrases

Rauchen verboten!	No smoking.
Du hast recht.	You're right.
Das stimmt.	That's right.
Ich bin ganz deiner Meinung.	I agree with you completely.
keineswegs	by no means
vor allem	above all
Gewiß!	Certainly.
Also!	Well then.
in dieser Hinsicht	in this respect

MODEL SENTENCES

I

Kennst du **diese** Bilder da drüben?	Do you know these pictures over there?
Jeder Mensch weiß das.	Everybody knows that.
Welche Zeitung lesen Sie?	Which newspaper do you read?
Alle Leute sind hier. **Alle** sind hier.	All the people are here. All are here.

II

Kommt ihr mit **meinem** Vater?	Are you coming with my father?
Ist das **eure** Mutter?	Is that your mother?
Was für einen Winter habt ihr gehabt?	What kind of winter did you have?
Viele Menschen haben oft eine **andere** Meinung.	Many people often have a different opinion.
Das ist **mein** Mantel. Wo ist **Ihrer?**	That's my coat. Where is yours?

III

Bleibt **gesund!**	Stay healthy.
Seine Gesundheit ist **ausgezeichnet.**	His health is excellent.
Das Museum ist **wirklich** einmalig.	The museum is really unique.

Grammar Explanations

I. der-WORDS

German has a group of noun modifiers called "**der**-words" because they are declined like the definite article, **der, die, das.** The most common of these are the following.

> dieser (this; that)
> jeder; *pl.* alle (each; every; *pl.* all)
> jener (that; the former)
> mancher (many a; *pl.* several, some)
> welcher (which)

To determine the form of a **der**-word, take the stem, for instance **dies–,** and add the appropriate case ending of the definite article.

Declension of **der**-Words: **dieser**

	Masculine	*Feminine*	*Neuter*	*All Genders*
		Singular		*Plural*
nom.	dies**er**	dies**e**	dies**es**	dies**e**
acc.	dies**en**	dies**e**	dies**es**	dies**e**
dat.	dies**em**	dies**er**	dies**em**	dies**en**
gen.	dies**es**	dies**er**	dies**es**	dies**er**

Hast du **diese** Bilder da drüben gesehen? Did you see those pictures over there?

In **mancher** Hinsicht ist die Sammlung einmalig. In some respect the collection is unique.

Der Wert **jener** Gemälde ist ganz beträchtlich. The value of those paintings is quite considerable.

A few indefinite numerical adjectives occur mainly in the plural and take the same endings as the plural **der**-words. These are **alle** (all), **beide** (both), and **solche** (such).

Alle Leute sind hier.	All the people are here.
Beide Bilder sind interessant.	Both pictures are interesting.
Solche Fragen sind sehr wichtig.	Such questions are very important.

Notice that **der**-words may also function as *pronouns*, that is, they may replace nouns, in which case the adjective endings are retained.

Alle sind hier.	All are (everyone's) here.
Beide sind interessant.	Both are interesting.

Check Your Comprehension

A. *Decline the* **der-*words*** **jeder** *and* **welcher** *in the singular and in the plural, according to the following chart.*

	Masculine	Feminine	Neuter	All Genders
nom.	_____	_____	_____	_____
acc.	_____	_____	_____	_____
dat.	_____	_____	_____	_____
gen.	_____	_____	_____	_____

B. *Decline* **alle, beide,** *and* **solche** *according to the following chart.*

	Plural
nom.	_____
acc.	_____
dat.	_____
gen.	_____

C. *Add the correct* **der**-*word ending.*

1. Die Sammlung hat all_____ Gemälde.
2. In dies_____ Hinsicht ist sie einmalig.
3. Manch_____ Bilder finde ich schön.

4. Jen_____ Trend nimmt seit einigen Jahren zu.
5. Auf dies_____ Gebiet ist euer Museum weltberühmt.
6. Der Wert beid_____ Bilder ist sehr groß.

II. ein-WORDS

The term "**ein**-words" refers to a group of noun modifiers that are declined like the singular of the indefinite article, **ein, eine, ein,** and the plural of **kein.** These fall into two categories, the possessive adjectives

mein (my)	unser (our)
dein (your)	euer (your)
sein (his; its)	ihr (their)
ihr (her)	Ihr (your)

and "others."

kein (no; not a; not any)
solch ein (such [a])
was für ein, was für (what [a])
welch ein (what [a]; which)

Was für eine Sammlung!   What a collection!
Solch eine Entwicklung mußte allerdings   Such a development, however, had to
   kommen.   come.

To determine the form of an **ein**-word, take the stem, for instance **mein-,** and add the appropriate case ending of the indefinite article in the singular and of **kein** in the plural.

Declension of **ein**-Words: **mein**

	Masculine	*Feminine*	*Neuter*	*All Genders*
		Singular		*Plural*
nom.	mein	meine	mein	meine
acc.	meinen	meine	mein	meine
dat.	meinem	meiner	meinem	meinen
gen.	meines	meiner	meines	meiner

When **euer** takes a declensional ending, it drops the **–e–** in front of the **–r**: **euere** becomes **eure, eueren** becomes **euren**. In conversation, **unser** also often drops the first **–e**: **unserem** becomes **unsrem**.

Man kann unser Museum gut mit eurem Landesmuseum vergleichen.	One can very well compare our museum with your state museum.

Certain indefinite numerical adjectives occur only in the plural and take the same endings as the plural **ein**-words. These are

andere (other[s])
einige (some)
mehrere (several)
viele (many)
wenige ([a] few)

Die Sammlung hat **viele** Gemälde.	The collection has many paintings.
Einige Gemälde finde ich schön, **andere** nicht.	Some paintings I like, others (I do) not.
Seit **einigen** Jahren nimmt jener Trend zu.	That trend has been growing for several years.

All **ein**–words can replace nouns and thus function as pronouns. When this occurs, the endings differ from the normal declension of **ein**-words in the nominative masculine and the nominative and accusative neuter singular.

Declension of **ein**-Words as Pronouns

	Masculine	*Feminine*	*Neuter*	*All Genders*
		Singular		*Plural*
nom.	mein**er**	meine	mein**(e)s***	meine
acc.	meinen	meine	mein**(e)s***	meine
dat.	meinem	meiner	meinem	meinen
gen.	meines	meiner	meines	meiner

Das ist dein Volkswagen.	That's your Volkswagen.
Meiner ist in der Garage.	Mine is in the garage.

---

* In spoken German, the contracted forms **meins, deins,** and **seins** are preferred.

Das ist euer Flugzeug.	That's your plane.
Unseres kommt in einer Stunde.	Ours comes in an hour.
Hast du dein Gemälde?	Do you have your painting?
Nein, ich habe **sein(e)s.**	No, I have his.

Check Your Comprehension

A. *Decline the* **ein-words dein, unser,** *and* **was für ein** *in the singular and in the plural, according to the following chart.*

	Masculine	Feminine	Neuter	All Genders
nom.	____	____	____	____
acc.	____	____	____	____
dat.	____	____	____	____
gen.	____	____	____	____

B. *Decline* **einige, mehrere,** *and* **viele** *according to the following chart.*

	Plural
nom.	____
acc.	____
dat.	____
gen.	____

C. *Add the correct* **ein-**word *ending.*

1. Was für ein_____ Sammlung!
2. Ich glaube ihm kein_____ Wort.
3. Ich weiß, euer_____ Museum ist weltberühmt.
4. Man kann es gut mit unser_____ Museum vergleichen.
5. Unser_____ Einfluß in der Wirtschaft nimmt ab.
6. Ich bin ganz Ihr_____ Meinung.

III. PREDICATE ADJECTIVES AND ADVERBS

An adjective is said to be in the predicate position when it is separated by a verb from the noun or pronoun that it modifies. It is called a *predicate adjective* because it "predicates" or asserts something about a noun or pronoun. Most often the predicate adjective occurs after **sein** (to be), but it is also found with **werden** (to become) and **bleiben** (to remain).

Eure Sammlung ist **ausgezeichnet.**	Your collection is excellent.
Der Mann wird **alt,** aber er bleibt **gesund.**	The man is getting old, but he's keeping [staying] healthy.

The predicate adjective may also be found with a verb such as **finden** (to find) in the sense of expressing an opinion.

Ich finde manche Bilder **schön.**	I find some pictures beautiful.

In contrast to attributive adjectives, those that directly precede the noun they modify, as in "a beautiful picture" (*see* Chapters 10 and 11), predicate adjectives are not declined.

As the name implies, an *adverb* is a linguistic component that modifies a verb. It can also modify an adjective or another adverb. In English, the adverb is usually distinguished from its corresponding adjective by the ending **–ly** (tremendous, tremendous**ly**); in German, the adverb has the same form as the undeclined adjective.

The position of the adverb within a sentence is determined by the word that it qualifies. The adverb is placed directly before

1. a *verb,*

Man kann es **gut** vergleichen.	One can well compare it.

2. an *adjective,*

Das Museum ist **wirklich** einmalig.	The museum is really unique.

3. or another *adverb.*

Das hast du **wirklich** gut gemacht.	That you have done really well.

Notice that the adverb is spelled the same as the predicate adjective; the difference between the two is their function in the sentence, not their form.

Adverbs and adverbial expressions frequently indicate time (**morgen**), manner (**mit dem Auto, bestimmt**), or place (**nach Berlin**), and a sentence can contain one, two, or all three indications. The pattern in word order is generally T̲ime, M̲anner, P̲lace.

	T	M	P	
Er fährt	morgen	mit dem Auto	nach Berlin.	He's driving to Berlin by car tomorrow.

Any one of the three adverbial expressions may be placed at the beginning of the sentence, for emphasis, and the word order pattern of the other adverbs remains the same.

	M	P	
Morgen fährt er	mit dem Auto	nach Berlin.	He's driving by car to Berlin *tomorrow*.

	T	P	
Mit dem Auto fährt er	morgen	nach Berlin.	He's driving to Berlin *by car* tomorrow.

	T	M	
Nach Berlin fährt er	morgen	mit dem Auto.	He's driving by car *to Berlin* tomorrow.

The expression of time is found at the beginning of the sentence more often than the other two.

Check Your Comprehension

A. *Substitute the predicate adjective in parentheses for the word in boldface.*

1. Euer Landesmuseum ist wirklich **ausgezeichnet.** (weltberühmt)
2. Diese Ausstellung finde ich **interessant.** (einmalig)
3. Manche Gemälde sind **wertvoll.** (schön)
4. Die Sammlung ist nicht **übel.** (schlecht)
5. Dieser Urlaub wird **billig.** (teuer)

B. *Substitute the adverb in parentheses for the word in boldface.*

1. Diese Sammlung ist **wirklich** schön. (tatsächlich)
2. Die Bilder sind **einmalig** gut. (sehr)
3. Solch eine Ausstellung ist **immer** wertvoll. (sicher)

C. *Place the adverbs or adverbial expressions in the proper sequence in the sentence.*

1. Ich gehe _____. (sicher / heute abend / ins Theater)
2. Er kommt _____. (zu mir / mit dem Auto / morgen)
3. Sie ist _____. (bestimmt / morgen früh / zu Hause)
4. Wir fahren _____. (dahin / übermorgen / schnell)
5. Er studiert _____. (auf der Universität / immer / im Sommer)

CONVERSATION

Im Landesmuseum

CHARLIE   Was für eine Sammlung! Ich muß sagen, Herbert, euer Landesmuseum ist wirklich ausgezeichnet. Ich glaube, man kann es gut
mit unserem „Museum of Modern Art" vergleichen. Meinst du
nicht?

HERBERT   Gewiß! Unsere Sammlung hat vor allem viele Gemälde aus der   5
Romantik. In dieser Hinsicht ist sie tatsächlich einmalig. Aber
manche Werke aus der Nachkriegszeit sind sicher ebenso bedeutend.

CHARLIE   Ja, auf diesem Gebiet ist euer Museum ja weltberühmt!

HERBERT   Das stimmt. Hast du übrigens die Bilder da drüben gesehen?   10
Das sind alles Gemälde von Künstlern aus Amerika. Manche finde
ich sehr schön, andere finde ich allerdings nicht so gut. Aber das
ist sicher auch Geschmacksache!

CHARLIE   Ja, ich habe mehrere gesehen. Es scheint, der Einfluß der USA
auf dem Gebiet der Kultur ist wirklich nicht nur auf die Holly-   15
wood Westerns und die Fernseh-Krimis beschränkt!

HERBERT   Sicher nicht! Ich glaube, seit einigen Jahren nimmt dieser Trend
immer mehr zu.

CHARLIE   Das ist wirklich interessant! Unser Einfluß in der Wirtschaft
Europas nimmt ständig ab und unser Einfluß in der Kunst und   20
Kultur nimmt immer mehr zu. Wie ist das möglich?

HERBERT   Ja, es sieht tatsächlich so aus. Solch eine Entwicklung mußte
allerdings kommen! Europa ist heute nicht mehr ganz so abhängig von den USA wie noch vor wenigen Jahren. Nehmen wir
einmal an: wenn Amerika . . .   25

CHARLIE   Weißt du, ich finde das alles sehr interessant. Aber wollten wir
nicht die Ausstellung besichtigen?

HERBERT   Du hast recht. Bin ganz deiner Meinung. Also: zurück zur Kultur!

ORAL PRACTICE

A. *Substitute the correct form of the items in parentheses for the word in boldface.*

1. In **diesem** Museum habt ihr viele Gemälde.
   (euer / jener / kein / mancher / welcher / was für ein / solch
   ein / Ihr / jeder)
2. Der Wert **mehrerer** Bilder ist sehr groß.
   (einige / viele / manche / beide / alle / andere / solche / wenige)
3. In der Sammlung **eures** Museums sind viele Bilder aus Amerika.
   (unser / dein / Ihr / sein / kein / ihr / mein / was für ein)

B. *Supply the possessive pronoun as indicated in parentheses.*

EXAMPLE   Das ist mein Haus. Wo ist _____? (dein)
            Wo ist **deines** (*or* **deins**)?

1. Das ist unser Hund. Wo ist _____? (euer)
2. Das ist sein Problem. Was ist _____? (ihr)
3. Das ist dein Ball. _____ ist kaputt. (mein)
4. Das ist seine Aktentasche. Wo sind _____? (euer)
5. Das ist Ihr Auto. _____ steht in der Garage. (unser)

C. *Substitute the item in parentheses for the word in boldface and make any necessary changes.*

1. Sie ist gerade in eurem **Museum.** (Küche)
2. Er ist gerade in unserem **Badezimmer.** (Toilette)
3. Wir sind in unserer **Wohnung.** (Haus)
4. Ihr seid mit seinem **Flugzeug** gereist? (Auto)
5. Kommst du gerade von deiner **Schule?** (Universität)
6. Das ist Ihr **Zug.** (Garage)
7. Was ist der Name deines **Vaters?** (Freundin)
8. Ist das das Bild eurer **Mutter?** (Professor)
9. Dort ist das Gebäude meiner **Schule.** (Universität)
10. Ich warte auf die Ankunft unserer **Eltern.** (Zug)

D. *Substitute the items in parentheses for the word in boldface and make any necessary changes in the verb and adjective.*

1. **Ich** habe meine Zigaretten vergessen.
   (er / ihr / du / Sie / wir / die Dame / der Taxifahrer /
   ihr beide / die Eltern)
2. **Andere Leute** lesen ihre Zeitung.
   (wir / du / Herr Kuhn / der Arzt / meine Freundin / jedes Kind /
   die Studentin / deine Frau / sie / ihr / Sie beide)

E. *Substitute the items in parentheses for the word in boldface.*

1. Solch eine Diskussion finde ich **interessant.**
   (toll / gut / einmalig / wertvoll / schön / richtig / ausgezeichnet /
   prima)

2. Solch eine Entwicklung nimmt **ständig** zu.
   (wirklich / immer mehr / vielleicht / tatsächlich / oft / keineswegs / wahrscheinlich / sehr)

F. *Substitute or add each phrase as it is introduced into the previous sentence and make any necessary structural changes.*

Unsere Sammlung hat vor allem   viele   Gemälde aus der Romantik.

Eure_____

_____ Museum _____

_____ keineswegs _____

_____ wenige _____

_____ Bilder _____

_____ Nachkriegszeit.

Dieses _____

GUIDED CONVERSATION

A. Is there a current art exhibit somewhere on campus or in your city? Discuss the exhibit with someone in your class. If you both have seen it, discuss what you liked about it and what you did not like, and why. If only one of you has seen the exhibit, try to convince the other that it is worth seeing, or that it is not worth seeing. If neither of you has seen an exhibit recently, you might discuss famous paintings that you like or do not like. Use as many **der**-words and **ein**-words during your discussion as you can.

B. Assume that you are the host or hostess of a party to which the entire class has been invited. The party is now over and you must help everyone gather up his/her things. Point to various coats and/or accessories in the classroom and ask to whom they belong. The following might give you a start.

> Gehört dieser Mantel dir, Bob?
> Nein, das ist nicht mein Mantel.
> Ist das Ihr Mantel, Herr Professor?
> Ja, das ist meiner.

The following words may help you.

der Handschuh, –e (glove)
der Hut, ⸚e (hat)
die Jacke, –n (jacket, coat)
der Mantel, ⸚ ([over] coat)
der Regenmantel, ⸚ (raincoat)
der Schal, –s (scarf)

READING

Im Wartezimmer

Kein Wartezimmer ist immer so furchtbar voll wie dieses. Da muß ich sicher noch einige Stunden warten. Ich bin sehr ungeduldig, ich weiß.

Schon wieder diese Illustrierten! Beinahe jeder Patient liest diese „Kultur"-Magazine. Dort drüben liegt noch ein SPIEGEL. Manche mögen ihn nicht, andere finden ihn ausgezeichnet. Schade, ein anderer Herr greift   5
gerade zum SPIEGEL. Ich lese die FRANKFURTER ALLGEMEINE und warte . . .

Kennen Sie meinen Arzt? Natürlich nicht! Wissen Sie, der Mann fragt immer so viel: „Schon wieder etwas mit Ihrem Magen, Herr Kuhn? So? Was haben Sie denn gestern abend gegessen und getrunken? Na, sagen Sie 10 es mir ehrlich! Schließlich ist es ja Ihr Magen, nicht meiner."

Natürlich ist es mein Magen! Immer diese Fragen! Jeder Mensch ist schließlich für seine Gesundheit verantwortlich. Wie kann denn mein Arzt mir meine Martinis verbieten? Ich brauche sie doch wie andere Leute ihre Zigaretten. Ach ja, Zigaretten! Rauchen wir noch eine! Wo sind denn meine 15 Streichhölzer? Ein Herr zeigt auf ein Schild neben dem Eingang: „Rauchen verboten!" Natürlich. Es ist jener Herr mit dem SPIEGEL. Ich stecke meine Zigaretten wieder weg.

„Der Nächste, bitte!" Wer ist denn noch vor mir? Ich glaube, die Dame da drüben mit der Brille und dann das Mädchen da in der Ecke. Moment 20 mal! Diese Haare, diese Augen, diese Nase! Ist das nicht die Tochter meines Kollegen?

Au! Mein Magen! Warum bin ich eigentlich hier? Mein Arzt sagt ja doch immer: „Herr Kuhn, ein Glas ist genug! Und nehmen Sie diese Pillen drei- mal am Tag!" 25

Diese Pillen helfen ja doch nicht. Ich gehe . . .

Zu spät! Mein Arzt steht in der Tür und sagt: „Ach, Herr Kuhn, Sie sind wieder da? Bitte, kommen Sie herein! Schon wieder etwas mit Ihrem Magen? . . . "

QUESTIONS

1. Wo wartet Herr Kuhn?
2. Hat er viel Geduld?
3. Wie nennt Herr Kuhn die Illustrierten?
4. Welche Zeitschrift möchte er lesen?
5. Warum ist er beim Arzt?
6. Was verbietet ihm der Arzt immer?
7. Raucht er noch eine Zigarette?
8. Kennt er das Mädchen in der Ecke?
9. Wohin will Herr Kuhn gerade gehen?
10. Warum war es zu spät?

VOCABULARY EXERCISES

Supply the appropriate word from the list on the right.

1. Manche Werke aus der _____ sind sehr wertvoll.
2. Der _____ der USA auf die Wirtschaft Europas war beträchtlich.
3. Manche finden den SPIEGEL gut. Das ist sicher _____.
4. Die _____ Amerikas ist wirklich interessant.
5. Ich bin ganz deiner _____.
6. Das _____ ist heute furchtbar voll.
7. Der _____ von Herrn Kuhn ist nicht ganz gesund.
8. Er sucht seine _____.
9. Neben dem Eingang ist ein _____ : „Rauchen verboten!"
10. Der _____ gibt Herrn Kuhn Pillen.

a. Einfluß
b. Schild
c. Magen
d. Geschmacksache
e. Meinung
f. Arzt
g. Wartezimmer
h. Kunst
i. Streichhölzer
j. Nachkriegszeit

Review Exercises

A. *Supply the appropriate possessive adjective.*

EXAMPLE Die Illustrierten gehören meinem Arzt.
Es sind seine Illustrierten.

1. Der SPIEGEL gehört ihm. Es ist _____ SPIEGEL.
2. Die Streichhölzer gehören dir. Es sind _____ Streichhölzer.
3. Der Wagen gehört Ihnen. Es ist _____ Wagen.
4. Die Zigaretten gehören dem Mädchen. Es sind _____ Zigaretten.
5. Die Pillen gehören dem Patienten. Es sind _____ Pillen.
6. Das Schild gehört dem Arzt. Es ist _____ Schild.

B. *Supply the correct* **der-** *or* **ein-***word ending.*

1. Die Sammlung hat viel _____ Gemälde.
2. Was für ein_____ Gemäldesammlung!
3. In dies_____ Hinsicht ist sie einmalig.
4. Ich glaube ihm kein_____ Wort.
5. Manch_____ Bilder finde ich schön, ander_____ nicht.
6. Ich weiß, euer_____ Museum ist weltberümt.
7. Jen_____ Trend nimmt seit einigen Jahren zu.
8. Man kann dies_____ Museum gut mit unser_____ vergleichen.
9. Der Wert mehrer_____ Bilder ist ganz beträchtlich.
10. Unser_____ Wirtschaft ist abhängig von den USA.
11. Vor wenig_____ Jahren war das genau so wichtig.
12. Ich bin ganz dein_____ Meinung!

C. *Supply the German equivalents for the words in parentheses.*

_____ (no) Wartezimmer ist immer so furchtbar voll wie _____ (this one). Da muß ich sicher noch _____ (some) Stunden warten. Immer _____ (these) Illustrierten! Fast _____ (every) Mensch liest _____ (those) „Kultur"-Magazine! _____ (some) mögen den SPIEGEL, _____ (others) ihn nicht. Schade! Gerade greift ein _____ (other) Herr zum SPIEGEL. _____ (my) Arzt fragt immer soviel. Wie geht es _____ (your) Magen? Haben Sie wieder _____ (your) drei Martinis mit Eis getrunken? Sehr schön! Schließlich ist es ja _____ (your) Magen, nicht _____ (mine).

D. *Supply the German equivalent for the English predicate adjective or adverb in parentheses.*

1. Ich kenne die Tochter meines Kollegen _____. (well)
2. Sie spielt _____ Bridge und Tennis. (excellently)
3. In dieser Hinsicht ist sie wirklich _____. (world famous)
4. Ja, die Familie meines Kollegen ist sehr _____. (interesting)
5. Sie fliegt zum Beispiel _____ jede Woche nach London. (almost)
6. Der Bridge-Club dort ist _____. (unique)
7. Aber der Tennis-Club dort ist auch nicht _____. (bad)
8. Sagen Sie mir ganz ehrlich: Finden Sie Deutsch _____ interessant? (really)

GUIDED COMPOSITION

A. Have you seen a doctor or dentist (**Zahnarzt**) recently? Write a brief composition explaining the reason you made the appointment, and the thoughts that entered your mind as you were waiting to see the doctor or dentist. The following terms may help you.

das Auge, –n (eye)
das Bein, –e (leg)
der Fuß, ⸚e (foot)
der Hals, ⸚e (neck)
das Herz, –en (heart)
der Kopf, ⸚e (head)
der Mund, ⸚er (mouth)
das Ohr, –en (ear)
der Zahn, ⸚e (tooth)

B. Write a short composition characterizing the members of your family or class. The following pattern may give you some ideas on how to proceed.

Alle sind . . .
Jeder ist . . .
Einige sind . . .
Wenige haben . . .
Manche sind . . .
Viele haben . . .
Dieser ist . . .
Jener hat . . .

Chapter 10

Miltenberg

Useful Phrases

gar nicht	not at all
zum Glück	luckily
Wie bitte?	What did you say?
Genau!	Precisely.
Keine Sorge!	Don't worry.
Da steht es . . .	There it says. . . .
Lassen Sie mich mal sehen!	Let me see.
Es gibt* nichts zu lachen.	There is nothing to laugh (about).
Hier gibt es eine gute Sammlung.	Here there's a good collection.
Es gibt hier keine guten Restaurants.	There aren't any good restaurants here.

MODEL SENTENCES

Das ist meine **neue** Krawatte.	That's my new tie.
Es gibt diese **amerikanische** Zeitschrift hier nicht.	This American magazine isn't (available) here.
Diesen **langweiligen** Roman kenne ich.	I'm familiar with [know] this boring novel.
Sie liebt keine **großen** Autos.	She doesn't like big cars.
Die **modernen** Uhren sind gut konstruiert.	Modern watches are well made.
Welches **neue** Gemälde hast du gekauft?	Which new painting did you buy?
Ich habe meinem **alten** Freund einen **langen** Brief geschrieben.	I've written a long letter to my old friend.

---

* **Es gibt** (there is, there are), expressing mere existence, may be followed by a singular or plural object in the accusative case.

Grammar Explanations

ATTRIBUTIVE ADJECTIVES: WEAK DECLENSION

The definite and indefinite articles, **der-**words, and **ein-**words are adjectives that do not describe the noun they modify; they merely specify or identify a certain class or category of the noun and thus are called *limiting* words.

Adjectives followed by a noun are called *attributive* because they attribute certain characteristics to the noun they modify. They are also called *descriptive* adjectives. In contrast to predicate adjectives, attributive adjectives must be declined.

In German there are two types of adjective endings: weak and strong. Weak endings occur when the attributive adjective is preceded by a limiting word (a **der-**word or an **ein-**word *with* an ending). Strong endings occur on attributive adjectives following an **ein-**word *without* an ending in the masculine nominative or neuter nominative and accusative singular or when there is *no* limiting word. Strong adjective endings will be discussed in full detail in Chapter 11.

Since the limiting word already indicates the number, gender, and case of the noun, the descriptive adjective does not need to. There are thus only two weak adjective endings: **–e** and **–en.**

Weak Declension: Adjectives Following **der-**Words

	Masculine	Feminine	Neuter
Singular			
nom.	dieser groß**e** Bahnhof	jene neu**e** Uhr	welches schön**e** Haus
acc.	diesen groß**en** Bahnhof	jene neu**e** Uhr	welches schön**e** Haus
dat.	diesem groß**en** Bahnhof	jener neu**en** Uhr	welchem schön**en** Haus
gen.	dieses groß**en** Bahnhofs	jener neu**en** Uhr	welches schön**en** Hauses

	All Genders
Plural	
nom.	beide schön**en** Häuser
acc.	beide schön**en** Häuser
dat.	beiden schön**en** Häusern
gen.	beider schön**en** Häuser

Weak Declension: Adjectives Following **ein**-Words with Endings

	Masculine	Feminine	Neuter
Singular			
nom.	——*	ihre schön**e** Blume	——*
acc.	seinen langweilig**en** Roman	ihre schön**e** Blume	——*
dat.	seinem langweilig**en** Roman	ihrer schön**en** Blume	eurem neu**en** Kleid
gen.	seines langweilig**en** Romans	ihrer schön**en** Blume	eures neu**en** Kleides

All Genders

Plural	
nom.	kein**e** modernen Autos
acc.	kein**e** modernen Autos
dat.	kein**en** modernen Autos
gen.	kein**er** modernen Autos

Weak Adjective Endings

	Masculine	Feminine	Neuter	All Genders
		Singular		*Plural*
nom.	**–e**	**–e**	**–e**	–en
acc.	–en	**–e**	**–e**	–en
dat.	–en	–en	–en	–en
gen.	–en	–en	–en	–en

Notice that the **–e** ending occurs in five places; otherwise the ending is always **–en.**

If the noun has a series of attributive adjectives, all of them take the same weak endings.

das neu**e** rot**e** Kleid	the new red dress
unserem gut**en** alt**en** Freund	to our good old friend

---

* There are endings that are required in these three cases, but they are strong endings since **ein** has no ending in the singular masculine nominative and the singular neuter nominative and accusative. See Chapter 11 for the completion of this chart. The declension of adjective endings following **ein**-words is often called a *mixed* declension.

A. *Decline the noun and the preceding* **der**–*word and attributive adjective in all cases in the singular.*

1. jener gute Uhrmacher
2. diese wertvolle Uhr
3. manche elegante Frau
4. der schlechte Sommer
5. jedes billige Auto

B. *Decline the noun and the preceding word and attributive adjective in all cases in the plural.*

1. alle schlechten Sommer
2. solche schönen Bilder
3. diese wertvollen Uhren
4. die eleganten Frauen

C. *Supply the missing forms in the chart, disregarding the nominative masculine and the nominative and accusative neuter forms in the singular.*

	Masculine	*Feminine*	*Neuter*
Singular			
nom.		meine neue Uhr	
acc.	meinen neuen Wagen	_____	
dat.	_____	_____	meinem neuen Auto
gen.	_____	_____	_____
Plural			
nom.	_____	meine neuen Uhren	_____
acc.	_____	_____	_____
dat.	_____	_____	meinen neuen Autos
gen.	meiner neuen Wagen	_____	_____

CONVERSATION

Beim Uhrmacher

UHRMACHER	Guten Tag, Frau Lenz! Bitte sehr?
FRAU LENZ	Guten Tag, Herr Beuse! Ich fürchte, diese neue Uhr hier ist kaputt. Sehen Sie mal, sie geht nicht mehr.
UHRMACHER	Lassen Sie mich mal sehen! Ja, das ist eine teure[1] Uhr. „Made in Switzerland".
FRAU LENZ	Wie bitte?
UHRMACHER	Ich sagte: „Made in Switzerland". Sehen Sie, da steht es.
FRAU LENZ	Ach so! Ja, die Uhr ist aus der Schweiz.
UHRMACHER	Hat Ihr Mann diese Uhr nicht vor einigen Monaten hier gekauft?
FRAU LENZ	Ja, genau! Aber wie kann denn eine neue Uhr stehenbleiben? Bei meiner alten Uhr ist das nie passiert.
UHRMACHER	Keine Sorge, Frau Lenz! Die modernen Uhren sind sehr gut konstruiert. Da kann nicht viel passieren. Ich will sie mal öffnen.
FRAU LENZ	Zum Glück ist auf dieser Uhr noch Garantie.
UHRMACHER	Wie lange haben Sie diese Uhr jetzt schon, Frau Lenz?

5

10

15

FRAU LENZ	Seit dem letzten Sommer. Das ist ungefähr ein Jahr.
UHRMACHER	Dann müssen wir wahrscheinlich die alte Batterie durch eine neue ersetzen. Das ist alles.
FRAU LENZ	Ach, dann ist die Uhr gar nicht kaputt?
UHRMACHER	Keineswegs. Die Batterie muß man bei diesen elektronischen Uhren alle ein bis zwei Jahre ersetzen. Sehen Sie: die Uhr geht wieder. Das macht zwölf Mark fünfzig.
FRAU LENZ	Das war ja einfach. Vielen Dank, Herr Beuse! Auf Wiedersehen!
UHRMACHER	Auf Wiedersehen, Frau Lenz!

20

25

---

[1] The adjective is **teuer;** but when **teuer** takes a declensional ending, the **-e-** before the **-r** is dropped: **teueres** becomes **teures.** (See **euer** and **unser,** Chapter 9.)

ORAL PRACTICE

A. *Substitute the items in parentheses for the noun in boldface and make the necessary changes in adjective endings.*

  1. Ihr habt einen neuen **Wagen.**
       (Uhr / Tisch / Vase / Wohnung / Auto)
  2. Die Blumen sind in meiner alten **Vase.**
       (Wohnung / Haus / Küche / Wagen / Garten / Wohnzimmer)
  3. Der Wert dieser schönen **Bilder** ist groß.
       (Autos / Häuser / Wohnungen / Bücher / Gemälde / Zeitschriften)

B. *Supply the appropriate attributive adjective ending following a* **der-***word.*

  1. In diesem groß_____ Bahnhof ist ein Zeitungsstand.
  2. Jenes schön_____ Gemälde kostet einhundert Dollar.
  3. Der Wert beider alt_____ Häuser ist groß.
  4. Diese neu_____ Uhren gehen nicht.
  5. Gehört jenes schön_____ Haus tatsächlich Ihnen?
  6. Welche modern_____ Gemälde gefallen dir?
  7. Die modern_____ Uhren sind sehr gut konstruiert.

C. *Supply the appropriate attributive adjective endings following an* **ein-**-*word.*

1. Meine neu_____ Uhr ist kaputt.
2. Das ist wirklich eine sehr wertvoll_____ Uhr.
3. Was für eine elegant_____ Uhr Sie haben, Fräulein Meyer!
4. Zum Glück ist auf Ihrer neu_____ Uhr noch Garantie.
5. Der Wert solch einer modern_____ Uhr ist groß.
6. Ich habe leider keinen neu_____ Wagen.
7. Er liest schon seit gestern seinen langweilig_____ Roman.

D. *Supply the appropriate attributive adjective ending.*

1. Ich fürchte, diese neu_____ Uhr hier ist kaputt.
2. Das ist wirklich eine wertvoll_____ Uhr.
3. Hat Ihr Mann diese elegant_____ Uhr hier gekauft?
4. Wie kann denn eine neu_____ Uhr stehenbleiben?
5. Zum Glück ist auf dieser teur_____ Uhr noch Garantie.
6. Ich habe sie seit dem letzt_____ Sommer.
7. Wir müssen die alt_____ Batterie durch eine neu_____ ersetzen.
8. Die Batterie muß man bei diesen modern_____ Uhren etwa alle ein bis zwei Jahre ersetzen.

E. *Change the predicate adjective into an attributive adjective.*

EXAMPLE   Diese Uhr ist neu.   **diese neue Uhr**

1. Jene Uhr ist kaputt. _____
2. Die Uhr ist wertvoll. _____
3. Die Schweiz ist schön. _____
4. Das Buch ist amerikanisch. _____
5. Die Zeitschrift ist deutsch. _____
6. Meine Uhr ist alt. _____
7. Alle Uhren sind modern. _____
8. Die Batterie ist drei Jahre alt. _____
9. Diese teure Uhr ist modern. _____
10. Der letzte Sommer war warm. _____

F. *Substitute or add each phrase as it is introduced into the previous sentence and make any necessary structural changes.*

Hat Ihr Mann diese   elegante Uhr hier gekauft?
_____ Sie_____?
_____ solch eine _____?
_____ wertvolle _____?
_____ Wagen _____?
_____ gefunden?

GUIDED CONVERSATION

A. Assume that you are a new student in the class. Ask the person sitting next to you who is who. Use descriptive phrases to identify the person you are asking about.

> Wer ist der junge Mann da mit dem langen Bart?
> Das ist Herr . . .
> Wer ist die junge Dame da mit der eleganten Uhr?
> Das ist Fräulein . . .

The following new terms may help you.

> gelb (yellow)
> grau (gray)
> grün (green)
> kurz (short)
> das Hemd, –en (shirt)
> der Ring, –e (ring)

B. Assume that you have just returned from a trip, and you find that your car is not in the airport parking lot where you left it. Assume that one of the students in your class is an airport security guard. Explain the situation and describe your car as completely as possible, answering all questions the guard may ask of you. The conversation might take a course such as the following.

> War es ein neuer Wagen?
> Nein, es war kein neuer Wagen.
> War es ein großer Wagen?
> Ja, es war ein großer Wagen.

By now you should be familiar with the following adjectives which may be helpful in your conversation.

alt (old)	groß (big; great)
amerikanisch (American)	gut (good)
billig (cheap, inexpensive)	klein (small, little)
deutsch (German)	modern (modern)
einmalig (unique)	neu (new)
elegant (elegant)	teuer (expensive)
englisch (English)	wertvoll (valuable)

Be sure to use the colors you have learned, too.

READING

Das neue Vorlesungsverzeichnis

Gisela Wegner möchte Lehrerin werden. Seit zwei Jahren studiert sie schon Englisch, Deutsch und Pädagogik.

Sie blättert gerade im neuen Vorlesungsverzeichnis für das nächste Semester. Welche Seminare soll sie belegen? Schließlich findet sie ein Seminar mit dem interessanten Titel „Die neuen Methoden des Sprachunterrichts" von Professor Korff. Das ist der junge Mann mit dem langen Bart und den blauen Augen. Er behandelt die neuen empirischen Untersuchungen zum Sprachunterricht von Kalifornien. Er hat drei Jahre an der amerikanischen Universität Stanford studiert. Seine interessanten Seminare sind immer voll.   5

In Deutsch möchte Gisela Wegner einmal den neuen Professor von der österreichischen Universität Innsbruck hören. Er hält ein Seminar mit dem modernen Thema „Sprachliche Kommunikation und Gesellschaft". Unter „Englisch" findet Gisela im neuen Vorlesungsverzeichnis „Images of America: Prejudice and Reality". Diese Vorlesung hält Professor Cathey, jener bekannte   10

Gastprofessor aus den USA. Die meisten Studenten sind begeistert von ihm. 15
Er spricht das amerikanische Englisch mit einem östlichen Akzent, genau
wie die Einwohner von Boston.

Am nächsten Montag beginnt die Einschreibung mit dem langweiligen
Ausfüllen von Formularen. Im letzten Semester war dieser furchtbare Papierkrieg sehr anstrengend. 20

QUESTIONS

1. Was möchte Gisela Wegner werden?
2. Was studiert sie?
3. Wie lange studiert sie schon?
4. Wer ist Professor Korff?
5. Wo hat er drei Jahre studiert?
6. Woher kommt der neue Deutsch-Professor?
7. Was für ein Seminar hält er?
8. Wer ist Professor Cathey?
9. Was für einen Akzent hat er?
10. Wann beginnt die Einschreibung für das neue Semester?

VOCABULARY EXERCISES

Supply the appropriate word from the list on the right.

1. Ich fürchte, diese neue Uhr ist _____.
2. Kann eine neue Uhr _____?
3. Keine Sorge, da kann nicht viel _____.
4. Haben Sie schon das neue _____?
5. Haben Sie einen langen _____?
6. Professor Korff behandelt die neuen_____ in Kalifornien.
7. Der Gastprofessor aus den USA hält eine _____.
8. Die meisten Studenten sind _____ von ihm.
9. Vor Beginn des Semesters ist die _____.
10. Der Papierkrieg ist immer sehr _____.

a. Untersuchungen
b. Vorlesung
c. Einschreibung
d. anstrengend
e. kaputt
f. Vorlesungsverzeichnis
g. begeistert
h. stehenbleiben
i. Bart
j. passieren

Review Exercises

A. *Supply the* **der-** *or* **ein-***word ending and the appropriate attributive adjective ending.*

1. Ich fürchte, dies_____ neu_____ Tisch hier ist kaputt.
2. Ich möchte in d___ _ schön_____ Schweiz Skilaufen.
3. Zum Glück ist auf solch ein_____ teur_____ Uhr noch Garantie.
4. Seit d_____ letzt_____ Sommer bin ich nicht zu Hause gewesen.
5. Ich kann mein_____ alt_____ Wagen nicht mehr fahren.
6. Dies_____ drei Jahre alt_____ Uhr ist kaputt.
7. Ich blättere gerade in unser_____ neu_____ Telefonbuch.
8. Sein_____ interessant_____ Seminare sind immer voll.
9. Kennen Sie jen___ _ bekannt_____ Gastprofessor aus den USA?
10. Fräulein Smith, Sie sprechen mit d_____ gleich_____ einmalig schön_____ Akzent wie mein Freund aus Houston/Texas.

B. *Use the adjective in parentheses as an attributive adjective preceding the noun in boldface.*

1. Ich fürchte, dieses **Auto** ist kaputt. (neu)
2. Das ist eine **Uhr.** (wertvoll)
3. Zum Glück ist auf dieser **Uhr** noch Garantie. (teuer)
4. Seit dem **Sommer** bin ich nicht zu Hause gewesen. (letzt)
5. Die Batterie muß man bei diesen **Autos** alle fünf Jahre ersetzen. (modern)
6. Gisela kannte jenen **Studenten** nicht so gut. (amerikanisch)
7. Ich finde das **Ausfüllen** von Formularen nicht interessant. (langweilig)
8. Die Studenten sind begeistert von dem **Professor** aus Innsbruck. (neu)
9. Haben Sie schon einmal etwas über die **Kommunikation** gehört? (sprachlich)
10. Kennen Sie die **Untersuchungen** der kalifornischen Universität Stanford? (neu, empirisch)

11. Was für eine **Sammlung** Sie haben! (schön)
12. Von eurem **Museum** habe ich noch nie etwas gehört. (ausgezeichnet)
13. Wir haben viele **Gemälde** in unserem Museum. (alt)
14. Sehen Sie oft diese **Fernseh-Krimis**? (furchtbar)
15. Die Inkas sind wegen ihrer **Kultur** bekannt. (groß)

C. *Join the two sentences to make one sentence and use the predicate adjective as an attributive adjective.*

EXAMPLE   Diese Uhr ist teuer. Sie hat eine Batterie.
          Diese teure Uhr hat eine Batterie.

1. Jene Uhr ist neu. Sie ist kaputt.
2. Die Uhren sind modern. Sie sind gut konstruiert.
3. Die Batterie ist alt. Man muß sie durch eine neue Batterie ersetzen.
4. Das Auto ist alt. Es fährt nicht mehr.
5. Ein Wein ist gut. Er muß alt sein.
6. Diese Gemälde sind einmalig. Sie sind wertvoll.
7. Seine Tochter ist intelligent. Sie studiert Medizin.
8. Die Tomaten sind frisch. Sie sind billig.
9. Die Zigarren sind gut. Sie kommen aus Kuba.
10. Das Öl ist wertvoll. Es ist teuer geworden.

D. *Change the noun and its attributive adjective from the plural to the singular and make the necessary structural changes.*

1. Ich fürchte, **diese neuen wertvollen Uhren** sind kaputt.
2. Er liest **seine langweiligen Romane.**
3. Ich habe **diese furchtbaren Fernseh-Krimis** schon einmal gesehen.
4. **Diese kleinen deutschen Autos** sind nicht schlecht.
5. **Welche wertvollen Gemälde** wollten Sie kaufen?
6. Auf **jenen neuen Batterien** ist noch Garantie.
7. Viele österreichische Studenten studieren an **diesen deutschen Universitäten.**
8. **Die amerikanischen Gastprofessoren** sind weltberühmt.
9. Gisela blättert in **den neuen Vorlesungsverzeichnissen.**
10. **Diese frischen Apfelsinen** sind wirklich billig.

⑬ Service „Westminster"
Ein herrliches, ganz dem Zeitgeschmack entsprechendes Original-englisch-Service aus
feinstem Hartsteingut in der beliebten eckigen Formgebung. Das entzückende Blumendekor ist von handgravierten Kupferplatten
abgenommen und eingebrannt. Dieses wunderbare Geschirr ist absolut säurebeständig
und spülmaschinenfest.

| Kaffeeserv. f. 6 Pers., 15 tlg. | 99550 | DM | 65.- |
| Speiseserv. f. 6 Pers., 22 tlg. | 04272 | DM | 109.- |

GUIDED COMPOSITION

A. The tableware advertisement is taken from a catalogue by QUELLE, which is a large mail-order business in Germany. Read the description carefully, then make a list of all the predicate and attributive adjectives and adverbs. Look up unfamiliar words in a German–English dictionary. Use some of these words to write your own description of a set of dishes, or anything else, that you would like to advertise for sale in the want ad section of a newspaper.

B. Cut out a picture from a magazine and write a precise description of what it shows and/or what is taking place. Give as many details as possible, using descriptive adjectives and adverbs.

Chapter II

Luzern

Useful Phrases

Prost!	Cheers!
Guten Appetit!	[Good appetite!] Eat hearty.
Es sieht gut aus.	It looks good.
leider nicht	unfortunately not
Sonst noch etwas?	Anything else?
und so weiter (*abbrev.* usw.)	and so on (*abbrev.* etc.)
Ich kann das nicht vetragen.	It doesn't agree with me.

MODEL SENTENCES

I

Grüner Salat ist gesund.	Green salad is healthy.
Eiskaltes Bier ist ungesund.	Ice cold beer is unhealthy.
Bei **warmem** Wetter kann man schwimmen gehen.	In warm weather you can go swimming.
Spargel schmeckt gut mit **frischer** Butter.	Asparagus tastes good with fresh butter.

II

Das Ei muß fünf Minuten in **kochendem** Wasser liegen.	The egg must be boiled [in boiling water] for five minutes.
Sie erhielt das **bestellte** Kochbuch.	She received the cookbook that she (had) ordered.
Eis schmeckt [ist] **erfrischend**.	Ice cream tastes [is] refreshing.

III

Der Alte ist blind.	The old man is blind.
Ich glaube an **das Gute** im Menschen.	I believe in the goodness in man.
Er darf nichts **Gebratenes** essen.	He is not permitted to eat any fried foods.
Alles **Gekochte** ist gesund.	Everything (that is) cooked is healthy.

Grammar Explanations

I. ATTRIBUTIVE ADJECTIVES: STRONG DECLENSION

As noted in Chapter 10, attributive adjectives following an **ein**-word in the masculine nominative singular and the neuter nominative and accusative singular require strong endings. This is because the limiting **ein**-word does not show number, gender, or case. Thus the attributive adjective endings in these three instances become as follows.

Singular
nom. masc.: **ein** grün**er** Salat
nom. neut.: **ein** kalt**es** Bier
acc. neut.: **ein** kalt**es** Bier

Because adjectives following **ein**-words take both weak *and* strong endings, this is called a mixed declension.

Mixed Declension: Adjectives Following **ein**-Words

	Masculine	*Feminine*	*Neuter*
Singular			
nom.	ein grün**er** Salat	meine frisch**e** Milch	sein kalt**es** Bier
acc.	einen grün**en** Salat	meine frisch**e** Milch	sein kalt**es** Bier
dat.	einem grün**en** Salat	meiner frisch**en** Milch	seinem kalt**en** Bier
gen.	eines grün**en** Salates	meiner frisch**en** Milch	seines kalt**en** Bieres

	All Genders
Plural	
nom.	keine klein**en** Flaschen
acc.	keine klein**en** Flaschen
dat.	keinen klein**en** Flaschen
gen.	keiner klein**en** Flaschen

When a noun is not preceded by a limiting adjective, the attributive adjective ending must indicate the syntactics of the noun (number, gender, and case). These endings are termed the *strong declension* of adjectives. In most cases the adjective takes the ending of the omitted **der**-word to indicate the proper case.

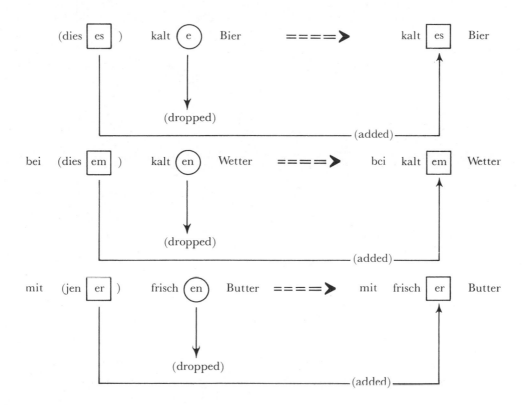

The strong declension endings are identical to the **der**-word endings, except in the masculine and neuter genitive singular.

Strong Declension: Adjectives

	Masculine	Feminine	Neuter	All Genders
		Singular		*Plural*
nom.	scharf**er** Käse	frisch**e** Butter	kalt**es** Bier	klein**e** Flaschen
acc.	scharf**en** Käse	frisch**e** Butter	kalt**es** Bier	klein**e** Flaschen
dat.	scharf**em** Käse	frisch**er** Butter	kalt**em** Bier	klein**en** Flaschen
gen.	scharf**en** Käses	frisch**er** Butter	kalt**en** Bieres	klein**er** Flaschen

Strong Adjective Endings

	Masculine	Feminine	Neuter	All Genders
		Singular		Plural
nom.	–er	–e	–es	–e
acc.	–en	–e	–es	–e
dat.	–em	–er	–em	–en
gen.	–en	–er	–en	–er

If there is more than one attributive adjective preceding a noun, all of them take the same strong endings.

Heute haben wir schön**es** warm**es** Wetter.   Today we have nice warm weather.

Several indefinite numerical words that occur only in the plural take strong endings (*see* Chapter 9): **andere, einige, mehrere, viele,** and **wenige.** All adjectives that follow these indefinite adjectives take the same strong endings.

Er hatte viel**e** gut**e** kalt**e** Biere.   He had many good, cold beers.
Ander**e** grün**e** Salate sind dort.   Other green salads are there.

After **alle,** another word that occurs only in the plural, the attributive adjectives take weak endings.

Der Mann sieht all**e** gut**en** Kinder.   The man sees all the good children.
Alle alt**en** weltberühmt**en** Professoren   All the old, world-famous professors are
sind da.   there.

Check Your Comprehension

A. *Supply the missing singular forms of the following mixed declensions.*

1. nom. _____
   acc. _____
   dat. einem guten Bier
   gen. _____

2. nom. _____
   acc. _____
   dat. _____
   gen. keines scharfen Käses

3. nom. _____   4. nom. mein frisches Ei
   acc. einen grünen Salat   acc. _____
   dat. _____   dat. _____
   gen. _____   gen. _____

B. *Omit the* **der-** *or* **ein-***word and make the necessary changes.*

1. Diese frische Butter ist gut.
2. Jener grüne Salat ist frisch.
3. Er trinkt jedes kalte Bier.
4. Ich esse gern Spaghetti mit einem scharfen Käse.
5. Mit der frischen Butter backt sie einen Kuchen.
6. Ich habe Appetit auf dieses dunkle Bier.
7. Bei diesem schönen warmen Wetter gehen wir schwimmen.

II. PARTICIPLES USED AS ATTRIBUTIVE ADJECTIVES

In German, as in English, participles of verbs may be used as attributive adjectives.

der gebratene Fisch	the fried fish
ein gekochtes Ei	a boiled egg
das kochende Wasser	the boiling water
ein lachendes Kind	a laughing child

As you may note, there are two types of participles: past and present.

A. Past Participle

The formation of the past participle in German was discussed in Chapter 5. To use the past participle as an adjective, take the complete form and add the appropriate adjective ending.

verbrennen, verbrannte, **verbrannt** (to burn)

Er suchte das **verbrannte** Gepäck.   He was looking for the burnt luggage.

stehlen, stahl, **gestohlen** (to steal)

Die Polizei fand das **gestohlene** Auto.   The police found the stolen car.

A past participle may also function as a predicate adjective with no ending.

Dieser Fisch schmeckt [ist] besser **ge-braten** als **gekocht.**

This fish tastes [is] better fried than boiled.

B. Present Participle

In English, the present participle is formed by adding the ending **–ing** to the verb stem:

to bark	barking
to boil	boiling

In German, the present participle is formed by adding the suffix **–d** to the *infinitive* form of the verb.

fahren	**d**	(driving)
kochen	**d**	(boiling)

To use the present participle as an adjective, add the appropriate attributive adjective ending. The present participle may also be used as a predicate adjective—with no ending.

| Das Ei ist im kochenden Wasser. | The egg is in boiling water. |
| Das Fondue sah **einladend** aus. | The fondue looked inviting. |

The present participle is often used as an adverb to express an action that occurs simultaneously with another.

Er kam **lachend** ins Zimmer.   He entered the room laughing.

The use of the participle as an adjective is widespread in German, much more common than in English. Present participles, especially, are used almost solely in this manner.

As you noticed, for easier reading you may need to convert the participle used as an attributive adjective into a relative clause in English.

Sie erhielt das **bestellte** Kochbuch.   She received the cookbook *that she* (had) *ordered.*

In German, the past or present participle frequently occurs with other parts of speech in a so-called *extended participial phrase*, which can only be rendered in English as a relative clause.

Sie erhielt das **von ihm bestellte** Kochbuch.	She received the cookbook that had been ordered by him.
Sie erhielt das **von ihm in Deutschland bestellte** Kochbuch.	She received the cookbook that had been ordered by him in Germany.

Check Your Comprehension

A. *Form the past participle of the verb and use it as a predicate adjective in the sentence.*

1. _____ schmeckt Fisch besser als Fleisch. (braten)
2. Fisch esse ich lieber _____ als roh. (kochen)
3. _____ schmeckt Fisch besser als gekocht. (grillen)
4. _____ sieht der Brief besser aus als getippt. (schreiben)

B. *Form the past participle of the verb and add the appropriate adjective ending.*

1. der _____ Fisch (braten)
2. mit dem _____ Ei (kochen)
3. die _____ Bratwürste (grillen)
4. den _____ Brief (schreiben)
5. die _____ Uhr (reparieren)

C. *Form the present participle of the verb and add the appropriate adjective ending.*

1. Das ist der _____ Vater. (lieben)
2. Hier sind die _____ Eier. (kochen)
3. Er sprang aus dem _____ Zug. (fahren)
4. Ich kenne den Namen des _____ Mädchens. (lachen)
5. Der _____ Mann dort ist ein Gangster. (rauchen)

D. *Form the present participle of the verb and use it as an adverb in the sentence.*

1. Der Mann sagte _____ zu mir: . . . (lachen)
2. Die Kinder liefen _____ durch den Wald. (singen)
3. Er trug schwer _____ die Koffer. (atmen)
4. Er kam _____ in die Klasse. (pfeifen)
5. Er fuhr _____ zur Universität. (nachdenken)

III. ADJECTIVES USED AS NOUNS

In German, almost any descriptive adjective, including those formed from participles, may be capitalized and used as a noun. When this occurs, and it does frequently, the adjective used as a noun retains the same adjective endings as when used as an attributive adjective.

Adjectival nouns may be masculine, feminine, or neuter. If they refer to human beings or pets, they are masculine or feminine; if they refer to abstract concepts or inanimate objects, they are neuter.

Der alte Mann ist blind.   The old man is blind.
Der **Alte** ist blind.

Die schöne Frau kocht ausgezeichnet.   The beautiful woman cooks excellently.
Die **Schöne** kocht ausgezeichnet.

Fondue ist eine gute Speise.   Fondue is a good dish.
Fondue ist etwas **Gutes.**

Notice that adjectives used as nouns are frequently found after **etwas, nichts, viel,** and **wenig.** Adjectival nouns following these words are neuter and take *strong* endings. Adjectival nouns following **alles,** however, take *weak* endings.

etwas Gut**es** (something good)   alles Gut**e** (everything good)
nichts Neu**es** (nothing new)   alles Neu**e** (all [that is] new)
viel Wertvoll**es** (much worthwhile)   alles Wertvoll**e** (everything worthwhile)
wenig Interessant**es** (little [of] interest)   alles Interessant**e** (all [that is] interesting)

Some examples of present and past participles as nouns include the following.

etwas Kochendes (something boiling)   alles Kommende (everything coming)
nichts Gebratenes (nothing fried)   alles Geschriebene (everything written)
viel Geschriebenes (much written material)   alles Gekochte (everything boiled)

A. *Form an adjectival noun from the adjective by omitting the modified noun.*

> EXAMPLE   Mozart, der weltberühmte Komponist
> Mozart, der **Weltberühmte**

1. Friedrich, der große König
2. unser kleines Kind
3. ein blinder Mann
4. von einer schönen Frau
5. für meine liebe Freundin
6. der Appetit eines dicken Mannes

B. *Form an adjectival noun from the predicate adjective by using the word in parentheses.*

1. Fondue is gut. (etwas)
2. Das ist schlecht. (nichts)
3. Das war wertvoll. (wenig)
4. Schlafen ist gesund. (etwas)
5. Das ist neu. (nichts)
6. Das ist gebraten. (etwas)

CONVERSATION

Im Supermarkt

FRAU HELMS   Sag mal, Ernst, was hältst du von grünem Salat und frischem Obst für heute zum Mittagessen? Du weißt doch, der Arzt hat gesagt . . .

HERR HELMS   Ja, ja. Nichts Fettes, nichts Süßes, nichts zu Scharfes, kein gebratenes Fleisch und so weiter und so weiter.   5

FRAU HELMS   Ganz recht. Aber ein frisches Joghurt oder ein gekochtes Ei darfst du natürlich auch essen.

HERR HELMS   Ich weiß, ich weiß.—Du, Ilse, wollten wir nicht die Meyers mal zum Fondue einladen? Wir haben es ihnen doch schon so lange versprochen!   10

FRAU HELMS	Aber Ernst, du weißt doch, in Öl gekochtes Fleisch kannst du nicht vertragen.
HERR HELMS	Natürlich! Ich dachte auch nicht an Fleisch-Fondue, sondern an ein schönes Käse-Fondue.
FRAU HELMS	Ach so! Ja, das ist etwas anderes. Wollen wir dann die Meyers für morgen abend einladen? Was brauchen wir denn für ein Fondue?
HERR HELMS	Ich glaube, man braucht ungefähr ein Pfund Schweizer Käse und ein Pfund Gruyère.
FRAU HELMS	Und was für Wein nimmt man? Einen weißen?[1]
HERR HELMS	Natürlich weißen! Es muß ein schöner herber Weißwein sein. Ich habe noch einen guten im Keller.
FRAU HELMS	Hast du auch Kirschwasser im Haus?
HERR HELMS	Leider nicht. Aber da drüben auf dem Regal stehen einige Flaschen.
FRAU HELMS	Gut! Es muß ja nichts Teures sein. Brauchen wir sonst noch etwas?
HERR HELMS	Wie ist es mit frischem Weißbrot?
FRAU HELMS	Wir haben noch tief gefrorenes Weißbrot zu Hause. Das ist genau so gut wie frisches.
HERR HELMS	Wunderbar! Ich kann kaum bis morgen abend warten. Endlich gibt es wieder einmal etwas Leckeres.

Line numbers: 15, 20, 25, 30

---

[1] When an adjective used as a noun refers back to, but does not replace, a noun *that has already been mentioned* the adjective is not capitalized.

ORAL PRACTICE

A. *Substitute the nouns in parentheses for the one in boldface and make the necessary changes.*

1. Ein frischer **Salat** liegt auf dem Tisch.
   (Tomate / Ei / Wurst / Weißbrot / Fisch / Apfelsine)
2. Das ist ein grüner **Volkswagen.**
   (Baum / Wald / Flasche / Salat / Haus / Sofa / Gebäude)
3. Unser neues **Auto** ist kaputt.
   (Volkswagen / Uhr / Batterie / Haus / Vase / Wirtschaft / Fernseher / Glas)
4. Spaghetti mit frischem **Salat** ist etwas Gutes.
   (Butter / Käse / Weißbrot / Tomaten / Milch)
5. Ich esse gerne scharfe **Pizza.**
   (Currywurst / Suppe / Käse / Fleisch / Steak / Salat / Zwiebeln)
6. Er trinkt gerne kaltes **Bier.**
   (Kaffee / Milch / Tee / Wodka / Coca-Cola / Wasser / Weißwein)

B. *Supply the appropriate adjective ending.*

1. Frisch_____ Salat ist gesund.
2. Kühl_____ Bier schmeckt gut.
3. Fondue ist etwas Lecker_____.
4. Wir brauchen noch sechs frisch_____ Eier.
5. Teur_____ Weißwein ist meistens gut.
6. Gut_____ Weißwein ist meistens teuer.
7. Ein schön_____ herb_____ Rotwein ist etwas Gutes.
8. Manchen rot_____ Wein trinkt man bei Zimmertemperatur.
9. Eiskalt_____ Milch ist nicht gesund.
10. Mit zu heiß_____ Kaffee soll man auch vorsichtig sein.

C. *Change the predicate adjective to an attributive adjective by using a form of the* **ein-** *word.*

1. Der Hut ist neu. Das ist ein _____.
2. Das Auto ist alt. Das ist ein _____.

3. Das Glas ist kaputt. Das ist ein _____.
4. Ich finde die Wohnung schön. Das ist eine _____.
5. Der Sommer war warm. Das war ein _____.
6. Die Uhr ist sehr wertvoll. Das ist eine _____.
7. Der Wein ist wirklich teuer. Das ist ein _____.
8. Der Wind war eiskalt. Es war ein _____.
9. Der Kaffee war heiß. Das war ein _____.
10. Das Fondue ist lecker. Das ist ein _____.

D. *Supply the inflected adjective indicated in parentheses.*

1. Bei _____ Wetter soll man zu Hause bleiben. (kalt)
2. Nach _____ Kaffee kann ich nicht schlafen. (stark)
3. Im Wohnzimmer steht ein _____ Tisch. (neu)
4. Das ist unser _____ Fernseher. (alt)
5. Er arbeitet gerne bei _____ Musik. (leise)
6. Wir schwimmen oft in _____ Wasser. (warm)
7. Ihr springt oft in _____ Wasser. (eiskalt)
8. Ich liebe das Aroma _____ Kirschwassers. (gut)
9. Ihr habt wirklich ein _____ Badezimmer. (schön)

E. *Supply the inflected present participle of the verb in parentheses.*

1. Tee macht man nur mit _____ Wasser. (kochen)
2. Sie gibt ihrem _____ Kind einen Kuß. (schlafen)
3. Bitte, springen Sie nicht aus dem _____ Zug. (fahren)
4. Der _____ Student hat seinen Reisepaß vergessen. (lesen)
5. Das _____ Kind läuft über die Straße. (spielen)
6. Der _____ Herr war mein Arzt. (rauchen)

F. *Supply the inflected past participle of the verb in parentheses.*

1. Ich esse jeden Morgen ein _____ Ei. (kochen)
2. Das ist unser neu _____ Auto. (kaufen)
3. Hier sehen Sie das _____ Haus. (verbrennen)

4. Heute schreibst du an deine _____. (lieben)
5. Wie ist das mit dem _____ Brief? (versprechen)
6. Darfst du _____ Fisch essen? (braten)
7. Ich muß viel _____ Fleisch essen. (grillen)
8. Die _____ Freundin kommt morgen abend. (einladen)
9. _____ Fisch kann ich gut vertragen. (kochen)

G. *Substitute an adjectival noun for the words in boldface.*

1. Der **alte Mann** ist blind.
2. Der **blinde Mann** ist alt.
3. Der Vater spielt mit dem **kleinen Jungen.**
4. Die Blumen sind von dem **dicken Herrn** da drüben.
5. Das ist ein **weißer Mann.**
6. Sie ist eine sehr **intelligente Frau.**

H. *Add the appropriate ending to the adjectival noun.*

1. Ich wünsche dir alles Gut_____.
2. Das ist für uns nichts Neu_____.
3. Man hört viel Interessant_____ über ihn.
4. Orangensaft ist bestimmt etwas Gesund_____.
5. Sie weiß nur wenig Neu_____ zu erzählen.

I. *Substitute or add each phrase as it is introduced into the previous sentence and make any necessary structural changes.*

Was hältst du von frischem   Obst?
_____ ihr_____?
_____ Tomaten?
_____ rot _____?
_____ Sie_____?
_____ Wein?
_____ französisch ____?
_____ Zwiebelsuppe?

GUIDED CONVERSATION

A. Begin a conversation with your neighbor and discuss your favorite menus. You might also mention the ingredients you need for the main dishes and how you prepare them.

B. Begin a conversation with someone in your class regarding foreign foods. Discuss the types of cuisine you like and do not like. You might also mention the restaurants in your city, which you have visited, that serve foreign dishes.

The following new vocabulary may help you.

chinesisch (Chinese)
holländisch (Dutch)
italienisch (Italian)
japanisch (Japanese)
die Küche, –n (cuisine)

READING

Ein Rezept

Möchten Sie einmal in gemütlicher Atmosphäre essen? Dann laden Sie doch[1] nette Freunde zu einem Fondue-Abend ein. Fondue ist ein Käsegericht aus der Schweiz. Man kennt es inzwischen auch schon in anderen Ländern. Das Schöne ist, die Zubereitung eines Käse-Fondues ist wirklich ganz einfach. Probieren Sie es einmal aus! Sie sind bestimmt nicht enttäuscht.   5

Zutaten:
etwas Knoblauch
3 Tassen herber Weißwein
ungefähr ein Pfund Schweizer Käse
ein Pfund Gruyère   10
1 Teelöffel Stärke
1 kleines Glas Kirschwasser
etwas Salz, Pfeffer und Paprika
frisches Weißbrot

Zubereitung:

Eine feuerfeste Schüssel mit Knoblauch ausreiben. Den Wein in der Schüssel auf kleiner Flamme erhitzen. Den geriebenen Käse langsam hinzugeben und immer gut rühren. Dann auf großer Flamme aufkochen lassen. Einen Teelöffel Stärke mit dem Kirschwasser mischen und in die Schüssel rühren, und noch einmal kurz erhitzen. Etwas Salz, Pfeffer und Paprika hinzugeben. 20

Man ißt dieses Gericht mit langen Fondue-Gabeln. Mit den Gabeln taucht man klein geschnittenes Weißbrot in das kochende Fondue.

Zu einem Käse-Fondue empfehlen wir einen schönen herben Rheinwein. Und nun: Guten Appetit! 25

---

[1] The word **doch** may occur in statements or commands for purposes of emphasis. It does not alter the content of the statement and cannot be translated.

QUESTIONS

1. Wie soll die Atmosphäre bei einem Fondue-Essen sein?
2. Wen kann man zu einem Fondue-Abend einladen?
3. Woher kommt dieses Käsegericht?
4. Welche Zutaten braucht man für ein Fondue?
5. Wie ißt man Fondue?
6. Welchen Wein kann man zu einem Fondue trinken?

VOCABULARY EXERCISES

A. *Supply the appropriate word from the list on the right.*

1. Fondue ist ein _____ aus der Schweiz.
2. Die _____ eines Fondues ist wirklich einfach.
3. Eine feuerfeste Schüssel muß man mit _____ ausreiben.
4. Dann muß man den Wein in der _____ erhitzen.
5. Man ißt dieses Käsegericht mit langen _____.
6. Dies ist ein _____ aus einem Kochbuch.

a. Fondue-Gabeln
b. Schüssel
c. Käsegericht
d. Rezept
e. Knoblauch
f. Zubereitung

B. *Do the same with the following sentences.*

1. Die Schüssel muß _____ sein.
2. Den _____ Käse muß man gut rühren.
3. Dann muß man alles auf _____ Flamme aufkochen lassen.
4. Man taucht klein _____ Weißbrot in das Fondue.
5. Man taucht es in das _____ Fondue.

a. kochende
b. geschnittenes
c. feuerfest
d. großer
e. geriebenen

Review Exercises

A. *Supply the German equivalents of the words in parentheses.*

1. Er trinkt jeden Abend _____. (his cold beer)
2. _____ ist bestimmt sehr gesund. (green salad)
3. Diesen Orangensaft gibt es nur in _____. (small bottles)
4. Der Wert ____ ist sehr groß. (of fresh milk)
5. Trinke nie _____ nach _____! (cold beer / fresh fruit)
6. Bei _____ gehen wir schwimmen. (warm weather)
7. Mit _____ bin ich meistens sehr vorsichtig. (spicy cheese)
8. _____ ist nicht sehr gesund. (fat meat)
9. Mit _____ oder Eis macht man eigentlich keine richtige Diät. (sweet pudding)
10. Ein _____ muß nicht immer teuer sein. (good wine)

B. *Omit the* **der-** *or* **ein-***word in each sentence and make the necessary changes in the attributive adjective.*

1. Der scharfe Käse ist nicht immer gesund.
2. Dieser frische Salat hat viele Vitamine.
3. Dieses alte Obst ist nicht gesund.
4. Das eiskalte Bier ist schlecht für den Magen.
5. Eine gemütliche Atmosphäre gibt es beim Fondue-Essen.
6. Die feuerfesten Schüsseln sind nicht billig.
7. Der teure Wein ist nicht immer gut.
8. Der schöne heiße Kaffee ist etwas Gutes.

C. *Omit the* **der-** *and* **ein-***words in each sentence and make the necessary changes in the attributive adjectives.*

1. Zu einem guten Essen trinkt man oft einen guten Wein.
2. Mit einem guten Käse kann man auch ein gutes Fondue machen.
3. Wegen des schlechten Wetters sind wir zu Hause geblieben.
4. Seid ihr bei dem starken Wind Ski laufen gegangen?

5. Das dunkle Bier ist besser als das helle.
6. Der herbe Rheinwein ist für Fondue besser als der französische Rotwein.

D. *Change the predicate adjective to an attributive adjective.*

> EXAMPLE   Dieser Käse ist frisch.
> **Dies ist frischer Käse.**

1. Dieser Wein ist drei Jahre alt.
2. Dieser Käse ist mild.
3. Dieser Kaffee ist heiß.
4. Diese Milch ist eiskalt.
5. Dieses Öl ist teuer.
6. Dieses Bier ist dunkel.
7. Dieses Fondue ist einmalig.
8. Diese Butter ist frisch.

E. *Supply the adverb or adjectival form of the present participle of the verb in parentheses.*

1. Er stand _____ auf der Straße. (rauchen)
2. Sie kamen _____ aus dem Kino. (lachen)
3. Die über New York _____ Maschine konnte eine halbe Stunde nicht landen. (fliegen)
4. Die _____ Kinder sind aus Wien. (singen)
5. Die Feuerwehr fuhr zu dem _____ Auto. (brennen)
6. _____ Hunde soll man nicht wecken. (schlafen)

F. *Supply the adjectival form of the past participle of the verb in parentheses.*

1. Er hatte das _____ Geld im Gepäck. (stehlen)
2. Der _____ Wagen steht schon vor der Tür. (bestellen)
3. Sie konnte das _____ Bier nicht mehr trinken. (bezahlen)
4. Endlich fanden sie die _____ Uhr. (suchen)
5. Wir aßen _____ Fisch. (kochen)
6. Mein Freund bestellte eine _____ Ente. (braten)

G. *Express the sentence in German by using an adjectival noun.*

1. The old man is blind.
2. The blind man is old.
3. The father plays with the little girl.
4. The flowers are from the fat man over there.
5. That's a white man.
6. She's a very intelligent woman.
7. I wish you all the best.
8. Orange juice is certainly something healthy.
9. She likes only very expensive things.
10. One hears many good things about him.

GUIDED COMPOSITION

A. Write down one of your favorite recipes. First write a list of the required ingredients, then explain clearly and concisely how the dish should be prepared. Follow the form of the recipe provided in the reading passage. Look up any words you need in an English-German dictionary.

B. Are you, or is someone you know, on a special diet? Write a brief composition explaining the types of food you and your friend are and are not allowed to have. You might also explain the reasons for the restrictions or limitations.

Chapter 12

Kloster Melk

Useful Phrases

einem recht geben	to agree that a person is right
ehrlich gesagt	to be quite honest
von mir aus	that's fine with me [from my point of view]
zum Kuckuck mit	to hell with
immer schlimmer	worse and worse
beim besten Willen	with the best intentions
so schnell wie	as fast as
noch nie	never before
noch einmal	once again
schon einmal	ever; once before

MODEL SENTENCES

I

Dieser Zug fährt **schneller** als unser Auto.	This train goes faster than our car.
Du verstehst Deutsch **besser** als ich.	You understand German better than I do.
Dieser Texas-Hut ist **am größten.**	This Texas hat is the biggest.
Studieren Sie **am liebsten** Deutsch?	Do you like to study German best of all?
Sibille ist ihre **liebste** Freundin.	Sibille is her dearest friend.
Heute ist der **kälteste** Tag des Jahres.	Today is the coldest day of the year.
Sie trägt ein **teureres** Kleid als ich.	She wears a more expensive dress than I do.
„Moby Dick" ist ein **längerer** Roman als „Der alte Mann und das Meer".	*Moby Dick* is a longer novel than *The Old Man and the Sea*.
Sie gibt **mehr** Geld für Reisen als für Kleidung aus.	She spends more money on traveling than on clothes.
Der Mount Everest ist der **höchste** Berg der Welt.	Mount Everest is the highest mountain in the world.

Es **hatte** vor einem Jahr noch wärmere Tage als heute **gegeben.**	A year ago there were [had been] even warmer days than today.
Wir **hatten** vor dem Examen schon alles **vergessen.**	We had already forgotten everything before the exam.
Damals **waren** die Freunde ins Schwimmbad **gegangen.**	At that time the friends had gone to the swimming pool.
Er **war** immer am liebsten **geflogen.**	He always had liked to fly best of all.

Grammar Explanations

I. COMPARISON OF ADJECTIVES AND ADVERBS

In German, as in English, there are three degrees of comparison: the *positive*, the basic form, which is listed in the dictionary, the *comparative*, which compares two unlike objects, and the *superlative*, which denotes the utmost degree of all levels. English forms the comparative and the superlative in two ways: short adjectives add **–er** and **–est,** and adjectives with two or more syllables use "more" and "most." In German, however, there is only one basic way to form the comparative and superlative: by adding the ending **–er** and **–st–**.

Positive		*Comparative*		*Superlative*	
lieb	dear	lieb**er**	dearer	lieb**ste**	dearest
klein	small	klein**er**	smaller	klein**ste**	smallest
schön	beautiful	schön**er**	more beautiful	schön**ste**	most beautiful

When used as *attributive* adjectives in German, both the comparative and superlative forms add the regular attributive adjective endings.

Julia ist eine schön**e** Frau.	Julia is a beautiful woman.
Brigitte ist eine schöner**e** Frau.	Brigitte is a more beautiful woman.
Helena ist die schönst**e** Frau.	Helena is the most beautiful woman.

Das kleine Auto gehört Karl.	The small car belongs to Karl.
Das kleinere Auto gehört Fred.	The smaller car belongs to Fred.
Das kleinste Auto gehört Heinrich.	The smallest car belongs to Heinrich.

The comparative of the attributive adjective may occur with the definite or the indefinite article.

Dies ist **ein schöneres** Hotel.	This is a more beautiful hotel.
Dies ist **das schönere** Hotel.	This is the more beautiful hotel.

But, in German, the superlative is used most often with the definite article only.

Dies ist **das schönste** Hotel.	This is the most beautiful hotel.

When used as a *predicate* adjective or adverb, the comparative form, as the positive form, takes no ending, and the superlative form always occurs as the phrase **am . . .–sten.**

Positive	*Comparative*	*Superlative*
lieb	lieb**er**	am lieb**sten**
schön	schön**er**	am schön**sten**

Julia ist schön.	Julia is beautiful.
Brigitte ist schön**er**.	Brigitte is more beautiful.
Helena ist **am** schön**sten**.	Helena is the most beautiful.

Karls Auto ist klein.	Karl's car is small.
Freds Auto ist klein**er**.	Fred's car is smaller.
Heinrichs Auto ist **am** klein**sten**.	Heinrich's car is the smallest.

m & Evchen / Von Edit Lankor

There are, of course, exceptions to the basic rule, and these occur primarily for easier pronunciation.

1. Adjectives with stems ending in **–e** merely add an **–r** in the *comparative* form.

leise   leiser   am leisesten

2. Adjectives with stems ending in **–el** and **–er** drop the **–e–** in the *comparative*.

dunk**el**   dunkler   am dunk**el**sten

teu**er**   teurer   am teu**er**sten

3. Adjectives with stems ending in **–s, –ß, –sch, –x, –z, –t,** and **–d** add an **–e–** in the *superlative*.

heiß   heißer   am heiß**e**sten

kurz   kürzer   am kürz**e**sten

In diesem Zimmer sind die **leiseren** Kinder.	The quieter children are in this room.
Er trägt einen **dunkleren** Anzug.	He's wearing a darker suit.
Sie trägt ein **teureres** Kleid.	She's wearing a more expensive dress.
Heute ist der **heißeste** Tag des Jahres.	Today's the hottest day of the year.
Morgen ist der **kürzeste** Tag des Jahres.	Tomorrow is the shortest day of the year.

In addition, most monosyllabic adjectives and adverbs with the stem vowels **a** and **u** form the comparative and superlative by adding an Umlaut to the vowel as well as by adding the endings.

lang   länger   am längsten

alt   älter   am ältesten

kurz   kürzer   am kürzesten

jung   jünger   am jüngsten

Er liest den **längeren** Roman.	He's reading the longer novel.
Klara trägt das **kürzere** Kleid.	Klara is wearing the shorter dress.

There are a number of adjectives and adverbs that form irregular comparatives and superlatives; all of these adjectives occur frequently in German, so be sure to memorize their irregular forms.

groß	größer	am größten
gut	besser	am besten
hoch (hoh-)	höher	am höchsten
nah(e)	näher	am nächsten
oft	öfter	am meisten
viel *or* viele	mehr	am meisten
gern	lieber	am liebsten

The adverb form is often indicated by an **–e** in parentheses: **nah(e)** or **lang(e)**. Note that in the positive form, **hoch** is the predicate adjective and adverb; **hoh–** is the attributive adjective.

Der Berg ist **hoch.**	The mountain is high.
Das ist **hoch** interessant.	That is most [highly] interesting.
Der **hohe** Berg ist Mount Rainier.	The high mountain is Mount Rainier.

The irregular adverb **gern** adds the meaning of "to like to" to the verb; the comparative **lieber** adds the meaning of "to prefer to"; the superlative **am liebsten** adds the meaning of "to prefer to most of all" or "to like to best of all."

Sie schreibt **gern** Briefe.	She likes to write letters.
Er trinkt **lieber** Bier.	He prefers to drink beer.
Wir essen **am liebsten** Fisch.	We like to eat fish best of all.

To indicate equality of the items being compared, the positive form of the adjective with the phrase **so . . . wie** is used.

Er ist **so groß wie** ich.	He's as tall as I am.
Sie fährt nicht **so schnell wie** ich.	She's not driving as fast as I am.

When the word **als** occurs in a comparison, the comparative form of the predicate adjective or adverb is used.

Der Zug fährt **schneller als** unser Auto.	The train goes faster than our car.
Du verstehst Deutsch **besser als** ich.	You understand German better than I do.

In conjunction with the comparative, the phrase **immer** suggests a progressive increase. Note the equivalent in English.

Es wird **immer schlimmer.**	It gets worse and worse.
Die Preise steigen **immer höher.**	The prices are climbing higher and higher.

A. *Give the comparative form of the predicate adjective or adverb.*

1. heiß
2. lange
3. schlimm
4. klein

5. warm
6. gern
7. teuer
8. hoch

B. *Give the superlative form of the predicate adjective and adverb.*

1. schlimm
2. natürlich
3. teuer
4. sauber

5. gut
6. viel
7. gern
8. hoch

C. *Supply the comparative form of the adjective in parentheses.*

1. das _____ Kleid (schön)
2. der _____ Zug (schnell)
3. die _____ Hitze (erträglich)
4. die _____ Temperatur (hoch)
5. die _____ Tomaten (billig)
6. das _____ Wasser (kühl)

D. *Supply the superlative form of the adjective in parentheses.*

1. der _____ Tag des Jahres (kurz)
2. das _____ Mädchen von Georgia (nett)
3. der _____ Roman (lang)
4. der _____ Sommer (warm)
5. der _____ Tag (heiß)
6. das _____ Schwimmbad (sauber)
7. der _____ Berg der Alpen (hoch)

II. PAST PERFECT TENSE

A. Usage

As in English, the past perfect tense in German is used to describe a past event or situation that occurred before another past event or situation. Situation *b* precedes Situation *a*.

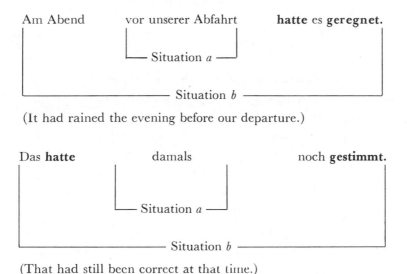

(It had rained the evening before our departure.)

(That had still been correct at that time.)

The past perfect tense is also often used with an expression of time, such as yesterday, last week, and last month, to emphasize the decidedly past character of an action or situation.

Hattest du letztes Jahr nicht   Didn't you say [had you not said]
   gesagt, . . . ?   last year . . . ?

B. Formation

Formation of the past perfect tense is similar to the present perfect tense in the combination of the auxiliary verb and the past participle of the principal verb; in the past perfect, however, the auxiliary verb, **haben** or **sein** is in the past tense.

| hören | hörte | **hatte** gehört |
| fahren | fuhr | **war** gefahren |

As in the present perfect tense, the past participle occurs at the end of the sentence or clause, and the double infinitive construction occurs with a modal auxiliary.

Wir **hatten** unseren Freunden **geholfen.**　We had helped our friends.

Wir **hatten** unseren Freunden **helfen** **können.**　We could [had been able to] help our friends.

Past Perfect Tense

	With **haben**	*With* **sein**
Singular		
	ich **hatte** gesagt	ich **war** abgefahren
	du **hattest** gesagt	du **warst** abgefahren
	er ⎱	er ⎱
	sie ⎰ **hatte** gesagt	sie ⎰ **war** abgefahren
	es ⎰	es ⎰
Plural		
	wir **hatten** gesagt	wir **waren** abgefahren
	ihr **hattet** gesagt	ihr **wart** abgefahren
	sie **hatten** gesagt	sie **waren** abgefahren
Singular/Plural		
	Sie **hatten** gesagt	Sie **waren** abgefahren

Check Your Comprehension

A. *Form the past perfect tense of the verb using the person indicated in parentheses.*

1. aushalten (er)
2. glauben (Sie)
3. aufhören (wir)
4. gehen (sie, *pl.*)
5. laufen (ihr)
6. stimmen (es)
7. sagen (du)
8. abfahren (er)
9. gehen dürfen (ich)
10. bezahlen müssen (sie, *sing.*)

B. *Underline the phrase in the sentence that indicates the situation or event that occurred prior to the other situation or event.*

1. Er hatte vor seiner Abfahrt mit mir telefoniert.
2. Vor der Reise hatte sie zwei Aspirin-Tabletten genommen.
3. Sie hatten vor dem Essen hart gearbeitet.
4. Am letzten Tag vor seinem Examen war er die Treppe hinuntergefallen.
5. Als Kinder waren wir immer vor Mitternacht ins Bett gegangen.

CONVERSATION

Die Hitzewelle

PETER   Heute ist bestimmt der heißeste Tag des Jahres! Ich halte diese Hitze nicht länger aus! Das ist ja schlimmer als letztes Jahr.

ROLF   Ich weiß nicht. Ich glaube, letztes Jahr gab es noch wärmere Tage als heute.

PETER   Nun ja, vielleicht war es damals tatsächlich noch ein bißchen heißer als heute. Aber das macht die Hitze auch nicht erträglicher.   5

ROLF   Ich schlage vor, wir hören jetzt auf, für das Examen zu arbeiten. Weißt du, was das Schlimmste ist?

PETER   Du meinst, bis morgen haben wir doch alles vergessen?

ROLF   Genau! Zum Kuckuck mit dieser blöden Geometrie! Den Euklid[1]   10
verstehe ich beim besten Willen nicht! Kapierst du das Zeug?

PETER   Nicht viel besser als du. Komm, laß uns ins Schwimmbad gehen! Da ist es kühler.

ROLF   Gute Idee! Die Frage ist nur, wohin? Wollen wir ins Odenwald-Bad[2] gehen?   15

PETER   Ja, von mir aus. Ehrlich gesagt, da gehe ich lieber hin als ins Olympia-Bad. Ich glaube, da ist das Wasser am saubersten.

ROLF   Außerdem sind da wahrscheinlich auch weniger Leute.

PETER   Das kann sein. Allerdings ist es im Odenwald-Bad auch teurer.

ROLF   Wieso? Hattest du kürzlich nicht gesagt, dort ist es billiger?   20

PETER Nun ja, damals hatte es auch noch gestimmt. Inzwischen ist aber alles
teurer geworden.

ROLF Es ist verrückt. Im Winter müssen wir mehr Geld für die Heizung
bezahlen und im Sommer mehr für kühleres Wasser! Alles wird teurer!
Unsere Inflation wird wirklich immer schlimmer!   25

---

[1] Euclid, the mathematician.
[2] Odenwald, a forest in southern Germany; Odenwald-Bad, the name of the swimming pool.

ORAL PRACTICE

   A. *Substitute the comparative form of the adjectives in parentheses for the predicate
adjective in boldface.*

      1. Dieser Baum ist **kleiner** als jener.
         (schön / kurz / lang / hoch / groß / dunkel / nahe / gut)
      2. Heute ist es **wärmer** als gestern.
         (kalt / heiß / kühl / mild / leise / laut / gut / schlimm)

3. Die Tomaten waren gestern **teurer** als heute.
      (billig / schlecht / gut / sauber / klein / grün / schön / groß)

B. *Substitute the comparative form of the adverbs in parentheses for the adverb in boldface.*

  1. Fräulein Baker, Sie sprechen ja beinahe **besser** Deutsch als Englisch.
     (schnell / gern / lange / viel / schön / leise / schlecht / natürlich)
  2. Ein Phantom-Jet fliegt **schneller** als eine Boeing 707.*
     (hoch / gut / leise / laut / lange / weit / kurz / schlecht / sicher)
  3. Er ist mit dem BMW **besser** gefahren als mit dem Mercedes.
     (schnell / gern / viel / schlimm / billig / lange / kurz / sicher)

C. *Substitute the comparative form of the adjectives in parentheses for the attributive adjective in boldface.*

  1. Das **schönere** Schwimmbad ist dort drüben.
     (klein / groß / billig / teuer / warm / nahe / kalt / gut)
  2. Im letzten Jahr hatten wir einen **kühleren** Sommer.
     (heiß / warm / erträglich / kalt / kurz / gut / mild / schlimm)
  3. Wir fahren heute mit einem **schnelleren** Zug.
     (lang / sauber / teuer / gut / groß / kurz / leise / kühl / schön)

D. *Substitute the superlative form of the words in parentheses for the predicate adjective in boldface.*

  1. Im Blausee ist das Wasser **am kühlsten.**
     (kalt / sauber / gut / schön / frisch / warm / tief / klar / heiß / schlimm)
  2. Das Öl aus Arabien ist **am besten.**
     (teuer / billig / nahe / schlecht / sauber / schön / uns lieb / im Preis hoch)
  3. Der Mount Rainier ist **am schönsten.**
     (hoch / groß / gut / nahe / natürlich / schlimm)

---

* Read: sieben-null-sieben.

E. *Substitute the superlative forms of the adjectives in parentheses for the adjective in boldface.*

1. Die **natürlichsten** Mädchen wohnen in Georgia.
    (schön / nett / lieb / gut / intelligent / elegant)
2. Ich habe das **kleinste** Haus der Stadt gekauft.
    (groß / hoch / billig / teuer / lang / gut / schön / alt)
3. Das Park-Hotel ist das **beste** Hotel in der Stadt.
    (teuer / groß / sauber / nahe / hoch / schön / billig / elegant / interessant)

F. *Change the predicate adjective or adverb in boldface into the comparative form.*

1. Heute ist es **heiß.**
2. Diese Hitze wird **schlimm.**
3. Im letzten Jahr war es um diese Zeit **warm.**
4. Das Odenwald-Bad ist natürlich **teuer.**
5. Ich liege **gern** mit vielen Menschen auf dem Rasen.
6. Dieses Schwimmbad ist nicht **billig.**
7. Wir müssen **viel** schwimmen gehen.
8. Das Olympia-Bad ist **nahe.**

G. *Change the predicate adjective or adverb in the above exercise (F) into the superlative form.*

H. *Change the superlative form into the comparative.*

1. Der Mount Rainier ist bestimmt am höchsten.
2. Die Mädchen aus Georgia sind bestimmt am schönsten.
3. Das Wasser des Blausees ist bestimmt am klarsten.
4. Das Bier in München ist bestimmt am teuersten.
5. Das Öl ist in Kuweit bestimmt am billigsten.
6. Die Spaghetti sind in Italien bestimmt am besten.
7. Die Pizza sind in Amerika bestimmt nicht am schlechtesten.
8. Der Phantom-Jet ist bestimmt am schnellsten.
9. Klaras Kleid ist bestimmt am kürzesten.
10. Ich rauche bestimmt am meisten.

I. *Complete the sentence by using the item in parentheses for comparison.*

1. Der Volkswagen ist klein, aber . . . (der Fiat)
2. Der Mercedes ist ein schneller Wagen, aber . . . (der Porsche)
3. Der Eiffelturm ist hoch, aber . . . (das Empire State Building)
4. Chicago ist nahe, aber . . . (Denver)
5. Berlin ist schön, aber . . . (München)
6. Der Mount Rainier ist hoch, aber . . . (der Mount McKinley)
7. Wasser ist kalt, aber . . . (Eis)
8. Skilaufen ist gesund, aber . . . (Schwimmen)
9. Ein Lincoln ist teuer, aber . . . (ein Rolls Royce)
10. Fliegen ist billig, aber . . . (Fahren)

J. *Compare the items in parentheses with the item in the sentence. Put the first item in parentheses into the comparative and the second into the superlative.*

EXAMPLE **Du** bist intelligent. (Brigitte / Peter)
Brigitte ist intelligenter.
Peter ist am intelligentesten.

1. Mein Haus ist groß. (dein Haus / das Schloß)
2. Coca-Cola ist gut. (Bier / Weißwein)
3. Das Examen ist nahe. (die Weihnachtsferien / mein Geburtstag)
4. Sie kaufen viel. (wir / ihr)
5. Die Mädchen aus München sind schön. (Salzburg / Zürich)
6. Fahren ist interessant. (Zu Hause bleiben / Fliegen)
7. Ein Volkswagen ist teuer. (Audi / Mercedes)
8. Der Roman ist langweilig. (der Film / die Oper)
9. Ich wohne hier schon lange. (du / Sie)
10. Der Mount Rainier ist hoch. (der Mount McKinley / der Mount Everest)

K. *Compare the items in parentheses with the item in the sentence, as in the above exercise (J), adding the appropriate attributive adjective endings.*

1. Brigitte ist das intelligente Mädchen. (Ilse / Angelika)
2. In München steht das alte Restaurant. (Freiburg / Miltenberg am Main)
3. In Milwaukee macht man gutes Bier. (München / Dortmund)

4. In Deutschland hat man schönes Wetter. (Italien / Kalifornien)
5. Das „Park-Hotel" ist ein teures Hotel. (das „Ambassador" / das „Hilton")
6. Der Dezember ist ein kalter Monat. (Februar / Januar)
7. Dies ist ein neues Buch von Siegfried Lenz. (das / jenes)
8. Der Volkswagen ist ein gutes deutsches Auto. (BMW / Porsche)
9. Die Zugspitze ist ein hoher Berg. (das Matterhorn / der Mont Blanc)
10. Kalifornien ist ein großer amerikanischer Staat. (Texas / Alaska)

L. *Put the sentence into the past perfect tense.*

1. Er hält die Hitze nicht mehr aus.
2. Wir schliefen den ganzen Tag.
3. Sie gingen um elf Uhr nach Hause.
4. Wir sind nach Stuttgart gefahren.
5. Die Donau sieht blauer aus.
6. Der Zug fährt pünktlich ab.
7. Im Café aßen wir Eis und tranken Tee.
8. Sie hatten noch nie solch ein großes Auto.
9. Das Wetter war letzte Woche sehr schlecht.
10. Es regnete nicht mehr.

M. *Substitute or add each phrase as it is introduced into the previous sentence and make any necessary structural changes.*

Die heißen   Tage waren   immer   im Juli   am schlimmsten.
_____ kürzesten.
_____ gewesen.
___ milde   Wetter _____
___ schönere _____
_____ längsten _____
_____ noch nie _____
___ höheren Temperaturen _____ Winter _____

GUIDED CONVERSATION

A. **Die dümmsten Bauern ernten die dicksten Kartoffeln.** What does this German proverb mean? Discuss it with someone in your class. Once you feel you understand the proverb, take turns modifying it or changing it completely by substituting different adjectives, different nouns, and/or a different verb. Make as many variations as you can. How does the meaning change each time?

B. Discuss with someone in your class your special interests: things you like to do, places you like to go, people you like to be with. Rate your interests according to what you like, what you prefer, and what you like most of all.

READING

Eine Dampferfahrt

Österreich ist bestimmt eines der schönsten Länder Europas. Wir hatten schon häufig von einer Dampferfahrt auf der Donau[1] gehört. Aber wir hatten bisher nie die Gelegenheit gehabt, an solch einer Fahrt teilzunehmen. Dieses Mal aber hatten wir die Chance, mit dem Dampfer auf der Donau von Linz bis Melk[2] zu fahren. Diese Strecke ist wahrscheinlich am schönsten.   5

Am Abend vor unserer Abfahrt hatte es geregnet, aber am nächsten Morgen war das Wetter wieder besser. Unser Schiff hieß „Prinz Eugen". Zur Zeit von Johann Strauß hatte die Donau wahrscheinlich blauer ausgesehen als heute.

Jetzt ist das Wasser beinahe braun. Um elf Uhr war der Dampfer pünktlich abgefahren. Wir mußten unseren Bekannten recht geben, eine schönere Land- [10] schaft gibt es wahrscheinlich kaum irgendwo auf der Welt. Zwischen dunklen Wäldern und grünen Wiesen lagen hier und da versteckte Dörfer und Städtchen. Größere Industriegebiete mit der üblichen Umweltverschmutzung gab es kaum. In Linz war mit uns eine Gruppe junger Männer eingestiegen. Sie tranken Wein und sangen zu einer Gitarre. [15]

Der Dampfer hielt kurz an verschiedenen Orten, wo Passagiere ein- und ausstiegen.[3] Ungefähr fünf Stunden später kamen wir in Melk an. Wir beschlossen gleich nach unserer Ankunft, eine solche Fahrt bei nächster Gelegenheit noch einmal zu machen.

---

[1] Danube River.
[2] Towns in Austria; Melk is especially known for its famous abbey.
[3] einstiegen und ausstiegen

QUESTIONS

1. Wozu hatten die Leute nie die Gelegenheit gehabt?
2. Von wo bis wo sind sie mit dem Dampfer gefahren?
3. In welchem Land liegen diese Städte?
4. Wie war das Wetter am Abend vor der Abfahrt gewesen?
5. Wie hatte das Schiff geheißen?
6. Wann hatte die Donau wahrscheinlich blauer ausgesehen?
7. Wann war das Schiff in Linz abgefahren?
8. Was gab es an der Donau zwischen Linz und Melk zu sehen?
9. Wer war in Linz auch eingestiegen?
10. Was beschlossen die Leute gleich nach ihrer Ankunft in Melk?

VOCABULARY EXERCISES

A. *Supply the appropriate word from the list on the right.*

1. Ich liege nicht gern mit so vielen Menschen auf dem _____.
2. Die _____ ist fast unerträglich.
3. Haben Sie schon einmal eine _____ auf der Donau gemacht?

a. Wetter
b. Landschaft
c. Rasen
d. Bekannten
e. Gelegenheit

4. Nein, wir hatten bisher noch nie die _____ dazu gehabt.

5. Die _____ von Linz bis Melk ist wahrscheinlich am schönsten.

6. Am Abend vor unserer _____ hatte es geregnet.

7. Aber am nächsten Morgen war das _____ wieder besser.

8. Wir hatten unseren _____ recht geben müssen.

9. Eine schönere _____ gibt es kaum irgendwo auf der Welt.

10. Größere Industriegebiete mit der üblichen _____ gab es kaum.

f. Hitzewelle
g. Abfahrt
h. Umweltverschmutzung
i. Strecke
j. Dampferfahrt

B. *Do the same with the following sentences.*

1. Wir hatten schon _____ von einer Dampferfahrt auf der Donau gehört.

2. Diese Strecke ist _____ am schönsten.

3. Jetzt ist das Wasser _____ braun.

4. Um elf Uhr war das Schiff _____ in Linz abgefahren.

5. Eine schönere Landschaft gibt es _____ irgendwo in der Welt.

6. Wir beschlossen, eine solche Fahrt _____ zu machen.

7. _____ waren die Temperaturen damals tatsächlich höher.

8. _____ gehe ich am liebsten.

a. vielleicht
b. noch einmal
c. pünktlich
d. häufig
e. dorthin
f. kaum
g. wahrscheinlich
h. beinahe

Review Exercises

A. *Supply the appropriate endings for the definite or indefinite article, and supply the appropriate comparative form of the adjective in parentheses.*

1. Du hast ein_____ _____ Wagen als ich. (neu)

2. Wir fahren mit d_____ _____ Intercity-Zug. (schnell)
3. Ich fliege gern mit ein_____ _____ Flugzeug. (klein)
4. Unsere Freunde reisen gern mit ein_____ _____ Schiff nach Afrika. (groß)
5. D_____ _____ Inflation ist im Moment in Deutschland. (schlimm)
6. D_____ _____ Monat ist wahrscheinlich der Januar. (kalt)
7. Italien hat oft ein_____ _____ Wetter als Österreich. (gut)
8. Australien ist ein_____ _____ Land als die Schweiz. (groß)
9. Der Mercedes ist ein_____ _____ Auto als der Audi. (teuer)
10. Sie trinkt lieber d_____ _____ Kaffee. (gut)

B. *Supply the appropriate ending for the definite or indefinite article, and supply the appropriate superlative form of the adjective in parentheses.*

1. Österreich ist eines d_____ _____ Länder Europas. (schön)
2. Heute abend essen wir in d_____ _____ Hotel in dieser Stadt. (elegant)
3. Ich bin jetzt in d_____ _____ Schule der Stadt. (gut)
4. In New York steht d_____ _____ Gebäude der Welt. (hoch)
5. San Franzisko ist d_____ _____ Stadt Kaliforniens. (schön)
6. In München gibt es d_____ _____ Currywurst Deutschlands. (teuer)
7. „Der Riese" in Miltenberg am Main ist d_____ _____ Restaurant Deutschlands. (alt)
8. Die Zugspitze ist d_____ _____ Berg in Deutschland. (hoch)
9. Schwimmen ist d_____ _____ Sport. (gesund)
10. D_____ _____ Zug der Welt gibt es in Japan. (schnell)

C. *Supply first the comparative and then the superlative form of the adjective in parentheses.*

1. Hier sind die _____ Tomaten. (frisch)
2. Das ist der _____ Roman von Siegfried Lenz. (neu)
3. Dort ist das _____ Modell von Mercedes. (jung)
4. Das ist die _____ Strecke. (kurz)
5. Dies ist die _____ Straße. (gut)
6. Das ist der _____ Wein. (teuer)
7. Dort sehen Sie den _____ Berg. (hoch)

8. Peter ist der _____ Student. (intelligent)
9. Hohenschwanstein* ist das _____ Schloß in Bayern. (interessant)
10. Sie hat immer _____ Geld (viel).

D. *Express in German.*

1. Oil is as expensive as wine.
2. The inflation in the USA is as bad as in Germany.
3. A Mercedes is as good as a Lincoln.
4. I don't speak German as well as you (do).
5. You eat more than I (do).
6. The weather is getting worse and worse.
7. Your German is getting better and better.

E. *Put the verb into the past perfect tense.*

1. Um elf Uhr fährt der Dampfer pünktlich ab.
2. Wir geben unseren Bekannten recht.
3. In Linz steigt eine Gruppe junger Männer ein.
4. Sie trinken Wein und singen zu einer Gitarre.
5. Der Dampfer hält an verschiedenen Orten für einige Minuten.

GUIDED COMPOSITION

A. Describe an excursion you once took by boat, train, plane, or car. Where did you go? What did you see? How did you feel about the trip? What impressed you most? least? Write your composition in the past perfect tense.

B. Write a comparative study of your closest friends. First briefly describe each person individually. Then draw comparisons among them using the positive, comparative, and superlative forms of adverbs and adjectives.

---

* One of Ludwig II's castles in Bavaria (Bayern).

Chapter 13

Göttingen

Useful Phrases

nie wieder	never again
bis zu	up to
bis vor kurzem	until recently
zehnter November	November 10
seit einigen Jahren	for several years
so etwas	something like that
aus diesem Grund	for this reason
auf den Markt bringen	to put on the market
eine Prüfung ablegen	to take an examination
eine Prüfung bestehen	to pass an examination

MODEL SENTENCES

I

Er will nach China reisen, **und** da braucht er wohl einen Paß.	He wants to travel to China, and so he probably needs a passport.
Ich brauche einen Paß, **denn** ich will nach Europa reisen.	I need a passport, because I want to go to Europe.
Sie ist nicht ledig, **sondern** sie ist seit einem Jahr verheiratet.	She is not single, but (on the contrary) she's been married for a year.
Wohin wollen Sie **denn** reisen?	Where (actually) do you want to go?
Das habe ich **doch** nicht gewußt.	I (really) didn't know that.

II

Er füllte das **Antragsformular** für seinen **Reisepaß** aus.	He filled out the application form for his passport.
Er hatte das **Reisepaßantragsformular** ausgefüllt.	He had filled out the passport application form.
Die Sekretärin bestellte ein **Farbband** für ihre **Schreibmaschine.**	The secretary ordered a ribbon for her typewriter.
Sie bestellte ein **Schreibmaschinenfarbband.**	She ordered a typewriter ribbon.

Grammar Explanations

I. COORDINATING CONJUNCTIONS

Conjunctions are important structural elements in a language, comparable to the cement that holds building blocks together. As the term implies, conjunctions "conjoin"—they connect words, phrases, and clauses. In addition, conjunctions express relationships among the various parts of a complex sentence: qualification, attribution, restriction, causality, and temporality. In this sense, conjunctions add an element of sophistication to the sentence structure. Without their presence, the fabric of a language would consist largely of a juxtaposition or succession of practically independent, coequal statements; with their aid, the succession of statements is turned into a sequence or a "dynamic, linguistic pattern."

For instance, the statement "Helga had studied the menu. She called the waiter." is a rather childlike stringing together of two events; using a conjunction links the two events together in a temporal sequence: "**After** having studied the menu, Helga called the waiter."

German makes a careful structural distinction between two groups of conjunctions: *coordinating* conjunctions, which connect clauses of equal value and which *do not* affect word order, and *subordinating* conjunctions, which denote the dependency of one phrase upon another and which *do* affect the word order (*see* Chapter 14).

In English, there is practically no difference between the two groups except in punctuation. The coordinating conjunctions—**and, but, or,** and **nor**—require a preceding comma if they connect two independent clauses; there is generally no comma used with the subordinating conjunctions—**because, when, before, after,** and so on. In German, a comma precedes *all* coordinating conjunctions if an independent clause follows and *all* subordinating conjunctions.

The most common coordinating conjunctions in German are the following.

aber (but)	oder (or)
denn (for, because)	sondern (but, on the contrary)
doch (yet, however)	und (and)

Sondern is always used after a negative clause and indicates a contrast.

The coordinating conjunctions are most frequently used to connect two independent clauses, and they are not considered to be a part of either clause. Thus they do not affect the word order; the following verb remains in second place, whether in regular or inverted word order.

      1   2
. . . , **aber** *ich will* nach West-Berlin   . . . , but I intend to go to West Berlin.
    fahren.
      1 2
. . . , **denn** *ich habe* nichts zu tun.   . . . , because I don't have anything to do.
      1   2
. . . , **und** *da brauche* ich wohl einen   . . . , and so I'll probably need a pass-
    Reisepaß.   port.

Quite often, in a simple, declarative sentence, the conjunction **und** connects two verbs governed by the same subject. The subject is then only used once, there is no comma before the conjunction, and the second verb always directly follows the conjunction. This parallels English usage.

     Ich   *kannte* die Bestimmungen nicht genau und *wußte* nur, daß . . .
     ↑   ↑   ↑
  common verb 1   verb 2
   subject
(I did not know the regulations exactly and was only aware of the fact that . . . .)

The coordinating conjunctions **aber, denn,** and **doch** may also be used as emphatic particles which cannot be directly translated into English. Since these words merely add stress to the verb, they are not considered an important part of the sentence and thus do not affect word order.

Das ist **aber** wirklich sehr nett von Ihnen.   This is (indeed) really very kind of you.
Wohin wollen Sie **denn** reisen?   Where (actually) do you want to go?
Das habe ich **doch** nicht gewußt.   I (really) didn't know that.

While in English these emphatic particles are practically superfluous, they are widely used in spoken German, but they do not have the meanings or connotations of the corresponding coordinating conjunctions.

Use the coordinating conjunction in parentheses to connect the set of independent clauses.

1. Ich bin hungrig. Ich habe nichts zu essen. (aber)
2. Ich kenne diese Stadt. Ich bin hier zu Hause. (denn)
3. Jemand stiehlt das Geld. Dann sieht man es nie wieder. (und)
4. Das ist für sie keineswegs immer günstig. Sie müssen den Banken dafür viel Geld bezahlen. (denn)
5. In Amerika gibt es die Bankamericard. So etwas gibt es in Deutschland nicht. (doch)
6. Soll ich nach Hause gehen? Soll ich hier bleiben? (oder)
7. Jeder weiß das. Niemand sagt etwas. (aber)
8. Man braucht keine Reiseschecks. Man kann überall mit Euro-Schecks bezahlen. (sondern)

II. NOUN COMPOUNDS

One of the most characteristic features of German is the abundance of noun compounds. Though English offers the possibility of combining more than two words into one (as, for instance, in Mid/summer/night's Dream), the practice is much more common in German, especially in administrative jargon and legal codes. The last component determines the gender, number, and case ending of the entire compound.

die Reise (trip)	+	der Paß (passport)	=	der Reisepaß (passport for a trip)
der Antrag (application)	+	das Formular (form)	=	das Antragsformular (application form)
der Reisepaß (passport)	+	das Antragsformular (application form)	=	das Reisepaßantragsformular (application form for a passport)

Noun compounds may consist of any of the following elements.

noun + noun: der Antrag + das Formular = das Antragsformular
adjective + noun: weiß + der Wein = der Weißwein

adverb + noun: lang(e) + der Schläfer = der Langschläfer

verb + noun: wohnen + der Ort = der Wohnort

prefix + noun: vor + der Name = der Vorname

They may also be composed of combinations of these.

adjective + noun + noun: hoch + die Schule + die Reform = die Hochschulreform

At times an **–(e)s** or **–(e)n** ending is added to the first noun of a compound: das **Antragsformular, die Straßenbahn.** Infinitives usually drop the suffix **–en: der Wohnort.** There is no hard and fast rule to know when this is done; correct usage will come with observation and practice.

Check Your Comprehension

Form a noun compound from the following elements and add the appropriate article.

1. eine Reise + ein Paß
2. die Reise + das Zicl
3. der Antrag + das Formular
4. schreiben + die Maschine
5. der Bahnhof + die Straße

6. die Straße + die Bahn
7. nach + der Name
8. eine Bank + ein Angestellter
9. der Paß + das Bild
10. wohnen + dcr Ort

CONVERSATION

Im Rathaus

Herr Schneider	Guten Morgen! Ich möchte einen Reisepaß beantragen.
Der Beamte	So? Wohin wollen Sie denn reisen? Für die meisten europäischen Länder genügt nämlich der Personalausweis.
Herr Schneider	Ich weiß, aber ich will mit dem Auto durch die DDR[1] nach West-Berlin fahren, und da brauche ich wohl einen Reisepaß.
Der Beamte	Das ist natürlich richtig. Bitte, füllen Sie dieses Antragsformular aus!

5

HERR SCHNEIDER	Danke. Ach, jetzt habe ich meinen Kugelschreiber nicht bei mir. Können Sie mir einen geben?
DER BEAMTE	Natürlich! Aber ich kann das Antragsformular auch gleich mit der Schreibmaschine ausfüllen, denn ich habe im Moment nichts zu tun.
HERR SCHNEIDER	Das ist wirklich sehr nett von Ihnen.
DER BEAMTE	Ihren Nachnamen und Vornamen, bitte!
HERR SCHNEIDER	Schneider, Helmut.
DER BEAMTE	Postleitzahl, Wohnort und Straße?
HERR SCHNEIDER	Sieben Stuttgart, Bahnhofstraße zehn.
DER BEAMTE	Ihr Geburtsort, Herr Schneider?
HERR SCHNEIDER	Oberammergau in Bayern.
DER BEAMTE	Und Ihr Geburtstag?
HERR SCHNEIDER	Zehnter November, neunzehnhundertfünfzig.
DER BEAMTE	Beruf?
HERR SCHNEIDER	Bankangesteller.
DER BEAMTE	Bitte, unterschreiben Sie hier. Danke! Jetzt brauche ich noch Ihren Personalausweis und zwei Paßbilder.
HERR SCHNEIDER	Hier ist mein Personalausweis. Ich kannte die Bestimmungen nicht genau und wußte nicht, wieviele Paßbilder man braucht. Aber zum Glück habe ich zwei mitgebracht.
DER BEAMTE	Gut. Dann ist ja alles in Ordnung. Wir schicken Ihnen den Reisepaß in den nächsten Tagen zu.
HERR SCHNEIDER	Vielen Dank! Auf Wiedersehen.
DER BEAMTE	Auf Wiedersehen, Herr Schneider.

---

[1] Deutsche Demokratische Republik (German Democratic Republic, East Germany).

ORAL PRACTICE

A. *Combine the two sentences into one by using the German coordinating conjunctions indicated by the English equivalents in parentheses.*

1. Ich weiß das. Ich habe das gelesen. (for)
2. Ich kannte die Bestimmungen nicht. Ich habe keine Paßbilder mitgebracht. (and)
3. Ich kann das Antragsformular nicht ausfüllen. Ich habe im Moment viel zu tun. (for)
4. Er trinkt nicht. Er raucht. (but)
5. Er raucht nicht Zigaretten. Er raucht Zigarren. (but, on the contrary)
6. Ißt er Pizza? Trinkt er Bier? (or)
7. Sie hat seit Januar ihren Eltern nicht geschrieben. Sie hat viel mit ihnen telefoniert. (yet)
8. Wir möchten ins Restaurant gehen. Wir haben kein Geld. (but)
9. Ich will durch die DDR fahren. Da brauche ich wohl einen Reisepaß. (and)
10. Ich kann das machen. Ich habe im Moment nichts zu tun. (for)

B. *Form a noun compound from the set of two elements and add the appropriate article. The meaning of the compound is indicated by the English equivalent in parentheses.*

1. der Kredit + die Karte (credit card)
2. das Geld + der Beutel (purse)
3. der Brief + die Tasche (wallet)
4. die Straße + die Bahn (streetcar)
5. das Geschäft + die Leute (businessmen)
6. die Tankstelle + der Besitzer (gas station owner)
7. die Konkurrenz + der Kampf (competitive battle)
8. der Kredit + das System (credit system)
9. das Auto + die Vermietung (car rental [agency])
10. das Land + die Währung (national currency)
11. die Reise + der Scheck (traveler's check)
12. der Urlaub + die Reise (vacation trip)

C. *Form a noun compound from the set of three elements in the same way as in the above exercise (B).*

1. der Kredit + die Karte + das System (credit card system)
2. die Straße + die Bahn + die Haltestelle (streetcar stop)
3. schreiben + die Maschine + das Papier (typewriter paper)
4. hoch + die Schule + die Reform (college reform)
5. der Paß + das Bild + die Größe (size of a passport picture)

D. *For review practice, change the sentence to the past tense.*

1. Er spricht gut Deutsch.
2. Ich finde meinen Reisepaß nicht.
3. Du fährst zu schnell, Maria!
4. Kennen Sie Gary Cooper?
5. Er rennt so schnell wie er kann.
6. Jemand stiehlt sein Geld.
7. Sie studiert Medizin.
8. Sie bringen alle eine Flasche Weißwein mit.
9. Er nennt seinen Vornamen nicht.

E. *For review practice, change the sentences in the above exercise (D) to the present perfect tense.*

F. *Substitute or add each phrase as it is introduced into the previous sentence and make any structural changes.*

1. Ich weiß das, aber ich will   mit dem Auto durch die DDR fahren.
   _____, denn _____
   Wir _____
   _____, und _____ doch ___ _____

2. Ich brauche einen Personalausweis und   zwei Paßbilder.
   _____ keinen _____, sondern _____
   Er_____
   _____ ein Visum.

GUIDED CONVERSATION

A. Study the monstrous noun compound on the poster advertising the German railroad **(Bundesbahn)**. Discuss it with several members of your class and try to figure out what it means. You might begin by writing the word on the board in a single line without the hyphens. Then start at the end and break the word down into all its single components. Analyze each component and determine how the addition of each affects the meaning of the noun compound. What English equivalent would you give this word?

Bitte eine Rundfahrtumweglongtimepreissenkungsunterbrechungsrückfahrkarte.

B. Assume that you are a civil servant employed in the city hall of a German town and that one of the members in your class is a German citizen who has come to you to apply for a passport. Exchange greetings and comments on how you feel, what you think of the weather, and so on; then interview him/her by asking for the information required on the application form.

The following terms will help you understand the form.

die Anschrift, –en (address)
der Antrag, ⸗e (application)
der Antragsteller, – (applicant)
    begleiten (to accompany)
die Blockschrift (print)
der Buchstabe, –n (letter)
    deutlich (clear)
die Ehefrau, –en (spouse)
    eventuell (*abbrev.* evtl.) (possibly)
die Geburt, –en (birth)
das Geschlecht, –er (sex)
der Hauptwohnort, –e (main residence)
das Reiseziel, –e (destination)
der Reisezweck, –e (purpose of trip)
die Staatsangehörigkeit, –en (nationality)
die Urkunde, –n (document)

Antrag auf Ausstellung ~~Verlängerung der Gültigkeit~~
eines Reise- ~~Familien~~ Fremden-Passes ~~oder Kinder-Ausweises~~

	Antragsteller	Ehefrau (nur ausfüllen, wenn gleichzeitig ein F oder Fam.-Paß beantragt wird)
1. Familienname		
2. Mädchenname (bei Ehefrauen)		
3. Sämtl. Vornamen nach Geburtsurkunde		
4. Familienstand verheiratet/ledig		
5. Staatsangehörigkeit (auch frühere)		
6. Geburtstag		
7. Geburtsort (Kreis/Land)		

Ausfertigung der Pässe.

8. Beruf				
9. Personenbeschreibung	Größe in cm		Größe in cm	
	Gesichtsform	Augenfarbe	Gesichtsform	Augenfarbe
10. Unveränderliche Kennzeichen				
11. Hauptwohnort				
12. Anschrift (Straße und Hausnummer)				
13. Evtl. 2. Wohnort				
14. Wohnort und Anschrift in den letzten 12 Monaten				
15. Wohnort am 31. 12. 1937				
16. Nr. und sämtl. Buchstaben des Personal-Ausweises				
17. Reiseziel (ggf. Anschrift)				
18. Reisezweck				

19. Begleitende Kinder unter 15 Jahren (nur eigene Kinder oder Mündel; Bestallungsurkunde vorlegen)	Rufname	Familienname	Geburtsdatum und -ort	Geschle
	1.			
	2.			
	3.			
	4.			
	5.			

20. Haben Sie nach 1945 schon einen Reisepaß besessen: Ja — Nein. Falls ja, ist dieser Reisepaß beim Paßamt mit vorzulegen.

(Ort, Datum)

(Unterschrift der Ehefrau) (bei Antrag auf Paß)

(Unterschrift des Antragstellers)

(Bei Minderjährigen Unterschrift beider Elternteile oder des Vormundes und Personalausweise vorlegen)

Dem Antrag sind beizufügen:

1. **2** Paßbild **er** je Person (bei Familien-Paß keine Bilder für Kinder), Aufnahme ohne Kopfbedeckung, im Halbprofil, so daß ein Ohr sichtbar ist (Größe 4 × 5,5 cm) **und**

2. Personalausweis **und**

3. Geburts- oder Heiratsurkunde oder Familienbuch

4. ggf. Einbürgerungsurkunde oder Staatsangehörigkeitsausweis

5. und 10,— DM.

Zu beachten: Bei Minderjährigen unter 21 Jahren — außer Ehefrauen sind die Einwilligung beider Elternteile bzw. des Vormundes (Gegenzeichnung) sowie die Personalausweise u die Bestallungsurkunde des Vormundes erforderlich.

Antrag auf Ausstellung — Verlängerung der Gültigkeit eines Reise- — Familien- — Fremden-Passes oder Kinder-Ausweises

Das Eurocheque-System

In Amerika ist das Kreditkartensystem weit verbreitet, denn niemand möchte zuviel Bargeld in der Brieftasche haben. Viele fürchten, jemand stiehlt das Geld, und dann sieht man es nie wieder. Aber nicht jeder ist so pessimistisch. Andere fürchten, sie verlieren das Geld, denn schon viele haben ihr Geld im Zug, in der Straßenbahn oder in einem Restaurant verloren. Aus diesem Grund hat Amerika die Kreditkarte eingeführt. Das ist für die Geschäftsleute und Tankstellenbesitzer keineswegs immer günstig, denn sie müssen den Banken Prozente dafür bezahlen, aber der Konkurrenzkampf verlangt es.

In Europa hat man solch ein Kreditsystem bis vor kurzem noch nicht gekannt. Aber seit einigen Jahren haben die amerikanischen Autovermietungen (wie „Hertz", „Avis" und andere) solche Kreditkarten auch an deutsche Geschäftsleute gesandt. Doch so etwas wie die „Bankamericard" oder „Mastercharge" gibt es in Deutschland nicht. Aber es gibt die Eurocheque-Karte und die Euro-Schecks. Das ist praktisch, denn man kann in allen europäischen Ländern (ausgenommen Albanien, die DDR, Polen und die Sowjetunion) nicht nur an jeder Bank, sondern auch an fast allen Bahnhöfen und Flughäfen Bargeld bekommen. Für jeden Scheck bekommt man bis zu dreihundert Mark in der Landeswährung. Das ist ungefähr einhundert Dollar. Man braucht also für die europäischen Länder keine Reiseschecks, sondern man kann überall für Euro-Schecks Bargeld in der Landeswährung bekommen.

Das Eurocheque-System ist besonders praktisch für Urlaubsreisen; denn wer will schon mit viel Geld in der Tasche in andere Länder reisen?

QUESTIONS

1. Warum ist in Amerika das Kreditkartensystem so weit verbreitet?
2. Was fürchtet mancher?
3. Was fürchten andere?
4. Warum ist das Kreditkartensystem für die Geschäftsleute und Tankstellenbesitzer nicht immer günstig?
5. Wer verlangt es?

6. Hat man dieses System in Europa schon lange gekannt?
7. Was haben amerikanische Autovermietungen in den letzten Jahren getan?
8. Was kann man mit einer Eurocheque-Karte und Euro-Schecks machen?
9. Wieviel Mark kann man für jeden Scheck bekommen?
10. In welchen Ländern außerhalb Deutschlands kann man die Euro-Schecks benutzen?
11. Wo kann man sie nicht benutzen?

VOCABULARY EXERCISES

Supply the appropriate word from the list on the right.

1. Für die meisten europäischen Länder genügt der _____.
2. Ich kann nicht schreiben, denn ich habe meinen _____ vergessen.
3. Wann ist Ihr _____, Herr Schneider?
4. Herr Schneider ist von Beruf _____.
5. Ich kannte die _____ nicht genau.
6. Wie ist Ihr Vorname und _____, bitte?
7. Der _____ verlangt es.
8. Niemand möchte zuviel _____ haben.
9. Gibt es hier eine _____ wie Hertz oder Avis?
10. Wann machen Sie Ihre nächste _____?

a. Bestimmungen
b. Autovermietung
c. Bargeld
d. Personalausweis
e. Nachname
f. Konkurrenzkampf
g. Geburtstag
h. Urlaubsreise
i. Bankangestellter
j. Kugelschreiber

Review Exercises

A. *Supply the appropriate coordinating conjunctions in the following passage.*

In Amerika ist das Kreditkartensystem weit verbreitet, _____ niemand möchte zuviel Bargeld im Geldbeutel oder in der Brieftasche haben. Mancher fürchtet, jemand stiehlt das Geld, _____ er sieht es nie wieder. _____ nicht jeder ist so pessimistisch. Andere fürchten, sie verlieren das Geld, _____ schon viele haben ihr Geld im Zug, in der Straßenbahn oder in einem Restaurant verloren. Aus diesem Grund hat Amerika die Kreditkarte auf den Markt gebracht. Das ist für die Geschäftsleute und Tankstellenbesitzer keineswegs immer günstig, _____ sie müssen den Banken viel Geld dafür bezahlen, _____ der Konkurrenzkampf verlangt es.

B. *Form a noun compound from the set of elements and add the appropriate article. Supply the English equivalent for the German compound.*

1. der Bus + der Fahrer
2. baden + das Zimmer
3. das Blut + die Probe
4. der Bahnhof + die Halle
5. der Curry + die Wurst
6. der Flug + der Platz
7. die Feuerwehr + der Wagen
8. fahren + die Karte + der Schalter
9. der Fuß + der Ball + das Spiel
10. fern + sehen + das Programm
11. der Flug + der Hafen + das Gebäude
12. das Gemüse + der Stand
13. der Geschmack + die Sache
14. der Gast + der Professor
15. die Geburt + der Tag
16. die Kultur + das Magazin

17. kochen + die Gelegenheit
18. das Land + das Museum
19. landen + die Bahn
20. nach + der Krieg + die Zeit
21. die Orange + der Saft
22. der Paß + die Kontrolle
23. die Stadt + das Theater
24. die Sprache + der Unterricht
25. der Staat + das Eigentum
26. das Telefon + das Gespräch
27. warten + das Zimmer
28. schlafen + das Zimmer
29. wohnen + das Zimmer
30. essen + das Zimmer

C. *For review practice, change the following text into the past tense.*

In Europa kennt man ein solches Kreditsystem nicht. Aber seit einigen Jahren senden amerikanische Autovermietungen solche Kreditkarten auch an deutsche Geschäftsleute. Doch so etwas wie die Bankamericard gibt es in Deutschland nicht.

Aber es gibt die Eurocheque-Karte und dazu die Euro-Schecks. Das ist sehr günstig, denn man kann dafür in allen europäischen Ländern an jeder Bank Bargeld bekommen. Für jeden Scheck bekommt man ungefähr dreihundert Mark. In Deutschland kann man eigentlich in fast jedem Geschäft sowie in Hotels und Restaurants mit Euro-Schecks bezahlen.

D. *For review practice, change the text in the above exercise (C) into the present perfect tense.*

GUIDED COMPOSITION

If you were to apply to a German university, you would be asked to fill out a form similar to the one shown on the following pages. On a separate sheet of paper, supply all the information necessary to complete this portion of the form. Look up the meaning of unfamiliar words in a German-English dictionary.

In addition to this form, an applicant would also be required to submit a curriculum vitae (in German of course). For further practice, write your own curriculum vitae. It should be brief but comprehensive, including whatever information you feel would increase your chances of being accepted by the German university.

Westfälische Wilhelms-Universität Münster, Akademisches Auslandsa

4400 Münster (Westf.), Schloßplatz 1, Ruf-Nr. 4 90 22 27

In dreifacher Ausfertigung einzureichen

(Bitte in Druckbuchstaben ausfüllen; Nichtzutreffendes streichen)

Antrag auf Zulassung

zum Studium in der Fachrichtung ....

für das Sommer- / Wintersemester 19..............

1. Familienname: .... Vorname: ....

2. Geburtsdatum: .... Geburtsort: ....

3. Nationalität: ....

4. Geschlecht: männlich / weiblich

5. Familienstand: ledig / verheiratet / geschieden   Kinder: ....

6. Heimatadresse: ....

....

7. Gegenwärtige Adresse: ....

....

8. Name und Beruf des Vaters: ....

Studienziel

9. Welche Universitätsexamina wollen Sie in Münster ablegen? ....
   Diplom / Staatsexamen / Magister / Promotion

10. Welches Berufsziel haben Sie? ....

Vorbildung

ame und Datum der Schulabschlußzeugnisse
bitur, Bachelor, Baccalaureat, Maturität, Apolyterion, G. C. E., S. M. A., usw.)

....

ame und Ort der Schule: ....

usbildung und Tätigkeit nach dem Abitur: ....

....

üheres Universitätsstudium:

niversität / Ort   Fach   von — bis

....

....

elche Prüfungen haben Sie an den obengenannten Universitäten abgelegt?

t der Prüfung   Ort   Datum   Ergebnis

....

....

cht bestandene Prüfungen: ....

elche deutschen Sprachkenntnisse besitzen Sie?..
hulkenntnisse, privates Studium, Universitätsbesuch)

ie lange haben Sie Deutsch gelernt? ....

Chapter 14

Bad Waldsee

Useful Phrases

Hör mal!	Listen!
Appetit auf etwas haben	to be hungry for something
eine Diät machen	to go on a diet
Mir ist übel *or* schlecht.	I feel sick to my stomach.
Glück haben	to be lucky
Einkäufe machen	to go shopping
auf keinen Fall	by no means
nicht übel	not bad

MODEL SENTENCES

I

Ich weiß, **daß** ich nichts **weiß.**	I know that I don't know anything.
Daß ich nichts **weiß,** weiß ich.	
Sie möchte Pizza essen, **weil** sie hungrig ist.	She would like to eat pizza because she is hungry.
Weil sie hungrig **ist,** möchte sie Pizza essen.	
Ich weiß nicht, **ob** er seine Schwester **abgeholt hat.**	I don't know whether he picked up his sister.
Ob er seine Schwester **abgeholt hat,** weiß ich nicht.	
Peter rief den Ober, **nachdem** Helga die Speisekarte **gelesen hatte.**	After Helga had read the menu, Peter called the waiter.
Nachdem Helga die Speisekarte **gelesen hatte,** rief Peter den Ober.	

II

Ich kann **auf den Wein** nicht verzichten.	I can't forgo the wine.
Ich kann **darauf** nicht verzichten.	I can't forgo it.
Auf was warten Sie, mein Herr?	What are you waiting for, sir?
Worauf warten Sie, mein Herr?	

Grammar Explanations

I. SUBORDINATING CONJUNCTIONS AND DEPENDENT WORD ORDER

The second type of connecting words, subordinating conjunctions, affect the word order of the clause that they introduce. Subordinating conjunctions show the dependency of one statement upon another, and this dependency is reflected in the word order. Clauses introduced by subordinating conjunctions are, as one would expect, in *dependent word order* (at times also called "subordinate" word order). In dependent word order, the inflected (or conjugated or finite) verb stands at the very end of the dependent clause. The following points are important.

1. In the present or past tense, the principal verb comes at the end of the clause.

Ich weiß, **daß** du wirklich gerne Fisch **ißt.**   I know that you really like to eat fish.

2. When the present or past tense verb is one with a separable prefix, the prefix and stem reunite, and the complete inflected form stands at the end of the clause.

Er **nahm** sechs Kilo **zu.**   He's gained six kilograms.
Er weiß, **daß** er sechs Kilo **zunahm.**   He knows that he gained six kilograms.

3. In the present perfect or past perfect tense, the inflected form of the auxiliary **haben** or **sein** comes at the end of the clause.

Ich weiß das, **weil** ich hier schon oft **ge-**   I know that because I've eaten here quite
gessen habe.   often already.
Ich glaube, er ist gegangen, **weil** das   I think he's gone, because the airplane
Flugzeug schon **abgeflogen ist.**   has departed already.

4. When a modal auxiliary is used with the verb, the modal *always* falls at the end of the clause.

Er weiß nicht, **ob** man hier frische Fo-   He doesn't know if he [one] can get
rellen bekommen **kann**.   fresh trout here.

It is also possible for the dependent clause to precede the main clause, but the dependent clause always retains dependent word order. Since the finite verb of the main clause must be in second place in the sentence, and the dependent clause is considered to be in the first position, the main clause is automatically in inverted word order.

         1   2

Wenn du willst, kannst du gern ein   If you wish you may gladly have a piece
   Stück davon haben.   of it.

The dependent clause, whether preceding or following the main clause, is always separated by a comma.

Frequently used subordinating conjunctions include the following.

> als (when, as)
> als ob, als wenn (as if)
> auch wenn (even if)
> bevor (before)
> bis (until)
> da (since, *causal*; as)
> damit (so that)
> daß (that)
> ehe (before)
> falls (if, in case)
> indem (by *plus English progressive form*)
> nachdem (after)
> ob (whether)
> obwohl, obgleich, obschon (although)
> seit, seitdem (since, *temporal*)
> sobald, sowie (as soon as)
> so daß (so that)
> solange (as long as)
> sooft (as often as)
> während (while)
> weil (because)
> wenn (if; when, whenever)
> wenn auch (even if)
> wie (as, like)

Most of these subordinating conjunctions are parallel in usage to their English equivalents; some, however, pose special problems.

There are two subordinating conjunctions that mean "when." **Als** is used to denote a single action or situation in the *past* and is used with the past or past perfect tense. **Wenn** is used to denote a single action in the present or future and is used with the present or future tense.

Der Ober kam, **als** Peter noch die Speisekarte studierte.	The waiter came as (when) Peter was still studying the menu.
Als Helga die Speisekarte studiert hatte, rief Peter den Ober.	When Helga had studied the menu, Peter called the waiter.
Wenn wir bestellen möchten, rufen wir den Ober.	When we wish to order, we'll call the waiter.

Wenn is also used to indicate repeated, habitual actions and can be used to introduce clauses in any tense. It is often used in conjunction with **immer** and can be expressed in English as "whenever."

Immer **wenn** ich in dieses Restaurant gehe, esse ich Forelle.	I always eat trout when(ever) I go into this restaurant.
Jedes Mal, **wenn** ich in dieses Restaurant ging, aß ich Forelle.	Everytime I went to this restaurant I ate trout.

The English "if" also has two equivalents in German. **Wenn** is used to denote a conditional if.

Wenn es nicht regnet, gehen wir.	If it doesn't rain, we'll go.

When "if" can be substituted by the word "whether," the conjunction **ob** is always used.

Sie weiß nicht, **ob** es hier Forellen gibt.	She doesn't know if (whether) they have [there's] trout here.

The conjunctions **bevor, bis, ehe, nachdem, seit, seitdem,** and **während** indicate time relationships between the main and dependent clauses, and, since time relationships are frequently unequal, the main and dependent clauses may use different tense forms. This occurs especially with **nachdem.** When the main clause is in the present tense, the subordinate **nachdem** clause is in the present perfect tense; when the main clause is in the past the subordinate is in the past perfect.

Sie gehen in ein Café, **nachdem** sie Einkäufe gemacht haben.	They go into a café after they've gone shopping.
Ich trank Kaffee, **nachdem** ich meine Zeitung gelesen hatte.	I drank coffee after I had read my newspaper.

Notice that **seit** and **seitdem** mean "since" only in a temporal sense and never in the causal. The causal relationship expressed by "since" in English is usually indicated by the conjunctions **da** and **weil**.

Seit(dem) ich hier bin, ist viel passiert.	Since I've been here much has happened.
Mir ist übel geworden, **weil** ich zuviel gegessen habe.	Since I ate too much I got sick to my stomach.

Check Your Comprehension

A. *Use the subordinating conjunction* **daß** *to combine the main and dependent clauses, and make the necessary structural changes.*

1. Wir wissen, Helga hat heute Geburtsag.
2. Ich weiß, du möchtest heute Forelle essen.
3. Jeder weiß, du mußt deine Kalorien zählen.
4. Peter weiß, Helga möchte keine Ente.
5. Alle wissen, man kann hier frische Forellen bekommen.

B. *Combine the two sentences using the conjunction* **weil** *and making the second subordinate to the first.*

EXAMPLE   Sie gehen ins Restaurant. Helga hat Geburtstag.
   Sie gehen ins Restaurant, weil Helga Geburtstag hat.

1. Sie gehen ins Restaurant. Es regnet.
2. Sie gehen ins Restaurant. Sie haben Hunger.
3. Sie gehen ins Restaurant. Helga möchte Forelle essen.
4. Sie gehen ins Restaurant. Es ist dort gemütlich.

C. *Combine the two sentences by using the conjunction* **da** *and making the first subordinate to the second.*

> EXAMPLE   Helga hat Geburtstag. Sie gehen ins Restaurant.
> **Da Helga Geburtstag hat, gehen sie ins Restaurant.**

1. Es regnet. Sie gehen ins Restaurant.
2. Sie haben Hunger. Sie gehen ins Restaurant.
3. Helga möchte Forelle essen. Sie gehen ins Restaurant.
4. Es ist dort gemütlich. Sie gehen ins Restaurant.

D. *Transpose the clauses in the sentence and make the necessary changes.*

1. Ob du Schweinshaxe möchtest, weiß ich nicht.
2. Solange wir uns kennen, redest du von deiner Diät.
3. Das ist eine gebratene Forelle, während „Forelle blau" gekocht ist.
4. Ich vergesse nicht, daß du deine Kalorien zählen mußt.
5. Weil sie weniger Kalorien hat, ist Forelle besser für dich.

E. *Combine the two sentences using the appropriate German equivalent of the subordinating conjunction in parentheses. Watch the sense of each sentence to determine which one is dependent on the other and be careful of the word order.*

1. Ich hatte Hunger. Ich ging ins Restaurant. (when)
2. Wir hatten die Speisekarte gelesen. Peter bestellte das Essen. (after)
3. Er ist im Juli umgezogen. Er ist sehr glücklich. (since)
4. Er hat Fisch essen wollen. Sie bestellte Steak. (although)
5. Die zwei Freunde sind immer schwimmen gegangen. Sie mußten Deutsch studieren. (whenever)
6. Er ißt nur. Er hat Hunger. (if)

II. da– AND wo–COMPOUNDS

As you recall, in German certain prepositions require the dative case of the following noun or pronoun in a prepositional phrase; others the accusative; and some others either the dative or the accusative, depending on the meaning of the verb. After these prepositions, it is important to use the correct form of the noun or pronoun. For instance, with pronouns, say **mit ihm** and **mit ihr** but **für ihn** and **für sie.**

This use of a declined pronoun occurs only when the pronoun refers to a person. But with most prepositions, when the pronoun refers to an inanimate, nonhuman object or idea, the pronoun is replaced by a **da**-compound: **da** + preposition or, if the preposition begins with a vowel, **dar** + preposition.

auf der Speisekarte⎫ auf ihr⎭	dar + auf

Die Preise stehen **auf der Speisekarte.** The prices are (listed) on the menu.
Die Preise stehen **darauf.** The prices are (listed) on it.

in dem Wagen⎫ in ihm⎭	dar + in

Wer ist **in dem Wagen?** Who's in the car?
Wer ist **darin?** Who's in it?

Läßt du mich **von deinem Rumpsteak** probieren? — Will you let me try a piece of your rumpsteak?

Läßt du mich **davon** probieren? — Will you let me try a piece of it?

Mußt du mich schon wieder **an meine Diät** erinnern? — Do you have to remind me of my diet once again?

Mußt du mich schon wieder **daran** erinnern? — Do you have to remind me of it again?

Note that prepositions governing the genitive and the prepositions **außer, ohne,** and **seit** do *not* form **da**-compounds.

The **da**-compounds are used in written and spoken German. There is nothing colloquial about them. They are a built-in, structural feature of the language. But remember they refer to an *impersonal* object or an idea, *never* to a person, and only occasionally to an animal. Thus, if you say, "Ich fahre **mit ihm** nach Berlin," the inference is automatically that you intend to travel with a companion. However, if you say, "Ich fahre **damit** nach Berlin," the reference is to an object (or idea), probably a vehicle, such as your automobile.

Notice that the accent of a **da**-compound can fall either on the first or the second syllable. If the noun replaced by the **da**-compound is unstressed in the original sentence, then the accent falls on the second syllable.

Hier ist mein Wagen. Morgen fahre ich **damit′** nach Berlin. — Here's my car. Tomorrow I'm driving to Berlin with it.

If the **da**-compound is used to replace a stressed noun, the accent falls on the first syllable.

Fahren Sie mit **dem** Auto? Ja, ich fahre **da′mit**.

Are you taking *that* car? Yes, I'm driving with *that* one.

In replacing a stressed noun, you have a choice of using **da′mit** or an emphatic **der**-word, **dieser** or **jener,** to express "this" or "that."

Ja, ich fahre damit.
Ja, ich fahre mit dem.
Ja, ich fahre mit diesem.
Ja, ich fahre mit jenem.

Yes, I'm driving with *that* one.

In the same manner and with the same rules as with **da**-compounds, **wo**-compounds can be formed by combining **wo-** or **wor-** with a preposition. This occurs when the question word **was** (what) is preceded by a preposition.

Auf was hast du Appetit?
Worauf hast du Appetit?

What are you hungry for?

Über was spricht er?
Worüber spricht er?

What is he speaking about?

An was denkst du?
Woran denkst du?

What are you thinking about?

Either form can be used, but for stylistic reasons the **wo**-compounds are generally preferred.

At times, the **da**- and **wo**-compounds may refer to the specific location of an object.

Sie sitzt **auf dem Sofa.**
Davor steht ein kleiner Tisch.
Worauf sitzt sie, und **wovor** steht ein kleiner Tisch?
Sie sitzt **darauf,** und er steht **davor.**

She's sitting on the sofa.
In front of it there's a small table.
What's she sitting on, and what's the small table in front of?
She's sitting on it, and it's standing in front of it.

In some cases, the **da**- or **wo**-compound refers to the whole idea expressed in a previous sentence or following clause.

Ich muß auf meine Kalorien achten. Denk doch **daran!**

I have to pay attention to calories. Think of that (fact).

Woran soll ich denken?

What am I supposed to remember?

Du sollst **daran** denken, daß ich auf meine Kalorien achten muß.

You should remember that I have to pay attention to calories.

In the examples above, the compounds obviously refer to the *fact* of having to count calories and not to the word "calories." In the last sentence, the **da**-compound anticipates a dependent clause.

When the **da**-compound **damit** is used to introduce such a dependent clause, do not confuse it with the subordinating conjunction **damit** (so that).

da-compound: Was heißt das? Ach so, **da'mit** meint man gebratene Forellen.

What does that mean? I see, they mean fried trout (by that).

subord. conj.: Ich esse Forelle, **damit'** ich nicht noch mehr zunehme.

I eat trout so that I won't gain more weight.

With verbs of motion, especially **gehen** and **kommen,** the directional compounds **dahin, dorthin, daher, dorther, wohin,** and **woher** are used rather than **da-** and **wo-**compounds.

Woher kommst du?

Where are you coming from?

Ich komme aus der Schule. Kommst du auch **daher**?

I'm coming from school. Are you coming from there too?

Wohin gehst du?

Where are you going?

Ich gehe ins Kino. Gehst du auch **dahin**?

I'm going to the movies. Are you going there too?

Check Your Comprehension

A. *Form a* **da**-*compound using the preposition.*

1. an
2. durch
3. gegen
4. bei
5. nach
6. aus
7. hinter
8. vor
9. neben
10. zwischen
11. zu
12. in
13. auf
14. für
15. unter

B. *Form a **wo**-compound using the preposition.*

1. mit
2. aus
3. über
4. von
5. zwischen
6. bei

7. durch
8. zu
9. gegen
10. vor
11. auf
12. nach

C. *Substitute a **da**-compound for the prepositional phrase in the expression.*

1. an den Geburstag denken
2. auf etwas Appetit haben
3. von der Diät reden
4. etwas unter einer gebratenen Forelle verstehen
5. ein kleines Stück von dem Rumpsteak probieren
6. jemand an seine Diät erinnern
7. etwas von einer Sache verstehen
8. mit diesen Worten sagen

D. *Ask a question that refers to the assertion by using a **wo**-compound.*

EXAMPLE   Ich verstehe nichts davon.
   Wovon verstehst du nichts?

1. Ich weiß nichts darüber.
2. Unser Haus steht dazwischen.
3. Dein Geld ist darin.
4. Mein Herr, Sie sitzen darauf!
5. Ihr wart doch dabei!
6. Ich warte darauf.
7. Ich bin absolut dagegen.

STUHLMACHER

Hausgemachte Spezialitäten

Erbsensuppe	2,10
Erbsensuppe mit Einlage	2,50
Bayrische Leberknödelsuppe	4,00
Goulaschsuppe „Hausmacher"	3,75
STUHLMACHER's Wurstbrötchen	2,50
Münsterisches Kalbskopf-Töttchen nach altem Hausrezept	3,50
Hausmacher Blut- oder Leberwurst auf Brot . .	4,00
Hausmacher Kochkäse nach Tante Anna	4,50
Hausmacher Sülze mit Röstkartoffeln, Teufelssoße	5,00
geeiste Heringsfilets in Sahne, Butter und Brot oder Salzkartoffeln	5,00

Belegte Brote

mit

gekochtem Schinken	4,75
rohem Schinken, Schweinebraten oder Zunge, gut garniert	5,50
Münsterland-Schnittchen Schinken und Mettwurst, Gurke	5,50
Roastbeef, Remouladensauce, gut garniert . . .	6,00
Holländer Käse, Schweizer Käse Camembert oder Gervais, mit Butter und Brot	4,00
altem Holländer	5,00

CONVERSATION

Die Speisekarte

Peter und Helga sitzen im Restaurant „Stuhlmacher" und studieren die Speisekarte.

PETER   Schau, Helga, hier—die Speisekarte. Hm! Spezialität des Hauses: „Schweinshaxe vom Grill". Meinst du, daß das etwas für uns ist?

HELGA   Für mich bestimmt nicht. Denk doch daran, daß ich nicht soviel 5 essen kann. Worauf ich jetzt wirklich Appetit habe,[1] ist Fisch.

PETER   Na, gut. Obwohl ich weiß, daß du tatsächlich gerne Fisch ißt, verstehe ich nicht, wie man auf eine schöne gegrillte Schweinshaxe verzichten kann! Möchtest du vielleicht eine Ente?

HELGA	Aber nein! Weißt du eigentlich, wieviel Kalorien eine Ente hat? 10

HELGA Aber nein! Weißt du eigentlich, wieviel Kalorien eine Ente hat? 10
Wenn du mich fragst, worauf ich Appetit habe, dann ist meine
Antwort Forelle. Ich weiß allerdings nicht, ob man hier frische
Forellen bekommen kann.

PETER Aber sicher! Ich weiß das, weil ich hier schon oft gegessen habe.
Aber bevor ich bestelle, muß ich wissen, ob du „Forelle blau" oder 15
„Forelle nach Müllerin Art"[2] haben möchtest.

HELGA Du meinst also, gekocht oder gebraten.

PETER Genau! Übrigens, wenn du wissen willst, worauf ich Appetit habe.
Ich möchte gern ein schönes Rumpsteak mit Zwiebeln und gemisch-
tem Salat. 20

HELGA Hm, nicht übel! Also gut, ich nehme Forelle „Müllerin Art". Aber
wie du weißt, esse ich Rumpsteak auch furchtbar gern. Läßt du mich
ein kleines Stück davon probieren?

PETER Aber natürlich! Wenn du willst, kannst du gern ein Stück davon
haben. 25

HELGA Gut! Du, ich finde das wirklich ganz gemütlich hier.

PETER Ich auch. Ich glaube, dann können wir wohl bestellen. Herr Ober,
bringen Sie uns bitte auch die Weinkarte.

---

[1] Note the use of a comma after the dependent clause even though the whole clause is the
subject of the sentence.
[2] Two ways of cooking trout.

ORAL PRACTICE

A. *Transpose the clauses so that the subordinate clause begins the sentence. Watch the
word order in the main clause.*

1. Du darfst heute Forelle essen, da du Geburtstag hast.
2. Ich weiß nicht, ob man hier Forellen bekommen kann.
3. Ich sagte dir doch, daß ich meine Kalorien zählen muß!
4. Du redest von deiner Diät, solange wir uns kennen.
5. Ich verstehe nicht, wie man auf eine gegrillte Ente verzichten kann.
6. Ich weiß das, weil ich hier schon oft gegessen habe.
7. Dies ist eine gebratene Forelle, während eine „Forelle blau" gekocht
ist.
8. Ich verstehe die Frauen manchmal nicht, obwohl ich sie gut kenne.

9. Ich muß wissen, was du haben möchtest, bevor ich bestelle.
10. Ich bestelle noch ein Rumpsteak, wenn du willst.

B. *Use the subordinate conjunction* **daß** *to combine the main and dependent clauses and make the necessary changes.*

1. Ich glaube, du hast Appetit auf Schweinshaxe.
2. Ihr merkt, ich bin krank.
3. Wir wissen, ihr seid alle furchtbar intelligent.
4. Ich bin sicher, morgen regnet es.
5. Helga sagt, sie möchte Forelle essen.
6. Peter meint, Ente ist besser für sie.

C. *Combine the two sentences into one by using the subordinating conjunction in parentheses.*

EXAMPLE   Sie ißt die Suppe. Ich esse den Pudding. (während)
Sie ißt die Suppe, während ich den Pudding esse.

1. Peter hat Helga eingeladen. Sie hat Geburtstag. (weil)
2. Helga hat Forelle nicht gegessen. Sie kennt Peter. (seit)
3. Helga ißt jedesmal Fisch. Sie geht in ein Restaurant. (wenn)
4. Sie weiß. Peter ißt lieber Rumpsteak mit Zwiebeln. (daß)
5. Peter erinnert Helga an ihre Diät. Sie vergißt es. (sooft)
6. Er aß noch eine Ente. Er hatte schon eine Schweinshaxe gegessen. (nachdem)
7. Er weiß nicht. Hat Helga Appetit auf eine Ente? (ob)
8. Der Ober kam. Peter studierte noch die Speisekarte. (als)
9. Du mußt auf deine Kalorien achten. Du willst so schlank werden wie ein Mannequin. (wenn)
10. Peter sagte das. Er aß die Schweinshaxe. (indem)

D. *Combine the two sentences into one, using the subordinating conjunction in parentheses and making the first sentence dependent on the second.*

EXAMPLE   Ich esse den Pudding. Sie ißt die Suppe. (während)
Während ich den Pudding esse, ißt sie die Suppe.

1. Helga geht in ein Restaurant. Sie ißt immer Fisch. (wenn)

2. Helga hat Geburtstag. Peter hat sie eingeladen. (weil)
3. Peter ißt lieber Rumpsteak mit Zwiebeln. Sie weiß. (daß)
4. Sie kennt Peter. Helga hat Forelle nicht gegessen. (seit)
5. Sie vergißt es. Peter erinnert Helga an ihre Diät. (sooft)
6. Er hatte die Schweinshaxe gegessen. Er aß noch eine Ente. (nachdem)
7. Peter studierte noch die Speisekarte. Der Ober kam. (als)
8. Hat Helga Appetit auf eine Ente? Er weiß nicht. (ob)
9. Du willst so schlank werden wie ein Mannequin. Du mußt auf deine Kalorien achten. (wenn)
10. Peter sagte das. Er aß die Schweinshaxe und zwei gebratene Enten. (indem)

E. *Replace the prepositional phrase with a* **da-***compound.*

1. Peter hat Helga zum Abendessen eingeladen.
2. Sie fahren mit dem Zug.
3. Auf dem Tisch liegt die Speisekarte.
4. Die Mäntel legen sie über einen Stuhl.
5. Sie warten auf den Wein.
6. Peter ist mehr für Rotwein.
7. Helga hat nichts gegen einen guten Weißwein.
8. Nach dem Essen machen sie noch einen Spaziergang.
9. Helga lädt Peter zu einer Tasse Kaffee ein.
10. Sie denken an den schönen Abend.

F. *Replace the prepositional phrase with a* **da-***compound, if possible, or a preposition plus a personal pronoun, if a* **da-***compound cannot be used.*

1. Die Forelle ist für Helga.
2. Peter hat nichts gegen ein Rumpsteak mit Zwiebeln.
3. Er redet den ganzen Abend mit seiner Freundin.
4. Auf der Speisekarte stehen auch gute Weine.
5. In dem Restaurant ist es sehr gemütlich.
6. Sie warten auf den Ober.
7. Über dem Kamin hängt eine Uhr.
8. Unter einem anderen Tisch liegt ein Hund.

9. Mit Helga geht Peter immer gern spazieren.
10. Bei seiner Freundin bekommt er immer guten Kaffee.

G. *Substitute a* **wo**-*compound for the prepositional phrase with* **was.**

1. Auf was warten Peter und Helga?
2. Zu was hat Peter seine Freundin eingeladen?
3. Mit was fahren die Freunde zum „Ratskeller"?
4. An was denken die Mädchen?
5. Für was bezahlt Peter?
6. Gegen was hat Helga absolut nichts?
7. Auf was muß Helga besonders achten?

H. *Substitute or add each phrase as it is introduced into the previous sentence and make any necessary structural changes. Pay particular attention to verb changes.*

Da Helga   auf ihre Diät   achten muß, ißt sie jeden Tag Fisch.
Weil _____ _____
Seit __ _____
_____, muß _____ essen.
____ Peters Freundin __ _____
_____ Kalorien __ _____

GUIDED CONVERSATION

A. Study the menu that illustrates the conversation in this chapter. Suppose that you are sitting at a table in the restaurant with one of your class members trying to decide what to order. Discuss the various items on the menu, what you might like, what you would not like, what you would especially like but feel for one reason or another you should not order, what you would recommend to one another, and so on.

B. Exchange greetings with someone in your class. Ask him/her where he/she is just coming from; what he/she is thinking of; and/or where he/she would like to go, with whom, and how; comment on the person's replies and ask any additional questions. Use **da-** and **wo-**compounds whenever possible.

Der Leserbrief

Während es draußen regnet, wartet Fräulein Seidel auf ihren Verlobten. Er hat sie heute zum Theater eingeladen, weil sie Geburtstag hat. Bis ihr Verlobter kommt, dauert es aber bestimmt noch eine halbe Stunde. Er hat nämlich noch etwas in der Stadt zu tun, ehe er sie abholen kann.

Fräulein Seidel sitzt im Wohnzimmer auf dem Sofa. Davor steht ein kleiner 5 Tisch, und darauf liegen Illustrierte, eine Schachtel Zigaretten und Schokolade. Während sie eine Zigarette raucht, blättert sie in einer Illustrierten. Nachdem sie das Fernsehprogramm studiert hat, liest sie die Leserbriefe an „Frau Barbara". Einer davon ist der folgende:

Liebe Frau Barbara, 10

ich heiße Ursula M. und bin fast zwanzig Jahre alt. Ich glaube, daß ich recht gut aussehe, aber leider wiege ich sechs bis acht Kilo zuviel. Damit will ich nicht sagen, daß ich zu dick bin, nur etwas rundlich. Mein Freund sagte immer, wenn er mich sah, daß ich endlich eine Diät machen soll, damit wir auch einmal zusammer schwimmen gehen können. 15

Ich gebe zu, ich konnte einfach auf die vielen Süßigkeiten nicht verzichten, so daß mich mein Freund vor einigen Wochen verlassen hat. Jetzt esse ich dafür noch mehr als früher, weil ich sehr unglücklich bin.

Ich möchte Sie nun fragen, ob ich vielleicht Diätpillen nehmen soll wie meine Freundin. In den letzten vier Wochen hat sie tatsächlich beinahe zehn Kilo ab- 20 genommen, und dabei ißt sie fast pausenlos. Schaden solche Pillen wirklich nicht der Gesundheit? Ich kann nicht recht daran glauben. Aber wenn ich sechs bis acht Kilo abnehme, kommt mein Freund sicher wieder zurück.

Ursula M., Berlin

,,Frau Barbara" antwortet: 25

Liebe Ursula,

nehmen Sie auf keinen Fall die Diätpillen von Ihrer Freundin! Vielleicht hat sie mehr Glück als Verstand. Die meisten Pillen dieser Art schaden wirklich der Gesundheit. Wenn Sie tatsächlich abnehmen wollen, dann gehen Sie zu einem Arzt und fragen ihn, ob Sie eine Diät machen sollen und welche. Sprechen Sie offen mit ihm 30 darüber. Ihre Gesundheit ist wichtiger als Ihr Gewicht. Aber vielleicht genügt es schon, wenn Sie einfach etwas weniger Süßigkeiten essen.

Und nun zu Ihrem Freund. Wenn er Sie wirklich verlassen hat, weil Sie sechs bis acht Kilo zuviel wiegen, wie Sie schreiben, dann vergessen Sie ihn lieber!

QUESTIONS

1. Auf wen wartet Fräulein Seidel, während es draußen regnet?
2. Warum hat ihr Verlobter sie zum Abendessen eingeladen?
3. Was liegt auf dem Tisch im Wohnzimmer?
4. Was tut Fräulein Seidel?
5. Was ist Ursulas Problem?
6. Glaubt sie, daß sie wirklich zu dick ist?
7. Was sagt ihr Freund immer, wenn er sie sieht?
8. Warum soll sie schlanker werden?
9. Worauf konnte Ursula auf keinen Fall verzichten?

10. Was tut sie, seitdem sie unglücklich ist?
11. Was fragt sie „Frau Barbara"?
12. Woran glaubt sie nicht ganz?
13. Worauf hofft Ursula?
14. Wozu rät „Frau Barbara"?
15. Worüber soll Ursula mit dem Arzt offen sprechen?
16. Wie kann sie vielleicht am besten abnehmen?
17. Liebt der Freund das Mädchen wirklich?

VOCABULARY EXERCISES

Supply the appropriate word from the list on the right.

1. Fräulein Seidel wartet auf ihren _____.	a. Gewicht
2. Sie hat ihr Examen _____.	b. gedauert
3. Es hat noch eine halbe Stunde _____.	c. schaden
4. Der Verlobte will sie gleich _____.	d. bestanden
5. Auf dem Tisch liegt eine _____ Zigaretten.	e. Süßigkeiten
6. Ursula glaubt, daß sie zuviel _____.	f. Ober
7. Sie meint, daß sie zuviel _____ ißt.	g. wiegt
8. Diätpillen _____ bestimmt ihrer Gesundheit.	h. Verlobten
9. Ihre Gesundheit ist wichtiger als ihr _____.	i. abholen
10. Der _____ bringt das Rumpsteak mit Zwiebeln.	j. Schachtel

Review Exercises

A. *Combine the two sentences into one by using the subordinating conjunction in parentheses and making the second clause dependent on the first.*

1. Fräulein Seidel wartet auf ihren Verlobten. Es regnet draußen. (während)
2. Es dauert noch eine halbe Stunde. Er kommt. (bis)

3. Er muß zuerst nach Hause fahren. Sie gehen in den „Ratskeller". (bevor)
4. Sie hört Musik. Sie raucht eine Zigarette. (während)
5. Sie liest Leserbriefe an „Frau Barbara". Sie hat das Fernsehprogramm studiert. (nachdem)
6. Sie legt die Schokolade unter das Sofa. Sie hat das gleiche Problem wie Ursula. (weil)
7. Sie wiegt zuviel. Sie glaubt. (wie)
8. Sie weiß. Weniger Schokolade essen kann nichts schaden. (daß)
9. Sie ist nicht sicher. Ihr Verlobter verläßt sie. (ob)
10. Sie geht lieber in die Sauna. Sie geht zum Arzt. (ehe)

B. *Combine the two sentences into one by using the subordinating conjunction in parentheses and making the first clause dependent on the second. Watch the word order.*

1. Ich kam nach Hause. Die Tür stand offen. (als)
2. Ich wurde Millionär. Ich hatte nie einen Revolver bei mir. (bevor)
3. Ich habe meine Juwelen im Safe. Ich bin vorsichtig. (scitdem)
4. Ich hatte meinen Revolver aus der Tasche genommen. Ich ging leise ins Wohnzimmer. (nachdem)
5. Ich fand den Dieb. Es dauerte einige Sekunden. (bis)
6. Er mußte sehr schnell machen. Er wurde etwas nervös. (da)
7. Niemand hörte ihn. Er öffnete den Safe ganz leise. (damit)
8. Er rauchte eine Zigarette. Er nahm das Geld und die Juwelen aus dem Safe. (indem)
9. Er sah mich plötzlich. Er wurde wieder etwas nervös. (als)
10. Er sollte aus dem Fenster springen. Er wußte nicht. (ob)
11. Ich wollte meine Juwelen zurück haben. Er verstand. (daß)
12. Er legte die Juwelen wieder in den Safe. Ich rief den Sheriff an. (während)

C. *Express in German.*

1. Helga ate trout when she was in the "Ratskeller."
2. When I go to the "Ratskeller," I always eat fried duck.
3. Do you know if one can get fish here?
4. If you want, I'll order something for you.
5. I'm not sure whether they have trout.

6. After leaving the restaurant they took a walk.
7. When they came home, they drank a cup of coffee.
8. They always drink coffee when they come home from a restaurant.

D. *Substitute a directive compound (**dahin** or **dorthin**) for the prepositional phrase and then ask the respective question.*

EXAMPLE   Morgen fahre ich nach Berlin.
    Ich fahre dorthin. Wohin fahre ich?

1. Ursula geht jeden Tag zur Sauna.
2. Sie gehen heute abend in den „Ratskeller".
3. Du fährst zum Hauptbahnhof.
4. Wir fahren zusammen zum Flugplatz.
5. Er geht mit ihr ins Schwimmbad.

E. *Substitute a directive compound (**daher** or **dorther**) for the prepositional phrase and then ask the respective question.*

EXAMPLE   Ich kam gestern aus Berlin.
    Ich kam dorther. Woher kam ich?

1. Peter kommt jeden Tag um zwölf Uhr von der Schule.
2. Das Taxi kommt gerade vom Hauptbahnhof.
3. Der Wind kommt heute von Westen.
4. Der Zug kommt aus Hamburg.
5. Ich komme gerade vom Landesmuseum.

F. *Substitute a **da-** or **wo-***compound for the prepositional phrase.*

1. Ursula schreibt an Frau Barbara über ihr Problem.
2. Frau Barbara sagt etwas zu dieser wichtigen Frage.
3. Ihre Antwort auf dieses Problem ist ein Leserbrief.
4. An was denkt das Mädchen nur?
5. Es denkt immer nur an ihr Gewicht.
6. Auf was warten Sie eigentlich schon eine halbe Stunde?

7. Ich warte auf den nächsten Zug.
8. Über was spricht denn der Mann dort drüben?
9. Er spricht über die deutsche Politik.
10. Mit was schreiben Sie eigentlich da?
11. Ich schreibe mit einer neuen Schreibmaschine von IBM.
12. Was denken Sie eigentlich über die deutsche Grammatik?

GUIDED COMPOSITION

A. Do you have a problem of some sort, or are you concerned about a problem one of your friends has? Write a letter to Frau Barbara explaining the problem and seeking advice.

   For further practice, exchange letters with someone in your class and answer as if you were Frau Barbara.

B. Write a brief critique on your favorite restaurant. You might comment on the seting, the atmosphere, the service, and/or the prices. But most importantly, focus on the menu: explain what items are featured, which are the house specialities, which items you have tried, and which one is your favorite. Recommend a particular lunch or dinner, and try to convince your reader that he/she should go to the restaurant and order what you suggest.

Chapter 15

Zürcher See

Useful Phrases

recht gut	quite well
ein andermal	another time
jedes Mal	every time
zum ersten Mal	for the first time
schon wieder	already; once again
soviel wie möglich	as much as possible
Tja!	Well.
zu Besuch kommen	to come for a visit

MODEL SENTENCES

I

Holst du deine Schwester **ab?**	Are you going to pick up your sister?
Willst du deine Schwester **abholen?**	Do you want to pick up your sister?
Es ist richtig, daß ich zuviel Geld **ausgebe.**	It's correct that I spend too much money.
Es ist richtig, daß ich zuviel Geld **ausgegeben habe.**	It's correct that I spent too much money.
Beantworten Sie die Frage!	Answer the question.
Wollen Sie bitte die Frage **beantworten!**	Would you please answer the question.
Stimmt es, daß diese Frau ihn **beeindruckt?**	Is it true that this woman impresses him?
Stimmt es, daß diese Frau ihn **beeindruckt hat?**	Is it true that this woman impressed him?

II

Das ist das Haus, in **dem** ich wohne.	That's the house [in which] I live in.
Dort ist der Herr, **dessen** Brieftasche der Dieb gestohlen hat.	There is the gentleman whose wallet was stolen by the thief [the thief stole].
Das sind die Kinder, **denen** er geholfen hat.	These are the children [whom] he helped.

Wer Auto fährt, muß vorsichtig sein.	He who drives [a car] must be careful.
Was er tut, ist richtig.	What he is doing is right.

III

Ich warte, **um zu sehen,** was passiert.	I'm waiting to see what will happen.
Ohne auf mich **zu warten,** ging sie ins Kino.	She went to the movies without waiting for me.
Er ist mit dem Zug nach Italien gefahren, **statt** mit dem Flugzeug **zu fliegen.**	He went to Italy by train instead of flying (by plane).

Grammar Explanations

I. VERBS WITH SEPARABLE AND INSEPARABLE PREFIXES

A. Separable Prefixes

Verbs with separable prefixes have already been treated in some detail (*see* Chapters 3 and 5). Separable prefixes may be related to prepositions, examples being **ab-, an-, auf-, aus-, bei-, mit-, vor-, über-, um-, zu-,** and others; to adverbs, examples being **hin-, her-,** and **vorbei-**; and at times even to adjectives, as, for instance, in "**hoch**heben" (to lift up). Less frequent is the combination of two verbs such as "**kennen**lernen" (to get to know), in which the first verb of the combination is treated syntactically like a separable prefix.

Ich **lerne** ihn **kennen.**	I'm getting to know him.
Ich habe ihn **kennengelernt.**	I got to know him.

Using the three basic rules for word order, the position of the separable prefix is as follows. In the *normal* and *inverted* word order, if the verb is in a simple tense (present or past), the separable prefix is separated from the verb and is placed at the very end of the clause or sentence. If the verb is in a compound tense (present perfect or past perfect), the separable prefix is joined to the past participle of the verb.

	Present	*Present Perfect*
normal:	Man **gibt** viel Geld **aus.**	Man **hat** viel Geld **ausgegeben.**
inverted:	**Gibt** man viel Geld **aus?**	**Hat** man viel Geld **ausgegeben?**

In *dependent* word order, the separable prefix stays with the verb, and in the compound tenses the past participle precedes the auxiliary.

	Present	*Present Perfect*
dependent:	Es stimmt, daß man viel Geld **ausgibt.**	Es stimmt, daß man viel Geld **ausgegeben hat.**

B. Inseparable Prefixes

A large number of German verbs begin with the inseparable prefixes **be–, emp–, ent–, er–, ge–, über–, ver–,** and **zer–** (*see* Chapter 5). In this lesson you will find the following verbs with inseparable prefixes.

beantworten (to answer)
beeindrucken (to impress)
beherrschen (to dominate)
bekämpfen (to fight against)
bekommen (to get, receive)
beraten (to advise, counsel)
bereisen (to travel through)
besuchen (to visit)
betrachten (to look at; to consider)
bewohnen (to live in)
bezahlen (to pay for)
empfangen (to receive)
erhalten (to receive)
erleben (to experience)
ermüden (to make *or* get tired)
erobern (to conquer)
erwischen (to catch)
überqueren (to cross)
überzeugen (to convince)
verbieten (to forbid)
verlangen (to demand, ask for)
zerstören (to destroy)

At times, the prefix **be–** converts an intransitive verb (that is, a verb that cannot take a direct object but, rather, takes a prepositional phrase) into a transitive verb (one that can take a direct object).

Man **kämpft gegen** die Bevölkerungs- explosion.

Man **bekämpft** die Bevölkerungsexplo- sion.

They fight against the population ex- plosion.

The difference between the two alternative constructions is largely one of style.

In most cases, however, inseparable prefixes add a distinctive new mean- ing to the basic verb.

Basic Verb	*Prefixed Verb*
fangen (to catch)	**emp**fangen (to receive)
halten (to hold)	**er**halten (to receive)
herrschen (to rule)	**be**herrschen (to dominate)
kommen (to come)	**be**kommen (to obtain, get)
leben (to live)	**er**leben (to experience)
suchen (to look for)	**be**suchen (to visit)

Syntactically, verbs with inseparable prefixes do not present the same prob- lems as those with separable prefixes. The inseparable prefix, as the name suggests, always remains attached to the verb.

pres.:	Er **er**lebt viel.
past:	Er **er**lebte viel.
pres. perf.:	Er hat viel **er**lebt.
past perf.:	Er hatte viel **er**lebt.
with modal:	Er muß viel **er**leben.
in an infinitive clause with **zu:**	Es ist schön, so viel zu **er**leben.

In a compound tense, verbs with inseparable prefixes do not have the **ge–** of the past participle.

	Infinitive	*Past Participle*
weak verb:	bezahlen	bezahlt
strong verb:	empfehlen	empfohlen
irreg. weak verb:	verbrennen	verbrannt

Notice that verbs with inseparable prefixes may be weak, strong, or irregular weak. Be careful to distinguish between the present tense and the past participle in verbs that have identical forms for the two functions.

Sie **empfangen** mich sehr freundlich.	They receive me very kindly.
Sie **haben** mich sehr freundlich **emp-fangen.**	They (have) received me very kindly.

At this point we can recapitulate the three types of sentence construction (word order) in German.

Normal, Inverted, and Dependent Word Order

Normal Word Order	*simple tense:*	Helga **ißt** gern Fisch.
	with *sep. prefix:*	Helga **nimmt** etwas **ab.**
	with *modal:*	Helga **kann** hier Fisch **bekommen.**
	compound tense:	Helga **hat** gern Fisch **gegessen.**
	with *sep. prefix:*	Helga **hat** etwas **abgenommen.**
	with *modal:*	Helga **hat** hier Fisch **bekommen können.**
Inverted Word Order	*simple tense:*	Heute **hat** Helga Geburtstag.
	with *sep. prefix:*	Heute **nimmt** Helga etwas **zu.**
	with *modal:*	Heute **kann** Helga viel **essen.**
	compound tense:	Gestern **hat** Helga Geburtstag **gehabt.**
	with *sep. prefix:*	Gestern **hat** Helga etwas **zugenommen.**
	with *modal:*	Gestern **hat** Helga viel **essen können.**
	in a *question:*	**Hat** Helga heute Geburtstag?
		Hat Helga gestern Geburtstag **gehabt?**
Dependent Word Order	*simple tense:*	Ich weiß, **daß** Helga gern Fisch **ißt.**
	with *sep. prefix:*	Ich weiß, **daß** Helga etwas **zunimmt.**
	with *modal:*	Ich weiß, **daß** Helga hier Fisch **bekommen kann.**
	compound tense:	Ich weiß, **daß** Helga Fisch **gegessen hat.**
	with *sep. prefix:*	Ich weiß, **daß** Helga etwas **zugenommen hat.**
	with *modal:*	Ich weiß, **daß** Helga hier Fisch **hat bekommen können.**

A. *Form the past tense of the verb with a separable prefix. Then turn the sentence into a question. Then form the present perfect tense of the original sentence. Then turn that sentence into a question.*

1. Wir geben viel Geld aus.
2. Du erkennst sie an.
3. Er paßt gut auf.

B. *Form the present tense of the verb with an inseparable prefix. Then turn the sentence into a question. Then form the past perfect tense of the original sentence. Then turn that sentence into a question.*

1. Sie beeindruckte mich.
2. Jeder erhielt zweihundert Mark.
3. Sie verboten ihm alles.

C. *Form the past participle of the verb.*

1. bekämpfen
2. erobern
3. zerstören
4. empfehlen

D. *Substitute a verb with an inseparable prefix for the prepositional phrase.*

1. gegen etwas kämpfen
2. auf etwas antworten
3. in einem Haus wohnen
4. jemand zu etwas raten

II. RELATIVE PRONOUNS, wer, was, AND INTERROGATIVE CONJUNCTIONS

A relative pronoun introduces a relative clause, which relates to and further characterizes an element in the main clause. In English, the form of the relative pronoun required depends on the item referred to: if the reference is to a person, English uses a form of "who," if to a thing, "which" or "that."

German too requires a form of the relative pronoun that depends on the antecedent, and, generally, these forms are similar to those of the definite article. Gender and number of the pronoun are determined by the antecedent— the same for both people and things; the case of the pronoun is determined by its function in the dependent clause. Thus, if the antecedent is masculine singular, so is the relative pronoun; if the pronoun is used as the subject of the dependent clause, it is in the nominative case, and so on.

Masculine Singular

nom.: Der amerikanische Freund, **der** Hans besucht, ist beeindruckt.

The American friend who is visiting Hans is impressed.

acc.: Jerry, **den** Hans schon lange kennt, kommt zu Besuch.

Jerry, whom Hans has known for a long time, is coming for a visit.

dat.: Er führt Jerry, mit **dem** er studiert hat, durch die Stadt.

He leads Jerry, with whom he has studied, through the city.

gen.: Jerry, **dessen** Freund Hans ist, hat in den USA studiert.

Jerry, whose friend is Hans, has studied in the United States.

Feminine Singular

nom.: Die Freundin, **die** ihn besucht, . . .

The friend who is visiting him. . . .

acc.: Helga, **die** er schon lange kennt, . . .

Helga, whom he has known for a long time, . . .

dat.: Die Tasse, aus **der** er getrunken hat, . . .

The cup from which he drank, . . .

gen.: Die Firma „Zeiss", **deren** Produkte jeder Experte kennt, . . .

The firm of Zeiss, whose products are known by every expert, . . .

Neuter Singular

nom.: Das Geschäft, **das** die Schaufenster dekoriert hat, . . .

The business that has decorated its shop windows. . . .

acc.: Das Schaufenster, **das** sie sehen, . . .

The shop window that they see. . . .

dat.: Das Geschäft, in **dem** er arbeitet, . . .

The business in which he is working. . . .

gen.: Das Geschäft, **dessen** Name ich vergessen habe, . . .

The business whose name I've forgotten, . . .

All Genders (*Plural*)

nom.: Die Schaufenster, **die** sehr attraktiv sind, . . .

The store windows, which are very attractive, . . .

acc.: Die Kameras, **die** du da im Schaufenster siehst, . . .

The cameras that you see there in the store window. . . .

| | dat.: | Die Ideen, von **denen** niemand etwas wissen will, . . . | The ideas that no one wants to know about. . . . |
| | gen.: | Die Eltern, **deren** Sohn ich bin, . . . | The parents whose son I am. . . . |

Relative Pronoun Forms

| | Masculine | Feminine | Neuter | All Genders |
		Singular		Plural
nom.	der	die	das	die
acc.	den	die	das	die
dat.	dem	der	dem	**denen**
gen.	**dessen**	**deren**	**dessen**	**deren**

In the table and examples above, note that certain forms differ from those of the definite article: the genitive in all four instances and the dative plural. The rest are identical to the definite article forms.

Note that a comma is used in English to distinguish between essential and nonessential clauses; in German, as with all subordinate clauses, the relative clause is set off by commas. And, again, as is true of all dependent clauses, the inflected verb stands at the end of the clause.

In English the relative pronoun may sometimes be omitted. This omission is not permissible in German.

| Der Freund, **den** ich in Amerika habe, kommt zu Besuch. | The friend [whom] I have in America is coming for a visit. |

The question words **wer** (who, whoever) and **was** (what, whatever) can also be used as indefinite relative pronouns to introduce clauses for which there is no identifiable or specific noun antecedent. **Wer** refers to people (who *or* he who) and **was** to things (what *or* that which).

| Ich weiß nicht, **wer** die Schaufenster dekoriert hat. | I don't know who decorated the store window. |
| **Wer** die Firma „Zeiss" nicht kennt, versteht nichts von Fotografie. | Whoever doesn't know of the firm "Zeiss" doesn't know anything about photography. |

Wer is declined like **der,** although since it is indefinite, it has no gender or number.

Declension of **wer**

nom.	wer
acc.	wen
dat.	wem
gen.	wessen

acc.: Er sagt nicht, **wen** er besuchen will.

He isn't saying who he intends to visit.

dat.: Wir wissen, **wem** das Geld gehört.

We know who the money belongs to.

gen.: Ich weiß nicht, **wessen** Freund er ist.

I don't know whose friend he is.

The relative pronoun **was** is used to refer to (1) a whole clause,

Was mich wirklich beeindruckt, sind die Schaufenster.

What really impresses me are the shop windows.

Was er auch sagt, glaub ihm nicht!

Whatever he says, don't believe him.

(2) a preceding indefinite **das, alles, nichts,** or **etwas,**

Sie reden über **das, was** sie gesehen haben.

They talk about that which they have seen.

Er ist von **allem, was** er sieht, begeistert.

He is enthusiastic about everything he sees.

or (3) a superlative adjective.

Natürlich ist **das erste, was** sie brauchen, Schweizer Geld.

Of course, the first thing [which] they need is Swiss money.

If **was** follows a preposition in introducing a relative clause, the respective **wo-**compound may be used.

Die meisten Geschäfte dekorieren ihre Schaufenster sehr attraktiv, **wofür** man allerdings auch höhere Preise bezahlen muß.

Most shops decorate their windows quite attractively, for which, however, you also have to pay higher prices.

Wer, was, and the other interrogative words, such as **wann, warum, wie, wieviel, wo, woher,** and **wohin,** can also be used as *subordinating conjunctions*.

In this case, they are not considered relative pronouns but interrogative conjunctions. Such usage occurs most frequently, but not exclusively, with indirect discourse (*see* Chapter 21).

Laß uns doch mal sehen, **wieviel** man hier für Kameras verlangt.	Let's see how much they're asking for cameras here.
Ich bin nicht sicher, **wo** er hingegangen ist.	I'm not sure where he went.

The use of **wann** (when?) as a subordinating conjunction must not be confused with **wenn** (when).

Ich weiß nicht, **wann** er kommt.	I don't know *when* (at what time) he's coming.
Ich rufe dich an, **wenn** er kommt.	I'll call you *when* he comes.

Check Your Comprehension

A. *Supply the appropriate form of the definite relative pronoun.*

1. Das ist das Haus, _____ ich gestern gekauft habe.
2. Der Käse, _____ du da ißt, ist aus Holland.
3. Der Kuchen, von _____ ich ein Stück gegessen habe, ist lecker.
4. Das ist der Professor, bei _____ ich studiere.
5. Das Auto, _____ Preis ich nicht kenne, ist neu.
6. Die Autoren, _____ Bücher wir lesen, sind Amerikaner.

B. *Supply the appropriate form of the indefinite relative pronoun.*

1. _____ A sagt, muß auch B sagen. (he who)
2. _____ will, soll kommen. (whoever)
3. _____ er sagt, ist richtig. (what)
4. _____ Sie tun, ist bestimmt richtig. (whatever)
5. _____ ich nicht weiß, macht mich nicht heiß. (what)
6. Ich weiß etwas, _____ du nicht weißt. (which)
7. Nichts, _____ Sie sagen, ist richtig. (what)

III. INFINITIVE PHRASES AND CLAUSES

The infinitive is often used in German, as in English, with the preposition **zu** (to).

Da braucht man kein teures Hotelzimmer **zu nehmen**.	There you don't need to take an expensive hotel room.
Das ist leicht **zu lernen**.	That's easy to learn.

In an infinitive clause when a verb with a separable prefix is used, **zu** is placed between the prefix and the infinitive, and the whole compound is written as one word.

Er vergaß die Schecks **einzulösen**.	He forgot to cash the checks.

With *modals* and with **lassen, gehen, sehen, hören, lehren,** and **lernen,** when used with an infinitive, the preposition **zu** is dropped.

In sechs Wochen wollen sie soviel wie möglich **kennenlernen**.	They want to get to know as much as possible in six weeks.
Laß uns doch erst mal ins Hotel **gehen!**	Let's go to the hotel first of all.
Er lernt gut Deutsch **sprechen**.	He's learning to speak German well.

In some of these instances, the infinitive is equivalent to the English **–ing** form of the verb.

Ich sehe den Zug **kommen**.	I see the train coming.
Sie geht zum ersten Mal **schwimmen**.	She's going swimming for the first time.

When the infinitive with **zu** is used to introduce a more complete infinitive phrase, such as one with a direct or indirect object, the phrase is set off by a comma and is called an *infinitive clause*.

Er bittet seine Frau, **auf das Gepäck aufzupassen**.	He asks his wife to look after the luggage.

Three conjunctions are generally used to introduce infinitive clauses: **um** (in order to), **ohne** (without), and **(an)statt** (instead of). The infinitive preceded by **zu** always stands at the end of the clause.

Die Freunde gehen über die Straße, **um** die Kameras **zu sehen**.	The friends go across the street [in order] to see the cameras.

Sie ging über die Straße, **ohne** das Schaufenster **anzusehen.**	She went across the street without looking at the store window.
Statt Einkäufe **zu machen,** trank er eine Tasse Kaffee.	Instead of going shopping he drank a cup of coffee.

Um . . . zu always refers to an intended action and is usually given the English equivalent "in order to," although English usage eliminates "in order" and prefers the shorter, simpler "to."

Wir wollen ein Auto kaufen. Wir sind in die Stadt gegangen.	We intend to buy a car. We went downtown.
→ Wir sind in die Stadt gegangen, um ein Auto zu kaufen.	→ We went downtown to buy a car.

Check Your Comprehension

A. *Supply the appropriate infinitive form of the English equivalent in parentheses.*

1. Brauchen wir Geld, um ins Kino _____? (to go)
2. Sie möchte soviel wie möglich _____. (to see)
3. Er ist hergekommen, um mit mir den Film _____. (to watch)
4. Ich gehe nach Deutschland, um Deutsch _____! (to learn to speak)
5. Statt in die Klasse _____, gehen wir heute _____! (going, swimming)
6. Lassen Sie ihn nicht länger _____! (to wait)
7. Er ist zur Bank gegangen, ohne die Schecks _____. (cashing)
8. Haben sie den Zug _____ gehört? (coming)

B. *Combine the two sentences using* **um . . . zu** *to form an infinitive clause that indicates intention.*

1. Sie gehen über die Straße. Sie wollen Kameras sehen.
2. Wir brauchen ein Auto. Wir wollen in die Stadt fahren.
3. Er ging ins Geschäft. Er möchte einen Film kaufen.

CONVERSATION

Vor dem Fotogeschäft

Hans führt seinen amerikanischen Freund Jerry Thompson, den er in den USA kennengelernt hat, durch die Geschäftsstraßen seiner Heimatstadt. Jerry, der zum ersten Mal Deutschland besucht, spricht recht gut Deutsch.

JERRY   Was mich wirklich beeindruckt, sind die Schaufenster hier, die ich sehr attraktiv finde. 5

HANS Ja, das stimmt. Die meisten Geschäfte dekorieren ihre Schaufenster tatsächlich sehr attraktiv, wofür man allerdings auch höhere Preise bezahlen muß.

JERRY Ja, für Werbung gibt man sehr viel Geld aus. Du, laß uns doch mal sehen, wieviel man hier für die Kameras verlangt, die da drüben im Schaufenster stehen.   10

    Die beiden Freunde überqueren die Straße, um zu sehen, was die Kameras kosten. Plötzlich kommt ein Taxi um die Ecke. Mit quietschenden Bremsen hält es direkt vor ihnen an.

HANS Paß auf!   15

JERRY Mensch, der Kerl hat uns aber beinahe erwischt! Natürlich ein Taxifahrer! Wer so wild fährt, ist verrückt. Oder bekämpft man hier die Bevölkerungsexplosion mit Autos?

HANS Na ja, ganz so schlimm ist es wohl nicht.

JERRY Aha! Hier sind die Kameras. Mensch, die Preise sind ja astronomisch!   20
Ganz wie bei uns. Da in der Ecke steht eine „Rolleiflex", die man bei uns nicht unter dreihundert Dollar erhält. Und sieh mal dort die vielen japanischen Kameras!

HANS Tja, Japans optische Industrie beherrscht wohl den Weltmarkt. Da kommt man nicht mehr mit.   25

JERRY Wieso? Die Firma „Leica", deren Produkte doch beinahe jeder kennt, ist doch sicher ebenso gut wie „Nikon".

HANS Oh, damit erinnerst du mich, daß ich ja noch einen Farbfilm brauche.

JERRY Und ich will mal sehen, ob ich hier einen „Kodak"-Film für meine Kamera bekommen kann.   30

ORAL PRACTICE

A. *Put the sentence into the present perfect tense.*

1. Ich steige aus.
2. Das Taxi hält an.
3. Sie fährt hin.

4. Er kommt her.
5. Wir laden ihn ein.
6. Sie geben zuviel Geld aus.
7. Dieses Wort kann er nicht aussprechen.
8. Ich rief dich gestern an.
9. Er lernt sie heute abend kennen.

B. *Put the sentence into the past perfect tense.*

1. Sie beantworteten die Fragen.
2. Ich bezahlte ihm das Bier.
3. Niemand bekämpft die Bevölkerungsexplosion.
4. König William eroberte England.
5. Sie verstehen nicht viel von Fotografie.
6. Du zerstörst deine Gesundheit.
7. Man empfahl uns dieses Hotel.
8. Ich erhielt deinen Brief.

C. *Turn the sentence into a question.*

1. Sie fährt bestimmt hin.
2. Sie ist bestimmt hingefahren.
3. Ich steige hier aus.
4. Ich bin hier ausgestiegen.
5. Er paßt gut auf.
6. Er hat gut aufgepaßt.
7. Der Bus fährt am Bahnhof vorbei.
8. Der Bus ist am Bahnhof vorbeigefahren.
9. Sie betrachten die Kameras.
10. Er hat die Emanzipation der Frau bekämpft.

D. *Substitute each verb in parentheses for the verb in boldface.*

1. Er hat das Taxi **bestellt.**
   (anrufen / erwarten / reparieren / empfehlen / bezahlen / verlangen)

2. Man hat den Studenten **eingeladen.**

(anerkennen / beeindrucken / abholen / erwischen / hinbringen / empfehlen / mitnehmen / beraten)

3. Ich **schrieb** den Brief, den du suchst.

(erhalten / durchlesen / verbrennen / hinbringen / bekommen / verlieren / empfangen)

E. *Substitute each item in parentheses for the noun in boldface and make the necessary changes.*

1. Das **Auto,** das ich gekauft habe, ist neu.

(Tisch / Vase / Buch / Haus / Schüssel / Maschine / Stuhl / Sofa)

2. Der **Wagen,** mit dem du fährst, ist kaputt.

(Bus / Taxi / Straßenbahn / Zug / Fahrrad / die Autos)

3. Das **Hotel,** dessen Name ich vergessen habe, ist wirklich gut.

(Kamera / Busfahrer / Schwimmbad / Dampfer / Speise / Restaurant / Pilot / die Kinder)

F. *Supply the appropriate form of the relative pronoun.*

1. Die Milch, _____ sie trinken, ist frisch.
2. Der Ball, mit _____ wir spielen, ist kaputt.
3. Hunde, _____ bellen, beißen nicht.
4. Das Auto, _____ Besitzer ich nicht kenne, ist ganz neu.
5. Die Frau, _____ Uhr kaputt ist, hat viel Geld.
6. Die Autoren, _____ Bücher wir lesen, sind Schweizer.
7. Die Leute, bei _____ ich wohne, sind sehr nett.

G. *Supply the appropriate form of the indefinite relative pronoun* (**wer** *or* **was**).

1. _____ das gesagt hat, ist sehr intelligent.
2. Er weiß nicht, _____ das Geld gehört.
3. _____ immer du tust, ist leider vergeblich.
4. Das Wichtigste, _____ Sie jetzt brauchen, ist Geld.
5. Du hast an alles gedacht, _____ (for which) ich dir danke.
6. Ich glaube Ihnen alles, _____ Sie sagen.

H. *Transform each sentence with the subordinating conjunction* **weil** *into a sentence with the infinitive phrase* **um . . . zu.**

    EXAMPLE   Er tut das, weil er Geld bekommen will.
                  Er tut das, um Geld zu bekommen.

1. Ich gehe zu Fuß, weil ich gesund bleiben möchte.
2. Wir gehen ins Konzert, weil wir Beethoven hören wollen.
3. Sie gehen ins Café, weil sie Eis essen möchten.
4. Er achtet auf seine Diät, weil er nicht zunehmen will.
5. Ihr geht jeden Tag schwimmen, weil ihr fit bleiben wollt.

I. *Substitute or add each phrase as it is introduced into the previous sentence and make any necessary structural changes.*

Hans,   dessen Vater ich kenne, reist viel, um etwas zu erleben.
Sonja, _____
_____ Mutter _____ _____
_____ nicht _____
_____, statt zu Hause zu bleiben.
Die Freunde, _____
_____ Eltern _____

GUIDED CONVERSATION

A. Begin a discussion with someone in your class regarding camera equipment. Among other things, you might comment on the following: whether you have a camera, what kind of camera it is, your reasons for choosing it, where it was made, whether it takes good pictures, how it compares with other cameras, what type of camera or camera equipment you would like and why, which brands impress you most or least and why, and so on.

B. Think of a popular item on the market today (small, compact cars, for example) and discuss it with someone in your class. Exchange views on why people want the item, what various companies are asking for it, what impresses you about it, how it compares with similar items on the market, and so on.

AUSLÄNDISCHE BANKNOTEN			ANKAUF	VERKAUF
Belgien	100	bfrs	6.35	6.65
England	1	£	6.08	6.33
Frankreich	100	FF	53.00	56.00
Holland	100	hfl	94.75	97.00
Italien	1000	Lit	3.55	3.77
Östereich	100	öS	13.40	13.75
Schweden	100	skr	57.00	59.50
Schweiz	100	sfrs	84.25	86.25
Spanien	100	Ptas	4.60	4.85
USA	1	$	2.72	2.83

READING

In der Wechselstube

Herr und Frau Stein aus Milwaukee bereisen zum ersten Mal Europa. In sechs Wochen wollen sie soviel wie möglich kennenlernen, was natürlich sehr anstrengend sein kann. Die vielen Museen und Kathedralen, die man gesehen haben muß; die Exkursionen, die man mitmachen möchte; die fremden Speisen, an die man nicht gewöhnt ist—all das ermüdet sehr, beson- 5
ders wenn man nicht mehr der Jüngste ist wie Herr Stein.

Gerade eben sind Herr und Frau Stein mit dem Trans-Europa-Express (TEE) von München kommend in Zürich eingetroffen. Das erste, was sie brauchen, ist natürlich Schweizer Geld. Herr Stein geht in eine Wechselstube, um einige Reiseschecks einzulösen. 10

Vor dem Schalter stehen eine Menge Touristen, von denen viele Englisch sprechen. Sie reden über das, was sie hier und da erlebt haben; wieviel sie für dieses oder jenes Hotel bezahlen mußten; und darüber, ob man sie freundlich oder unfreundlich empfangen hat. Unter den Leuten am Schalter sind auch einige Gastarbeiter[1] aus Italien, Jugoslawien und der Türkei, die sehr 15
schnell in ihren fremden Sprachen sprechen. In einer Ecke steht eine Gruppe

junger Leute mit hohen Rucksäcken. Sie lachen darüber, daß ein Mädchen auf ihrem Rucksack eingeschlafen ist.

„Wie schön, wenn man jung ist", denkt Herr Stein. „Da braucht man keine teuren Hotelzimmer zu nehmen, wenn man ausruhen will." Er be- [20] trachtet etwas melancholisch seine Reiseschecks und fragt den Beamten am Schalter, wieviele Schweizer Franken er für den Dollar bekommt. Der junge Mann, der sehr gut Englisch spricht, beantwortet die Frage, worauf Herr Stein zweihundert Dollar einwechselt. Dann geht er zu seiner Frau zurück, die in der Bahnhofshalle gewartet hat, um auf das Gepäck aufzupassen. [25]

Frau Stein empfängt ihren Mann mit den Worten: „Da bist du ja! Du, ich habe gehört, die Geschäfte in der Bahnhofstraße sollen ausgezeichnet sein. Da können wir gleich einige Souvenirs kaufen. Du weißt doch, ich wollte schon immer eine Schweizer Uhr." Herr Stein ist nicht besonders begeistert von diesem Gedanken. Er meint: „Laß uns doch erst mal ins Hotel gehen! [30] Vielleicht kann man da ein Schnäpschen bekommen", worauf Frau Stein erwidert: „Aber Max, schon wieder?"

---

[1] Laborers from countries outside Germany, generally the Mediterranean countries. Presently, there are over two million "Gastarbeiter" in West Germany.

QUESTIONS

1. Was machen Herr und Frau Stein?
2. Warum ist das Reisen für die Steins etwas anstrengend?
3. Wo sind die beiden gerade angekommen?
4. Was ist das erste, was sie brauchen?
5. Was macht Herr Stein in der Wechselstube?
6. Worüber reden die Leute vor dem Schalter?
7. Worüber lachen die jungen Leute?
8. Was denkt Herr Stein?
9. Was fragt er den Beamten am Schalter?
10. Wieviel Dollar wechselt er ein?
11. Warum wartet Frau Stein in der Bahnhofshalle?
12. Was möchte sie am liebsten sofort tun?
13. Wie reagiert ihr Mann darauf?
14. Was möchte Herr Stein am liebsten zuerst tun?
15. Was denkt seine Frau über diese Idee?

VOCABULARY EXERCISES

Supply the appropriate word from the list on the right.

1. Die Steins _____ zum ersten Mal Europa.
2. In sechs Wochen wollen sie soviel wie möglich _____.
3. Die Exkursionen, die man _____ möchte, sind sehr anstrengend.
4. Herr und Frau Stein sind gerade mit dem Zug _____.
5. Herr Stein geht zu einer Wechselstube, um einige Reiseschecks _____.
6. Die Leute reden darüber, ob man sie nett oder unfreundlich _____ hat.
7. Sie lachen, weil ein Mädchen auf ihrem Rucksack _____ ist.
8. Herr Stein _____ zweihundert Dollar.
9. Seine Frau muß auf das Gepäck _____.
10. "Aber Max, schon wieder?", _____ Frau Stein.

a. einzulösen
b. aufpassen
c. bereisen
d. erwidert
e. kennenlernen
f. eingeschlafen
g. mitmachen
h. empfangen
i. angekommen
j. wechselt

Review Exercises

A. *Put the sentence into the past tense.*

1. Sie sind aus dem Bus ausgestiegen und haben ein Taxi gerufen.
2. Nach dem Essen trinken sie einen schönen warmen Kaffee.
3. Wir wechseln Geld und machen einige Einkäufe.
4. Dieses Wort haben Sie sehr gut ausgesprochen.
5. Ich habe diese junge Dame gestern abend kennengelernt.
6. Wir hatten ihn nach seinem Examen zu einer Party eingeladen.
7. Wenn wir nach Europa fliegen, geben wir immer sehr viel Geld aus.
8. Sie hatte alle Fragen ausgezeichnet beantworten können.

9. Der Krieg hat viele Städte und Dörfer zerstört.
10. Die Polizei hat leider zu gut aufgepaßt.

B. *Put the sentence into the present perfect tense.*

1. Er bezahlte das Bier und fuhr nach Hause.
2. Sie kam, sah ihn und eroberte ihn in wenigen Stunden.
3. Dieses blonde Mädchen beeindruckte ihn so sehr, daß er sie eine Woche später heiratete.
4. Wir vergaßen das Fußballspiel ganz.
5. Sie verbrennt immer seine Briefe, nachdem sie sie gelesen hat.
6. Ich lese die Zeitung nur selten ganz durch.
7. Verstehen Sie die Vorlesung über sprachliche Kommunikation?
8. Mein Freund ruft mich jedes Mal an, wenn er in Stuttgart ist.
9. Du holtest mich ab, um mit mir ins Kino zu gehen.
10. Wir gehen oft schwimmen, um gesund zu bleiben.

C. *Supply the appropriate form of the relative pronoun.*

1. Das sind die Studenten, _____ ich meine.
2. Das sind die Studenten, mit _____ wir reden wollen.
3. Das sind die Studenten, _____ immer zu wenig Geld haben.
4. Das sind die Studenten, _____ Interesse Deutsch ist.
5. Das sind die Studenten, _____ wirklich sehr intelligent sind.
6. Das sind die Studenten, gegen _____ ich nichts habe.
7. Das sind die Studenten, von _____ man viel Gutes gehört hat.
8. Das ist die Summerhill Schule, über _____ man viel gelesen hat.
9. Das ist die Summerhill Schule, in _____ so wenige Schüler sind.
10. Das ist die Summerhill Schule, _____ so ausgezeichnet ist.
11. Das ist die Summerhill Schule, in _____ die Schüler gerne gehen.
12. Das ist die Summerhill Schule, _____ so weltberühmt ist.
13. Das ist die Summerhill Schule, von _____ man so viel hört.
14. Das ist die Summerhill Schule, _____ Schüler emanzipiert sind.

D. *Supply the appropriate form of the indefinite relative pronoun* (**wer** *or* **was**).

1. Ich weiß nicht, von _____ du das gehört hast.
2. Sie weiß genau, _____ sie will.

3. Weißt du, _____ Eltern aus Schottland in die USA eingewandert sind?
4. Ich weiß wirklich nicht, _____ ich getan habe.
5. Sie will ihren Eltern nicht sagen, _____ sie heiraten will.
6. Wir wissen genau, an _____ du einen Brief geschrieben hast.
7. _____ Chinesisch versteht, muß sehr intelligent sein.
8. Ich weiß nicht, _____ von euch beiden ich glauben kann.

E. *Transform the sentence by using the infinitive phrase* **um . . . zu.**

1. Er will nach Hause gehen, weil er das Fußballspiel sehen will.
2. Viele Leute fahren nach Arizona, weil sie den Grand Canyon sehen möchten.
3. Manche Leute bereisen Europa, weil sie die alten Kathedralen sehen wollen.
4. Ich fahre in die DDR, weil ich die Städte Leipzig und Dresden besuchen möchte.
5. Viele Menschen leben, weil sie arbeiten möchten.
6. Manche Menschen arbeiten, weil sie leben möchten.
7. Wir lernen Deutsch, weil wir einmal deutsche Literatur lesen möchten.
8. Andere lernen Deutsch, weil sie einmal deutsche Zeitschriftenartikel lesen wollen.
9. Einige lernen Französisch, weil sie in Frankreich studieren wollen.
10. Manche wollen viel Geld haben, weil sie einmal Europa bereisen wollen.

F. *Express in German.*

1. Don't spend too much money in Europe.
2. He is doing that in order to travel through Germany.
3. This is the camera that I talked to you about last night.
4. The most important thing (that) I can recommend to you is to remain healthy.
5. I believe everything he says.
6. The letter, for which I thank you, arrived yesterday.
7. Whatever he does, it is always excellent.
8. I can't tell to whom this luggage belongs.
9. I don't know yet who I'm going to marry.
10. These are the children whose parents are in the hospital.

GUIDED COMPOSITION

A. The etching is of seventeenth-century Munich. Write a short composition regarding this picture. You might describe the various buildings and how they differ from those you see in modern American cities, suggest what the people in the market place are doing, and give your overall impressions of the scene.

B. Is there a city in East or West Germany, Austria, or Switzerland you would especially like to visit? Look the city up in an encyclopedia or travel guide and read about the main attractions. Then write an itinerary of the things you would like to do and see, and the places within the city you would like to visit during an extended stay there.

Der Marckt zu München.

Chapter 16

Lübeck

Useful Phrases

frühstücken	to have breakfast
zu Mittag essen*	to have lunch
zu Abend essen	to have dinner
Entschuldigung!	Excuse me.
Verzeihung!	Pardon me.
gerade eben	just now
sich Sorgen machen um	to worry about
Es klingelt.	The bell rings.
um Punkt zwölf Uhr	at twelve o'clock sharp

MODEL SENTENCES

I

Ich erinnere **ihn** an den Film.	I remind him of the film.
Ich erinnere **mich** an den Film.	I remember the film.
Er **freut sich auf** seinen Urlaub.	He's looking forward to his vacation.
Sie **freut sich über** die Blumen.	She's very pleased about the flowers.
Du mußt **dich** heute dem Chef **vorstellen**.	You have to introduce yourself to the boss today.
Ich **stelle mir** das sehr interessant **vor**.	I imagine that is quite interesting.

II

In unserer Klasse sind über **fünfund-dreißig** Studenten.	There are over thirty-five students in our class.
Heute ist **Montag, der 22. Januar 1985.****	Today is Monday, January 22, 1985.

III

Um Punkt 8 Uhr stehe ich auf.	I get up at 8 o'clock on the dot.
Ich esse Frühstück **um halb neun**.	I eat breakfast at 8:30 a.m.

---

* Most German families serve a big meal at lunch time, comparable to the American dinner. The evening meal is usually a lighter meal, similar to the American supper.

** Read: Heute ist Montag, der zweiundzwanzigste Januar neunzehnhundertfünfundachtzig.

Um wieviel Uhr fängt der Film an?	[At] what time does the movie start?
Wir unterhielten uns **den ganzen Abend** darüber.	We spoke about it [for] the entire evening.
Heute morgen bin ich spät aufgestanden.	This morning I got up late.

Grammar Explanations

I. REFLEXIVE PRONOUNS AND VERBS

Reflexive pronouns reflect, or refer to or turn back to, the subject of the verb: the reflexive pronoun and the subject are the same person or thing. In English, the addition of the suffix **–self** or **–selves** to the personal pronoun forms the reflexive pronoun.

> I overworked myself.
> He hurt himself.
> They excused themselves.

In German, a set of reflexive pronouns is used rather than suffixes. The first- and familiar second-person forms are identical to the accusative and dative personal pronouns; but the third- and polite second-person forms use a special reflexive: **sich.**

Reflexive Pronouns

	Accusative	*Dative*	*Accusative and Dative*
	Singular		*Plural*
1st pers.	mich	mir	uns
2nd pers. fam.	dich	dir	euch
3rd pers.	sich	sich	sich
2nd pers. pol.	sich	sich	sich

| Ich kämme **mich.** | I comb my hair [myself]. |
| Ich wasche **mir** die Hände. | I wash my hands. |

Hast du **dich** am Muttertag an deine Mutter erinnert?	Did you remember your mother on Mother's Day?
Wie stellst du **dir** das vor?	How do you envision that?
Er erinnert **sich** an den Film.	He remembers the film.
Wir freuen **uns** auf den Urlaub.	We're looking forward to the vacation.
Ihr kämmt **euch.**	You comb your hair [yourselves].
Sie stellen **sich** etwas Fantastisches vor.	They imagine something fantastic.
Haben Sie **sich** der Chefin vorgestellt?	Did you introduce yourself to the (female) boss?

Often reflexive verbs are logical extensions of nonreflexive verbs.

waschen (to wash)

sich waschen (to wash oneself)

But notice that the verb is reflexive only when the subject and object refer to the *same* person or thing.

Not reflexive	*Reflexive*
Sie wäscht den Hund.	Sie wäscht sich.
(She's washing the dog.)	(She's washing herself.)

The reflexive pronoun can be either in the accusative or dative case, depending on whether the pronoun is used as a direct or an indirect object. Usually the reflexive is in the accusative, but if the sentence already has an accusative object, the reflexive pronoun will be in the dative case.

Accusative

Max, zieh **dich** mal an!   Max, now get dressed.

	Dative	*Accusative*	
Hast du	**dir**	die Filmanzeige	angesehen?	Have you looked at the movie advertisement?

Certain reflexive verbs always take the dative case; certain others take the accusative. In this chapter and in the end vocabulary, only the reflexive pronouns that must be in the dative case are indicated. The other reflexive verbs take reflexive pronouns in the accusative case according to the rules above.

sich **freuen**   to be glad *or* pleased

sich **überlegen** (*dat.*)   to ponder

acc.: Ich freute **mich** riesig.	I was quite happy.
dat.: Ich überlege **mir** eben, ob ich hier bleiben soll.	I'm just thinking whether I should stay here.

In rare instances, a verb used reflexively may have the reflexive pronoun either in the accusative or the dative. With the change in case, the meaning of the verb also changes.

dat.: Stell **dir** das vor!	Just imagine that!
acc.: Ich stellte **mich** vor.	I introduced myself.

In certain instances, the same verb used nonreflexively and reflexively has two different meanings.

Not Reflexive	*Reflexive*
Ich **erinnere** meinen Bruder **an** den Film.	Ich **erinnere mich an** den Film.
(I remind my brother about the movie.)	(I remember the movie.)
Er **setzte** das Glas **hin.**	Er **setzte sich hin.**
(He put down the glass.)	(He sat down.)

In German, when an action refers to a part of the body, possessive pronouns are not used. Instead of saying "I wash my face," the German speaker says, literally, "I wash the face to myself." Thus, the definite article is used in conjunction with the part of the body, and both are preceded by a dative reflexive pronoun.

	Dative	*Accusative*	
Ich wasche	mir	das Gesicht.	I wash my face.
Du kämmst	dir	die Haare.	You comb your hair.

At times, a dative reflexive pronoun is used *affectively* to stress the significance of the action for the performer or subject. This is also true in English colloquial usage.

Ich kaufe **mir** ein neues Kleid.	I'm going to buy me a new dress.
Ich nehme **mir** ein Buch vom Regal.	I'm taking [me] a book from the shelf.

In these instances, the reflexive pronoun is used for emphasis and doesn't change the meaning of the sentence. The pronoun in these cases could be omitted, but most German speakers include it to clarify for whom the action is done.

Wir haben die Mäntel angezogen.	
Wir haben **uns** die Mäntel angezogen.	We put on our coats.
Ich kaufe ein neues Auto.	
Ich kaufe **mir** ein neues Auto.	I'm buying (me) a new car.

In order to add emphasis to the actor, the word **selbst** or **selber** (self), which is the same for all persons and numbers, can be used. Usually, the use of either word stresses the fact that the actor did the action alone, without any help. This usage occurs very often with the reflexive pronoun to add double emphasis.

Ich wasche mich **selbst.**	I wash myself (all by myself).
Das Kind zog sich **selbst** an.	The child dressed himself (all by himself).
Wir emanzipierten Frauen zünden uns **selber** die Zigaretten an.	We emancipated women light our own cigarettes.

Many reflexive verbs occur in conjunction with a preposition, some always and some only in certain instances. The preposition must be memorized as part of the complete phrase. The accusative prepositions (**für, gegen,** and so on) govern the accusative case, and the dative prepositions (**aus, von,** and so on), the dative case. Those prepositions that take either the dative or the accusative generally take the accusative case when used in conjunction with a reflexive verb, but this is not always true, so be sure to note which case is required. Some of these reflexive verbs and their prepositions included in this chapter are the following.

sich **ärgern** (**über** + *acc.*)   to be upset *or* angry (about)
sich **entscheiden** (**für** + *acc.*)   to decide (on)
sich **entschließen** (**für** + *acc.*) to decide (on)
sich **freuen** (**auf** + *acc.*; **über** + *acc.*)   to be glad (look forward to; be happy about)
sich **fürchten** (**vor** + *dat.*)   to be afraid (of)
sich **interessieren für** + *acc.*   to be interested in
sich **kümmern um** + *acc.*   to worry *or* be concerned about

Note that the preposition in parentheses may or may not be used with the verb. The preposition not in parentheses must always be used in the phrase.

In the plural, the reflexive pronoun can also have a reciprocal meaning: "one another" or "each other."

Sie begrüßten sich.   They greeted each other.

A. *Supply the appropriate reflexive pronoun.*

1. Ich kümmere _____ darum.
2. Sie freuen _____.
3. Du kämmst _____.
4. Er wäscht _____.
5. Wir entschuldigen _____.
6. Ihr ärgert _____ über den Regen.
7. Ich entscheide _____ dagegen.
8. Interessierst du _____ für Deutsch?
9. Ich entschließe _____ abzufahren.
10. Sie erinnern _____ an diesen Tag.
11. Du ziehst _____ an.
12. Wir fühlen _____ frisch.

B. *Supply the appropriate reflexive pronoun.*

1. Ich kämme _____ die Haare.
2. Du wäschst _____ das Gesicht.
3. Wir ziehen _____ die Schuhe aus.
4. Ihr seht _____ den Film an.
5. Ich schaue _____ die Post an.
6. Du hast _____ den Film anders vorgestellt.
7. Ich zünde _____ eine Zigarette an.

II. CARDINAL AND ORDINAL NUMBERS AND DATES

Cardinal numbers are used for counting and indicating quantity. As noted in the discussion of indefinite articles, **ein** means both "one" and "a"; it is declined just as an **ein**-word, even when it refers to the number one. When **ein** stands alone as a pronoun or noun, it takes the strong **der**-word endings. In counting, the form becomes **eins**. All other cardinal numbers cannot be declined.

Er hat nur **einen** Koffer.		He has only one suitcase.	
Einer der beiden Koffer kam nicht an.		One of the two [both] suitcases did not arrive.	
Eins und **eins** sind **zwei.**		One and one are two.	

Cardinal Numbers

0	null	19	neunzehn
1	eins (ein–)	20	**zwan**zig
2	zwei	21	**ein**undzwanzig
3	drei	30	dreißig
4	vier	40	vierzig
5	fünf	50	fünfzig
6	sechs	60	**sech**zig
7	sieben	70	**sieb**zig
8	acht	80	achtzig
9	neun	90	neunzig
10	zehn	100	(ein)hundert
11	elf	101	(ein)hunderteins
12	zwölf	200	zweihundert
13	dreizehn	1000	(ein)tausend
14	vierzehn	1100	(ein)tausendeinhundert
15	fünfzehn	1101	(ein)tausendeinhunderteins
16	**sech**zehn	2000	zweitausend
17	**sieb**zehn	1000000	eine Million
18	achtzehn	2000000	zwei Millionen

Compound numbers are always written as one word. Notice that the unit number precedes the ten number.

66	sechsundsechzig
124	hundertvierundzwanzig
4210	viertausendzweihundertzehn
1925	neunzehnhundertfünfundzwanzig

A space may be used to separate units: **1 000, 2 500 000.** A comma is used to indicate the English decimal point: **$325,25.** The percentage **5,6 Prozent** is read as **fünf Komma sechs Prozent** (five point six percent). Cardinal numbers may be used as nouns and such nouns are always feminine.

Für mich ist **die Dreizehn** eine Glückszahl.   Thirteen is a lucky number for me.

Ordinal numbers refer to a specific number in a series and are declined just like adjectives. They rarely occur without a preceding **der-** or **ein-**word.

Er trinkt schon die **dritte** Tasse Kaffee.	He's already drinking his third cup of coffee.
Ihr **zweiter** Mann hieß Eugen.	Her second husband's name was Eugen.

Notice that ordinal numbers when written in figures are followed by a period.

Lincolns Geburtstag ist am **12.** Februar.   Lincoln's birthday is on February twelfth.

Ordinal numbers are formed by adding **–t** to the cardinal numbers one to nineteen and **–st** to twenty and above plus the adjective ending. Note the slight irregularities in **erste, dritte, siebte,** and **achte;** also note the formation of **hunderterste** (hundred and first).

Ordinal Numbers

1. der die das } **erste**	19. der die das } neunzehnte
2. zweite	20. zwanzigste
3. **dritte**	21. einundzwanzigste
4. vierte	30. dreißigste
5. fünfte	40. vierzigste
6. sechste	50. fünfzigste
7. **siebte**	60. sechzigste
8. **achte**	70. siebzigste
9. neunte	80. achtzigste
10. zehnte	90. neunzigste
11. elfte	100. (ein)hundertste
12. zwölfte	101. (ein)hundert**erste**
13. dreizehnte	200. zweihundertste
14. vierzehnte	1000. (ein)tausendste
15. fünfzehnte	2000. zweitausendste
16. sechzehnte	1000000. millionste
17. siebzehnte	2000000. zweimillionste
18. achtzehnte	

Ordinal numbers can be used as nouns, in which case they follow the same rules as adjectives used as nouns (*see* Chapter 11) and are capitalized.

Er ist **der Dritte** in seiner Klasse.   He's third in his class.

Ihr Dritter hieß Eugen.   Her third (husband)'s name was Eugen.

Roman numerals may be used with names of royalty.

Elizabeth II.
Elizabeth die Zweite } Elizabeth the 2nd

References to parts of the day, days of the week, and months and seasons of the year are all masculine except for "the night."

The Day

> der Morgen (morning)
> der Vormittag (before noon)
> der Mittag (noon)
> der Nachmittag (afternoon)
> der Abend (evening)
> die Nacht (night)
> die Mitternacht (midnight)

Days of the Week

der Montag (Monday)	am Montag (on Monday)	montags (on Mondays)
der Dienstag (Tuesday)	am Dienstag (on Tuesday)	dienstags (on Tuesdays)
der Mittwoch (Wednesday)	am Mittwoch (on Wednesday)	mittwochs (on Wednesdays)
der Donnerstag (Thursday)	am Donnerstag (on Thursday)	donnerstags (on Thursdays)
der Freitag (Friday)	am Freitag (on Friday)	freitags (on Fridays)
der Samstag *or* Sonnabend (Saturday)	am Samstag *or* Sonnabend (on Saturday)	samstags *or* sonnabends (on Saturdays)
der Sonntag (Sunday)	am Sonntag (on Sunday)	sonntags (on Sundays)

Months and Seasons of the Year

der Januar (January)	der Juli (July)	der Frühling (spring)
der Februar (February)	der August (August)	der Sommer (summer)
der März (March)	der September (September)	der Herbst (fall)
der April (April)	der Oktober (October)	der Winter (winter)
der Mai (May)	der November (November)	
der Juni (June)	der Dezember (December)	

Dates are always written in the order day, month, year.

Die Weihnachtsferien fangen am 18. Dezember an.	Christmas vacation begins on December 18.
Er flog am 5. Juni 1976 (5. 6. 1976) nach Europa.	He flew to Europe on June 5, 1976.

It is impossible to say "in 1978" in German; say either **1978** or **im Jahre 1978.**
Units of currency and measurement do not have plural forms when used with numbers.

Es kostet vier Mark.	It costs four marks.
Zwei Dutzend Eier kosten jetzt fast drei Dollar.	Two dozen eggs cost almost three dollars now.
Wieviele Zentimeter hat ein Meter?	How many centimeters are in a meter?

Adverbs of time can be made from the days of the week and parts of the day to denote habitual or repetitious action. When used as adverbs, the nouns are lower-cased and an **–s** is added.

Ich fahre **montags** meistens nach Köln.	Mondays I usually drive to Cologne.
Er schläft **abends** sehr früh ein.	He falls asleep evenings very early.

Check Your Comprehension

Supply the complete spelling of the figure in parentheses.

1. Ich wohne in der Leopoldstraße _____. (74)
2. Wir brauchen _____ Kisten. (85)

3. Dieses Auto hat _____ Mark gekostet. (5500)

4. _____ dieser beiden Fahrräder gehört mir. (1)

5. Die _____ ist meine Glückszahl. (7)

6. Ihr habt wirklich nur _____ Auto? (1)

7. Ja, wir haben wirklich nur _____ Wagen; der andere ist kaputt. (1)

8. Ich habe genau _____ Mark auf der Bank. (100)

9. Er raucht schon die _____ Zigarette. (3)

10. Sie hat bestimmt nicht am _____ Februar Geburtstag. (30.)

III. TIME

A. Telling Time

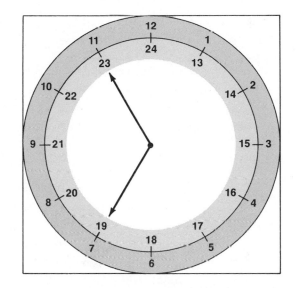

Telling time is based on a twenty-four hour clock in Germany when the expression of time is read as o'clock; a.m. and p.m. are not used.

Es ist jetzt dreizehn Uhr.	It's 1:00 p.m.
Ich gehe um 19.20 (neunzehn Uhr zwanzig) ins Kino.	I'm going to the movies at 7:20 p.m.

Such usage of the twenty-four hour clock is especially widespread in official use: in timetables, theater programs, and, as in America, in the military.

Der Film fängt um 20.00 (zwanzig Uhr) an.	The movie begins at 8:00 p.m.
Der Bus fährt um 15.30 (fünfzehn Uhr dreißig) ab.	The bus is departing at 3:30 p.m.

As in English, however, the twelve-hour clock is generally used in conversation to indicate both morning and afternoon. Sometimes an adverb of time is used to indicate a.m. and p.m.

Er fährt um neun Uhr morgens ab.   He's leaving at 9 o'clock in the morning.

German is similar to English in its use of **nach** and **vor** to indicate minutes past or before the hour.

Es ist zwanzig Minuten nach neun.   It's twenty minutes after nine.
Es ist zehn Minuten vor acht.   It's ten minutes before eight.

Fractions are more commonly used to express the English "quarter after," "half past," and "quarter to."

Es ist viertel nach zwei.   It's quarter after two.
Es ist viertel vor eins.   It's quarter to one.
Es ist dreiviertel vier.   It's 3:45 [*lit.* three-quarters of the way to four].
Es ist halb acht.   It's 7:30 [*lit.* half way to eight].

Thus, the time 7:45 p.m. can be expressed in all of the following ways.

Es ist fünfzehn Minuten vor acht.
Es ist sieben Uhr fünfundvierzig.
Es ist viertel vor acht.
Es ist dreiviertel acht.
Es ist neunzehn Uhr fünfundvierzig.

With official indication of time, fractions cannot be used.

Study the following sentences very carefully and observe especially how the time is expressed in German in contrast to English.

MEIN TAGESLAUF
(The Course of My Day)

Um sechs (Uhr) wache ich auf.　　At six (o'clock) I wake up.

Um viertel nach sechs stehe ich auf.　　At a quarter past six I get up.

Um viertel vor sieben frühstücke ich.　　At a quarter to seven I have breakfast.

Um zwanzig nach sieben lese ich die Zeitung.　　At twenty (minutes) past seven I read the paper.

Um halb acht fahre ich zum Büro.　　At half past seven I go to my office.

Um acht oder **fünf nach acht** beginne ich mit der Arbeit.　　At eight or five past eight I start working.

Von **eins** (*or* von **ein Uhr**) bis **halb zwei** esse ich zu Mittag.　　From one (o'clock) to one-thirty I have lunch.

Von **halb zwei** bis **fünf** arbeite ich wieder im Büro.　　From one-thirty to five I work in my office again.

Um viertel vor sechs komme ich meistens nach Hause.　　At a quarter to six I usually get home.

Von **sechs** bis **halb sieben** arbeite ich meistens im Garten.　　From six to six-thirty I usually work in the garden.

Um halb sieben essen wir gewöhnlich zu Abend.　　At half past six we usually eat dinner.

Um sieben schaue ich mir die Nachrichten im Fernsehen an.　　At seven I watch the news on TV.

Von **zwanzig nach sieben** bis **zehn** lese ich ein Buch, höre Musik oder schaue mir einen Fernseh-Krimi an.

From twenty past seven to ten I read a book, listen to music, or watch a detective story on TV.

 Zwischen **halb elf** und **elf** gehe ich gewöhnlich zu Bett.

Between ten-thirty and eleven I usually go to bed.

B. Expressions of Time

There are two expressions that can be used (1) to ask for the time,

Wie spät ist es?
Wieviel Uhr ist es? } What time is it?

(2) to ask for the date,

Der wievielte ist heute?
Welches Datum haben wir heute? } What's the date today?

or (3) to ask when (at what time) something is to be done.

Wann gehen wir ins Kino?
Um wieviel Uhr gehen wir ins Kino? } When (at what time) are we going to the movies?

Note that **um** denoting "at" is not a contraction of preposition plus article as is **im** for **in dem.**

Um Mitternacht ist es dunkel.
Im Frühling ist es warm.

It's dark at midnight.
It's warm in spring.

Certain time expressions are used without any preposition to specify when something happened; when these occur, they are called *definite time* expressions and are in the accusative case.

Er ist **jedes Jahr** hergekommen.
Wir fahren **nächsten Montag** in Urlaub.

He has come here every year.
We're going on vacation next Monday.

The expressions **heute morgen** (this morning), **gestern abend** (last night), **morgen nachmittag** (tomorrow afternoon), and so on are considered adverbs of time and are thus not capitalized. Other expressions refer to *indefinite* time and take the *genitive* case.

Eines Tages wird er zurückkommen. He'll come back some day.
Eines Abends ging ich sehr früh zu Bett. One evening I went to bed early.

Check Your Comprehension

A. *Tell what time it is in German.*

1. 6:15 a.m.
2. 8:20 a.m.
3. 10:30 a.m.
4. 12:00 noon

5. 3:45 p.m.
6. 4:47 p.m.
7. 11:22 p.m. (official time)
8. 12:00 midnight

B. *Tell at what time you do each of the following activities.*

1. frühstücken
2. zu Mittag essen
3. zur Universität gehen

4. in die Deutschklasse gehen
5. eine Pause machen
6. zu Bett gehen

C. *Ask the question for which the answer is given.*

1. Ich studiere von sechs Uhr abends bis Mitternacht.
2. Die Filme fangen immer pünktlich an.
3. Er geht um acht Uhr ins Kino.
4. Gestern war der 22. Juli.

D. *Supply the expression of time in parentheses.*

1. Die Firma war _____ wegen Ferien geschlossen. (one week)
2. _____ blühen die Blumen. (in spring)
3. Wir machen _____ eine Autofahrt. (every weekend)
4. _____ fahre ich mit meiner Freundin nach Europa. (some day)
5. Sind Sie _____ in der Stadt gewesen? (yesterday afternoon)

CONVERSATION

Der Chef

CHEF	Guten Morgen, Fräulein Hansen!
SEKRETÄRIN	Guten Morgen, Herr Neumann! Ich freue mich, daß Sie wieder da sind. Wie war Ihre Geschäftsreise?
CHEF	Danke! Ein bißchen anstrengend, aber sonst ganz erfolgreich. Hoffentlich haben Sie sich nicht überarbeitet, während ich acht Tage weg war.
SEKRETÄRIN	Keineswegs! Ich habe mich nur geärgert, daß die Lieferung von Brinkmann und Co. noch nicht angekommen ist, die man uns für den 23. Mai versprochen hatte.
CHEF	Was? Brinkmann hat die Kisten noch nicht geliefert? Welches Datum haben wir denn heute?
SEKRETÄRIN	Heute ist schon der 30. Mai.

CHEF	Da will ich gleich mal anrufen. Geben Sie mir bitte mal die Nummer! Wieviele Kisten haben wir denn bestellt?
SEKRETÄRIN	40 große und 85 kleine. Die Telefonnummer von Brinkmann ist Vorwahl 025034 und dann 7071.
CHEF	Danke! Ich kümmere mich sofort darum. Sonst noch etwas Wichtiges?
SEKRETÄRIN	Ja, die Firma Brandt hat am 26. Mai geschrieben. Sie erkundigt sich, ob wir nächste Woche 18 Geräte des Typs LS 34 liefern können.
CHEF	Die Lieferung ist wahrscheinlich kein Problem, aber ich muß erst mit dem Abteilungsleiter sprechen. Haben Sie sich sonst noch wichtige Termine notiert?
SEKRETÄRIN	Ja, am Montag, dem 6. Juni um 11 Uhr ist eine Konferenz. Herr Krause hat sich entschuldigt, weil er schon am 4. Juni in Urlaub fährt.
CHEF	Gut. Im Moment finde ich keine Zeit, die Post zu lesen. Ach, Fräulein Hansen, machen Sie mir doch bitte eine Tasse Kaffee, dann geht die Arbeit besser!
SEKRETÄRIN	Ach so! Ihre Arbeit! Der Kaffee ist in drei Minuten fertig.

ORAL PRACTICE

A. *Substitute the item in parentheses for the noun or pronoun in boldface and make the necessary changes.*

1. **Der Chef** interessiert sich für die Sekretärin.
   (wir / ihr / ich / Sie / er / die Firma)
2. **Ich** möchte mich dem Chef vorstellen.
   (wir / du / er / ihr / sie (*pl.*) / die Sekretärin)
3. **Fräulein Hansen** hat sich gerade gebadet.
   (wir / Herr Neumann / du / ihr / die Kinder / ich / Sie)
4. **Sie** hat sich das Datum notiert.
   (ich / ihr / der Chef / du / wir / sie (*pl.*) / er)
5. **Wir** haben uns gestern den Film angeschaut.
   (du / Sie / ich / die Freundinnen / ihr / er)
6. **Ihr** habt euch einen Audi gekauft.
   (ich / Sie / wir / du / Fräulein Hansen / die Eltern)

B. *Supply the appropriate reflexive pronoun.*

1. Hoffentlich hast du _____ nicht überarbeitet.
2. Ich freue _____, daß Sie wieder da sind, Herr Neumann.
3. Wir kümmern _____ sofort um die Kinder.
4. Ich möchte _____ entschuldigen, daß ich zu spät komme.
5. Zieh _____ bitte die Schuhe aus, wenn du hereinkommst.
6. Setzen Sie _____ bitte da drüben aufs Sofa.
7. Haben Sie _____ schon angezogen, Fräulein Hansen?
8. Ich habe _____ gestern einen neuen Teppich gekauft.
9. Hast du _____ schon die Hände gewaschen?
10. Ich habe _____ alle wichtigen Termine notiert.
11. In Deutschland gibt es ein Spiel, das heißt ,,Mensch, ärgere _____ nicht!''
12. Erinnert ihr _____ noch an die letzte Inflation?
13. Ich habe _____ entschlossen, ein Jahr in Zürich zu studieren.
14. Hast du _____ gerade dieses Buch gekauft?
15. Manchmal wundern wir _____, wie leicht das Lernen der deutschen Sprache ist.

C. *Supply the correct spelling of the number in parentheses.*

1. Diese beiden Koffer gehören mir. _____ davon ist kaputt. (1)
2. Du brauchst nicht beide Koffer zu tragen. _____ kannst du mir geben. (1)
3. Wenn man in den Automaten _____ Pfennig steckt, dann kommt da unten eine Flasche Coca-Cola heraus. (60)
4. Dieser Herr raucht schon seine _____ Zigarre. (5.)
5. Der _____ ist für Frankreich ein wichtiges Datum. (14. 7. 1789)
6. Dieses Fahrrad habe ich mir für DM* _____ gekauft. (127,35)
7. Die _____ ist immer meine Glückszahl gewesen. (13)
8. Ihr habt zwei Autos? Wir haben nur _____. (1)
9. George Orwell schrieb den utopischen Roman _____. (,,1984'')
10. Meine Bekannte wohnt in der Königsberger Straße _____. (116)
11. Haben Sie auch am _____ Februar Geburtstag? (29.)
12. Der _____ Dezember heißt in Deutschland ,,Silvester''. (31.)

---

* Deutsche Mark

13. Am _____ Oktober beginnt das Wintersemester. (17.)
14. Der _____ Besucher bekommt einen Mercedes von der Firma. (1000000.)
15. Meine Telefonnummer ist _____. (322-4680)

D. *Supply the appropriate German equivalent of the phrase in parentheses.*

1. König Wilhelm _____ hat lange gelebt. (the second)
2. Kürzlich habe ich gelesen, daß _____ Prozent der Frauen emanzipiert sind. (25.6)
3. Heutzutage erhält man etwas mehr als _____ für _____. (two marks / one dollar)
4. Jede Woche kaufen wir _____ Eier. (two dozen)
5. Nelson Jr. ist _____ dieses Namens in seiner Familie. (the third)

E. *Supply the time, date, or time expression in parentheses.*

1. _____ _____ wasche ich mir die Haare. (Sundays, at 10:00 p.m.)
2. Fast _____ _____ verabschiede ich mich von meinen Freunden, um nach Hause zu gehen, so daß ich studieren kann. (every day, at 3:00 p.m.)
3. Sie geht _____ _____ von der Arbeit nach Hause, denn sie überarbeitet sich nicht. (at 5:00 p.m. on the dot)
4. _____ bin ich zu spät in die Deutschklasse gekommen. (Thursday afternoon)
5. Es war _____, als der Chef zurückkam. (Monday)

F. *Substitute or add each phrase as it is introduced into the previous sentence and make any necessary structural changes.*

Um Punkt fünf Uhr   verlasse ich mein Büro, das in der Parkstraße ist.
_____ sie (*sing.*)_____
Jeden Tag um fünf Uhr _____
_____ der Chef _____
Gerade eben _____
_____ wir _____
_____ ganz modern _____

GUIDED CONVERSATION

A. Assume you just had a minor car accident in which you bumped into your neighbor's car. Apologize and offer some explanation of what happened; then exchange addresses, phone numbers, driver's license numbers, automobile license numbers, insurance policy numbers, and so on.

B. Begin a conversation with someone in your class, and compare notes on what you do each morning before leaving the house.

The following terms may help you.

auf·wachen (to wake up)
auf·stehen, –stand, ist –gestanden (to get up)
sich waschen, wäscht, wusch, gewaschen (to wash [oneself])
sich baden (to take a bath)
sich duschen (to take a shower)
sich ab·trocknen (to dry [oneself])
sich die Zähne putzen (to brush one's teeth)
sich an·ziehen, –zog, –gezogen (to get dressed)
sich kämmen (to comb one's hair)
sich die Haare bürsten (to brush one's hair)
sich auf·regen über + *acc.* (to get excited about)
sich beeilen (to hurry)

To practice time expresssions, tell at precisely what time you do each of the above. Use either the **Sie–** or **du–** form throughout your conversation. For additional practice, carry on a similar conversation with someone else, and use the form you did not use in your first conversation.

READING

Ein Kinobesuch

Verzeihung, darf ich mich vorstellen? Ich heiße Uta Jung, bin 19 Jahre alt, wohne in der Leopoldstraße 74 in der 6. Etage und bin von Beruf Sekretärin bei Brinkmann & Co.

Peter hat gerade eben angerufen und mich zu einem Kinobesuch eingeladen. Ich freue mich schon sehr darauf. Er will wissen, für welchen Film   5 ich mich interessiere, weil vielleicht die Vorbestellung von Karten nötig ist. Ich kann mich noch gut an einen Abend erinnern, wo wir uns einen Film ansehen wollten, für den wir keine Karten mehr bekamen. Peter hatte sich damals furchtbar darüber geärgert, ich mich allerdings auch.

Peter und ich sind uns einig, daß es sich nur selten lohnt, in Deutschland ins Kino zu gehen, weil man dort fast nur Sex-Filme oder Thrillers zu sehen bekommt, bestenfalls mal einen billigen Western.

Um Punkt 16.30 Uhr[1] verabschiede ich mich von meinem Chef, der sich keine Sorgen macht, daß ich mich überarbeite. Ich setze mich in die Linie 23 und fahre bis zum Alexanderplatz. Fünf Minuten später bin ich zu Hause.

Ich schließe die Tür auf, schaue mir die Post an, ziehe mir den Mantel aus, zünde mir eine Zigarette an und blättere in der Zeitung, bis ich die Filmanzeigen finde. Wofür ich mich überhaupt nicht interessiere, sind Krimis und Westerns. Der Film „Der falsche Mann" von Alfred Hitchcock ist mir zu aufregend. Den Film „Adel verpflichtet" mit Alec Guinness habe ich mir 1974 schon einmal in Hamburg angeschaut. Für Romy Schneider kann ich mich überhaupt nicht begeistern. Aber wie ist es mit „Mein Name ist Nobody" mit Terence Hill und Henry Fonda? Der läuft schon die 6. Woche im Residenz-Kino. Ich kann mich nicht entschließen, ob ich mir nicht doch lieber den weltberühmten Film „Cabaret" mit Liza Minelli ansehen soll, der 8 Oscars erhalten hat und im Schloßtheater nun schon die 10. Woche läuft. Ich rufe Peter an und sage ihm, daß ich mich für „Cabaret" entschlossen habe.

Bevor Peter kommt, wasche ich mich, kämme mir das Haar und ziehe mir mein dunkelblaues Kleid an. Das dauert etwa eine halbe Stunde. Jetzt fühle ich mich wieder frisch. Es klingelt. Peter steht vor der Tür. Als wir uns hinsetzen und Peter mein Telefon sieht, fällt ihm plötzlich ein, daß er ganz vergessen hat, Karten vorzubestellen. Sofort ruft er an und erkundigt sich, ob man noch Karten bekommen kann. Alles außer 2. Parkett (das ist die 1. bis 3. Reihe) und außer einem Platz im Sperrsitz (das ist die 10. bis 21. Reihe) ist ausverkauft. Aber nach wenigen Minuten ruft die Kinokasse noch einmal an: Zwei Logenplätze für 7 Mark pro Karte sind frei geworden. So konnten wir uns diesen Film doch noch ansehen.

Der Film „Cabaret" war interessanter als ich mir vorgestellt hatte. Wir unterhielten uns noch den ganzen Abend darüber. Es muß wohl spät geworden sein, denn am nächsten Morgen bin ich erst um neun Uhr aufgewacht.

---

[1] Read: 16 Uhr 30.

QUESTIONS

1. Wie alt ist Uta Jung und wo wohnt sie?
2. Worauf freut sich Uta schon sehr?
3. Was will Peter wissen?
4. Woran kann sich Uta noch gut erinnern?
5. Worin sind sich die beiden einig?
6. Warum lohnt es sich nur selten, sich in Deutschland einen Film anzusehen?
7. Wann verabschiedet sich Uta Jung von ihrem Chef?
8. Worüber macht er sich keine Sorgen?
9. Wie ist Uta nach Hause gekommen?
10. Was tut Uta, als sie zu Hause ankommt?
11. Wofür interessiert sie sich überhaupt nicht?
12. Welcher Film ist ihr zu aufregend?
13. Welchen Film hat sie sich schon einmal in Hamburg angeschaut?
14. Für wen kann sie sich überhaupt nicht begeistern?
15. Wozu kann sie sich nicht entschließen?
16. Für welchen Film entscheiden sich die beiden schließlich?
17. Was tut Uta, bevor Peter sie abholt?
18. Was fällt Peter plötzlich ein, als er Utas Telefon sieht?
19. Wonach erkundigt er sich sofort?
20. Wie fand Uta den Film?

VOCABULARY EXERCISES

A. *Supply the appropriate word from the list on the right.*

1. Uta ist von _____ Sekretärin bei einer bekannten Firma.
2. Vielleicht ist die _____ von Karten nötig.
3. Um _____ 16.30 Uhr verabschiedet sich Uta von ihrem Chef.
4. Die _____ kann man in der Freitag-Zeitung finden.
5. Die Plätze im Kino von ungefähr der 10. bis zur 21. Reihe nennt man _____.
6. Die _____ ruft an wegen der vorbestellten Karten.

a. Sperrsitz
b. Beruf
c. Punkt
d. Vorbestellung
e. Kinokasse
f. Filmanzeigen

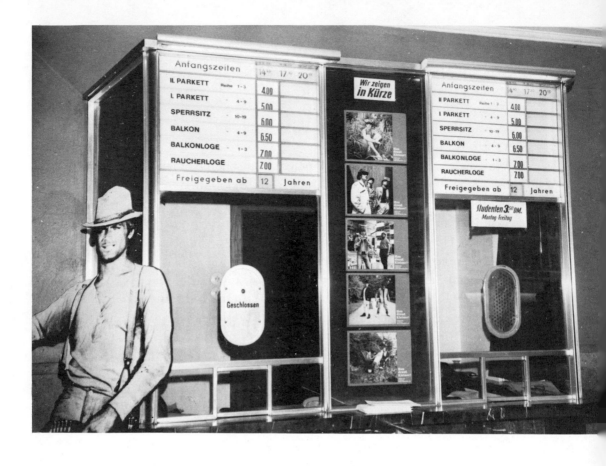

B. *Supply the appropriate word from the list on the right.*

1. Verzeihung, darf ich Ihnen Herrn Fleischer _____?
2. Wir _____ uns schon auf den Kinobesuch.
3. _____ Sie sich auch für gute Filme?
4. Ich kann mich nur an wenige gute deutsche Filme _____.
5. Ihr habt euch gestern einen Western _____?
6. Worüber hast du dich eigentlich so _____?
7. Ich kann mich für Alec Guinness sehr _____.
8. Verzeihung, darf ich mir eine Zigarette _____?
9. Ich habe mich _____, nach Spanien zu reisen.
10. Mein Lehrer macht sich keine Sorgen, daß ich mich _____ habe.

a. geärgert
b. erinnern
c. interessieren
d. vorstellen
e. angeschaut
f. überarbeitet
g. freuen
h. anzünden
i. entschieden
j. begeistern

Review Exercises

A. *Substitute the item in parentheses for the word in boldface and make the necessary changes.*

1. **Die Sekretärin** entschuldigt sich bei ihrem Chef. (wir)
2. **Der Mann** erkundigt sich nach dem Weg. (du)
3. **Wir** erinnern uns an den Film. (ihr)
4. Setz **dich** hin! (Sie)
5. **Ich** interessiere mich für Fußball. (die Leute)
6. **Er** freut sich auf seinen Urlaub. (Monika)
7. **Sie** entschließen sich, nach Hause zu gehen. (wir)
8. **Ich** fühle mich krank. (ihr)
9. Zieht **euch** schnell an! (du)
10. **Hans** unterhält sich mit seiner Freundin. (ich)

B. *Substitute the item in parentheses for the pronoun in boldface and make the necessary changes.*

1. **Wir** schauen uns die Bilder an. (er)
2. **Sie** ist sich mit ihrem Partner einig. (wir)
3. **Mir** fällt gerade eben ein, daß du heute Geburtstag hast. (er)
4. **Ihr** überlegt euch, ob ihr das Auto kaufen sollt. (du)
5. **Sie** hat sich alles Wichtige notiert. (ich)
6. **Ich** stelle mir vor, daß die Boeing 747 ein sehr großes Flugzeug ist. (sie, *pl.*)

C. *Express in German, paying close attention to the reflexive and nonreflexive uses of the verbs.*

1. The woman washes her clothes on Mondays, but she washes herself twice a day.

2. We took off our shoes and got undressed.
3. Put your own shoes on.
4. Introduce yourself to my friend.
5. Imagine how interesting that is.
6. They looked at each other.
7. Every day the two friends asked one another how they got together.
8. I remember well how happy you were then.
9. Please decide on the car you wish to buy.
10. Don't sit down because you have to go to work right away.

D. *Give each of the following dates first in numbers and then in words.*

EXAMPLE   Lenin's Birthday
Lenins Geburtstag ist am 22. 4.
Lenins Geburtstag ist am zweiundzwanzigsten vierten.

1. New Year's Day (Neujahr)
2. Washington's Birthday
3. Lincoln's Birthday
4. Easter (Ostern)
5. Whitsunday, Pentecost (Pfingsten)
6. beginning of the fall semester (or quarter)
7. Christmas
8. New Year's Eve (Silvester)

GUIDED COMPOSITION

A. Write a composition on the subject of **Mein Tageslauf.** You might follow the model provided in this chapter, but alter it to fit your own personal schedule and daily activities.

B. Write a composition regarding your plans for each day of the coming week. You might also mention some special events coming up in your life during the coming months.

C. Assume you just had a clash with your German professor regarding a grade you felt was unjustified. You were upset and lost your temper. Now that you have had a chance to think about it, however, you feel sorry about the incident and decide to write a letter of apology.

The following words may help you write your letter.

sich ärgern über (to be upset about)
sich entschuldigen (to apologize)
die Note, −n (grade)
der Test, −s (test)
sich überlegen (to think about)
ungerecht (unjust)
verdienen (to deserve)

Chapter 17

Useful Phrases

erst	just, only; first, at first
Bitte schön?	May I help you?
Voll, bitte!	Fill it up, please.
Gute Fahrt!	Have a good trip.
dreißiger Öl	thirty weight oil
nach einem Bericht	according to a report
aktiv Sport treiben	to be active in sports
Es macht mir Spaß.	I have fun.
Was das betrifft, . . .	As far as that is concerned. . . .

MODEL SENTENCES

I

Hier sind die **Schlüssel** für das Haus.	Here are the keys for the house.
Er hat schon sechs **Semester** studiert.	He has already studied six semesters.
Die **Läden** sind um 18.30 Uhr schon geschlossen.	At 6:30 the shops are already closed.
Sie hat sieben **Jahre** hier gelebt.	She lived here for seven years.
Die alten deutschen **Städte** sind ganz romantisch.	The old German towns are quite romantic.
Diese Herren bevorzugen **Zigarren.**	These gentlemen prefer cigars.

Ich brauche keine **Quittungen.**   I don't need any receipts.

Viele **Lehrerinnen** lieben ihren Beruf.   Many (female) teachers love their profession.

Diese **Häuser** sind erst drei Jahre alt.   These houses are just three years old.

Alte **Radios** haben oft einen guten Klang.   Old radios often have a good sound.

II

Ich fahre oft mit jenen **Studenten** spazieren.   I often go for a drive with those students.

Geben Sie dem **Herrn** da drüben und den zwei **Herren** hier keine Zigaretten!   Don't give that man over there and these two men here any cigarettes.

III

Bei kühlem Wetter ist das **Arbeiten** leichter.   Working is easier in cool weather.

Der **Forscher** brauchte Geld, um neue **Entdeckungen** zu machen.   The scientist needed money in order to make new discoveries.

Grammar Explanations

I. NOUN PLURALS

Nouns, also called "substantives," are generally categorized as *proper* nouns, names of specific places and persons, and *common* nouns, names of objects (concrete) and qualities or actions (abstract). More commonly in German, however, nouns are classed by the way they form their plurals.

In English, the plural is almost always formed by adding **–s** or **–es** to the singular form of the noun.

dog   dogs

class   classes

In contrast, German has no general rule, and the noun plurals should be memorized along with the singular form and the definite article of each noun. Most plural endings, however, can be classified according to the following major categories.

Classes of Noun Plurals

Class	Feature	Example
1a	no change	der Schlüssel, die Schlüssel
b	Umlaut (⸚)	der Laden, die Läden
2a	–e	der Rest, die Reste
b	⸚e	die Stadt, die Städte
3a	–er	das Bild, die Bilder
b	⸚er	das Buch, die Bücher
4a	–n	die Schule, die Schulen
b	–en	der Student, die Studenten
5	–s	das Auto, die Autos

Although there are quite a number of notable exceptions, it is possible to establish a few useful guidelines showing which nouns fall into which class. The following list of major rules is intended for reference purposes only. As you continue to study German, you may wish to consult these rules as necessary. They should help you in finding and memorizing the plurals of most nouns.

Class 1a and 1b: no ending, addition of Umlaut whenever possible

1. masculine and neuter nouns ending in **–el, –en,** and **–er**
2. nouns ending in **–chen** and **–lein,** always neuter
3. neuter nouns with the prefix **Ge–** and the suffix **–e**

Class 2a: **–e** ending

1. many monosyllabic masculine and some neuter nouns
2. nouns ending in **–ich, –ig** and **–ling,** always masculine
3. nouns ending in **–nis** and **–sal** always either feminine or neuter; nouns ending in **–nis** double the **s** in the plural
4. polysyllabic neuter nouns with the prefix **Ge–** but without the suffix **–e**

Class 2b: **–e** ending, addition of Umlaut

some masculine and feminine nouns, but no neuter nouns

Class 3a and 3b: **–er** ending, addition of Umlaut wherever possible

1. most monosyllabic neuter and some masculine nouns
2. nouns ending in **–tum**
3. no feminine nouns

Class 4a and 4b: **–n** or **–en** ending, no Umlaut possible

1. nouns ending in **–ei, –ion, –heit, –keit, –schaft, –tät, –ung,** and **–ie,** always feminine; feminine nouns with the suffix **–in** add **–nen**
2. a few masculine nouns (*see* Chapter 4), with the special declension of **–n** or **–en** in all cases but the nominative singular: **der Mensch, der Student,** and **der Herr,** for example
3. no neuter nouns, except one: **das Herz** (heart)
4. a few monosyllabic feminine nouns: **die Frau**

Class 5: **–s** ending, no Umlaut possible.

1. nouns of foreign origin that have recently been assimilated into German
2. proper names

There are *exceptions* to these rules.

Two feminine nouns add Umlaut and take no ending, as in class 1a.

die Mutter, die **Mü**tter
die Tochter, die **Tö**chter

A few irregular masculine and neuter nouns add **–n** or **–en,** as in class 4a and 4b. Their genitive form remains the regular **–s** or **–es.**

das Auge, die Auge**n**
der Staat, die Staate**n**
das Ohr, die Ohre**n**

A few irregular masculine nouns ending in **–e** add **–n** or **–en,** as in class 4a and 4b. Their genitive form is also irregular: **–ns.**

der Name, die Name**n**
der Gedanke, die Gedanke**n**

One irregular neuter noun adds **–en** as in class 4b.

das Herz, die Herzen

Many foreign nouns add **–en** or change their stem and add **–en** as in class 4b.

der Professor, die Professoren
das Museum, die Museen

The plurals of compound nouns are formed by pluralizing the last noun in the compound. (See Chapter 13.)

Check Your Comprehension

Form the plural of the noun.

1. der Liter
2. die Tankstelle
3. das Nummernschild
4. die Stadt
5. der Reifen
6. das Semester
7. die Quittung
8. der Arzt
9. der Volkswagen
10. das Auto
11. der Schlüssel
12. der Wunsch
13. die Entdeckung
14. die Gruppe
15. der Wissenschaftler
16. die Anthropologin
17. die Universität
18. der Taucher
19. die Küste
20. die Straße
21. der Stein
22. das Meer
23. der Forscher
24. die Expedition

II. NOUN DECLENSION SUMMARY

The following rules summarize the most important aspects of noun case endings.

1. Feminine nouns take no endings in the singular.

2. Most polysyllabic masculine and neuter nouns add an **–s** in the genitive singular; monosyllabic masculine and neuter nouns usually add an **–es.**

| nom.: | der Wagen | der Rest | das Semester | das Haar |
| gen.: | des Wagen**s** | des Rest**es** | des Semester**s** | des Haar**es** |

3. All nouns add an **–n,** in the dative plural, unless the plural already ends in **–n** or **–s.**

Nominative Plural	*Dative Plural*
die Schlüssel	mit den Schlüssel**n**
die Nummernschilder	mit den Nummernschilder**n**
die Studenten	mit den Studenten
die Autos	mit den Autos

4. A relatively small number of German nouns take endings in all cases of the singular and plural except the nominative singular. Most of these nouns are masculine and the case endings throughout are either **–n** or **–en.** Included in this category are nouns of Latin or Greek origin (**der Student, der Architekt, der Professor**); some masculine nouns ending in **–e** (**der Junge**); nouns denoting male citizens of countries (**der Franzose, der Chinese**); and the names of many animals (**der Löwe, der Bulle**).

	Singular	*Plural*
nom.:	der Student	die Student**en**
acc.:	den Student**en**	die Student**en**
dat.:	dem Student**en**	den Student**en**
gen.:	des Student**en**	der Student**en**
nom.:	der Herr	die Herr**en**
acc.:	den Herr**n**	die Herr**en**
dat.:	dem Herr**n**	den Herr**en**
gen.:	des Herr**n**	der Herr**en**

Two nouns are even more irregular in their declension: **das Herz** and **der Name.**

	Singular		*Plural*	
nom.:	das Herz	der Name	die Herzen	die Namen
acc.:	das Herz	den Namen	die Herzen	die Namen
dat.:	dem Herzen	dem Namen	den Herzen	den Namen
gen.:	des Herzens	des Namens	der Herzen	der Namen

Decline the noun in the singular and in the plural.

1. das Nummernschild
2. der Reifen
3. das Glas
4. die Expedition
5. der Arzt
6. die Sekretärin

7. das Meer
8. der Stein
9. das Radio
10. die Quittung
11. der Professor
12. das Motiv

III. NOUN FORMATION SUMMARY

The following rules summarize the most important aspects of noun formation.

1. Any German infinitive can be changed into a noun, whenever the meaning is logical, simply by capitalizing it and adding the correct form of the definite or indefinite article. The noun formed is always neuter. Sometimes the English equivalent of the noun changes slightly, but generally it is the same as the **–ing** form.

arbeiten (to work)	das Arbeiten (work)
sprechen (to speak)	das Sprechen (speech)
überlegen (to think)	das Überlegen (thinking)

Bei einer Tasse Kaffee geht das Arbeiten leichter.	Work goes easier with a cup of coffee.
Es gab keine Zeit zum Überlegen.	There was not time for thinking.

2. Agents, both male and female, can be formed from verbs and from other words that usually denote a nationality or a profession. A male agent always takes the ending **–er** and a female agent takes the ending **–erin**.

sprechen (to speak)	der Sprecher (male speaker)	die Sprecherin (female speaker)
schwimmen (to swim)	der Schwimmer	die Schwimmerin
fahren (to drive)	der Fahrer	die Fahrerin

laufen (to run)	der Läufer	die Läuferin
Amerika (America)	der Amerikaner	die Amerikanerin
die Schweiz (Switzerland)	der Schweizer	die Schweizerin
das Fleisch (meat)	der Fleischer (butcher)	die Fleischerin

If the masculine agent does not end in **–er,** the feminine agent can still be formed by adding the **–in** ending.

der Freund	die Freundin
der Architekt	die Architektin
der Philosoph	die Philosophin
der Anthropologe	die Anthropologin

Some nouns formed by adding the **–er** ending to the infinitive stem of the verb may denote a tool with which an action is performed.

bohren (to bore)	der Bohrer (drill)
rollen (to roll)	der Roller (scooter)
schieben (to slide)	der Schieber (slide)

3. Most any noun can be made diminutive by adding the endings **–chen** or **–lein;** the vowel is umlauted whenever possible. The ending **–chen** is more predominant than **–lein,** especially in the north of Germany. Whenever a noun adds the diminutive ending, it becomes neuter. Adding one of these endings to a proper name shows endearment and affection.

die Frau (woman)	das Fräulein ([*lit.* little woman], girl)
das Haus (house)	das Häuschen (little house)
die Gans (goose)	das Gänslein (little goose)
Hans	Hänschen (little Hans)

4. Compound nouns can be formed by uniting two or more nouns. Such nouns are used in abundance in German (*see* Chapter 13).

5. Foreign words are frequently assimilated into German, often by retaining the spelling and giving the noun a gender. Some American words in vogue in the everyday vocabulary of contemporary German include the following.

der Flirt	die Party	das Weekend
der Playboy	die City	das Happy-end
der Snob	die Story	das Training
der Appeal	die Ranch	das Handicap

and

der Song	das Baby
die Band	der Fan
das Camping	der Interviewer
der Catcher	der Gangster

Check Your Comprehension

A. *Form a noun from the verb in parentheses and use it with the definite article.*

1. Mir macht _____ Spaß. (tanzen)
2. Ich finde _____ schön. (wandern)
3. Wir haben _____ gern. (diskutieren)
4. Ich habe Freude an _____. (musizieren)
5. Uns gefällt besonders _____. (fernsehen)
6. Ich liebe vor allem _____ von Büchern und Krimis. (lesen)

B. *Supply the infinitive noun and the article. When prepositions are used, make use of contractions where possible.*

1. Er hat sich bei _____ _____ den Fuß verletzt. (skilaufen)
2. Sie hat nie Zeit zu _____ _____. (schlafen)
3. Ist _____ _____ hier verboten? (rauchen)
4. Für _____ _____ bezahlt man in Deutschland sehr viel Geld. (wohnen)

5. Zu _____ _____ der Post finde ich im Moment keine Zeit. (lesen)
6. Der Arzt hat mir _____ _____ empfohlen. (spazierengehen)
7. _____ _____ ist aber auch sehr gesund. (schwimmen)

C. *Form a masculine agent from the verb.*

1. tauchen   der _____ (diver)
2. forschen   der _____ (explorer)
3. finden   der _____ (finder)
4. arbeiten   der _____ (worker)
5. entdecken   der _____ (discoverer)

D. *Form an agent from the noun.*

1. die Wissenschaft   der _____ (scientist)
2. Holland   der _____ (Dutchman)
3. Spanien   der _____ (Spaniard)
4. das Fleisch   der _____ (butcher)
5. die Schule   die _____ (female pupil)
6. die Arbeit   die _____ (female worker)

E. *Form a diminutive from the noun.*

1. die Rose   5. das Haus
2. die Straße   6. die Blume
3. der Stein   7. der Tisch
4. das Kind   8. Fritz

CONVERSATION

An der Tankstelle

TANKWART	'n[1] Abend! Bitte schön?
GÜNTER	Voll, bitte! 10 Liter Super und den Rest Normalbenzin.
TANKWART	Ihr Tank ist noch abgeschlossen. Können Sie mir bitte den Schlüssel geben?
GÜNTER	Ach, natürlich! Das vergesse ich immer. Hier sind die Schlüssel. Dieser ist für den Tank.
TANKWART	Danke! Ich sehe an Ihrem Nummernschild, daß Sie aus Göttingen sind.[2] Schöne Stadt! Hab'[3] fünf Jahre dort gewohnt.
GÜNTER	Ja, da kann man's aushalten! Ich bin dort an der Uni.[4]
TANKWART	Ach so. Was studieren Sie denn?
GÜNTER	Medizin. Bin jetzt im siebten Semester.
TANKWART	Nun, Ärzte brauchen wir ja dringend. Wie ist es mit dem Öl?

GÜNTER	Ja, bitte prüfen Sie auch das Öl! Diese alten Volkswagen ver-
	brauchen eine ganze Menge. Das ist natürlich bei den neuen
	Autos besser.
TANKWART	Sicher! Ein halber Liter fehlt. Welches Öl nehmen Sie?
GÜNTER	Dreißiger, bitte. Ach, können Sie bitte auch die Reifen prüfen?
	Ich glaube, der rechte Vorderreifen hat zu wenig Luft.
TANKWART	Natürlich! Haben Sie sonst noch einen Wunsch?
GÜNTER	Nein danke. Das ist alles.
TANKWART	Möchten Sie eine Quittung haben?
GÜNTER	Danke, nicht nötig. Also, auf Wiedersehen!
TANKWART	Auf Wiedersehen! Gute Fahrt! Und grüßen Sie Göttingen von
	mir!

15

20

---

[1] In normal speech, as in English, often the endings and sometimes even the stems of words are dropped; **'n** here denotes **guten**; in line 9 **man's** equals **man es**. Frequent dropping of the **-e** ending in the first-person present tense verbs also occurs: Ich hab' kein Geld.

[2] License plates in Germany begin with one to three letters that denote the city in which the car is licensed. GÖ is the designation for Göttingen. Others, for example, are M, Munich; D, Düsseldorf; BN, Bonn; FR, Freiburg; and NOH, Nordhorn.

[3] In fast conversation sometimes the personal "I" reference is even dropped.

[4] Colloquial for **Universität**.

ORAL PRACTICE

A. *Put the noun in boldface into the plural and make the necessary structural changes.*

1. Ich glaube, der **Vorderreifen** hat zu wenig Luft.
2. Ein neues **Auto** braucht bestimmt weniger Öl als ein altes.
3. Er hat sonst keinen anderen **Wunsch.**
4. Brauchen Sie eine **Quittung?**
5. Die Zigarren habe ich von jenem **Herrn** bekommen.
6. Das kleine **Städtchen** in Österreich ist wunderschön.
7. Das **Nummernschild** an seinem Auto hat die Buchstaben GÖ.
8. Mit diesem **Schlüssel** kann man den Tank öffnen.
9. Der **Abend** wird im Sommer immer länger.
10. Das Benzin an der deutschen **Tankstelle** wird immer teurer.
11. Mancher **Arzt** kommt aus der DDR in die Bundesrepublik Deutsch-land.
12. Das Wasser des **Meeres** ist nicht mehr sauber.

13. Eine **Lehrerin** bekommt in Deutschland nicht weniger Geld als ein **Lehrer.**

14. Die **Entdeckung** der alten historischen **Stadt** ist ein wichtiges Kapitel in der Kulturgeschichte.

15. Am Anfang kocht die neue **Sekretärin** ihrem **Chef** gerne Kaffee.

16. In Deutschland schließt jeder **Laden** schon um 18:30 Uhr.

17. Die **Reform** der Schulen hat kein Ende.

18. An der **Universität** studieren zu viele Studenten.

19. Unser **Radio** ist kaputt.

20. Der Protest des **Professors** war erfolgreich.

B. *Add the noun in parentheses to the sentence using the appropriate case ending.*

1. Die Qualität dieses _____ ist ausgezeichnet. (Bier)
2. Ich habe gestern _____ Gantenbein kennengelernt. (Herr)
3. Die Farbe des _____ ist weiß. (Nummernschild)
4. Mit dieser _____ haben Sie ein Jahr Garantie. (Quittung)
5. In diesem _____ ist ein ausgezeichneter Rheinwein. (Glas)
6. Die Frage des _____ konnte er nicht beantworten. (Arzt)
7. Mit dem _____ planten wir unser Haus. (Architekt)
8. Die _____ sind meistens sehr charmant. (Schweizerinnen)
9. Die Fische des _____ können nicht mehr lange leben. (Meer)
10. Die Farbe ihres _____ war feuerrot. (Haar)

C. *Form a noun from the verb in parentheses and use it in the sentence.*

1. Der _____ Amerikas hieß Christoph Kolumbus. (entdecken)
2. Der _____ meiner Uhr erhält zehn Mark. (finden)
3. Alle _____ wollen mehr Geld für ihre Arbeit. (arbeiten)
4. Die beiden _____ fanden das Wrack eines Schiffes. (tauchen)
5. Ich habe von meinen _____ immer nur D's und E's bekommen. (lehren)
6. Die Hausfrau freut sich über die vielen _____. (essen)
7. Für den _____ ist die deutsche Sprache bestimmt nicht leicht. (anfangen)
8. Ich suche die _____ (*sing.*) dieses Wagens. (fahren)
9. Sein Sohn ist ein ausgezeichneter _____. (schwimmen)

D. *Change the noun in boldface to a female agent.*

1. Die **Schweizer** haben wenig Interesse an Politik, sagt man.
2. Ich habe dem **Studenten** ein Buch gekauft.
3. Es gibt viele **Amerikaner,** die nach Österreich reisen wollen.
4. Die **Lehrer** haben viel zu wenig Urlaub.
5. Von den **Anthropologen** kann man sehr viel lernen.

E. *Change the noun in boldface into a diminutive and make the necessary structural changes.*

1. Rothenburg ist eine kleine alte **Stadt,** nicht weit von Frankfurt.
2. Dies ist der Autor des kleinen **Buches,** das ich dir gegeben habe.
3. Möchten Sie noch ein **Glas** Kirschwasser?
4. Ich habe ein hübsches **Haus** gekauft.
5. Dieser **Hund** ist erst zwei Wochen alt.

F. *Substitute or add each phrase as it is introduced into the previous sentence and make any necessary structural changes.*

Keine Sekretärin kocht ihrem Chef   gerne Kaffee.
Alle _____
_____ Frau _____
_____ Mann _____
_____ Suppe.
Jede _____
_____ Freundin _____
_____ Student _____
_____ Abendessen.
Alle _____

GUIDED CONVERSATION

A. The advertisement of a symposium called "German Semester" at the University of Southern California shows how performances are announced in German. Notice particularly how the day, date, and time of a performance are given.

Study the advertisement, then discuss the advertised events with someone in your class. You might mention which event you would like to attend and why, with whom you would like to attend, which day would be most suitable, where the event takes place, whether or not parking space is available, who the various speakers are, whether you have heard of any of the speakers, what the lectures or films are about, what the admission fee is, and so on.

Wie Sie jetzt Ihren Partner finden können!

1.

Kreuzen Sie an, was Sie in Ihrer Freizeit bevorzugen. Denn Ihr Idealpartner soll in seinen Interessen zu Ihnen passen.

	sehr interessiert	gelegentlich	kein Interesse
aktiv Sport treiben	☐	☐	☐
Besuch von Sportveranstaltungen	☐	☐	☐
Funk und Fernsehen: Unterhaltungssendungen	☐	☐	☐
Sendungen über Politik und Wissenschaft	☐	☐	☐
Krimis	☐	☐	☐
Musiksendungen	☐	☐	☐
Naturwissenschaft/Technik	☐	☐	☐
Problemfilme	☐	☐	☐
Sportsendungen	☐	☐	☐
berufliche Weiterbildung	☐	☐	☐
Geisteswissenschaften	☐	☐	☐
Basteln/Handarbeiten	☐	☐	☐
Musizieren	☐	☐	☐
ernste Musik hören	☐	☐	☐
Unterhaltungsmusik hören	☐	☐	☐
Bildungslektüre	☐	☐	☐
Unterhaltungslektüre	☐	☐	☐
Theater-, Opernbesuch	☐	☐	☐
Tanzen	☐	☐	☐
Parties	☐	☐	☐
Diskussionen	☐	☐	☐
Wandern	☐	☐	☐
mit Auto spazierenfahren	☐	☐	☐
Urlaub: Körperl. Betätigung u. Sport	☐	☐	☐
Faulenzen	☐	☐	☐
Bildung	☐	☐	☐
Vergnügen	☐	☐	☐
Familienfeiern	☐	☐	☐

2.

☐ Sind Sie ledig   ☐ konfessionslos
☐ verwitwet   ☐ evangelisch
☐ geschieden   ☐ katholisch

andere _____

Wählen Sie aus den folgenden Eigenschaften 5 aus, die Sie von Ihrem zukünftigen Partner erwarten:

☐ temperamentvoll   ☐ strebsam
☐ fröhlich   ☐ natürlich
☐ intelligent   ☐ gütig
☐ ehrlich   ☐ sportlich
☐ sparsam   ☐ gutaussehend
☐ häuslich   ☐ selbstbewußt

Wesens-Test:
In das Feld der Farbe, die Ihnen am besten gefällt, schreiben Sie eine 1. Die Farbe, die Ihnen am zweitbesten gefällt, bekommt eine 2. Dann vergeben Sie die 3 und die 4, und zum Schluß die 5 für die Farbe, die Ihnen am wenigsten gefällt.

dunkelblau	leuchtend gelb	mittelgrau	feuerrot	grasgrün

Ihre Staatsangehörigkeit: _____

Geburtsdatum: _____

Körpergröße _____ cm

Ihr Beruf: _____

Wo sind Sie beschäftigt? _____

B. Part of a computer test from the German magazine *Stern* is offered here. The test is to give you some indication of your chances for finding your ideal partner and/or marriage. First look up any unfamiliar words in a German-English dictionary. Then go through the test orally with someone in your class. As you do so, try to formulate complete questions for each item.

> Treiben Sie aktiv Sport?
>
> Sind Sie konfessionslos?
>
> Erwarten Sie einen temperamentvollen Partner?

READING

Die verkehrte Welt

Ich stehe auf der Terrasse des Bundeshauses in Bern[1] und schaue auf das Häusermeer der Stadt, die tief unter mir liegt. Ja, vieles hat sich verändert: Der Stadtverkehr ist dichter, die Jugend emanzipierter und ihre Kleidung amerikanischer geworden. Auch der Schweizerfranken ist bedeutend teurer geworden. Aber vieles ist gleich geblieben: das gemütliche „Schwyzerdüütsch"[2] der Berner; die Altstadt mit ihren Lauben,[3] Riegelhäusern,[4] Stadttoren und Brunnen; die Aare,[5] die sich durch die Stadt windet. Den Bärengraben[6] nicht zu vergessen. Und am Horizont leuchten immer noch die Alpen und Voralpen im Abendrot—halb versteckt hinter Gewitterwolken. 5

„Sali Roobi",[7] höre ich hinter mir. Mein alter Schulkamerad ist eben angekommen und begrüßt mich in seinem breiten Baseldeutsch. „Wir müssen uns beeilen," sagt er „um halb neun Uhr erwarten uns die Freunde im Restaurant ‚Zum Rüden' in Zürich."—„Wann, wo? Das geht doch nicht, da müssen wir ja fliegen!"—„Mach dir keine Sorgen, mit dieser Maschine da werden wir gleich da sein," sagt er und zeigt auf ein „Mercedes"-Sportsmodell. Wir winden uns durch den Stadtverkehr und erreichen die Autobahn. Und nun geht's los: 100, 120, 160, 180, einmal sogar 200 km pro Stunde. Ich glaube auf der Rennstrecke in Le Mans zu sein. „Was ist die Abhebegeschwindigkeit deines Wagens?" frage ich.—„Ha, ha, in den Vereinigten Staaten fahrt ihr wohl nicht so schnell."—„Nein, nicht ganz, so 55 bis 65 Meilen pro Stunde."—„Schneckentempo!"—Mir läuft der Schweiß von der Stirn. 10 15 20

„Siehst du da in der Mitte der Autobahn die Eisenbarrieren? Die kann man entfernen. Und im Kriegsfall wird die Autobahn zum Flugplatz."—„Toll," denke ich bei mir, „aber schon zu Friedenszeiten ist die Autobahn fast eine Startbahn."—„Naja, im Kriegsfall," sage ich laut, „wer will denn die Schweiz heutzutage schon angreifen!?"—„Ja, also, man weiß nie."—„Höchstens wenn mal ein anderes Land das schweizer Bankgeheimnis erschließen will!" sage ich lachend. Mein Freund macht ein böses Gesicht. Er ist Bankpräsident. Stille. Man hört nur das Heulen des Mercedes.

In Zürich im Restaurant „Zum Rüden" gibt es viel Händedrücken, Erzählen und ein gutes Essen mit Wein. Wir kommen auf den Verkehr zu sprechen. „Wir leben in einer verkehrten Welt," meint ein alter Kamerad, „jetzt haben wir die schnellen Wagen, aber es dauert eine Ewigkeit, von den Wohnvierteln zur Innenstadt zu fahren."—„Fahrt doch mit dem Velo[8] zur Arbeit," schlage ich vor, „dann werdet ihr auch weniger Abgase einatmen müssen." „Was, du meinst, daß wir uns das Velo vom Estrich holen sollen. Das ist doch eine Schnapsidee! Erstens ist mein Drahtesel[9] verrostet, zweitens will ich nicht in den Tramschienen ein Foul machen[10] und drittens hat es im Spital nicht genügend Platz für Velounfälle."

„Na," denke ich „vielleicht sind nicht die Welt und der Verkehr verkehrt, sondern die Menschen."

---

[1] Federal building of Berne, where the Swiss parliament meets.
[2] Swiss-German differs considerably in structure, vocabulary, and pronunciation from standard German. The difference is as great as between the English of Chaucer and modern English. Moreover, there are many distinct dialects, which make the standardization of the spelling nearly impossible. But **Schwyzerdüütsch** for **Schweizerdeutsch** is a fairly accurate rendering of the pronunciation.
[3] Berne is known, among other things, for its **Lauben,** Swiss for arcades or covered sidewalks.
[4] Swiss expression denoting a type of house characterized by its half-timbered construction.
[5] A tributary of the Rhine, winding through the city.
[6] Bear pit, a tourist attraction located in the center of the city. The bear is the emblem of Berne.
[7] Rendering of the Basle-dialect for **Salü, Robi** (Swiss abbreviation, for Robert). Among friends, the Swiss use **Salü** from the French *salut* (greetings) for **Guten Tag.**
[8] Swiss expression for **Fahrrad** (bicycle).
[9] Colloquial Swiss expression for **Velo,** literally "wire-donkey."
[10] Expression borrowed from sports, here meaning to have a minor accident; **Tramschienen** is southern German for **Straßenbahnschienen,** streetcar tracks.

QUESTIONS

1. Wo stehe ich?
2. Wohin sehe ich?
3. Wie hat sich die Stadt verändert?
4. Was ist gleich geblieben?
5. Was leuchtet am Horizont?
6. Wann müssen wir in Zürich sein?
7. Wie schnell fahren wir?
8. Was sieht man in der Mitte der Autobahn?
9. Zu was wird die Autobahn im Kriegsfall?
10. Haben Sie schon vom schweizer Bankgeheimnis gehört?
11. Worauf kommen wir im Restaurant in Zürich zu sprechen?
12. Warum, meint ein alter Kamerad, leben wir in einer verkehrten Welt?
13. Was schlage ich vor?
14. Warum nennt mein Freund meinen Vorschlag eine „Schnapsidee"?
15. Was denke ich?

Bern

VOCABULARY EXERCISES

A. *Supply the appropriate word from the list on the right.*

1. Prüfen Sie bitte das _____.
2. Wenn die Sonne untergeht, leuchtet der Himmel im _____.
3. In den letzten Jahren ist der _____ dichter geworden.
4. In alten Städten gibt es viele _____.
5. Vom Empire State Building sieht man das _____ der Stadt New York.
6. Im Kriegsfall wird die Autobahn zur _____.
7. Fünfzig Meilen pro Stunde auf der Autobahn ist ein _____.
8. Es ist nicht weit von den _____ zur Innenstadt.
9. In der Innenstadt muß man viele _____ einatmen.
10. _____ sind für Fahrräder gefährlich.

a. Startbahn
b. Wohnvierteln
c. Häusermeer
d. Tramschienen
e. Schneckentempo
f. Abgase
g. Öl
h. Abendrot
i. Stadtverkehr
j. Stadttore

B. *Do the same with the following sentences.*

1. Wir _____ auf das Häusermeer der Stadt.
2. In den letzten Jahren hat sich vieles _____.
3. Der Verkehr ist dichter _____.
4. Der Film fängt gleich an, wir müssen uns _____.
5. In einer alten Stadt muß man sich im Auto durch den Verkehr _____.
6. Da ist die Autobahn, jetzt _____!
7. Wer will denn schon ein kleines Land wie Liechtenstein _____?
8. Es dauert lange, die Innenstadt im Auto zu _____.
9. Heute muß man in den Städten sehr viele Abgase _____.
10. Mein Fahrrad ist _____.

a. winden
b. beeilen
c. geht's los
d. angreifen
e. einatmen
f. verrostet
g. erreichen
h. schauen
i. verändert
j. geworden

Review Exercises

A. *Supply the plural form of the noun in parentheses.*

1. Hast du die drei _____ für mich? (das Foto)
2. Nennen Sie _____ von drei oder vier Ihrer Freunde! (der Name)
3. Wo hat er _____ hingelegt? (das Bild)
4. Wieviele _____ Deutschlands kennen Sie? (die Stadt)
5. Er hat einige _____ geschrieben. (das Buch)
6. Viele _____ in Deutschland sind weltbekannt. (das Museum)
7. _____ in der Innenstadt sind fast alle neu. (das Gebäude)
8. _____ meines Freundes studieren in Deutschland. (die Tochter)
9. Um wieviel Uhr schließen hier _____? (der Laden)
10. _____ sind verkehrt, nicht die Welt. (der Mensch)

B. *Supply the gender of the compound noun.*

1. Vorderreifen
2. Volkswagen
3. Stadttor
4. Gewitterwolke
5. Schulkamerad
6. Sportsmodell
7. Autobahn
8. Bankpräsident
9. Wohnviertel
10. Abgas

C. *Put the nouns in* (B) *above into the plural.*

D. *Supply the German equivalent for the item in English in parentheses, using the definite article and a preposition as required.*

1. Es gab keine Zeit _____. (for thinking)
2. Ich hatte nur fünf Minuten _____. (for getting dressed)
3. _____ im Park ist in Deutschland verboten. (sleeping)

4. _____ um 7 Uhr ist für viele Leute nicht leicht. (getting up)
5. _____ der Zeitung habe ich nur wenig Zeit. (for reading)
6. _____ von Briefen ist meistens billiger als _____. (writing / calling)
7. Sie findet _____ immer sehr anstrengend. (shopping)
8. _____ soll man am besten in die Sauna gehen. (after eating and drinking)

GUIDED COMPOSITION

A. Choose ten nouns from the list in the beer advertisement and write a paragraph explaining how the product might accompany each activity. Be sure to use the appropriate **der-** or **ein-**word. Then supply the definite article and the plural form of as many of the nouns on the list as possible.

TRINKEN SIE ISENBECK PILS

Anregung — Besuch — Camping — Club — Diskussion — Eisbein Entspannung — Feierabend — Fernsehen — Freundschaft — Frohsinn — Gemütlichkeit — Gesang — Gesellschaft — Gespräch Hausbar — Jubiläum — Kasino — Kegelbahn — Kühlschrank Lebensfreude — Lesen — Liebe — Party — Reise — Restaurant Schützenfest — Skat — Stammtisch — Stimmung — Theke Urlaub — Weidwerk — Zutrunk

DER NEUE TREND ISENBECK PILS

Faß — Flasche — Dose — Glas — Becher — Krug

BRAUEREI ISENBECK AG
47 HAMM · TELEFON (02381) 26853

B. The marriage advertisements are from the weekly German newspaper *Die Zeit*. Read through the advertisements, using a German-English dictionary to look up any unfamiliar words. Then write a response to the advertisement which attracts you most.

Ein Sommernachtstraum?

Liebe, Vertrauen, Zärtlichkeit, . . . das braucht für Sie kein Traum zu bleiben. — Anschmiegsam, fraulich, selbstsicher, gepflegt, beruflich engagiert, mit Liebe zu Kindern, Musik, Büchern, einem schönen Heim, das Gespräch suchend, Geborgenheit und die Liebe ersehnend . . . Könnte so Ihre „Traumfrau" aussehen? — Bitte schreiben Sie mir nach Raum 2 (Hamburgerin, mittelblond, 38/1,71, Abitur).

Raum Frankfurt

(nicht ortsgebunden). Attraktive Lady, schlank, 1,66, mit inneren und äußeren Werten. Interesse: Oper, Operette, Tanz, Reisen, Vorträge und an allem Zeitgeschehen in der heutigen Welt.

Suche adäquaten Lebenspartner, Ende 40, auch älter, der mir einen Hauch von Zärtlichkeit, Geborgenheit und Frohsinn gibt. Welcher Gentleman, der sonst so eine Art von Kennenlernen ablehnt, sendet doch einmal ein Echo mit oder ohne Bild.

Ich bin so eine

— die mit linker Logik liebäugelt
— die aber an bürgerlicher Kultur Spaß hat
— die die Beschäftigung mit den 3 K nicht negativ empfindet
— die aber nicht nur über Emanzipation (sondern auch . . .) reden möchte, sondern auch . . .
— die zwar nicht das hübscheste Cesicht hat
— die aber hübsch schmusen möchte

Fortsetzung folgt, wenn Sie sich ehewilliger Lehrerin (29/1,70/Raum 4) bemerkbar machen.

In München lebt eine glückliche, junge Familie, bestehend aus einer attrak., intell. Mutter (gesch.), schlank, sportl., künstl. Neigungen u. ganz schön anspruchsvoll; Sohn 12 J., Tochter 10 J., beide aufgeschlossen und liebenswert. Welcher mutige Individualist mit einer Menge Humor, Intelligenz, Toleranz, Kinder- u. Tierliebe, viel Sinn für Kunst, aufgeschlossen für alles Neue, frei von Engstirnigkeit und Spießbürgerlichkeit, hat Lust, in unsere fröhliche Runde als „Familienoberhaupt" aufgenommen zu werden?

Ich suche

ein Mädchen zum Heiraten! Ein recht schlankes Mädchen, das die Ehe als Partnerschaft mit viel Vertrauen und Toleranz versteht, das einen Beruf hat bzw. anstrebt, das recht selbständig ist und viel Zärtlichkeit braucht. Ein Mädchen, das mich optimistisch stimmt, mit mir Freuden teilt und Probleme bewältigt. Ich bin Junggeselle (31 Jahre, 178 cm) und zur Zeit Hochschulassistent (Ingenieurwissenschaften) in Aachen.

Richtiger Berliner,

34jähr. Mediziner, 169 cm, untersetzt-athletisch, mit beg. „Platte", beruflich engagiert, fröhlich, lebensbejahend, seit einiger Zeit geschieden, sucht aus Mangel an Gelegenheit ca. 25–30jähr. charmante, schlanke, lebendige und emanzipierte Akademikerin für eine gemeinsame Zukunft. Interessen: Ungewöhnliches, Musik, Segeln, Ski, Reisen etc. Bitte um Bildzuschriften. Garantiert Antwort.

Ihr Vertrauen sucht

Vorstandsmitglied, Akademiker, USA-Bürger, 38/1,78, Vermögen, z. Z. Deutschland. Sind Sie eine Lebensgefährtin, die sehr gut aussieht, sich in Jeans und Abendkleid wohl fühlt, in der Lage ist, ein sehr großes Haus zu führen, auch vor weltweiten Reisen nicht zurückschreckt? Sie sollen modern und aufgeschlossen sein, Temperament und Sinnlichkeit haben und gerne Sport treiben. Schreiben Sie mir bitte ausführlich mit Bild (natürlich zurück). Ihre Zuschrift wird beantwortet. Ich danke im voraus.

D—K—BN + 100 km

Freiberufler, 40/1,75/75, gesch., liebt frische Luft (nicht nur beim Segeln), Bücher, Musik, fremde Gewässer, aber auch Haus und Hof — sucht treues Eheweib, ± 30, ohne Anhang, natürlich, fröhlich, sportlich.

Wenn SIE dieses Jahr nicht wieder allein oder mit Ihrer besten Freundin Urlaub machen wollen, sondern auch ernsthaft den ersten Schritt zu einer Ehe, dann würde ich (Dipl.-Ing., 36, kinderlieb, Musikliebhaber, Nichtraucher, Wassersportler, Antifernsehtist) mich über Ihre Zuschrift mit Bild und/oder Telefonnummer freuen.

Chapter 18

Bremen

Useful Phrases

bis morgen	until tomorrow; by tomorrow
in Erfüllung gehen	to come true, be fulfilled
genug haben	to have enough
viel Spaß haben	to have a good time
keine Lust zu etwas haben	to have no desire to (do) something
Die Temperatur liegt um 16 Grad Celsius.	The temperature is [lies] around 16 degrees Centigrade.
wechselnd wolkig	partly [changing] cloudy
eine Neigung zu	a tendency to; a chance of

MODEL SENTENCES

I

Fährst du **morgen** nach Stuttgart?	Are you going to Stuttgart tomorrow?
Nein, ich **fahre** erst **nächsten Montag.**	No, I'm not going before next Monday.
Wie lange **wirst** du in Stuttgart **bleiben?**	How long will you stay in Stuttgart?
Ich **werde** nur zwei Tage dort **verbringen** und (**werde**) dann in die Schweiz **weiterreisen.**	I'll spend just two days there and then go on to Switzerland.
Du **wirst wohl** auch deine Freunde in Stuttgart **besuchen?**	You'll probably see your friends in Stuttgart too, (won't you)?

II

Nein, leider nicht. Sie haben Ferien und **werden** bis dahin schon an die Nordsee **abgereist sein.**	Unfortunately, no. They're on (have their) vacation and will have left for the North Sea by then.
Bis übernächstes Jahr **werden** wir sie hoffentlich **gesehen haben.**	Hopefully we'll have seen them by the year after next.

Grammar Explanations

I. FUTURE TENSE

In German, the present tense often expresses an action that occurs in the future (*see* Chapter 1), especially when an adverb of time (such as **gleich, heute abend, morgen,** and **nächste Woche**) is used in the sentence. The adverb specifies that the event is in the future time.

Morgen fahre ich in die Stadt.	Tomorrow I'll drive into the city.
Macht ihr nächste Woche eine Radtour?	Are you going on a bicycle tour next week?

When future time is not specifically designated by a time expression, the future tense of the verb is used.

Wir **werden** zehn Pfund **abnehmen.**	We'll lose ten pounds.
Die Höchsttemperatur **wird** bei 16 Grad Celsius **liegen.**	The highest temperature will be about 16 degrees Centigrade.

The future tense in German, however, is used not only to indicate futurity of time, but also to express probability. Its occurrences can be grouped into three categories.

1. Assurances

Ich verspreche dir, ich **werde kommen.**	I promise you I'll come.
Wir **werden** es schon **schaffen.**	We'll make it for sure.

2. Assumptions

Morgen **wird** es bestimmt nicht **regnen.**	It certainly won't rain tomorrow.
Das **wird** wohl **stimmen.**	That's probably right.

3. Commands

Du **wirst** das sofort **aufessen!**	You'll eat that up right away.
Werdet ihr endlich ruhig **sein!**	Will you finally be quiet.

Frequently expressions of probability contain the adverb **wohl** (probably); other adverbs also used are **hoffentlich** (hopefully), **möglicherweise** (possibly), **schon** (probably), **sicher** (certainly) **vielleicht** (perhaps), and **wahrscheinlich** (most likely).

The future tense in German is formed with the conjugated present tense of **werden,** here used as an auxiliary, and the infinitive of the main verb.

Future Tense of **abnehmen**

Singular
ich werde abnehmen
du wirst abnehmen
er
sie } wird abnehmen
es

Plural
wir werden abnehmen
ihr werdet abnehmen
sie werden abnehmen

Singular/Plural
Sic werden abnehmen

Check Your Comprehension

Form the future tense of the verb according to the person indicated.

1. Ich _____ _____. (beginnen)
2. Sie (*pl.*) _____ _____. (skilaufen)
3. Ihr _____ das Rauchen _____. (reduzieren)
4. Du _____ dich _____. (waschen)
5. Wir _____ _____. (schreiben)
6. Sie (*sing.*) _____ das wohl _____. (wissen)
7. Er _____ mit dem Auto _____. (hinfahren)

II. FUTURE PERFECT TENSE

The future perfect tense is rarely used in German. When it does occur, it usually expresses the probability that an action will be concluded sometime in the future.

Bis nächsten Monat **werden** wir sicher fünf Pfund **abgenommen haben.**	By next month we'll certainly have lost five pounds.

The future perfect tense is formed from the conjugated future tense of the auxiliary **werden,** the past participle of the principal verb, and the infinitive of the auxiliary **haben** or **sein: werden** + **geregnet** + **haben,** for example.

Bis morgen abend **wird** es sicher zweimal **geregnet haben.**	By tomorrow night it will probably rain [have rained] twice.
Bis morgen **werden** sie sicher **abgefahren sein.**	By tomorrow they will probably have left.

In the future and future perfect tenses, the present and past infinitives stand at the end when the sentence is in regular or inverted word order.

Wir werden zwei Tage in Stuttgart **bleiben.**	We'll stay two days in Stuttgart.
Bis dahin werdet ihr wohl schon wieder **abgereist sein.**	By then you'll probably be gone [have left] again.

In dependent word order, the finite verb, in this case the conjugated form of **werden,** moves to the end of the clause.

Weil er nach Stuttgart fahren **wird, . . .**	Because he will go to Stuttgart, . . .
Da du zwei Tage in Stuttgart bleiben **wirst, . . .**	Since you will stay in Stuttgart for two days, . . .
Nachdem ihr schon abgereist sein **werdet, . . .**	After you'll (already) have gone, . . .

As is to be expected, the separable prefix remains united with the infinitive or the past participle.

Ich hoffe, daß sie bald **abreisen** werden.	I hope they will soon leave.
Ich hoffe, daß sie bis morgen abend **abgereist** sein werden.	I hope they will have left by tomorrow night.

Form the future perfect tense of the verb according to the person indicated.

1. Sie (*pl.*) _____ es _____ _____. (versprechen)
2. Du _____ es _____ _____. (versuchen)
3. Ihr _____ nach Hause _____ _____. (gehen)
4. Ich _____ dorthin _____ _____. (schwimmen)
5. Er _____ es _____ _____. (brauchen)
6. Wir _____ es uns _____ _____. (überlegen)
7. Sie (*sing.*) _____ _____ _____. (abreisen)
8. Du _____ _____ _____. (hingehen)

CONVERSATION

Ein Silvesterabend

Es ist kurz vor Mitternacht. Draußen hört man schon das Knallen explodierender Feuerwerkskörper. Herr und Frau Schröder reden über ihre Vorsätze fürs Neue Jahr. Herr Schröder öffnet vorsichtig eine Flasche Sekt.

FRAU SCHRÖDER	Ich bin eigentlich sehr froh, daß wir dieses Mal den Silvesterabend ganz allein feiern.
HERR SCHRÖDER	Ja, ich habe auch genug von den üblichen Silvesterparties mit Tanzmusik und Feuerwerk. Bis Mitternacht können wir uns ja noch überlegen, was wir uns fürs nächste Jahr vornehmen wollen.
FRAU SCHRÖDER	Eines kann ich dir versprechen: ich werde jetzt endlich mit meiner Diät beginnen und auch ein bißchen Sport treiben.
HERR SCHRÖDER	Na, Luise, wenn du zu Ostern mit mir nach Garmisch[1] fahren und vierzehn Tage Ski laufen wirst, brauchst du wahrscheinlich mit deiner Diät nicht so streng zu sein.

	Was meinst du, wie wir beide bei einem Skiurlaub abneh-
	men werden!
FRAU SCHRÖDER	Ich weiß nicht, Rudi, ob ich noch Ski laufen werde in
	meinem Alter. Aber da wir ja in unserem Hotel ein
	Hallenbad haben werden, werde ich viel schwimmen 20
	gehen, während du auf dem Skihang bist.
HERR SCHRÖDER	Sag mal, willst du im nächsten Jahr nicht auch das
	Rauchen etwas reduzieren? Ich habe es mir doch inzwi-
	schen ganz abgewöhnt. Ich habe nun schon seit zwei Jah-
	ren keine Zigarren mehr geraucht. 25
FRAU SCHRÖDER	Wirklich bewundernswert! Seit dir der Arzt gesagt hat,
	daß... Aber du hast ja recht! Ich werde versuchen,
	es mir ebenfalls abzugewöhnen, obwohl es sicher nicht
	einfach sein wird.
HERR SCHRÖDER	Hörst du die Kirchenglocken? Es ist Mitternacht. Das neue 30
	Jahr hat begonnen. Hier, nimm dein Glas!
FRAU SCHRÖDER	Na, dann: Prost Neujahr! Ich hoffe, daß alle unsere
	Wünsche in Erfüllung gehen werden.
HERR SCHRÖDER	Das hoffe ich auch. Prost, Luise! Hier, komm ans Fenster
	und sieh dir das herrliche Feuerwerk an! 35

---

[1] Ski resort on the German/Austrian border.

ORAL PRACTICE

A. *Put the sentence into the future tense.*

1. Regnet es?
2. Gibt es Schnee?
3. Macht ihr eine Radtour?
4. Wird es wieder etwas wärmer?
5. An der See gibt es starken Wind.
6. In Köln steigen wir um.
7. Wir fahren in die Alpen.
8. Unseren Urlaub verbringen wir dieses Jahr in Spanien.
9. Ich schicke euch ein Telegramm.
10. Heiratest du im Mai oder im Juni?

B. *Put the sentence into the future tense and use the expression of probability in parentheses.*

1. Er ist hungrig. (vielleicht)
2. Ich nehme an, Ihr habt keine Lust, in die Schule zu gehen. (wahrscheinlich)
3. Wenn du krank bist, mußt du zu Hause bleiben. (wohl)
4. Ihr habt heute nicht viel zu tun, wie ich annehme. (sicher)
5. Er ist kein Dieb! (hoffentlich)
6. Ihr freut euch auf Weihnachten. (bestimmt)
7. Der Kandidat bekommt die Position. (wohl)
8. Ich glaube, mein Freund wird noch Präsident des Studentenparlamentes. (möglicherweise)
9. Wir fahren gleich in die Stadt. (wohl)
10. Das stimmt. (schon)

C. *Put the sentence into the future perfect tense.*

1. Bis morgen hast du den Brief geschrieben.
2. Bis Sonntag hast du die anderen Briefe geschrieben.
3. Bis zum 1. April muß er für das Auto dreitausend Mark bezahlen.
4. Im nächsten Sommer macht er seinen B.A.
5. In zwei Jahren macht sie ihr „Abitur".
6. Bis Freitag hast du eine Antwort von mir.
7. In 10 Jahren hat man viele Probleme der Umweltverschmutzung gelöst.
8. Bald haben die Europäer alle afrikanischen Kolonien zurückgegeben.
9. Im nächsten Sommer haben sie hier sicher drei Häuser gebaut.
10. In drei Wochen hast du dich bestimmt gut erholt.

D. *Put the sentence into the future perfect tense and use the expression of probability in parentheses.*

1. Er hat nicht daran gedacht. (vielleicht)
2. Der Milchmann hat geklingelt. (wohl)
3. Sie hat schon einen Reisepaß beantragt. (sicher)
4. Er hat eine Menge zu tun gehabt. (wahrscheinlich)
5. Bis wir in Stuttgart ankommen, seid ihr schon wieder abgereist. (sicher)

6. Du hast den Brief gefunden. (wohl)
7. Sie haben die Bombe rechtzeitig entdeckt. (hoffentlich)
8. Der Zug ist schon abgefahren. (wohl)
9. Du hast von meinem Auto-Unfall gehört. (wahrscheinlich)
10. Ihr habt euch keine Sorgen gemacht. (hoffentlich)

E. *Use the appropriate tense of the verb in parentheses. Sometimes only one blank needs to be completed.*

1. Ich glaube, nächstes Jahr _____ alle unsere Wünsche in Erfüllung _____. (gehen)
2. Bis nächstes Jahr _____ sich alle seine Träume. (erfüllen)
3. Wir _____ beim Skifahren bestimmt viel Spaß _____. (haben)
4. Er _____ gleich zehn Pfund _____. (abnehmen)
5. Übermorgen _____ er seinen Geburtstag _____. (feiern)
6. Obwohl du keine Lust dazu hast, _____ du es sofort _____! (aufessen)
7. Heute abend _____ ich mir im Kino einen guten Film _____. (ansehen)
8. Gestern habt ihr versprochen, daß ihr übermorgen _____ _____. (kommen)

F. *Substitute or add each phrase as it is introduced into the previous sentence and make any necessary changes.*

Morgen   besucht er   seine Freunde in Garmisch.
Nächste Woche _____
Wahrscheinlich _____
_____ anrufen.
Bis übermorgen _____
_____ sie (*pl.*) _____
Heute abend _____

GUIDED CONVERSATION

Begin a conversation with your neighbor regarding your immediate and distant future plans. You might compare notes on what you plan to do after class this evening, tomorrow, Saturday night, this summer, after finishing school (**nach Schulabschluß**), and later.

Zone 1: Meister heiter, Höchsttemperatur 17 Grad, morgen: zeitweise etwas wolkig.

Zone 2: Überwiegend freundlich, Höchsttemperatur 14 Grad, morgen: sonnig.

Zone 3: Heiter bis wolkig, Höchsttemperatur 16 Grad, morgen: wenig Änderung.

Zone 4: Heiter bis wolkig, Höchsttemperatur 16 Grad, morgen: wenig Änderung.

Zone 5: Geringe Niederschläge, Höchsttemperatur 18 Grad, morgen: örtlich Gewitter.

Zone 6: Gebietsweise Schauer, Höchsttemperatur 14 Grad, morgen: meist freundlich.

Zone 7: Nachmittags einzelne Gewitter, Höchsttemperatur 18 Grad, morgen: unverändert.

Zone 8: Wenige Niederschläge, Höchsttemperatur 18 Grad, morgen: veränderlich.

Zone 9: Gebietsweise Gewitter, Höchsttemperatur 12 Grad, morgen: wenig Änderung.

Zone 10: Wenige Regenfälle, Höchsttemperatur 19 Grad, morgen: gleichbleibend.

READING

Der Wetterbericht

Maria möchte übers Wochenende mit zwei ihrer Klassenkameradinnen eine Fahrradtour machen. Sie wollen von Düsseldorf nach Venlo fahren, einer kleinen Stadt gleich hinter der holländischen Grenze.

Maria möchte wissen, ob es morgen oder übermorgen regnen wird oder nicht. Wenn es nämlich in den nächsten Tagen keinen Regen gibt, dann wird sie natürlich auch keinen Regenmantel mitnehmen. Das Zelt wird schwer genug sein, so daß sie froh ist über alles, was sie zu Hause lassen kann.

Maria hat sich zwar auf dem Heimweg für 20 Pfennig eine BILD-Zeitung gekauft, aber sie möchte sich vergewissern, ob diese Wettervorhersage richtig

5

ist und sie mit dem Wetterbericht im Fernsehen vergleichen. Es ist gleich 10
19.15 Uhr. Maria hat den Fernseher angeschaltet. Im 2. Programm[1] sind
die Nachrichten gerade vorüber. Es folgt der Wetterbericht.

„Die Wettervorhersage für morgen, Samstag, den 28. März:

In den nördlichen Landesteilen wechselnd wolkig. Nur geringe Neigung
zu Niederschlägen. Die Höchsttemperatur wird um 16 Grad liegen, örtlich 15
ein bißchen darüber. An der See werden die Temperaturen nicht ganz so
hoch sein, da langsam kühle Meeresluft von Nordwesten nach Norddeutschland eindringt.

Im mittleren Deutschland, etwa vom Ruhrgebiet bis südlich des Mains,
wird es heiter bis wolkig sein. Die Tagestemperaturen werden zwischen 15 20
und 19 Grad liegen.

Im Süden Deutschlands beherrscht noch immer ein Mittelmeer-Hoch unser
Wetter. Dort wird es überwiegend sonnig und etwas wärmer sein als heute.
Die Temperaturen werden bis etwa 20 Grad ansteigen. Örtlich werden
einzelne Gewitter auftreten. 25

Und nun die Wettervorhersage bis übermorgen abend. Das Tief über
Schottland schwächt sich ab; daher wird es keine wesentliche Änderung
geben.

So weit der Wetterbericht für morgen, den 28. März. Guten Abend!

Zur Fortsetzung des Programms schalten wir jetzt um in unser Studio 30
in Köln.“

---

[1] German radio and TV is government owned and operated, and there are only three stations:
1. (read **erstes**) **Programm,** 2. **Programm,** and 3. **Programm.**

QUESTIONS

1. Was plant Maria fürs nächste Wochenende?
2. Mit wem wird sie fahren?
3. Womit werden sie fahren?
4. Wohin wollen sie fahren?
5. Was möchte Maria wissen?
6. Warum will sie wissen, ob es Regen geben wird?
7. Warum genügt ihr die Wettervorhersage in der Zeitung nicht?

8. Wann kann man den Wetterbericht im 2. Fernsehprogramm sehen?
9. Wie wird das Wetter in Norddeutschland sein?
10. Wie wird das Wetter im mittleren Deutschland sein?
11. Wie wird das Wetter im Süden Deutschlands sein?
12. Wie ist die allgemeine Wettervorhersage für übermorgen?

VOCABULARY EXERCISES

Supply the appropriate word from the list on the right.

1. Zwölf Uhr nachts oder 24 Uhr ist _____.
2. Hoffentlich werden unsere Wünsche im nächsten Jahr _____ gehen.
3. Er öffnet vorsichtig eine _____ Sekt.
4. Sie werden _____ nach Garmisch fahren.
5. Das Hotel hat ein großes _____.
6. Man kann die _____ der Kirchen hören.
7. Die Mädchen wollen am Wochenende eine _____ machen.
8. Das sind zwei _____ von Maria.
9. Flensburg ist eine deutsche Stadt an der _____ zu Dänemark.
10. Wir nehmen ein _____ mit für den Campingplatz.
11. Bei Regen braucht man einen _____ oder Regenschirm.
12. Die _____ für morgen ist: Schnee in den Bergen.
13. Dortmund, Essen und Bochum sind Städte im _____.
14. Die Türkei, Italien, Jugoslawien und Spanien sind Länder am _____.
15. In Süddeutschland wird es einzelne _____ geben.
16. Die _____ liegt bei 33 Grad.
17. Die _____ des Programms folgt in einer Minute.

a. Ruhrgebiet
b. zu Ostern
c. Fahrradtour
d. Zelt
e. Mittelmeer
f. Hallenbad
g. in Erfüllung
h. Glocken
i. Gewitter
j. Flasche
k. Grenze
l. Regenmantel
m. Fortsetzung
n. Höchsttemperatur
o. Wettervorhersage
p. Klassenkameradinnen
q. Mitternacht

Review Exercises

A. *Supply the appropriate future tense form of the verbs in parentheses.*

1. Was _____ Sie nach der Deutschstunde _____? (machen)
2. Was _____ du nach dem Abendessen _____? (tun)
3. Was _____ sie (*sing.*) heute abend _____? (kochen)
4. Sie (*pl.*) _____ alles _____ wollen. (wissen)
5. _____ Sie bald _____? (heiraten)
6. _____ du eine Menge Geld _____? (haben)
7. _____ seine Freundin Lehrerin _____? (werden)
8. Ich weiß noch nicht, ob ich dieses oder jenes Hotel _____ _____. (wählen)

B. *Supply the appropriate future perfect tense form of the verb in parentheses.*

1. Vielleicht _____ er Hunger _____ _____. (haben)
2. Möglicherweise _____ die Leute keine Lust _____ _____. (haben)
3. Nach dem anstrengenden Tag _____ du sicher müde _____ _____. (sein)
4. Bis Dienstag _____ ich den Brief bestimmt _____ _____. (beantworten)
5. Wenn ich nach Hamburg komme, _____ du wohl schon _____ _____. (abreisen)
6. Ihr _____ wahrscheinlich nicht genug Geld bei euch _____ _____. (haben)
7. Bis morgen _____ die Polizei den Dieb sicher _____ _____. (erwischen)

C. *Put the following passage into the future tense.*

Die Wettervorhersage für morgen, Samstag, den 28. März:

In den nördlichen Landesteilen **ist** es wechselnd wolkig. **Es gibt** nur geringe Neigung zu Niederschlägen. Die Höchsttemperaturen **liegen** um 16 Grad, örtlich ein bißchen darüber.

Im mittleren Deutschland **ist** es heiter bis wolkig. Die Tagestemperaturen **liegen** zwischen 15 und 19 Grad. Im Süden Deutschlands **beherrscht** ein Mittelmeer-Hoch auch morgen unser Wetter. Im Norden: Überwiegend sonnig und etwas wärmer. Örtlich **treten** einzelne Gewitter **auf.**

Und nun die Wettervorhersage bis übermorgen abend: Das Tief über Schottland **schwächt sich ab; es gibt** daher keine wesentliche Änderung.

D. *Express in German.*

1. I will probably be married by (**bis**) June.
2. They will go on a bike trip next week.
3. She will have taken her exam by Friday.
4. We will buy a bigger house.
5. In two years I will be a teacher.
6. What will you be doing tomorrow night?
7. What will the weather be like the day after tomorrow?
8. Will you still go to Europe this year?
9. Nobody will be able to tell you that.
10. He will become president next year.

GUIDED COMPOSITION

A. Write a short composition on what life might be like in the year 2000. You might make predictions regarding your personal life (how old you will be, what you will be doing, where you will be living, whether you will be married, whether you will have children, and so on), or you might write about life in general (the energy situation, traffic, housing, schools, politics, and so on).

B. Write a horoscope for someone you know. Include predictions for the immediate future as well as for the distant future.

Chapter 19

Oktoberfest in München

Useful Phrases

im folgenden	as follows; in the following passage
zum Verkauf	for sale
Na und?	So what?
das Fieber messen	to take (one's) temperature
Das versteht sich von selbst.	It goes without saying.

MODEL SENTENCES

I

Wird das Auto gerade repariert?	Is the car just being repaired?
Nein, es **ist** schon repariert.	No, it's already repaired.
Wurde die Lampe gestern repariert?	Was the lamp being repaired yesterday?
Nein, sie **war** gestern schon repariert.	No, it was already repaired yesterday.
Ist das Sofa vorgestern repariert **worden?**	Was the sofa being repaired the day before yesterday?
Nein, das Sofa **ist** vorgestern schon repariert **gewesen.**	No, the sofa was already repaired the day before yesterday.
War der Stuhl repariert **worden,** bevor er verkauft wurde?	Had the chair been repaired before it was sold?
Das Radio **wird** noch repariert **werden.**	The radio will still be repaired.
Es wird nicht **geredet!**	No talking!
Hier **wird** nicht **geraucht!**	No smoking here!

II

Die Tür **öffnet sich.**	The door is being opened.
Die Schreibmaschine **läßt sich** nicht reparieren.	The typewriter cannot be repaired.
Ich **lasse mir** die Haare schneiden.	I'm having my hair cut.

Grammar Explanations

I. PASSIVE VOICE

In English and in German, the active voice is used when the subject of the sentence acts or does something.

> John stellte mich deinem Freund vor.   John introduced me to your friend.

When the subject does *not* perform the action but is acted upon, or "suffers" the action, the sentence is in the *passive voice*.

Ich wurde deiner Freundin von John   I was introduced to your friend by John.
   vorgestellt.

In the passive voice there is usually a deemphasis on the performer of the action (the agent) and a focus of attention on the receiver of the action (the subject). The agent may therefore be omitted.

> Wir wurden (von ihnen) erkannt.   We were recognized (by them).

In passive constructions, the agent is used in conjunction with a preposition, in German usually **von**. Remember that **von** always governs the dative case.

> Es wurde **von ihr** angefertigt.   It was made by her.

The transformation from the active to the passive voice in German is similar to that in English; the subject of the active sentence becomes the agent of the passive sentence, and the direct object of the active sentence becomes the subject of the passive sentence. The subject of the sentence, whether in the active or the passive voice, is always in the nominative case.

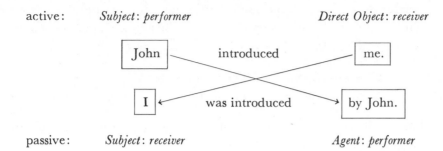

active: *Subject: performer*   *Direct Object: receiver*

passive: *Subject: receiver*   *Agent: performer*

In actual practice, nobody ever explicitly performs this mental operation. It is a purely analytic classroom exercise. The native speaker automatically uses either the active or the passive voice, depending on whether the focus of his attention is on the performer or the receiver of the action.

The passive in English is formed from the auxiliary **to be** and the past participle of the principal verb.

The picture is being painted.

In German the passive voice is formed by using the conjugated form of the auxiliary **werden** and the past participle of the principal verb. The passive voice can be formed in all six tenses merely by conjugating the auxiliary **werden.**

pres.:	Das Gemälde **wird gemalt.**	The picture is being painted.
pres. perf.:	Das Gemälde **ist gemalt worden.**	The picture has been painted.
past.:	Das Gemälde **wurde gemalt.**	The picture was being painted.
past perf.:	Das Gemälde **war gemalt worden.**	The picture had been painted.
fut.:	Das Gemälde **wird gemalt werden.**	The picture will be painted.
fut. perf.:	Das Gemälde **wird gemalt worden sein.**	The picture will have been painted.

In the perfect tenses, note that the past participle of the auxiliary **werden** drops the **ge–: worden;** this form occurs *only* in the passive and *only* in these tenses. Also notice that the auxiliary of **werden** is **sein.**

In English sometimes a sentence is ambiguous because it could refer either to the *action* of the verb or the *state* of being resulting from the action. Thus, it is not clear in the sentence "The picture is painted" whether the picture is in the process of being painted or is the finished, painted picture. In German, however, it is relatively easy to make the distinction. Use of the conjugated auxiliary **werden** + past participle indicates action; use of the conjugated auxiliary **sein** + past participle indicates result of the action. This use of **sein** is sometimes called the *statal passive*.

action: Die Gemälde **werden gemalt.**   The pictures are (being) painted.
state: Die Gemälde **sind gemalt.**   The pictures are (have been) painted.

English has not developed a simple system that allows the speaker to distinguish clearly between action and state. At times, the differentiation can be made by using the progressive rather than the simple form of the tense. Thus the sentence "A house **was being built** in the canyon" emphasizes the action of building, whereas the sentence "A house **was built** in the canyon" is ambiguous, because it could refer to the action of building or the result of it. In other cases, English makes the differentiation between action and state through word order.

action: In our zoo, the animals are fed well.
state: In our zoo, the animals are well fed.

Modal auxiliaries sometimes occur in the passive voice, especially in the present and simple past. In that case the word order is: conjugated form of the modal, past participle of the principal verb, and infinitive of the auxiliary **werden.**

Active	*Passive*
Er darf diese Bilder nicht ausstellen.	Diese Bilder **dürfen** nicht ausgestellt werden.
(He may not exhibit these pictures.)	(These pictures may not be exhibited.)
Sie konnte das Bild nicht verkaufen.	Das Bild **konnte** nicht verkauft werden.
(She couldn't sell the picture.)	(The picture couldn't be sold.)

In English the indirect object in the active voice can be made into the subject of the passive voice.

Indirect Object	*Subject*
They told *him* the truth.	*He* was told the truth.

In German this is not a permissible construction. The direct object of the active voice is always used as the subject of the sentence in the passive voice. The indirect object remains in the dative case.

Man sagte *ihm* die Wahrheit.   They told him the truth.
Die Wahrheit wurde *ihm* gesagt.   He was told the truth.

For the sake of emphasis the indirect object may move to first position in the sentence.

Ihm wurde die Wahrheit gesagt.   Him they told the truth.

This leads to certain constructions seemingly without a subject, often called *impersonal* sentences, which occur primarily with verbs that govern the dative case ("Mir wurde gedankt.") or in situations where the direct object is a subordinate clause ("Mir wurde gesagt, daß . . ."). Thus it is *not* possible to say "Ich wurde gesagt, daß . . ." (I was told that. . . .) because, in this instance, the verb **sagen** governs the dative case. The construction "Mir wurde gesagt, daß . . ." is used instead.

At times, in such elliptic clauses, the rather meaningless "filler" **es** can be used as a subject.

Es wurde **mir** gesagt, daß . . .   I was told that. . . .

But as long as some other expression is in first position in the sentence, such as an adverb of time or the indirect object, the **es** is not required. Note that **es,** however, is always the *implied subject,* and, therefore, the verb is always in the third-person singular.

Gestern abend wurde ihm gesagt, daß . . .   Last night he was told that. . . .
Ihnen wurde gesagt, daß . . .   They were told that. . . .

The passive voice of some verbs, such as **arbeiten, kämpfen, lachen** and so on, which do not normally govern an accusative object, may express an *activity as such.* This leads to a characteristically German construction that can hardly be translated.

Hier wird gearbeitet. ⎫   There is work going on here.
Es wird hier gearbeitet. ⎭   (*Lit.*: Here is being worked.)

Es wurde lange gekämpft.   There was fighting going on for a long time. (*Lit.*: It was being fought for a long time.)

Frequently such impersonal passive constructions are used as commands.

Hier wird nicht geraucht!   There will be no smoking here.
      or No smoking here!

Es wird nicht geredet!   There will be no talking.
      or No talking!

A. *Form the passive voice of the verb in the tense indicated in parentheses.*

1. Sie (*sing.*) _____ glücklich _____ _____. (machen, *present perfect*)
2. Er _____ _____ _____. (erkennen, *past perfect*)
3. Es _____ _____. (anfertigen, *past*)
4. Alles _____ _____ _____. (kaufen, *present perfect*)
5. Vieles _____ _____. (anbieten, *present*)
6. Die Halskette _____ _____. (tragen, *past*)
7. Die Pizza _____ _____. (aufessen, *past*)
8. Wir _____ _____. (anregen, *present*)
9. Sie (*pl.*) _____ _____ _____. (sehen, *present perfect*)
10. Die Gemälde _____ _____. (ausstellen *past*)

B. *Form the statal passive of the verb in the tense indicated in parentheses.*

1. Der Fisch _____ _____. (kochen, *present*)
2. Das Bild _____ _____. (ausstellen, *past*)
3. Das _____ selbst _____. (anfertigen, *present*)
4. Wir _____ _____. (einladen, *past*)
5. Die Tür _____ _____. (öffnen, *past*)
6. Der Laden _____ _____. (schließen, *present*)

C. *Change the sentence from active into the passive voice and use an impersonal construction.*

1. Er sagte mir etwas.
2. Jemand antwortete ihm.
3. Wir tanzten heute abend.
4. Niemand berichtete uns das.
5. Man kämpfte hart.
6. Sie rauchen hier nicht.

II. ALTERNATIVES TO THE PASSIVE

In many instances, the active voice is preferred in German, and there are several alternative constructions that can be used in lieu of the passive proper.

The indefinite pronoun **man** plus an active construction is probably the most common.

Es wurde mir gesagt, daß . . .	It was told to me that. . . .
Man sagte mir, daß . . .	Someone told me that. . . .
Hier wird abends getanzt.	There is dancing here nightly.
Man tanzt hier abends.	*Lit.*: One dances here nightly.

Another frequent construction consists of **sich lassen** or **lassen** plus the infinitive of another verb, with the meaning "to have something done by someone else." Here the underlying principle is passive, since the subject is not performing the action.

Er **läßt sich** die Haare **schneiden.**	He has his hair cut. (*Lit.*: He lets his hair be cut.)
Er **hat sich** nicht von einem Arzt **untersuchen** lassen.	He did not have himself examined by a physician.
Er **läßt sich** mit seinem Büro **verbinden.**	*Lit.*: He has himself connected with his office.
Er **läßt** seinen Wagen **reparieren.**	He has his car repaired.
Sie **läßt** den Brief **schreiben.**	She has the letter written.

One more alternative construction for the passive voice is the use of the principal verb with **sich.** This formation, however, can be made with only very few verbs, such as **öffnen** and **schließen,** but these verbs occur frequently.

Die Tür **wird geöffnet.**	The door is being opened.
Die Tür **öffnet sich.**	*Lit.*: The door opens itself.

Check Your Comprehension

A. *Change each sentence with passive construction to an active sentence using* **man.** *Be careful to use the same tense.*

1. Er wurde mit seiner Sekretärin verbunden.
2. Gestern sind seine Sachen geliefert worden.

3. Ich werde ihr vorgestellt.
4. Das Kind wird verwöhnt.
5. Es wird vor dem Rauchen gewarnt.

B. *Change the passive construction into an alternative construction with* **sich lassen,** *meaning "to have something done."*

1. Ihm werden die Haare geschnitten.
2. Sie wird untersucht.
3. Wir werden verwöhnt.
4. Ihr werdet bezahlt.
5. Du wurdest mit dem Büro verbunden.

CONVERSATION

Studenten in München-Schwabing[1]

ROLF   Siehst du, da drüben ist es schon. Ich sage ja: Wer Schwabing nicht gesehen hat, hat München nicht gesehen!

KATRIN   Du meinst die Gestalten da drüben auf dem Bürgersteig?

ROLF   Ja, aber von hier aus ist noch nicht viel zu erkennen. Laß uns mal näher 'rangehen[2]!   5

KATRIN   Rolf, schau mal, bei dem Langhaarigen da drüben sind ja eine ganze Menge Gemälde ausgestellt. Meinst du, daß die alle von ihm selbst gemalt sind?

ROLF   Ganz sicher. Die meisten von denen, die hier ihre Kunst und Handarbeit ausstellen, studieren an der berühmten Münchner   10 Kunst-Akademie. Manche verkaufen dann die Dinge, die von ihnen selbst gemacht worden sind.

KATRIN Ich muß sagen, das Bild da auf dem Bürgersteig gefällt mir. Die Farben sind wirklich einmalig!

ROLF Ja, die Farben gefallen mir auch, aber sonst ist mir das Bild ein 15 bißchen zu abstrakt.

KATRIN Na und? Ich finde, bei diesen abstrakten Bildern wird die Fantasie wenigstens ein bißchen angeregt.

ROLF Da hast du natürlich recht. Sieh mal, was hältst du von diesem Silberschmuck? 20

KATRIN Sehr schön! Ist der auch von den Studenten selbst hergestellt?

ROLF Aber sicher! Alles, was du hier siehst und was hier zum Verkauf angeboten wird, ist von den Studenten selbst angefertigt worden.

KATRIN Oh, schau mal, diese Halskette! Ist die nicht hübsch?

ROLF Ja, wirklich. Die paßt bestimmt gut zu deinem schwarzen Pullover. 25 Weißt du was? Ich kaufe sie dir, wenn ich von dir dafür heute abend zu einer selbstgemachten Pizza eingeladen werde.

KATRIN Nun, darüber läßt sich reden. —Danke, Rolf! Diese Halskette ist wirklich ganz toll! Ich werde sie heute abend tragen, wenn ich dir die selbstgemachte Pizza serviere. 30

---

[1] Schwabing is a section of Munich, known for its student life and artists.
[2] Short for **herangehen**.

ORAL PRACTICE

A. *Change the sentence from the active to the passive voice. Watch the change in subject and agent and be careful of the verb tense.*

1. Der Langhaarige hat eine Menge Gemälde ausgestellt.
2. Die Studenten verkaufen diese Dinge.
3. Sie machen diese Sachen selbst.
4. Regt die Grammatik Ihre Fantasie an?
5. Man bietet vieles hier zum Verkauf an.
6. Du hattest mich eingeladen.
7. Ich habe die Halskette gekauft.
8. Man dankte ihm schon.

B. *Change the sentence to the statal passive and use the tense in parentheses.*

1. Sie brät den Fisch. (*present*)
2. Er malt das Bild. (*past*)
3. Ich habe die Halskette selbst angefertigt. (*present*)
4. Du hast uns eingeladen. (*present*)
5. Man öffnet die Tür. (*present*)
6. Man schloß den Laden. (*past*)

C. *Change the sentence into the passive voice using any impersonal construction.*

1. Man sagte mir, heute ist Sonntag.
2. Man antwortete ihm auf seine Frage.
3. Man tanzte den ganzen Abend.
4. Man berichtete uns von der Kunst-Akademie.
5. Man kämpfte hart.

D. *Transform the sentence to an alternative construction for the passive voice with* **sich lassen.** *Watch the verb tense.*

1. Mir werden die Haare geschnitten.
2. Uns wird das Geld geschickt.
3. Sekt wurde uns gebracht.
4. Ein Taxi wird ihr geschickt.
5. Du wirst mit dem Büro verbunden.

E. *Change from the passive to the active voice; where no agent is indicated, use* **man** *as subject. Be careful to use the same tense.*

1. Das Auto ist repariert worden.
2. Dieser Satz wurde von den Studenten nicht verstanden.
3. Dieser Silberschmuck ist von ihm selber hergestellt worden.
4. Darüber wird sehr viel geschrieben.
5. Darüber wird wohl sehr viel diskutiert werden.
6. Er wird von seiner Frau verwöhnt.
7. Die Fantasie wird von diesen Bildern angeregt.
8. Das Essen wurde um acht Uhr serviert.

F. *Substitute or add each phrase as it is introduced into the previous sentence and make any necessary structural changes.*

Er hat sich von einem Arzt untersuchen lassen.

Ich _____

____ lasse _____

_____ Ärztin _____

_____ behandeln.

Wir _____

____ hatten _____

_____ zwei guten_____

_____ operieren _____

Du _____

____ läßt _____

GUIDED CONVERSATION

A. Is there a particular street or area in your city that attracts street artists, musicians, and/or actors? Discuss the various displays and/or performances with someone in your class. Exchange opinions on what is particularly interesting or impressive, what is not so interesting, what appeals to you and what does not.

B. Discuss student life on campus with someone in your class. What aspects do you find agreeable? What aspects are not so agreeable?

READING

Eine Erkältung

Sind Sie kürzlich einmal von einer schlimmen Erkältung oder Grippe gequält worden? Dann wissen Sie ja, wie man sich fühlt. Im folgenden wird von Herrn Sommer berichtet, der von einer scheußlichen Grippe heimgesucht wurde und acht Tage nicht ins Büro gehen konnte.

Herr Sommer liegt seit einer Woche im Bett und wird von seiner Frau gepflegt. Er hat eine schwere Erkältung: Husten, Schnupfen und Halsschmerzen. Er hat sich allerdings nicht vom Arzt untersuchen lassen, weil man gegen Erkältung bekanntlich im allgemeinen nicht viel mehr tun kann, als was von den meisten Ärzten immer wieder empfohlen wird: viel Ruhe, viel Wasser trinken, genug Vitamin C und Aspirin nicht zu vergessen.

Die letzte Nacht hat Herr Sommer ganz gut geschlafen. Er genießt es, von seiner Frau einmal so richtig verwöhnt zu werden. Gerade öffnet sich die Tür: das Frühstück wird ihm ans Bett gebracht. Orangensaft, Tee, ein weich gekochtes Ei, Toast, Vollkornbrot, Butter und Honig.

Herr Sommer will sich aber nicht länger von seiner Frau verwöhnen lassen, weil er sich wieder besser fühlt. Er möchte wieder ins Büro gehen, wo er bestimmt schon vermißt wird. Seine Frau verlangt jedoch, daß erst das Fieber gemessen wird. Glücklicherweise ist die Temperatur wieder normal, so daß ihm jetzt von seiner Frau erlaubt wird aufzustehen. Er greift zum Telefon und läßt sich mit seinem Büro verbinden. Von seiner Sekretärin werden ihm die wichtigsten Termine mitgeteilt, die er sich sofort notiert. Herr Sommer steht auf und zieht sich an, denn um 10 Uhr wird er bereits von seinem Chef erwartet.

QUESTIONS

1. Haben Sie kürzlich einmal eine Grippe gehabt?
2. Wissen Sie, wie man sich bei Grippe fühlt?
3. Von wem wird hier berichtet?
4. Wie lange konnte Herr Sommer nicht ins Büro gehen?
5. Von wem wird er gepflegt?
6. Was sind die Symptome für Herrn Sommers Erkältung?
7. Warum hat er sich nicht vom Arzt untersuchen lassen?
8. Was kann man im allgemeinen gegen eine Erkältung tun?
9. Was genießt Herr Sommer?
10. Woraus besteht das Frühstück, das ihm gerade ans Bett gebracht wird?
11. Warum möchte Herr Sommer wieder ins Büro gehen?
12. Was verlangt seine Frau?
13. Mit wem läßt er sich am Telefon verbinden?
14. Was wird ihm von seiner Sekretärin mitgeteilt?
15. Von wem wird er bereits um 10 Uhr erwartet?

VOCABULARY EXERCISES

A. *Supply the appropriate word from the list on the right.*

1. Gehen Sie bitte auf dem _____!	a. Halskette
2. Der _____ wird wohl ein Künstler sein.	b. Fieber
3. Dieser Schmuck ist eine wertvolle _____.	c. Bürgersteig
4. Die Bilder werden hier _____ angeboten.	d. Vollkornbrot
4. Die _____ ist aus Silber.	e. Langhaarige
6. Eine _____ kommt oft von einer Erkältung oder von einem Virus.	f. zum Verkauf
7. _____ ist sehr gesund.	g. Grippe
8. Mit 39 Grad Celsius hat man _____.	h. Handarbeit

B. *Do the same as in* (A) *above.*

1. Sind Sie schon einmal von einer Grippe _____ worden?	a. mitgeteilt
	b. untersuchen

2. Ich werde manchmal von meinen Eltern ein
   bißchen _____.
3. Lassen Sie sich lieber von einem Arzt _____!
4. Wir müssen noch die Temperatur _____.
5. _____ Sie mich bitte sofort mit der Polizei!
6. Sie hat ihm alle wichtigen Termine _____.

c. verbinden
d. gequält
e. verwöhnt
f. messen

Review Exercises

A. *Change the sentence into the passive voice. Be careful of the verb tense.*

1. Die Grippe quälte ihn.
2. Wir berichten über Herrn Sommer.
3. Eine scheußliche Erkältung suchte ihn heim.
4. Seine Frau pflegte ihn.
5. Der Arzt hat ihn allerdings nicht untersucht.
6. Die meisten Ärzte empfehlen viel Ruhe.
7. Seine Frau verwöhnt ihn.
8. Jemand öffnet die Tür.
9. Man bringt ihm das Frühstück ans Bett.
10. Man vermißt ihn schon im Büro.
11. Die Sekretärin teilte ihm die wichtigsten Termine mit.
12. Sein Chef erwartete ihn bereits.

B. *Supply the appropriate form of the statal passive in the past tense.*

1. Die Läden _____ um 19 Uhr schon _____. (schließen)
2. Die Pizza _____ von ihr selbst _____. (machen)
3. Alle Fenster _____ weit _____. (öffnen)
4. Die meisten Autos _____ schon _____. (verkaufen)
5. Die Stadt Dresden _____ vom Krieg fast völlig _____. (zerstören)
6. Das Haus _____ schon _____, als es von den Flammen zerstört
   wurde. (bezahlen)

7. Du _____ wirklich sehr _____. (verwöhnen)
8. Das Fahrrad _____ schon lange _____. (reparieren)

C. *Put the sentence into the passive voice using an impersonal construction.*

1. Man schrieb mir, ich soll warten.
2. Man hat mir von dem Unfall berichtet.
3. Man trank Wein, Bier oder Orangensaft.
4. Man hatte viele Zigaretten geraucht.
5. Man singt deutsche Volkslieder.
6. Man machte eine Blutprobe.

D. *Express in German.*

1. You're having your hair cut.
2. He has the house built.
3. I had my car washed this morning.
4. We have some pictures sent to us.
5. She had her picture painted.
6. They have their old Oldsmobile repaired.

GUIDED COMPOSITION

A. Have you had a bad cold or a bout with the flu recently? Write a brief composition describing your illness. You might mention what symptoms you had, what you took in the way of medicine, what you had to eat, if you stayed in bed and how long, who took care of you, and so on.

B. Write a short evaluation of your German course. Among other things, you might mention whether the lessons were well prepared, you were stimulated by the readings in the book, the additional readings were interesting, your questions were answered by your instructor, what can be improved in the course, and so on. Practice using the passive voice in writing your evaluation.

The following words may help you.

> an·regen (to stimulate)
> aus·wählen (to select)
> eine Note geben (to give a grade)
> der Kurs, −e (course)
> der Lehrer, − (instructor)
> die Leseübung, −en (reading)
> die Unterrichtsstunde, −n (lesson)
> verbessern (to improve)
> vor·bereiten (to prepare)
> zusätzlich (additional)

Chapter 20

Schloß Sans Souci in Potsdam

Useful Phrases

Es tut mir leid.	I'm sorry.
Er kommt zu spät.	He's too late.
nach meinem Geschmack	to my taste
eine Reise wert sein	to be worth a trip
nach dem Weg fragen	to ask directions

MODEL SENTENCES

I

Ich wünschte, ihr **kämet** sofort nach Hause.	
Ich wünschte, ihr **würdet** sofort nach Hause **kommen**.	I wish you would come home right away.
Es **täte** mir leid, wenn ihr nicht **kämet**.	
Es **würde** mir leid tun, wenn ihr nicht **kämet**.	I would be sorry if you didn't come.
Hätten Sie wohl einen Moment Zeit?	Would you have a minute?
Wären Sie so nett, die Tür zu schließen?	Would you be so kind as to close the door.
Er wünschte, er **wäre** gestern **abgefahren**.	He wished he had left yesterday.
Du **hättest** vorher **anrufen sollen**.	You should have called before.

II

Wenn wir ihn nicht **angerufen hätten**, **wäre** er bestimmt nicht **gekommen**.	
Hätten wir ihn nicht **angerufen**, **wäre** er bestimmt nicht **gekommen**.	If we hadn't called him he certainly wouldn't have come.
Er **wäre** gar nicht **gekommen, wenn** wir ihn nicht **angerufen hätten**.	He wouldn't have come at all if we hadn't called him.
Wenn ich doch nur mehr Zeit **hätte**!	If only I had more time!

Grammar Explanations

I. SUBJUNCTIVE II

A. Usage

The *subjunctive* is one mood or mode of the verb. Roughly speaking, mood signifies the manner in which a statement is made. In both German and English, there are three basic moods of the verb.

1. Imperative, used to express a command (*see* Chapter 3)

    Machen Sie bitte die Tür auf!   Please open the door.

2. Indicative, as the term suggests, used to indicate facts

    Meine Eltern wohnen in Deutschland.   My parents live in Germany.

3. Subjunctive, used to make statements that may contain an element of unreality, or "fancy," instead of fact

German grammar distinguishes between two forms of the subjunctive: I and II. *Subjunctive II* occurs more frequently. It is formed from the second principal part of the verb and expresses hypothetical situations—wishes, possibilities, doubt, conditions contrary-to-fact (if-clauses), or polite requests. It may also be used in indirect discourse, especially in spoken German. *Subjunctive I* is derived from the first principal part of the verb and is primarily used in indirect discourse in literary German (*see* Chapter 21 for a complete discussion of indirect discourse).

Compare the moods in the following set of sentences. In the indicative, the statements express facts; in the subjunctive, the statements express wishes that might or might not be realized.

Indicative	*Subjunctive*
Er kommt morgen.	Wenn er morgen nur käme!
(He's coming tomorrow.)	(If he only would come tomorrow.)

Indicative	*Subjunctive*
Peter hat genug Geld, um seinen Urlaub in Spanien zu verbringen.	Wenn Peter genug Geld hätte, würde er seinen Urlaub in Spanien verbringen.
(Peter has enough money to spend his vacation in Spain.)	(If Peter had enough money, he would spend his vacation in Spain.)

The subjunctive in English is not very common in speech, although it does occur in certain idioms and in formal resolutions and recommendations.

> If I **were** you, I **would do** that too.
> **Be** that as it may, ...
> I move that the motion **be** passed.
> We ask that he **act** in the interest of the community.
> If she knew, she **might** not go.
> **Had** we only **known** then what we know now!

The subjunctive is more common in German. The principal uses are three-fold.

1. Wishful thinking

| Ich wollte, er **käme** morgen. | I wish he would come tomorrow. |
| Ich wünschte, er **käme** morgen. | I wish he would come tomorrow. |

2. Contrary-to-fact statements

| Wenn er nicht **käme, täte** es mir leid. | If he didn't come, I would be sorry. |
| Wenn ich genug Geld **hätte,** ginge ich in die Ferien. | If I had enough money, I'd go on vacation. |

3. Polite requests, commands, or questions

Hätten Sie einen Moment Zeit?	Would you have a moment?
Wären Sie so nett, mir die Tür aufzumachen?	Would you be so kind as to open the door for me.
Könntest du mir bitte **sagen,** wo das Restaurant ist?	Could you please tell me where the restaurant is?

Note that wishful thinking is usually expressed by the introductory clauses **ich wollte, ich wünschte,** or, less frequently, **ich möchte.** Contrary-to-fact statements contain the subjunctive II in both the **wenn**-clause and the conclusion. The more polite form of a request is used especially with the verbs **haben** and **sein** and the modals **können** and **mögen.**

Many wishes or polite requests are, from a structural standpoint, contrary-to-fact or unreal conclusions, presupposing an implied but unexpressed "if this were possible." They frequently contain the adverbs **gern** (with pleasure, very much), **lieber** (rather, preferably), or **am liebsten** (most of all).

Ich **hätte gern** das Stück Kuchen.	I would (very much) like that piece of pastry.
Hätten Sie **lieber** Kaffee oder Tee?	Would you prefer coffee or tea?
Ich **hätte am liebsten** Bier.	I'd like beer most of all.
Möchten Sie **gern** ein Ei essen?	Would you like (very much) to eat an egg?

B. Formation: Present Subjunctive II

The subjunctive II is formed by adding the subjunctive personal endings to the second principal part of the verb (past indicative stem), and this is called the *present subjunctive II*.

Personal Endings: Subjunctive Mood

	Singular	*Plural*
1st pers.	–e	–en
2nd pers. fam.	–est	–et
3rd pers.	–e	–en
2nd pers. pol.	–en	–en

Regular *weak* verbs and the modals **sollen** and **wollen** are identical in form in the present subjunctive and in the past indicative.

Infinitive	*Past Indicative*	*Present Subjunctive II*
lachen	ich lachte	ich lachte
lieben	ich liebte	ich liebte
rauchen	ich rauchte	ich rauchte
sollen	ich sollte	ich sollte

In *strong* verbs, the remaining four modals, and *irregular weak* verbs, such as **bringen** and **denken,** the present subjunctive personal endings are added to the past indicative stem, and the stem vowel is umlauted wherever possible.

Infinitive	Past Indicative	Present Subjunctive II
tun	ich tat	ich täte
schließen	ich schloß	ich schlösse
fahren	ich fuhr	ich führe
laufen	ich lief	ich liefe
bringen	ich brachte	ich brächte
denken	ich dachte	ich dächte
wissen	ich wußte	ich wüßte
dürfen	ich durfte	ich dürfte
können	ich konnte	ich könnte
mögen	ich mochte	ich möchte
müssen	ich mußte	ich müßte
haben	ich hatte	ich hätte
sein	ich war	ich wäre
werden	ich wurde	ich würde

Examples of the declension of all three types of verbs in the present subjunctive are as follows.

Declension of Present Subjunctive II

Weak Verbs **lachen** (to laugh)		Strong Verbs **gehen** (to walk)		Irregular Weak Verbs **bringen** (to bring)	
ich lacht	e	ich ging	e	ich brächt	e
du lacht	est	du ging	est	du brächt	est
er lacht	e	er ging	e	er brächt	e
wir lacht	en	wir ging	en	wir brächt	en
ihr lacht	et	ihr ging	et	ihr brächt	et
sie lacht	en	sie ging	en	sie brächt	en
Sie lacht	en	Sie ging	en	Sie brächt	en

C. Substitute Construction: <u>würde</u> Plus Infinitive

Since the weak verbs are identical in the past indicative and the present subjunctive, a substitute construction of **würde** plus the infinitive of the principal verb is often used. Moreover, nowadays the pure subjunctive II forms have a literary flavor and occur more often in writing than in conversation even with strong verbs.

Ich wünschte, er **würde** mir das Geld **senden.**	I wish he would send me the money.
Wenn er nur **lachen würde!**	If he would only laugh!
Würden Sie mir bitte die Tür **aufmachen?**	Would you please open the door for me.
Ich wollte, er **würde** morgen **kommen.**	I wished he would come tomorrow.
Wenn er nicht käme, **würde** es mir leid **tun.**	If he didn't come, I would be sorry.
Wenn er nur nicht nach Hause **gehen würde!**	If he only wouldn't go home!

Note that the English form of **would** plus the infinitive corresponds to the **würde** construction.

The substitute construction is not generally used with **haben, sein, wissen,** and the modals, however; the present subjunctive II is preferred usage with these verbs.

Hätten wir doch einen Farbfernseher!	If only we had a color TV!
Wir **wären** glücklich, wenn wir das **wüßten.**	We would be happy if we knew that.
Er hoffte, sie **könnte** kommen.	He hoped she could come.

D. Past Subjunctive II

The past subjunctive II in German is similar to English usage; it generally indicates an unreal or hypothetical action that could have occurred in the past but did not. The perfect tense is used to indicate past subjunctive time.

Wir **hätten** gern **angerufen.**	We would have liked to call.
Er **wäre** lieber mit uns **gekommen.**	He would have preferred to come with us.

As one would expect, the past subjunctive in German consists of the subjunctive II form of the auxiliary **haben** or **sein** and the past participle of the principal verb.

The substitute construction with **würde** plus the infinitive is very rarely used in the past subjunctive, primarily because it is awkard.

Ich hätte ihn angerufen.

rather than   I would have called him.

Ich würde ihn angerufen haben.

When the past subjunctive occurs with a modal auxiliary, the double infinitive form is used.

Ich **hätte** gestern **kommen können.**   I could have come yesterday.
Wir **hätten** früher **kommen sollen.**   We should have come earlier.
Er **hätte** früher **kommen müssen.**   He would have had to come earlier.

In a **wenn-**clause, dependent word order is used and thus the auxiliary immediately precedes the double infinitive construction.

Wenn ich ihn nur **hätte sehen können!**   If only I could have seen him!

Check Your Comprehension

A. *Supply the present subjunctive II forms of the verb according to the person indicated in parentheses.*

1. schwimmen (ihr)
2. gchcn (er)
3. rauchen (wir)
4. finden (ich)
5. bekommen (sie, *pl.*)
6. kaufen (du)
7. arbeiten (ihr)
8. laufen (es)
9. sehen (er)
10. geben (wir)
11. bringen (sie, *sing.*)
12. annehmen (ihr)
13. abfahren (er)
14. schließen (ich)
15. lesen (du)

B. *Form the subjunctive II of the verbs in* (A) *above using the substitute construction with* **würde** *plus infinitive.*

C. *Form the past subjunctive II of the verbs in* (A) *above.*

D. *Form the past subjunctive II of the verb and modal.*

1. suchen sollen (wir)
2. wissen müssen (du)
3. hereinkommen dürfen (Sie)
4. abreisen können (ihr)
5. es nicht tun mögen (sie, *sing.*)

II. THE CONDITIONAL

The **würde** plus infinitive construction is often called the *conditional*, especially when used in the conclusion of a contrary-to-fact statement. Such a statement usually contains two clauses: the condition and the conclusion. The conditional clause describes the action necessary for the conclusion of the sentence to be true. Generally, the condition begins with **wenn** (if) and is thus frequently called the **wenn-** or if-clause.

Condition	*Conclusion*
Wenn ich das Buch hätte,	würde ich es dir schicken.
(If I had the book,	I would send it to you.)
Wenn ich viel Geld besäße,	würde ich dir etwas abgeben.
(If I possessed a lot of money,	I would give you some.)

Note that it is *only in the conclusion* that the **würde** form is used. It is considered bad style to use **würde** plus infinitive in the condition. On the other hand, in writing or in formal speech, it is possible to use the pure subjunctive II form in both clauses.

Wenn sie das wüßte, käme sie sofort nach Hause.

If she knew that, she would come home right away.

Remember that with **sein** and the modals the **würde** form is not used in the conclusion of a contrary-to-fact statement even in spoken German.

Wenn ich mehr Geld hätte, wäre ich zufrieden.

If I had more money I'd be satisfied.

Wenn du fertig wärest, könntest du jetzt gehen.

If you were finished you could go now.

The tenses in the condition and the conclusion of a sentence are not necessarily the same. The conditional sentence may be entirely in the present or in the past, or it may consist of a conditional clause in the past and a conclusion in the present.

Condition	*Conclusion*
Wenn er mich anriefe,	{ ginge ich jetzt.
	{ würde ich jetzt gehen.
(If he called me,	I would go now.)
Wenn er mich angerufen hätte,	wäre ich gegangen.
(If he had called me,	I would have gone.)
Wenn er mich angerufen hätte,	{ ginge ich jetzt.
	{ würde ich jetzt gehen.
(If he had called me,	I'd go now.)

Either clause may be in first position in the sentence.

Conclusion	*Condition*
Wir würden ihm helfen,	wenn es nötig wäre.
(We would help him	if it were necessary.)

When the conclusion begins the sentence, *normal* word order is used.

Ich **wäre** sehr glücklich, wenn ich mehr Geld hätte.

I'd be very happy if I had more money.

When the conclusion follows the conditional dependent clause, *inverted* word order is used.

Wenn ich mehr Geld hätte, **wäre** ich sehr glücklich.

If I had more money I would be very happy.

Note that since **wenn** is a subordinating conjunction, *dependent* word order is required; that is, the finite verb is in last position in the clause. Dependent word order occurs with **wenn** whether the condition begins the sentence or whether the conclusion does.

Ich wäre sehr glücklich, **wenn** ich mehr Geld **hätte.**

I would be very happy if I had more money.

Wenn ich mehr Geld gehabt **hätte,** wäre ich sehr glücklich gewesen.

If I had had more money I would have been very happy.

The conjunction **wenn** may be omitted in a contrary-to-fact sentence, in which case the finite verb is in first position. The conclusion then sometimes begins with **so** or **dann.**

Hätte ich das Geld, **(so)** würde ich ein Paar neue Schuhe kaufen.	If I had the money I'd buy a pair of new shoes.
Wäre er hier, **(dann)** würden wir einkaufen gehen.	If he were here we'd go shopping.
Hätte ich viel Geld **besessen, (so)** hätte ich dir etwas abgegeben.	If I had had a lot of money I'd have given you some.

Wenn-clauses also occur quite frequently alone and express a desire based on some dissatisfaction with an existing situation. In German these clauses invariably contain a **nur** or **doch nur,** or, in case the impatience expressed is particularly strong, even a **nur endlich** or **doch endlich.**

Wenn ich (doch) nur mehr Geld hätte!	If only I had more money!
Wenn du (doch endlich) nur kommen würdest!	If only you would finally come!

The conjunction **wenn** may also be omitted, resulting in inverted word order.

Hätte ich doch nur diese Möbel!	If I only had this furniture!
Wäre er nur endlich nach Hause gekommen!	If only he'd have finally come home!

It is important to note that conditional statements may also be in the indicative mood. When it is not certain whether the situation is real or unreal, the indicative is used. Compare the following conditional situations.

Indicative	*Subjunctive*
Wenn es morgen schön **ist, machen** wir einen Ausflug.	If the weather is nice tomorrow [but we don't know what it will be like] we'll take a trip.
Wenn das Wetter schön **wäre, würden** wir einen Ausflug **machen.**	If the weather were nice [but it isn't] we'd take a trip [but we're not going to].

In the first sentence, we know nothing about the weather; therefore, our intention may or may not be realized. In the second sentence, we know by implication that the weather is bad; therefore, our intention is contrary to fact, and the situation is hypothetical or unreal.

A. *Add the conclusion to each if-clause and use the appropriate tense.*

1. Wenn wir Zeit hätten, _____. (das schicken können)
2. Wenn ihr wolltet, _____. (etwas kaufen)
3. Wenn du es wünschtest, _____. (hinfahren können)
4. Wenn ich es gewußt hätte, _____. (gehen)
5. Wenn er mit dem Zug gefahren wäre, _____. (zu spät kommen)
6. Wenn wir nicht gefragt hätten, _____. (leid tun)

B. *Change from the indicative to the subjunctive II and use the appropriate tense.*

1. Wenn ich das Geld habe, kaufe ich mir das Auto.
2. Wenn er mehr Zeit hat, macht er eine Stadtrundfahrt.
3. Wenn Sie das wissen wollen, fragen Sie ihn.
4. Wenn er deine Nummer findet, ruft er dich an.
5. Wenn ihr mit dem Zug fahrt, kommt ihr am frühesten an.

CONVERSATION

Im Café

FRAU DAHL	Ach, da bist du ja, Luise! Es tut mir leid, daß ich eine Viertelstunde zu spät komme. Ich hätte schon längst hier sein können, wenn ich nicht die Straßenbahn verpaßt hätte.
FRAU CARLSEN	Na, das macht doch nichts, Gerda. Setz dich her und probier mal dieses herrliche Gebäck! Der Kaffee kommt gleich, ich habe ihn schon bestellt.
FRAU DAHL	Weißt du, Luise, ich war gerade bei Hamann—du weißt schon, dem Möbelgeschäft beim Rathaus—und da habe ich ein paar fabelhafte Stücke gesehen, wirklich ganz nach

5

	meinem Geschmack. Am liebsten hätte ich sie gleich mit- 10 genommen. Wir brauchen unbedingt einen Sessel fürs Wohn- zimmer und eigentlich auch neue Stühle für den Eßtisch.
FRAU CARLSEN	Heutzutage sollte man nicht zu lange zögern, denn die Preise gehen immer weiter 'rauf.
FRAU DAHL	Wenn ich nur das Geld gehabt hätte, dann hätte ich den 15 Sessel bestimmt gleich gekauft. Aber du weißt doch, wir müssen uns solch einen Kauf zweimal überlegen. Wenn mein Mann doch nur endlich einmal wieder eine Gehaltser- höhung erhielte! Mit unserem Einkommen können wir uns beinahe nichts mehr leisten. 20
FRAU CARLSEN	Ja, wenn ich gewußt hätte, wie die Lebenskosten eines Tages ansteigen würden, hätte ich damals meine Ausbildung als Bibliothekarin bestimmt abgeschlossen, und es ginge uns heute etwas besser.
FRAU DAHL	Ich denke auch manchmal, daß ich mir jetzt, wo wir noch 25 keine Kinder haben, eine Stellung suchen sollte. Dann brauchten wir nicht nur von der Hand in den Mund zu leben.
FRAU CARLSEN	Aber sag mal, Gerda, wie wär's, wenn wir dieses deprimie- rende Thema abschließen würden, damit wir unseren Kaffee 30 genießen können.
FRAU DAHL	Du hast wohl recht. Aber nächsten Montag werde ich ernsthaft nach einer Stellung suchen.

ORAL PRACTICE

A. *Put the sentence into subjunctive II by using the phrase* **Ich wünschte, . . .**

1. Paul raucht keine Zigarre.
2. Der Busfahrer fährt etwas schneller.
3. Sie bringen mir bessere Nachrichten.
4. Er ist freundlicher zu mir.
5. Du hast mehr Geduld.
6. Mein Freund mietet das Zimmer neben meiner Wohnung.
7. Wir sparen etwas mehr Geld.
8. Sie zögert nicht so lange.
9. Du kommst nicht immer zu spät.
10. Ihr besitzt dieses Ferienhaus.

B. *Change the sentences in (A) above into the substitute construction for the subjunctive II (* **würde** *plus infinitive).*

C. *Change from the indicative form to the subjunctive II.*

1. Ich **darf** lange schlafen.
2. Ihr **könnt** mit mir fahren.
3. Er **muß** das Bier bezahlen.
4. Sie **bringt** mir das Frühstück ans Bett.
5. Wir **wissen** gern, wie die Leute heißen.

D. *Express the request more politely using the subjunctive II.*

1. Haben Sie einen guten Rheinwein?
2. Können Sie mir sagen, wie spät es ist?
3. Darf ich mal bitte ans Fenster?
4. Bist du so nett und reichst mir mal den Zucker?
5. Sind Sie so freundlich und tragen meinen Koffer zum Ausgang?
6. Mögen Sie eine Tasse Kaffee?
7. Haben Sie gerade einen Moment Zeit?

E. *Express the request more politely using the substitute construction for the subjunctive II (**würde** + infinitive).*

1. Geben Sie mir bitte die Zeitung!
2. Setzen Sie sich bitte da drüben an den Tisch!
3. Fahren Sie bitte weiter!
4. Bringen Sie mir bitte die Speisekarte!
5. Machst du bitte das Fenster zu!
6. Kommt ihr bitte sofort nach Hause!
7. Geht ihr bitte einen Moment hinaus!

F. *Combine the pair of sentences to make a contrary-to-fact statement. Use the subjunctive II in both clauses. Put the condition in first position.*

EXAMPLE　Er kommt nicht. Es tut mir leid.
Wenn er nicht käme, täte es mir leid.

1. Ich habe viel Geld. Ich fliege nach Europa.
2. Sie ist gesund. Sie geht schwimmen.
3. Er ist Präsident. Wir haben keine Sorgen mehr.
4. Du bist zu Hause. Ich besuche dich einmal.
5. Es regnet nicht. Wir können eine Radtour machen.
6. Sie haben es mir nicht gesagt. Ich habe es vergessen.
7. Sie haben Hunger. Sie essen etwas.

G. *Combine the pair of sentences to make a contrary-to-fact statement. Use the substitute construction for the subjunctive II (**würde** plus infinitive) in the conclusion, but use the subjunctive II in the conditional clause. Put the conclusion in first position.*

EXAMPLE　Es tut mir leid. Er kommt nicht.
Es würde mir leid tun, wenn er nicht käme.

1. Ich fliege nach Europa. Ich habe viel Geld.
2. Sie geht schwimmen. Sie ist gesund.
3. Wir haben keine Sorgen mehr. Er ist Präsident.
4. Ich besuche dich einmal. Du bist zu Hause.
5. Sie essen etwas. Sie haben Hunger.

H. *Change the sentence from the present to the past (subjunctive II).*

> EXAMPLE   Ich würde ihn anrufen, wenn ich seine Nummer wüßte.
> **Ich hätte ihn angerufen, wenn ich seine Nummer gewußt hätte.**

1. Wir würden gern kommen, wenn es nicht regnete.
2. Sie würde die Schuhe kaufen, wenn sie Geld hätte.
3. Er würde nach Holland fahren, wenn er genug Benzin hätte.
4. Würden Sie nach Ost-Berlin reisen, wenn Sie einen Paß hätten?
5. Würden Sie zu Fuß gehen, wenn Sie kein Auto hätten?
6. Ich würde ihm einen Brief schreiben, wenn ich könnte.
7. Sie würde das Buch bestimmt lesen, wenn sie Zeit hätte.

I. *Omit the* **wenn** *in the sentence and make the necessary changes.*

> EXAMPLE   Wenn ich das doch endlich wüßte!
> **Wüßte ich das doch endlich!**

1. Wenn ich doch nur mehr Zeit hätte!
2. Wenn du mir das doch nur versprächest!
3. Wenn ihr doch endlich nach Hause kämet!
4. Wenn das doch nur wahr wäre!
5. Wenn ich nur nicht soviel gegessen hätte!
6. Wenn wir doch nur nicht so schnell gefahren wären!
7. Wenn ihr doch nur auf mich gehört hättet!

J. *Substitute or add each phrase as it is introduced into the previous sentence and make any necessary structural changes.*

Hätte er   mir   geholfen, so hätte ich   das   tun   können.
_____ Sie _____
_____ ihnen _____ sie (*pl.*) _____
_____ nicht _____ nicht _____
Wenn _____
_____ machen _____
_____ du _____

„.... wenn ich Uri Geller wäre!"

Die verbotenen Träume des Johnny X. zeichnete Klaus Pause für BRAVO auf

„Rosys Heino-Platten wären unspielbar!"

„Eine Band mit falschem Sound hätte bei mir nichts zu lachen!"

„In Fechten würde ich spielend Weltmeister!"

„Mein Nebenbuhler Emil hätte bei Lissy nichts zu lachen!"

„Muttis müde Mager-Suppen würde ich nicht mehr löffeln!"

„Gerda würde endlich auf mich aufmerksam!"

„Den Ladenbesitzer Krachmeier könnte ich herrlich ärgern!"

„... und der Schulbetrieb fiele häufig aus!"

GUIDED CONVERSATION

A. Uri Geller claims the ability to perform fantastic feats merely through the use of mental power. The jokes on the topic of **Wenn ich Uri Geller wäre . . .** are from the German youth magazine *Bravo*. Read through the jokes, then begin a conversation with someone in your class regarding some of the things you would do if you were Uri Geller.

B. Exchange greetings with one of your class members and carry on a conversation with him/her based entirely on wishful thinking. Express your wishes and desires with the forms **ich wollte** and **ich wünschte**.

READING

Ein Besuch in Ost-Berlin

Ich würde Ihnen ja das folgende gar nicht erzählen, wenn ich nicht so beeindruckt davon gewesen wäre.

Wissen Sie, ich war neulich in Berlin. Das ist wirklich eine Reise wert, wie die Prospekte sagen. Am liebsten wäre ich ja mit dem Auto gefahren, dann hätte ich in Berlin keinen Wagen zu mieten brauchen und hätte eine 5 Menge Geld gespart. Aber um Zeit zu sparen, bin ich von Hannover aus geflogen, denn an der Grenze zur DDR hätte ich wahrscheinlich doch ziemlich lange warten müssen. Das wollte ich vermeiden.

Es war gut, daß ich mir gleich am Flughafen Tempelhof in West-Berlin einen Wagen gemietet hatte, denn sonst hätte ich bestimmt vieles nicht 10 gesehen. Natürlich gibt es in West-Berlin viele Busse und Untergrundbahnen, aber wenn ich damit gefahren wäre, hätte ich wahrscheinlich nicht all die vielen interessanten Dinge fotografieren können, die ich auf meiner Autofahrt entdeckte.

Vor allem aber hätte ich nicht so viel von Ost-Berlin sehen können, selbst 15 wenn ich mit dem Bus eine Stadtrundfahrt gemacht hätte. An der Grenze nach Ost-Berlin ging alles schneller als erwartet. Ich mußte nur meinen Paß und meinen Führerschein vorzeigen und etwas Geld wechseln. Nach kurzer

Alexanderplatz

Wartezeit konnte ich weiterfahren. Hätte ich einen Stadtplan von Ost-Berlin gehabt, dann hätte ich nicht so oft anhalten und nach dem Weg fragen müssen. 20
Aber schließlich fand ich die breite Straße, die zum Brandenburger Tor und zum Museumsviertel führt.

Wenn ich doch nur mehr Zeit gehabt hätte! Ich hätte mir so gern den berühmten Pergamon-Altar[1] angesehen. Das Museum war leider schon ge-schlossen, als ich hinkam. 25

Sehr eindrucksvoll fand ich den Alexanderplatz[2] mit dem hohen Funkturm, den großen freien Plätzen und den vielen modernen Geschäften. Fasziniert

war ich vor allem von der großen Weltzeituhr, die wohl jedem aufgefallen wäre, weil sie in ihrer modernen Struktur wirklich einmalig ist.

Nach einem Spaziergang durch die Ost-Berliner Innenstadt kaufte ich mir noch eine Zeitung „Neues Deutschland" und fuhr dann über die Grenze nach West-Berlin zurück.

30

---

[1] Greek altar dedicated to Zeus and Athena. Erected ca. 200 B.C. in Pergamum and now exhibited in a museum in East Berlin.
[2] Famous square in the center of East Berlin.

QUESTIONS

1. Warum erzählt der Autor von seinem Besuch in Berlin?
2. Warum wäre er am liebsten mit dem Auto nach Berlin gefahren?
3. Warum ist er von Hannover aus geflogen?
4. Was mietete er sich gleich am Flughafen Tempelhof?
5. Warum ist er nicht mit der Untergrundbahn durch Berlin gefahren?
6. Was mußte er an der Grenze nach Ost-Berlin vorzeigen?
7. Warum hätte er gern einen Stadtplan von Ost-Berlin gehabt?
8. Was hätte er sich gern angesehen, wenn er mehr Zeit gehabt hätte?
9. Was fand er besonders eindrucksvoll?
10. Was kaufte er sich, bevor er nach West-Berlin zurückfuhr?

VOCABULARY EXERCISES

Supply the appropriate word from the list on the right.

1. Ich kann mir diese Preise nicht leisten; mein _____ ist zu niedrig.
2. In diesem Café gibt es herrliches _____.
3. Dieses Bild von Mondrian ist nicht mein _____.
4. Er hat seine _____ als Filmregisseur abgeschlossen.
5. Haben Sie mal eine _____ durch Ost-Berlin gemacht?
6. An der _____ zur DDR mußten wir lange warten.
7. Wie alt waren Sie, als Sie Ihren _____ bekamen?

a. Grenze
b. Einkommen
c. Führerschein
d. Gebäck
e. Ausbildung
f. Geschmack
g. Stadtrundfahrt

Review Exercises

A. *Change the sentence into subjunctive II.*

1. Ich bin gern mit dem Auto gefahren.
2. Mein Bruder fliegt lieber.
3. Meine Schwester blieb am liebsten zu Hause.

4. Wenn ich nicht immer so lange warten muß, gehe ich sogar gern zum Zahnarzt.
5. Wenn du weniger rauchst, lebst du länger.
6. Wenn das Wetter schön ist, gehen wir schwimmen.
7. Wenn Deutsch nicht schwer ist, lernt er es.
8. Was tust du, wenn du das Examen nicht bestehst?

B. *Change the statement to one indicating wishful thinking. Start with* **Ich wollte** *or* **Ich wünschte.**

EXAMPLE   Du bist hier.
              Ich wünschte, du wärest hier.

1. Sie ist wieder gesund.
2. Wir können noch heute nach Wien fliegen.
3. Du weißt, wie sehr ich dich liebe.
4. Ich kann solch ein Ferienhaus kaufen.
5. Sie will auch ein Instrument spielen.
6. Die Schweiz ist nicht so weit von hier.
7. Wir haben einen deutschen Schäferhund.
8. Ich bin noch einmal 17 Jahre alt.
9. Sie haben das laut gesagt.
10. Wir haben endlich Ferien.

C. *Express the request more politely by using the subjunctive II.*

1. Verzeihung, können Sie mir sagen, wie spät es ist?
2. Darf ich das Radio mitnehmen?
3. Haben Sie etwas dagegen, wenn ich rauche?
4. Verzeihung, haben Sie vielleicht Streichhölzer?
5. Wissen Sie vielleicht, wo mein Schlüssel ist?
6. Herr Ober, können Sie mir wohl einen Whiskey bringen?
7. Darf ich mir eben die Hände waschen?
8. Können Sie mir sagen, wo die Lindenstraße ist?

D. *Replace the subjunctive II form by the substitute construction* **würde** *plus infinitive.*

1. Ich wünschte, er **käme** sofort.
2. Wir wünschten, ihr **liefet** nicht so schnell.

3. Mein Vater wünschte, ich **fragte** nach dem Weg.
4. Ich wollte, du **bliebest** zu Hause.
5. Ich weiß, Sie wünschten, mein Hund **bellte** nicht so laut.
6. Sie wollte, sie **brauchte** nicht Deutsch zu studieren.
7. Wir wünschten, wir **flögen** morgen nach Zürich.
8. Du wolltest, es **gäbe** hier keine Autos.

E. *Combine the pair of sentences and make a contrary-to-fact statement using the subjunctive II or the substitute construction when possible.*

EXAMPLE   Ich habe das gewußt. Ich bin sofort gekommen.
   Hätte ich das gewußt, so wäre ich sofort gekommen.

1. Er hat das getan. Er muß es sagen.
2. Sie hat den Baum gesehen. Sie ist nicht dagegen gefahren.
3. Ihr habt gewußt, daß es regnet. Ihr seid zu Hause geblieben.
4. Du hast das gelesen. Du weißt das.
5. Du hast das Mädchen gesehen. Du hast dich sofort verliebt.
6. Wir haben von dem Skandal gehört. Wir haben einen anderen Kandidaten gewählt.
7. Das Öl ist nicht teurer geworden. Wir fahren heute einen Lincoln.
8. Ihr habt jetzt mehr Geld. Ihr reist nach Europa.

F. *Omit the* **wenn** *and make the necessary changes.*

1. Wenn du da gewesen wärest, wäre das bestimmt nicht passiert.
2. Wenn ich das gewußt hätte, hätte ich sofort angerufen.
3. Wenn das Auto billiger wäre, würde ich es mir vielleicht kaufen.
4. Wenn Deutsch nicht so schwer wäre, würde es mir vielleicht sogar Spaß machen.
5. Wenn Sie die letzte Nacht geschlafen hätten, wären Sie jetzt nicht so müde.

G. *Express in German.*

1. I could have come yesterday.
2. You should have told me that.
3. They would have had to call him right away.

4. If I had (possessed) a lot of money, I would give you some.
5. If only I had more time.
6. If only she had had more money!
7. Most of all I would like to go home now.
8. I would be quite unhappy if I had less money.
9. If I were you, I would buy the car.
10. She would have been quite unhappy if I had married her.

GUIDED COMPOSITION

A. Write a short essay on the topic **Wenn ich Präsident wäre, . . .** Or, if you prefer, choose your own variation of the topic by substituting a proper name or profession for **der Präsident.**

B. Write a composition on one or more of the following topics.

> Hätte ich viel Geld, . . .
> Am liebsten wäre ich, . . .
> Wenn ich doch nur mehr Zeit hätte, . . .
> Wenn ich doch nur mehr Zeit gehabt hätte, . . .

Chapter 21

Köln

Useful Phrases

Haben Sie keine Angst!	Don't be afraid.
Weiter!	Go on.
Es fällt mir ein.	It occurs to me.
Basta!	That's enough.
Fragen stellen	to ask questions
einen Bummel machen	to go for a stroll
Verständnis für etwas haben	to understand *or* appreciate something
aus den Augen verlieren	to lose sight of
nach Hause bringen	to take home

MODEL SENTENCES

Er sagte, er **komme** später.	
Er sagte, er **käme** später.	He said he would come later.
Er sagte, er **würde** später **kommen**.	

Sie sagte, sie **sei** krank.	She said she was sick.
Du sagtest, wir **seien** schon da.	You said we were there already.
Sie sagte, ich **hätte** viel Zeit.	She said I had a lot of time.
Er sagte, das **dürfe** ich nicht wissen.	He said I wasn't allowed to know that.
Er sagte, er **müsse** nach Hause.	He said he had to go home.

Er sagt: „**Ich** bin lange krank gewesen."	He says, "I've been sick a long time."
Er sagt, **er** sei lange krank gewesen.	He says he was sick a long time.
Er sagte: „**Mein** Auto ist kaputt."	He said, "My car is broken."
Er sagte, **sein** Auto sei kaputt.	He said his car was broken.

Er sagte zu mir: „**Geh** nach Hause!"	He told me, "Go home."
Er sagte zu mir, **ich solle** nach Hause gehen.	He told me I should go home.

Sie fragte mich: „**Wann** kommst **du** zurück?"	She asked me, "When are you coming back?"
Sie fragte mich, **wann ich** zurückkäme.	She asked me when I was coming back.
Sie fragte ihn: „Liebst du mich?"	She asked him, "Do you love me?"
Sie fragte ihn, **ob** er sie liebe.	She asked him if he loved her.

Grammar Explanations

SUBJUNCTIVE I: INDIRECT DISCOURSE

As stated in Chapter 20, subjunctive I forms are used in German for indirect discourse.

Direct discourse is used when you quote someone's words directly.

<blockquote>

Er sagte: „Ich bin sehr ärgerlich."   He said, "I'm very angry."

</blockquote>

But since it is cumbersome, repetitive, and somewhat primitive to speak or write with direct discourse—except, of course, for dramatic or imitative purposes—direct discourse is seldom used. In most cases, *indirect quotation* is preferred to give a second-hand report of someone else's words.

<blockquote>

Er sagte, er sei sehr ärgerlich.   He said he was very angry.

</blockquote>

In indirect discourse quite often a shift from the first to the third person occurs because the speaker reports to his interlocutor what a third person said.

English further requires a shift in the tense if the opening verb is in the past (**said,** or **told,** for example): the present tense in the words to be reported becomes past tense and *any* past tense (simple past, present and past perfect) is changed to the past perfect.

Tense Shift: Direct to Indirect Discourse

	Direct Discourse	Opening Verb	Indirect Discourse
Pres.:	"I am ill."	He said	he was ill.
Any past:	"I was ill." "I have been ill." "I had been ill."	He said	he had been ill.

In German, the shift from first to third person, as dictated by the situation, also occurs. But instead of a shift in indicative tenses, German operates with a *change of mood*.

The subjunctive I is used in German in the dependent clause to report a statement to someone else. The speaker suggests, by using the subjunctive, that he does not know whether what he is quoting is fact; he refuses to take responsibility for the statement, and he does not agree or disagree with it. In the sentence "I'm very angry," for instance, the person himself said he was angry, but we don't know definitely that he was.

Using the subjunctive I in indirect statements is generally restricted to formal literary style; it is not so common in informal conversation or writing. Since it does occur, however, in radio and television reports and in newspaper and magazine articles, close attention must be given to subjunctive I so you will be able to recognize it.

Subjunctive I is formed by adding to the first principal part (infinitive stem) the same set of subjunctive endings as the subjunctive II.

Personal Endings: Subjunctive I

	Infinitive Stem	Endings	Subjunctive I
ich	komm	e	komme
du	komm	est	kommest
er sie es	komm	e	komme
wir	komm	en	kommen
ihr	komm	et	kommet
sie	komm	en	kommen
Sie	komm	en	kommen

Subjunctive I Compared to Present Indicative

	kommen		**laufen**		**lesen**	
	Subjunctive	*Indicative*	*Subjunctive*	*Indicative*	*Subjunctive*	*Indicative*
ich	komme	(komme)	laufe	(laufe)	lese	(lese)
du	kommest	(kommst)	laufest	(läufst)	lesest	(liest)
er sie es	komme	(kommt)	laufe	(läuft)	lese	(liest)
wir	kommen	(kommen)	laufen	(laufen)	lesen	(lesen)
ihr	kommet	(kommt)	laufet	(lauft)	leset	(lest)
sie	kommen	(kommen)	laufen	(laufen)	lesen	(lesen)
Sie	kommen	(kommen)	laufen	(laufen)	lesen	(lesen)

Notice that the stem-vowel change of the second- and third-person singular forms is not carried over from the indicative into the subjunctive I. Since it is most important to *differentiate* between the indicative and the subjunctive, the subjunctive I is essentially limited to the third-person singular. And, because the first-person singular and plural and the third-person plural forms of the subjunctive I do not differ at all from the indicative forms, it is common practice to replace those forms by the subjunctive II. The basic principle is to *avoid ambiguous forms as much as possible.*

subj. I/pres. indic.:
  Ich sagte, ich **komme** heute.
subj. II: Ich sagte, ich **käme**
  heute.

I said I'd come today.

The verb **sein,** however, does have subjunctive I forms sufficiently different from the indicative so that they can be used throughout. It is not necessary to replace them by subjunctive II forms or the **würde-**substitute.

Subjunctive I of **sein**

ich sei
du seist
er
sie } sei
es
wir seien
ihr seiet
sie seien
Sie seien

The modals also have distinctive subjunctive I forms except in the first- and third-person plural and the second-person polite. Therefore subjunctive I forms are used largely in the singular and subjunctive II forms in the plural. The **würde-**substitute is not used.

subj. I: Er sagte, ich müsse kommen.   He said I had to come.
subj. II: Er sagte, wir müßten kommen.   He said we had to come.

Subjunctive I of modals

	dürfen	**können**	**mögen**	**müssen**	**sollen**	**wollen**
ich	dürfe	könne	möge	müsse	solle	wolle
du	dürfest	könnest	mögest	müssest	sollest	wollest
er						
sie }	dürfe	könne	möge	müsse	solle	wolle
es						
wir	dürfen	können	mögen	müssen	sollen	wollen
ihr	dürfet	könnet	möget	müsset	sollet	wollet
sie	dürfen	können	mögen	müssen	sollen	wollen
Sie	dürfen	können	mögen	müssen	sollen	wollen

Which tense of the subjunctive to use depends not on the tense of the opening verb but on the time of the reported action in relation to the speaker's time. If the times are *simultaneous*, use the present tense in the indirect statement. If the action reported is *prior* to the speaker's time, use the past tense. If the action reported is *subsequent* to the speaker's time, use the future tense. The opening verb may be any tense in all situations. Schematically, this system can be presented as follows.

Tense of Subjunctive in Indirect Discourse

Time	*Direct Discourse*	*Opening Verb* (any tense)	*Indirect Discourse*
Simultaneous:	„Ich **bin** krank."		er { **sei** / **wäre** } krank.
	„Ich **habe** genug Geld."		er { **habe** / **hätte** } genug Geld.
Prior:	„Ich **war** krank."	Er sagt, Er sagte,	er { **sei** / **wäre** } krank **gewesen**.
	„Ich **hatte** genug Geld."	Er hat gesagt, Er hatte gesagt, Er wird sagen,	er { **habe** / **hätte** } genug Geld **gehabt**.
Subsequent:	„Ich **werde** krank sein."		er { **werde** / **würde** } krank **sein**.
	„Ich **werde** genug Geld haben."		er { **werde** / **würde** } genug Geld **haben**.

Although there are three ways of stating past time in the indicative (simple past, present perfect, and past perfect), there is only one past tense in the subjunctive. Any one of the three tenses is reported as past subjunctive in the indirect statement.

„Ich **hatte** genug Geld."
„Ich **habe** genug Geld **gehabt**."   Er sagt, er { **habe** / **hätte** } genug Geld **gehabt**.
„Ich **hatte** genug Geld **gehabt**."

If a direct statement is projected into the future and contains a specification of time, the present subjunctive form is preferred to the **werde** or **würde** construction.

$$\text{Er sagte, er}\begin{cases}\textbf{komme}\\ \textbf{käme}\end{cases}\text{morgen.}$$

Lately there is an increasing tendency in *conversational* style to retain the indicative in indirect discourse.

$$\text{Er sagte, er \textbf{kommt} morgen.}$$

The shift from the first to the third person is not restricted to personal pronouns but also occurs with possessive adjectives.

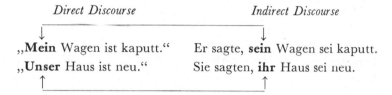

Direct Discourse	Indirect Discourse
„**Mein** Wagen ist kaputt.“	Er sagte, **sein** Wagen sei kaputt.
„**Unser** Haus ist neu.“	Sie sagten, **ihr** Haus sei neu.

If the direct discourse contains an imperative, it is converted into indirect discourse with the aid of the modals **sollen** or **müssen.**

Direct Discourse   *Indirect Discourse*

$$\text{„Geh nach Hause!“}\qquad\text{Sie sagte, ich}\begin{cases}\textbf{solle}\\ \textbf{müsse}\end{cases}\text{nach Hause gehen.}$$

Questions without a question word are rendered into indirect discourse with the help of the conjunction **ob** (if, whether). If there is a question word, it introduces the indirect clause.

Direct Discourse	Indirect Discourse
„Kommt dein Vater?“	Er fragte mich, **ob** mein Vater käme.
„Wann kommt dein Vater?“	Er fragte mich, **wann** mein Vater käme.

Notice that **ob** and **wann** are subordinating conjunctions; therefore, dependent word order, or verb-last position, is required. Dependent word order is also required in clauses beginning with **daß,** which is a variant means of introducing an indirect statement. When **daß** is omitted, the clause returns to regular word order, or verb in second position.

$$\text{Er sagt, \textbf{daß} er krank sei.}$$

but

$$\text{Er sagt, er sei krank.}$$

A. *Form the subjunctive I of the verb in parentheses.*

1. Sie sagte, er _____ gerade. (telefonieren)
2. Sie sagte, es _____ hier. (stinken)
3. Sie sagte, ihr _____ zuviel. (rauchen)
4. Sie sagte, ich _____ sofort. (kommen)
5. Sie sagte, sie (*sing.*) _____ nach Hause. (gehen)
6. Sie sagte, du _____ den Tee. (bringen)
7. Sie sagte, sie (*sing.*) _____ Musik. (hören)
8. Sie sagte, es _____. (regnen)
9. Sie sagte, er _____ Hunger. (haben)
10. Sie sagte, er _____ mit dem Zug. (fahren)

B. *Form the subjunctive I of the modal auxiliary in parentheses.*

1. Er hat gesagt, du _____ abreisen. (wollen)
2. Er hat gesagt, sie (*sing*) _____ nach Hause. (müssen)
3. Er hat gesagt, ihr beide _____ heiraten. (sollen)
4. Er hat gesagt, er _____ warten. (können)
5. Er hat gesagt, ich _____ mitfahren. (dürfen)
6. Er hat gesagt, du _____ Geduld haben. (mögen)
7. Er hat gesagt, sie (*sing.*) _____ sofort kommen. (sollen)
8. Er hat gesagt, man _____ das nicht wissen. (können)

C. *Form the subjunctive I of the verb* **sein.**

1. Ich sagte, ich _____ gesund.
2. Ich sagte, er _____ krank.
3. Ich sagte, sie (*sing.*) _____ charmant.
4. Ich sagte, du _____ hungrig.
5. Ich sagte, sie (*pl.*) _____ interessant.
6. Ich sagte, wir _____ müde.
7. Ich sagte, ihr _____ elegant.
8. Ich sagte, es _____ ausgezeichnet.

D. *Form the subjunctive I by using the verb and the time reference in parentheses.*

1. Sie hatte gesagt, sie _____ krank _____. (sein, *prior*)
2. Sie hatte gesagt, er _____ Hunger _____. (haben, *subsequent*)
3. Sie hatte gesagt, wir _____ müde. (sein, *simultaneous*)
4. Sie hatte gesagt, du _____ einen Unfall _____. (haben, *prior*)
5. Sie hatte gesagt, ich _____ hungrig _____. (sein, *subsequent*)
6. Sie hatte gesagt, ihr _____ einen Mercedes. (haben, *simultaneous*)
7. Sie hatte gesagt, es _____ interessant _____. (sein, *prior*)
8. Sie hatte gesagt, Sie _____ Aspirin. (haben, *simultaneous*)
9. Sie hatte gesagt, man _____ zu vorsichtig _____. (sein, *prior*)
10. Sie hatte gesagt, er _____ dann kein Geld _____. (haben, *subsequent*)

CONVERSATION

Der Kommissar

Für die deutschen Krimi-Freunde gibt es kaum eine spannendere Fernsehsendung als die Serie „Der Kommissar" am Freitagabend um 20.15 Uhr. Hier ist ein Ausschnitt.

Herr Scholz kommt heute abend sehr spät nach Hause. Seine Frau empfängt ihn ganz verstört. 5

FRAU SCHOLZ   Endlich bist du da, Herbert! Es war furchtbar! Ein Kommissar Keller war vor einer halben Stunde hier. Er sagte, er
sei von der Kriminalpolizei und müsse einige Fragen stellen.
Es gehe um Mord.

HERR SCHOLZ   Was? Um Mord? Wieso, wer ist denn ermordet worden? 10
Was haben wir denn damit zu tun? Was wollte der Kommissar wissen? Was hast du ihm gesagt?

FRAU SCHOLZ   Um halb zehn klingelt es. Ein Mann steht vor der Tür, der
sagt, er sei Kommissar Keller von der Mordkommission. Ich
sagte, er solle hereinkommen, das sei sicher ein Irrtum und 15
so weiter.

HERR SCHOLZ   Natürlich!

FRAU SCHOLZ   Dann fragte er, ob mein Mann zu Hause sei. Ich sagte, nein,
du seist heute auf einer Geschäftsreise und kämest erst später
zurück. 20

HERR SCHOLZ   Gut! Weiter. Was hat er noch wissen wollen, dieser Kommissar Keller?

FRAU SCHOLZ   Er fragte, ob ich eine Maria Korff kenne. Ich sagte, ja, das
sei doch die Sekretärin meines Mannes. Warum er danach
frage, wollte ich wissen. 25

HERR SCHOLZ   Und? Was hat er gesagt?

FRAU SCHOLZ   Fräulein Korff sei—oh, Herbert, das darf nicht wahr sein
—sei—sei gestern abend tot in ihrer Wohnung aufgefunden
worden. Ermordet! Herbert, ich kann das nicht glauben!
Sag doch etwas! 30

HERR SCHOLZ   Maria?—tot?—ermordet? Hat der Kommissar gefragt, wo
ich gestern abend gewesen sei?

FRAU SCHOLZ   Ja. Ich sagte ihm, du seist zum Kegeln gegangen wie jeden
Mittwoch. Er sagte: „Wieso? Gestern war doch Dienstag.''
Er hat mich ganz konfus gemacht. 35

HERR SCHOLZ   Hat er sonst noch etwas gesagt?

FRAU SCHOLZ   Nun, ich habe gefragt, was du eigentlich mit der ganzen
Sache zu tun habest. Er werde doch nicht annehmen, daß
du—Herbert! Was ist mit dir? Du bist ja so nervös!

HERR SCHOLZ   Nichts! Es ist nur der Schock, ja, der Schock! Arme Maria! 40
Hat der Kommissar gesagt, daß er mich sprechen müsse?

FRAU SCHOLZ   Ja, es sei dringend. Du sollest ihn anrufen, wenn du zurück seist. Er suche nach einem Zeugen.

HERR SCHOLZ   Ach, Gerda, mir fällt gerade ein, daß ich unbedingt noch einen Kunden besuchen muß. Wenn der Kommissar noch   45 einmal kommen sollte, sag ihm, ich sei . . .

KOMMISSAR KELLER   Nicht mehr nötig, Herr Scholz! Hände hoch und keine Bewegung! Ich muß Sie leider bitten mitzukommen.

ORAL PRACTICE

A. *Put the sentence into direct discourse.*

1. Sie hatte gesagt, die Polizei sei da gewesen.
2. Er sagte, er sei sehr müde.
3. Sie sagte, sie habe ein neues Kleid.
4. Sie sagten, sie hätten nichts gehört.
5. Ihr sagtet, wir kämen zu spät.
6. Du sagtest, du werdest morgen abreisen.
7. Er hat gesagt, Sie seien sehr aufgeregt.
8. Sie wird sagen, das habe sie schon gewußt.
9. Ich sagte, das sei nicht so schlimm.
10. Wir sagten, daß er ein neues Auto habe.

B. *Put the sentence into indirect discourse and use the opening phrase,* **Er sagte,** . . . *Avoid ambiguous forms by using the subjunctive II when necessary.*

1. „Wir werden das Haus verkaufen."
2. „Ich bleibe hier."
3. „Ich trinke einen Gin mit Soda."
4. „Wir kennen dich!"
5. „Wir fliegen morgen nach Atlanta."
6. „Du bist mein bester Freund."
7. „Ihr wißt, was ich meine."
8. „Ich werde ein Wiener Schnitzel braten."
9. „Wir haben zuviel Kaffee getrunken."
10. „Sie sind wirklich sehr nett."

C. *Put the subjunctive II form into subjunctive I.*

1. Er sagte, er käme später.
2. Sie sagte, sie gäbe mir keinen Kuß.
3. Sie hat gesagt, sie kochte mir ein Ei.
4. Er sagt, er wäre zufrieden mit mir.
5. Er hatte gesagt, ich telefonierte zu lange.
6. Sie sagt, sie nähme das Geld nicht an.
7. Er sagte, er ginge nach Hause.
8. Sie sagte, sie hätte die Musik gehört.
9. Ich sagte, er wäre immer sehr intelligent gewesen.
10. Man sagt, Deutsch wäre nicht so schwer.

D. *Put the sentence into indirect discourse by using the opening phrase,* **Er sagte,** ...

1. „Ich muß abreisen."
2. „Wir können Glück haben."
3. „Ich mag keinen Tee."
4. „Du darfst nichts trinken."
5. „Ich darf hier nicht rauchen."
6. „Ich weiß, was du denkst."
7. „Wir wollen nach Hamburg fahren."
8. „Du sollst nicht so lange schlafen."
9. „Ich muß immer früh aufstehen."
10. „Ich kann warten."

E. *Put the question into indirect discourse by using the opening phrase,* **Er fragte,** ...

1. „Hast du einen Moment Zeit?"
2. „Haben Sie eine Zigarette für mich?"
3. „Bist du gleich fertig?"
4. „Kann man hier Postkarten bekommen?"
5. „Haben Sie einen Briefumschlag für mich?"
6. „Wieviel kostet das?"
7. „Warum ist alles so teuer?"
8. „Kochen Sie gern?"
9. „Von wem wissen Sie das?"

10. „Fährst du morgen nach Salzburg?"

11. „Geht es Ihnen gut?"

12. „Wie geht es Ihrer Frau?"

13. „Wann kommt dein Vater zurück?"

14. „Hat dein Freund schon geschrieben?"

15. „Wie spät ist es?"

16. „Wo wohnen Sie?"

17. „Darf ich Sie nach Hause bringen?"

18. „Wozu studieren Sie Deutsch?"

19. „Wer hat das gesagt?"

20. „Darf ich Sie zu einer Tasse Kaffee einladen?"

F. *Put the command into indirect discourse by using the opening phrase,* **Sie hat gesagt,** *. . . and the correct form of either* **sollen** *or* **müssen.** *Do not use the conjunction* **daß.**

1. „Geh jetzt zu Bett!"

2. „Setzen Sie sich!"

3. „Bring mir das Frühstück ans Bett!"

4. „Schließ die Tür ab!"

5. „Warten Sie einen Moment!"

6. „Kauf ein paar Brötchen!"

7. „Bleiben Sie sitzen!"

8. „Haben Sie keine Angst vor mir!"

9. „Schreib mir mal!"

10. „Rufen Sie schnell einen Arzt!"

G. *Put the sentence into indirect discourse by using the opening phrase,* **Er sagte,** *. . .*

1. „Mein Auto ist kaputt."

2. „Unser Haus ist ganz neu."

3. „Das ist Ihre Uhr."

4. „Deine Frau ist wirklich sehr charmant."

5. „Mein Vater ist Zahnarzt."

6. „Eure Tochter ist sehr intelligent."

7. „Ihr Mantel liegt da drüben."

8. „Mein Sohn ist Flugkapitän."

9. „Unsere Eltern sind auf Urlaub."

10. „Dein Fahrrad steht im Keller."

H. *Substitute or add each phrase as it is introduced into the previous sentence and make any necessary structural changes.*

Wir   sagten, unsere Männer seien   verwöhnt.
Die Damen _____
Du _____
_____ mein _____
_____ Kinder _____
_____ nicht _____
Er _____
_____ sein _____

GUIDED CONVERSATION

A. Carry on a conversation with someone in your class concerning the day's news. Exchange news items you read in the morning newspaper and/or heard on radio or television news reports. Use indirect discourse to relate what was said by a newsman, reporter, and/or interviewer.

B. Tell your class members about a television program you watched recently. Give the highlights of what happened during the episode and relate through indirect discourse pieces of important conversations.

C. Relate to your class members a conversation or an argument that you had recently with your roommate, a friend, a professor, a member of your family, or whomever. Use indirect discourse to tell what was said.

READING

Die Kontrolle

Neulich machte ich mit meiner Freundin einen Schaufensterbummel auf der „Kö"—so nennen die Düsseldorfer ihre berühmte Geschäftsstraße, die „Königsallee", die in Deutschland so bekannt ist wie etwa die Fifth Avenue

in New York. Anschließend setzten wir uns in eines der Straßencafés, tranken
unseren Eiskaffee und beobachteten die Leute auf der Straße.   5

   Plötzlich stieß mich meine Freundin an und wollte wissen, ob ich denn
schon von meinem Kollegen, Herrn Lorenz, einen Brief bekommen hätte.
Ja, der gute Herr Lorenz hatte tatsächlich geschrieben, aus Dallas/Texas.
Nun wollte sie ganz genau wissen, was er geschrieben hätte, so daß ich für
uns noch einen Eiskaffee bestellte und ihr alles berichtete.   10

   Herr Lorenz schrieb, daß er zuerst mit der Lufthansa fliegen wollte, doch
der Flug sei ausgefallen, weil die Piloten wieder einen Streik gehabt hätten.
Daher habe er mit Pan Am bis Chicago fliegen wollen und von dort mit
United bis Houston. Doch das hätte leider nicht geklappt, weil die Pan Am-
Maschine voll ausgebucht gewesen sei, was natürlich manchmal vorkommt.   15
Schließlich habe er sich an KLM gewandt. Die Dame am Flugkartenschalter

sei sehr nett gewesen und hätte sofort einen Platz für ihn reserviert. Die Maschine sei auch pünktlich von Düsseldorf abgeflogen, habe allerdings in Amsterdam noch eine Zwischenlandung gemacht, ehe sie nach Chicago weiterge-
flogen sei. Über den Service hätte er sich nicht beklagen können. Mit der   20
Zollkontrolle hätte er überhaupt keine Schwierigkeiten gehabt.

Dann berichtete ich meiner Freundin, daß Herr Lorenz bei seinem Flug
nach Houston auf dem O'Hare Flughafen in Chicago beinahe als Luftpirat
verdächtigt worden sei. Das hätte ich lieber nicht sagen sollen, denn jetzt rief
meine Freundin den Ober und bestellte einen dritten Eiskaffee, und soviel   25
Eis und Sahne ist nichts für meine Figur! Sie wollte jetzt alles sehr genau
wissen. Nun, ich erzählte ihr, daß Herr Lorenz—wie es heute an den meisten
Flugplätzen üblich ist—an Sicherheitsbeamten vorbeigehen mußte, die ihn
und sein Handgepäck mit elektronischen Geräten überprüften. Dabei hätten
die Geräte ständig reagiert, obwohl er sein Kleingeld und sein Taschenmesser 30
auf den Tisch gelegt habe. Daraufhin wäre er von oben bis unten nach Waffen
untersucht worden, aber sie hätten natürlich nichts finden können. Schließlich
habe er die Jacke ausziehen müssen, und da sei endlich die Ursache für das
Reagieren der Geräte gefunden worden. Es seien die Metallknöpfe an seiner
Jacke gewesen, die ihn so verdächtig gemacht hätten.   35

Die Sicherheitsbeamten hätten sich entschuldigt und erklärt, daß sie dies
zur Sicherheit aller Passagiere täten. Schließlich sei der Kampf gegen die
„Hijackers", wie die Amerikaner die Flugzeugentführer nennen, in den letzten
Jahren durch diese unpopulären Kontrollen doch sehr erfolgreich gewesen.
Herr Lorenz habe dafür auch Verständnis gehabt.   40

Meine Freundin meinte, Fliegen sei doch etwas Schönes, wenn auch manchmal etwas aufregend.

QUESTIONS

1. Was ist die „Kö"?
2. Wo tranken der Erzähler und seine Freundin einen Eiskaffee?
3. Was wollte die Freundin wissen?
4. Mit welcher Fluggesellschaft, schrieb Herr Lorenz, habe er eigentlich fliegen wollen?
5. Warum habe er nicht mit Pan Am fliegen können?
6. Wo habe die KLM-Maschine noch eine Zwischenlandung gemacht?
7. Wie sei die Zollkontrolle in Chicago gewesen?

8. Was sei ihm beim Flug nach Houston in Chicago passiert?
9. Warum sei er von oben bis unten nach Waffen untersucht worden?
10. Was habe ihn so verdächtig gemacht?
11. Was sei in den letzten Jahren so erfolgreich?
12. Was meinte die Freundin des Erzählers?

VOCABULARY EXERCISES

A. *Supply the appropriate word from the list on the right.*

1. „Der Kommissar" ist eine spannende _____.
2. Ihm ist ein _____ passiert.
3. _____ ist ein populärer Sport.
4. Es ist noch ein _____ im Laden.
5. Ich freue mich auf einen _____ durch die Fifth Avenue.
6. In der Autoindustrie gibt es viele _____.
7. Da drüben ist der KLM–_____.
8. Haben Sie bei der Zollkontrolle _____ gehabt?
9. Mit diesem _____ wird man nach Waffen untersucht.
10. Jetzt kenne ich die _____ seiner Krankheit.

a. Streiks
b. Kunde
c. Gerät
d. Irrtum
e. Fernsehsendung
f. Kegeln
g. Ursache
h. Schaufensterbummel
i. Flugkartenschalter
j. Schwierigkeiten

B. *Do the same as in* (A) *above.*

1. Manchmal _____ wir die Leute auf der Straße.
2. Sie hat mir den Vorfall _____.
3. Die Lufthansa-Flüge sind wegen Streik _____.
4. Die Pan Am-Maschine war voll _____.
5. Niemand kann sich über den Service _____.
6. Herr Lorenz ist als Luftpirat _____ worden.
7. Das Handgepäck wurde mit einem elektronischen Gerät _____.
8. Die Sicherheitsbeamten haben sich bei Herrn Lorenz _____.

a. beklagen
b. entschuldigt
c. ausgebucht
d. verdächtigt
e. berichtet
f. untersucht
g. ausgefallen
h. beobachten

Review Exercises

Put the complete passage into indirect discourse.

1. Ärger mit der Hauswirtin

Heute morgen sagte meine Hauswirtin zu mir: „Herr Fischer, Sie hatten gestern abend Damenbesuch. Das wünsche ich nicht. Das wissen Sie doch." Ich antwortete: „Frau Neubauer, es tut mir leid, aber das ist wirklich meine Sache. Ich bezahle meine Miete, sogar eine sehr hohe Miete, für mein Studentenzimmer, und da kann ich einladen, wen ich will." Meine Hauswirtin war ärgerlich über diese Antwort und sagte: „Sie, junger Mann, hören Sie mal. Vielleicht verstehen Sie etwas von Musik oder was Sie studieren, aber von einer Hausordnung verstehen Sie offensichtlich nichts! Ich erwarte, daß Sie auf Ihrem Zimmer keinen Damenbesuch empfangen. Basta!" Ich war wütend und sagte: "Das ist Diskriminierung! Das ist unsozial! Ich habe mit jener Studentin nur für das Examen gelernt, und das ist ja wohl nicht verboten!" „So, fürs Examen gelernt haben Sie", sagte sie. „Kein Student lernt am Samstagabend mit einer Dame für ein Examen!" Ich sagte: „Dann müssen Sie Ihre Vorstellungen über die Studenten von heute revidieren!"

2. Die Verfolgung

Ich sprang in ein Taxi und sagte zum Taxifahrer: „Bitte, folgen Sie der schwarzen Limousine da drüben!" Der Taxifahrer wollte wissen: „Warum soll ich dem Auto folgen? Sind Sie denn von der Kriminalpolizei?" Ich antwortete: „Fragen Sie nicht soviel! Fahren Sie lieber etwas schneller, sonst verlieren wir den Wagen aus den Augen." Er sagte: „Scheußliches Wetter haben wir heute. Der Regen will überhaupt nicht aufhören." Ich sagte: „Passen Sie auf, Mann! Der schwarze Wagen ist gerade links abgebogen. Fahren Sie schneller!" Er sagte: „Es tut mir leid, mein Herr, aber ich muß die Straßenbahn zuerst vorbeifahren lassen." Ich sagte wütend: „Die Gangster sind uns entkommen. Fahren Sie mich ins Hotel zurück!"

3. Der Augenzeuge

Herr Beckmann, Co-Pilot einer DC-10, war Augenzeuge einer Flugzeug-entführung. Er mußte der Kriminalpolizei genau berichten, was geschehen war. Er erzählte:

„Plötzlich stand ein Mann im Cockpit mit einer Handgranate in der Hand und sagte: ‚Tun Sie, was ich sage. Dann passiert nichts. Fliegen Sie sofort nach Havanna!‘ Der Chefpilot sagte: ‚Das ist unmöglich! Soviel Benzin haben wir nicht.‘ Daraufhin sagte der Luftpirat: ‚ Ich habe gesagt, fliegen Sie nach Kuba! Sonst wird dieses kleine runde Ding explodieren.‘ Der Chefpilot sagte: ‚Sehen Sie doch selbst! Wir haben nur noch 800 Liter Benzin. Damit kommen wir bestenfalls noch bis Atlanta.‘ Der Luftpirat fluchte wie verrückt und sagte schließlich: ‚Okay. Landen Sie in Atlanta und tanken Sie voll! Sagen Sie dem Tower, daß ich die Maschine in die Luft jage, wenn die Polizei auf uns schießt.‘ Ich zeigte dem Luftpiraten die Flugkarte und sagte: ‚Sehen Sie, wir sind jetzt hier. In einer halben Stunde . . . ‘ In diesem Moment schlug unsere Stewardess den Mann mit einem Karate-Schlag nieder."

GUIDED COMPOSITION

A. Have you had a problem recently with your landlord or landlady regarding the rent, house rules, or some other matter? Give a written account of the problem, using indirect discourse to relate pieces of conversation.

B. Have you received a letter recently from a friend or family member? Write a letter to a fictional German friend and relate through indirect discourse what your friend or family member said in his/her letter to you.

C. Have you ever been an eye-witness to a burglary, robbery, or some other criminal act? Were you interviewed by the police? Write a brief report of the interview, using indirect discourse to relate what was said by whom. You may want to write a fictional account of such an interview, if you have never personally witnessed a criminal act.

For further practice, rewrite your composition—regardless of which of the above topics you choose—using direct discourse. Compare the two versions. Which do you prefer stylistically? Why?

Chapter 22
Review

An der Mosel

Tense System

I. PRESENT TENSE

- The present tense of a verb is formed by adding the appropriate personal ending (**–e, –st, –t; –en, –t, –en**) to the first principal part (infinitive stem).

> Du denk**st** zuviel.

- Many strong verbs with the stem vowels **a, au** or **e** undergo a stem-vowel change in the second- and third-person singular.

> Ich fahre. Du f**ä**hrst.
> Ich laufe. Er l**äu**ft.
> Ich sehe. Sie s**ie**ht.

- The prefix of a separable prefix verb, such as **ansteigen** (to increase), is detached from the basic verb and moves to the end of a clause with normal and inverted word order.

> Die Preise **steigen** wieder **an.**

- In dependent word order and with a dependent infinitive the prefix remains attached to the verb.

> Ich weiß, daß die Preise wieder **ansteigen.**
> Die Preise sollen wieder **ansteigen.**

- There is no progressive form or emphatic form in German.
- The present tense is used to indicate not only present events but also future events, especially with adverbs of time that point into the future.

> Nächste Woche **steigen** die Eierpreise wahrscheinlich wieder **an.**

Read the following passage and observe the use of the present tense.

Die Preise steigen an

Der Brotpreis steigt wieder an. Die Benzinpreise steigen wieder an. Die Telefongebühren steigen wieder an. Die Reparaturkosten steigen wieder an. Das Taxifahren
wird wieder teurer. Das Fliegen wird wieder teurer. Das Heizöl wird wieder teurer.
Schuhe werden wieder teurer. Die Preise für Fisch steigen wieder an. Die Eierpreise
steigen wieder an. Energie wird wieder teurer. Denkst du, die Steuern steigen nicht an?

II. PRESENT PERFECT TENSE

- The present perfect tense of a verb is formed by using the present tense inflected form of the auxiliary **haben** or **sein** and the past participle of the
  principal verb.

Du **hast** zuviel **gedacht.**

- The past participle of a *weak* verb is formed by placing the unchanged verb
  stem between the frame **ge———t.**

lachen   ge**lach**t

denken   ge**dach**t

- The past participle of a *strong* verb is formed by placing a changed, or in a
  few cases the unchanged, verb stem between the frame **ge———en.**

steigen   ge**stieg**en

- The prefix of a separable prefix verb remains attached to the past participle
  of the basic verb, but it precedes the **ge–** prefix.

ansteigen   **an**ge**stieg**en

- Verbs showing a change in the position or condition of the grammatical
  subject use the auxiliary verb **sein.** All other verbs (with the exception of
  sein and **bleiben**) use the auxiliary verb **haben.**

Du **hast** zuviel **gedacht.**

Die Preise **sind** wieder **angestiegen.**

- The past participle is placed at the end of the clause with normal or inverted order.
- The present perfect tense is particularly used in conversational German or
  in an informal type of writing.

Read the following passage and observe the use of the present perfect tense.

Die Preise sind angestiegen

Der Brotpreis ist wieder angestiegen. Die Benzinpreise sind wieder angestiegen. Die Telefongebühren sind wieder angestiegen. Die Reparaturkosten sind wieder angestiegen. Das Taxifahren ist wieder teurer geworden. Das Fliegen ist wieder teurer geworden. Das Heizöl ist wieder teurer geworden. Schuhe sind wieder teurer geworden. Die Preise für Fisch sind wieder angestiegen. Die Eierpreise sind wieder angestiegen. Energie ist wieder teurer geworden. Hast du gedacht, die Steuern steigen nicht an?

TEURER:

Teurer geworden ist eigentlich alles.

III. PAST TENSE

- The past tense of *weak* verbs is formed by adding the past forming element **–t–** and the personal endings (**–e, –est, –e; –en, –et, –en**) to the infinitive stem.

Er lacht**e** laut.

- Strong verbs have a special past stem, usually with a changed stem vowel. The personal endings to be added are different from those of weak verbs: (no ending), **–st,** (no ending), **–en, –t, –en.**

Present: Der Brotpreis steigt wieder an.
Past: Der Brotpreis stieg wieder an.

- As in the present tense, the prefix of a separable prefix verb is detached from the basic verb and is placed at the end of a clause with normal or inverted word order.
- The past tense is generally used only in narratives, rarely in conversation. The modal auxiliaries, however, are almost always used in the past tense, even in conversational style.

Past Time: Past or Present Perfect Tense

Narrative	*Conversation*
Das Benzin **wurde** gestern wieder um 3 Pfennig teurer. Und vor einer Woche **stiegen** die Telefongebühren ebenfalls wieder um 10% **an.**	**Hast** du das **gelesen?** Benzin **ist** gestern wieder um 3 Pfennig teurer **geworden.** Und vor einer Woche **sind** die Telefongebühren ebenfalls wieder um 10% **angestiegen.**

With Modals
Das Benzin sollte um 3 Pfennig teurer werden. Die Telefongebühren konnten leider nur um 10% ansteigen.

When it is clear that an action starts in the past and reaches into the present or is done in the past and has an effect in the present, the present perfect tense can be used even in formal style. In such cases, one usually encounters an adverbial expression, such as **schon** or **schon wieder.**

Er hat meine Adresse schon wieder vergessen.

On the other hand, in a conversation a speaker may temporarily turn into a a storyteller and switch from the present perfect to the simple past tense.

> Gestern bin ich in die Stadt gefahren.
> Ich parkte meinen Wagen vor einer Parkuhr.
> Da kam ein Polizist.
> Er sagte mir, ich dürfte da nicht parken.

Read the following passage and observe the use of the past tense.

> Die Preise stiegen wieder an

Der Brotpreis stieg wieder an. Die Benzinpreise sollten wieder ansteigen. Die Telefongebühren mußten natürlich wieder ansteigen. Die Reparaturkosten stiegen auch wieder an. Das Taxifahren wurde wieder teurer. Das Fliegen wurde ebenfalls teurer. Das Heizöl durfte nicht billiger werden. Auch Schuhe wurden teurer. Die Preise für Fisch stiegen wieder an. Die Eierpreise wollte man auch erhöhen. Energie mußte natürlich auch teurer werden. Dachtest du, die Steuern steigen nicht an?

IV. PAST PERFECT TENSE

- The past perfect tense is formed from the past tense inflected form of the auxiliary verb **haben** or **sein** and the past participle of the principal verb (*see* present perfect tense).

> Du **hattest** zuviel **gedacht.**
> Die Reparaturkosten **waren** wieder **angestiegen.**

- As in the present perfect tense, the past participle is placed at the end of a clause with normal or inverted word order.
- If a clause in the present or past perfect tense has a modal auxiliary, the past participle of the modal is identical to the infinitive form.

> Du **hattest** zuviel denken **müssen.**
> Die Preise **hatten** wirklich ansteigen **müssen.**

With the modals you can only use the auxiliary **haben,** never the auxiliary **sein.**

- The use of the past perfect in German corresponds to its use in English.

Read the following passage and observe the use of the past perfect tense.

Die Preise waren wieder angestiegen

Der Brotpreis war wieder angestiegen. Die Benzinpreise hatten wieder ansteigen sollen. Die Telefongebühren hatten natürlich wieder ansteigen müssen. Die Reparaturkosten waren natürlich auch wieder angestiegen. Das Taxifahren war wieder teurer geworden. Das Fliegen war ebenfalls teurer geworden. Das Heizöl hatte nicht billiger werden dürfen. Auch Schuhe waren teurer geworden. Die Preise für Fisch waren wieder angestiegen. Die Eierpreise hatte man auch erhöhen wollen. Energie hatte natürlich auch teurer werden müssen. Hattest du gedacht, die Steuern steigen nicht an?

V. FUTURE TENSE

- The future tense is formed from the inflected form of the auxiliary verb **werden** plus the infinitive of the principal verb.

> Du **wirst** zuviel **denken.**
> Die Preise **werden** wieder **ansteigen.**

- The future tense must not necessarily be used to indicate *futurity* because the present tense can take over that function, particularly if an adverb of time is involved expressing future events.

> future: Die Benzinpreise **werden** morgen wieder **ansteigen.**
> present: Die Benzinpreise **steigen** morgen wieder **an.**

- The future tense is more frequently used to indicate *probability* or *anticipation* of events. The speaker expresses that he anticipates or expects that prices will go up eventually; yet, it is not a factual statement.

> Die Eier **werden** wahrscheinlich teurer **werden.**
> Der Preis für Heizöl wird wohl **ansteigen.**

Read the following passage and observe the use of the future tense.

Die Preise werden wieder ansteigen

Der Brotpreis wird wieder ansteigen. Die Benzinpreise werden wieder ansteigen. Die Telefongebühren werden wieder ansteigen. Die Reparaturkosten werden auch wieder ansteigen. Das Taxifahren wird wahrscheinlich auch teurer werden. Das Fliegen wird sicherlich ebenfalls teurer werden. Das Heizöl wird wohl auch wieder teurer werden. Schuhe werden wieder teurer werden. Die Preise für Fisch werden wahrscheinlich auch wieder ansteigen. Die Eierpreise werden wieder ansteigen. Energie wird wohl auch wieder teurer werden. Wirst du vielleicht denken, die Steuern steigen nicht an?

VI. FUTURE PERFECT TENSE

- The future perfect tense is formed from the inflected form of the auxiliary verb **werden** and the present perfect infinitive of the principal verb.

> Du **wirst** wieder zuviel **gedacht haben.**
> Die Preise **werden** wieder **angestiegen sein.**

- This tense is rarely used in German. It is primarily used to express probability of a concluded action projected into the future.

Read the following passage and observe the use of the future perfect tense.

Die Preise werden wieder angestiegen sein

Der Brotpreis wird dann wieder angestiegen sein. Die Benzinpreise werden dann wieder angestiegen sein. Die Telefongebühren werden bis dahin wieder angestiegen sein. Die Reparaturkosten werden dann wohl auch wieder angestiegen sein. Das Taxifahren wird dann wahrscheinlich auch teurer geworden sein. Das Fliegen wird dann sicherlich auch wieder teurer geworden sein. Das Heizöl wird bis zum Winter auch teurer geworden sein. Schuhe werden dann sicher wieder teurer geworden sein. Die Preise für Fisch werden dann auch angestiegen sein. Die Eierpreise werden dann natürlich auch angestiegen sein. Energie wird dann wohl auch wieder teurer geworden sein. Wirst du vielleicht gedacht haben, die Steuern steigen nicht an?

A. *Read the following paragraph. List the verbs with their components, and note the tense of each. Then list the infinitive and the principal parts of each verb.*

Kennen Sie ein Land, wo es keine Inflation gibt? Fast überall sind die Preise angestiegen. Wird man die Löhne auch erhöhen? In einigen Ländern konnte man eine Wirtschaftskrise nicht verhindern. Man hatte gehofft, die Preise stabil halten zu können. Niemand weiß, wann diese Wirtschaftskrisen beendet sein werden.

B. *Rewrite the following paragraph first in the past tense, then in the present perfect tense, and finally in the future tense.*

Kennen Sie ein Land, wo es keine Inflation gibt? Fast überall steigen die Preise an. Erhöht man auch die Löhne? In einigen Ländern kann man eine Wirtschaftskrise nicht verhindern. Man hofft, die Preise stabil halten zu können. Niemand weiß, wann diese Wirtschaftskrisen beendet sind.

Case System

I. NOMINATIVE CASE

- The subject of a clause, noun or pronoun, is always in the nominative case.

Eine Stadt in Bayern ist Bamberg.

Read the following paragraph and observe the use of the nominative case (set off in italics).

Kennen Sie Bamberg? Bamberg ist *eine* sehr alte *Stadt* in Nordbayern. *Die Romantiker* von heute finden diese Stadt sehr attraktiv. *Der Tourist* ist überrascht: *Das Stadtbild* von Bamberg hat sich seit vielen hundert Jahren kaum verändert. *Ein Kunstwerk* ist besonders interessant: Das ist *der* Bamberger *Reiter*, *eine Statue*. Aber auch *die* Bamberger *Symphonie* ist sehr bekannt.

II. ACCUSATIVE CASE

- The direct object of a clause, noun or pronoun, is always in the accusative case. The accusative forms of the definite and indefinite articles differ from the nominative forms only in the masculine singular.

> Ich kenne **den** Bamberger **Reiter.**
> Ich habe **einen** Bamberger **Reiter** auf der Postkarte.

- Certain prepositions always require the accusative case (*see* Chapter 7).

> Bamberg ist **für einen Touristen** interessant.

Read the following paragraph and observe the use of the accusative case (set off in italics).

Kennen Sie *die Stadt* Bamberg? *Eine* solche *Stadt* muß man gesehen haben! Es gibt *keine Romantiker*, die *einen Ort* wie Bamberg nicht attraktiv finden. Das Stadtbild von Bamberg überrascht *den Touristen*: Man hat *einen* großen *Teil* der Stadt seit vielen hundert Jahren kaum verändert. Ich finde *ein Kunstwerk* besonders interessant: Ich meine, *den* Bamberger *Reiter*. Aber auch *die* Bamberger *Symphonie* liebe ich sehr.

III. DATIVE CASE

- An indirect object in a sentence, noun or pronoun, is in the dative case.

> Bamberg gibt **dem Touristen** einen guten Eindruck.

- A small number of German verbs govern the dative case.

> Die Stadt **gefällt dem Touristen.**

- Certain prepositions always govern the dative case.

> **Mit der** Bamberger **Symphonie** bin ich zufrieden.

- Certain prepositions take either the accusative case (motion *toward* a place) or the dative case (position or motion *in* a place) (*see* Chapter 8).

> accusative: Der Ball fällt **unter den Tisch.**
> dative: Der Ball liegt **unter dem Tisch.**

Bamberger Reiter

Read the following paragraph and observe the use of the dative case (set off in italics).

Ist *Ihnen* Bamberg bekannt? Bamberg gehört *zu den* ganz alten *Städten* in Bayern. *Einem Romantiker* muß diese Stadt gefallen. *Dem Touristen* fällt auf, daß sich *an dem Stadtbild seit den* letzten hundert *Jahren* kaum etwas verändert hat. *Von einem Kunstwerk* haben Sie vielleicht auch schon gehört: Ich meine, *von dem* Bamberger *Reiter*. Diese Statue finden Sie *in dem* Bamberger *Dom*. Wenn Sie in Bamberg sind, gehen Sie in den Dom! Aber auch *von der Symphonie* sind alle begeistert.

IV. GENITIVE CASE

● The genitive case denotes a possessive relationship.

Die Stadt liegt im Norden **Bayerns.**

- It also denotes a relationship in which one noun modifies or qualifies another noun.

> Die Schönheit **dieses Kunstwerkes** ist einmalig.

- Masculine and neuter nouns add **–s** or **–es** in the genitive singular.
- Certain prepositions always govern the genitive (*see* Chapter 7).

> **Während des Urlaubs** blieben sie zu Hause.

Read the following paragraph and observe the use of the genitive case (set off in italics).

Kennen Sie *Bambergs* Attraktionen? Diese Stadt liegt im Norden *Bayerns*. Sie fand schon immer das Interesse *der Romantiker*. Zur Überraschung *des Touristen* hat sich das Bild *dieser* Stadt während der letzten hundert *Jahre* kaum verändert. Die Schönheit *eines* einmaligen *Kunstwerkes* ist besonders bekannt: die Statue *des* Bamberger *Reiters*. Aber auch die Konzerte *der* Bamberger *Symphonie* sind ausgezeichnet.

V. ATTRIBUTIVE ADJECTIVE ENDINGS: ALL CASES

- Whenever a **der**-word or an **ein**-word *with* an ending precedes the attributive adjective, a *weak* ending is required. The weak adjective ending is **–en** throughout, with the exceptions of the nominative masculine and the nominative and accusative feminine and neuter where the weak ending is **–e.**

> Kennen Sie die **schöne alte** Stadt Bamberg?
> Lieben Sie die **engen** Straßen mit ihren **romantischen alten** Häusern?

- Whenever an **ein**-word takes no ending, in the nominative masculine singular and the nominative and accusative neuter singular, the ending of the following attributive adjective is *strong*, which means it is either **–em, –er,** or **–es.**

> Bamberg ist ein **schönes altes** Städtchen.
> Sein **größter** Teil ist unverändert.

Read the following paragraph and observe the use of the attributive adjectives in the various cases.

Kennen Sie die *hübsche alte* Stadt Bamberg? Es ist eine *wunderschöne* Stadt, die man gesehen haben muß. Kein *wirklicher* Romantiker wird behaupten, daß Bamberg nicht attraktiv sei. Das *mittelalterliche* Stadtbild ist seit vielen hundert Jahren kaum verändert. Ich finde ein *einmaliges* Kunstwerk besonders interessant: Ich meine, den *berühmten* Bamberger Reiter. Aber auch ein so *ausgezeichnetes* Orchester wie die Bamberger Symphonie liebe ich sehr.

Check Your Comprehension

A *Write a complete sentence using the elements separated by slashes.*

1. Kanada / für / Touristen / interessant / sein
2. Zug / durch / Tunnel / fahren
3. Vase / auf / Tisch / stehen
4. ich / Vase / auf / Tisch / stellen
5. Mädchen / mit / Ball / spielen
6. er / Auto / in / Garage / fahren
7. mein Fahrrad / in / Keller / bringen
8. Bus / zu / Bahnhof / fahren
9. Bus / vor / Eingang / halten
10. Flugzeug / vor / KLM-Gebäude / rollen

B. *Read the following passage. List the attributive adjective phrases and note the case of each. Explain why each case and ending was used.*

So sieht mein neues Zimmer aus: In der linken Ecke steht mein neues grünes Sofa, und neben dem Sofa ist eine große weiße Lampe. Vor das grüne Sofa habe ich einen braunen Tisch gestellt. Hinter diesem kleinen Tisch stehen zwei gemütliche Sessel. Auf den grauen Fußboden habe ich einen dunkelbraunen Teppich gelegt. In der rechten Ecke direkt gegenüber dem neuen Sofa steht ein großer brauner Schrank für meine vielen Wein- und Schnapsgläser. Auf das untere Regal dieses Schrankes habe ich den alten Fernseher gestellt, während mein neuer Plattenspieler auf dem oberen Regal steht. An den Wänden hängen einige moderne Bilder von bekannten Künstlern. Und neben die Tür habe ich einen schönen Kalender gehängt.

Word Order

I. NORMAL WORD ORDER

- Just as in English, the normal word order of the major parts of speech in a German sentence is subject, verb, direct object.

| *Subject* | *Verb* | *Direct Object* |
| Jeder Mensch | hat | eine Schwäche. |

- Normal word order is also used after coordinating conjunctions.

1   2
Ich weiß das, aber ich kann es nicht ändern.

II. INVERTED WORD ORDER

- Word order is inverted whenever a clause begins with an element *other* than the subject. The subject is then placed *behind* the verb.
- Any part of speech, except the verb can be placed in the first position of a clause. The conjugated verb, however, is always in second position.

1 2
Er hat heute mit seiner Hauswirtin eine Unterhaltung gehabt.

1   2
Heute hat er mit der Hauswirtin eine Unterhaltung gehabt.

1   2
Mit der Hauswirtin hat er heute eine Unterhaltung gehabt.

1   2
Eine Unterhaltung hat er heute mit der Hauswirtin gehabt.

- Questions always require inverted word order whether they are introduced by a question word or not, unless a sentence in normal word order is turned into a question by mere intonation.

> Kommt der Arzt?
>
> Wann kommt der Arzt?

but

> Der Arzt kommt?

III. DEPENDENT WORD ORDER

- Clauses introduced by a subordinating conjunction, an interrogative conjunction, or a relative pronoun require dependent word order, in which the inflected verb moves to the last position.

> Ich weiß, daß ich nichts **weiß.**
>
> Niemand sagt mir, wie sie **heißt.**
>
> Das ist der Mann, den ich gesucht **habe.**

Check Your Comprehension

A. *Label the principal elements of the sentence (subject, verb, direct object, indirect object, and adverb). Explain which type of word order is used and why.*

1. Wir fliegen noch in diesem Jahr nach Europa.
2. Nächste Woche fliegt mein Mann nach Zürich.
3. Ich wußte, daß wir heute schönes Wetter haben würden.
4. Wann mußt du nach Hause fahren?
5. Der Vater gibt dem Kind einen Apfel.
6. Gibt der Vater dem Kind einen Apfel?
7. Warum gibt der Vater dem Kind keine Schokolade?
8. Ich weiß, warum der Vater dem Kind keine Schokolade gibt.
9. Das ist der Bus, mit dem ich nach Innsbruck fahren will.
10. Wo haben Sie Ihren Reisepaß?

B. *Rewrite the sentence three times by making the following changes: change the sentence to a simple question; ask a question for which the statement is the answer by using a question word (for example, **wann, wie, warum,** or **wo**); change the original sentence to one with a dependent clause by using the opening phrase* **Ich weiß nicht, ob. . . .**

1. Ein Kind geht in Deutschland in die Schule, wenn es sechs Jahre alt ist.
2. Es kann nach vier Jahren auf ein „Gymnasium" gehen.
3. Man kann ein Gymnasium vielleicht mit einer „High School" vergleichen.
4. Man kann nach Abschluß des Gymnasiums an der Universität studieren.
5. Die meisten Schüler sind dann ungefähr achtzehn Jahre alt.
6. Ein Student studiert in Deutschland ungefähr acht Semester.
7. Er macht dann sein Staatsexamen.

C. *Combine the sentences using the coordinating conjunction in parentheses.*

1. Ein guter Wein ist etwas Schönes. Er ist auch teuer. (aber)
2. Morgen sollten Sie einmal nicht soviel arbeiten. Sie sollten spazierengehen. (sondern)
3. Ich riet ihm zu heiraten. Er hat es auch getan. (und)
4. Wir fotografieren nicht viel. Das ist sehr teuer. (denn)
5. Heute würde ich gern schwimmen gehen. Ich habe leider keine Zeit. (aber)
6. Wirst du hier bleiben? Wirst du nach Hause gehen? (oder)

D. *Combine the sentences using the subordinating conjunction in parentheses. Then begin the sentence with the second clause.*

1. Wir studieren Deutsch. Wir können in Deutschland mit den Leuten sprechen. (damit)
2. Ich studierte Spanisch. Ich studierte Deutsch. (bevor)
3. Sie studierte Deutsch. Sie lebte in Österreich und sprach mit den Leuten. (indem)
4. Wir wissen es. Deutsch ist nicht ganz leicht. (daß)
5. Er studierte Deutsch. Diese Sprache ist schwer. (obwohl)

6. Ich lerne am besten Deutsch. Ich höre einen deutschen Rundfunksender. (wenn)
7. Er lernte Französisch. Sie lernte Deutsch. (während)
8. Mein Freund sagte es mir. Er lernt am leichtesten Deutsch. (wie)
9. Ich lernte Deutsch. Ich hatte Russisch gelernt. (nachdem)
10. Wir alle lernen Deutsch. Wir wollen nächsten Sommer in die Schweiz reisen. (weil)

Mood and Style

I. INDICATIVE (ACTIVE VOICE)

• Most utterances in any given language are in the indicative mood.

The following passage is kept entirely in the indicative (of the active voice). Read the passage and observe the use of this mood.

Ein Engländer, ein Franzose und ein Bayer unterhalten sich über die Unterschiede zwischen Schreibweise und Aussprache.

,,Sehr schwierig bei uns", erklärt der Brite. ,,Wir schreiben zum Beispiel ,Bir-ming-ham', sprechen aber ,Bör-ming-häm'."

,,Kein Vergleich", trumpft der Franzose auf. ,,Wir schreiben ,Bor-de-aux' und sagen ,Bor-do'."

,,Ois nix!" erklärt der Bayer. ,,Mir schreim ,Wie meinen Sie bitte?' und sprechen ,Ha?' "*

II. PASSIVE VOICE

• The passive voice is formed by using an inflected form of the auxiliary verb **werden** plus the past participle of the principal verb.

---

* This is Bavarian dialect: **ois nix!** = **ist nichts!** and **mir schreim** = **wir schreiben.**

Das Auto **wird** verkauft.
Das Auto **wurde** verkauft.
Das Auto **ist** verkauft **worden.**
Das Auto **war** verkauft **worden.**
Das Auto **wird** verkauft **werden**
Das Auto **wird** verkauft **worden sein.**

- In the active voice, the subject of a clause is the "agent" that "acts"; in the passive voice it is the "receiver" that is "acted upon" or "suffers the action."

Mein Freund verkauft sein Auto.
Das Auto **wird** von meinem Freund **verkauft.**

- The statal passive is used to indicate that the action is in fact completed, and it uses the auxiliary **sein.**

Das Auto **ist** verkauft.
Das Auto **war** verkauft.
Das Auto **ist** verkauft **gewesen.**
Das Auto **war** verkauft **gewesen.**
Das Auto **wird** verkauft **sein.**
Das Auto **wird** verkauft **gewesen sein.**

Read the following passage and observe the use of the passive voice.

Es wurde von einem Engländer, einem Franzosen und einem Bayern eine Unterhaltung geführt über die Unterschiede zwischen Schreibweise und Aussprache.

„Sehr schwierig bei uns", wurde von dem Briten erklärt. „Bei uns wird zum Beispiel ‚Bir-ming-ham' geschrieben, aber ‚Bör-ming-häm' gesprochen."

„Kein Vergleich", wurde von dem Franzosen aufgetrumpft. „Bei uns wird ‚Bor-de-aux' geschrieben und ‚Bor-do' gesagt."

„Ois nix!" wurde von dem Bayern erklärt. „Bei uns wird ‚Wie meinen Sie bitte?' geschrieben und ‚Ha?' gesprochen."

III. SUBJUNCTIVE II

- The subjunctive II is formed by adding the subjunctive personal endings (**–e, –est, –e; –en, –et, –en**) to the stem of a verb. Stem vowels of the past stem of strong verbs, irregular weak verbs, and some modals are umlauted if possible.

Indicative	Past Stem	Subjunctive II
Sie liebt ihn.	(liebt–)	Sie **liebte** ihn.
Ich weiß es.	(wußt–)	Ich **wüßte** es.
Er kann es tun.	(konnt–)	Er **könnte** es tun.
Wir schreiben es.	(schrieb–)	Wir **schrieben** es.
Sie spricht Deutsch.	(sprach–)	Sie **spräche** Deutsch.

- Since the subjunctive II form of regular weak verbs is identical with the past tense form, the substitute form of **würde** plus the infinitive is preferred.

Sie würde ihn lieben.

- The principal uses of the subjunctive II are wishful thinking,

Ich wünschte, ich hätte einen Farbfernseher.

contrary-to-fact conditions,

present: Wenn ich Hunger **hätte, würde** ich es **sagen.**
past: Wenn ich Hunger **gehabt hätte,** dann **hätte** ich es **gesagt.**

and polite requests.

Würden Sie mir einen Gefallen tun?

Read the following passage describing a hypothetical situation and observe the use of the subjunctive II.

Wenn sich ein Engländer, ein Franzose und ein Bayer träfen und sich über die Unterschiede zwischen Schreibweise und Aussprache unterhalten würden, so könnten sie folgendes sagen:

„Sehr schwierig bei uns", würde vielleicht der Brite erklären. „Wir schreiben zum Beispiel ‚Bir-ming-ham‘, sprechen aber ‚Bör-ming-häm‘."

„Kein Vergleich", würde dann vielleicht der Franzose auftrumpfen und sagen: „Wir schreiben ‚Bor-de-aux‘ und sagen ‚Bor-do‘."

„Ois nix!" würde daraufhin der Bayer erklären. „Mir schreim ‚Wie meinen Sie bitte?‘ und sprechen ‚Ha?‘."

IV. INDIRECT DISCOURSE

- To express the indirect discourse, you may either use the subjunctive I or the subjunctive II. In some instances, you may even use the indicative, but its use is still relatively rare.
- The prime function of subjunctive I is to indicate indirect discourse. If the subjunctive I forms are identical with the indicative forms, however, subjunctive II is usually preferred.

dir. disc.:	Er sagte: „Ich habe kein Geld."
indir. disc. (subj. I):	Er sagte, **er habe** kein Geld.
indir. disc. (subj. II):	Er sagte, **er hätte** kein Geld.
dir. disc.:	Er sagte: „Sie verdienen zu wenig Geld."
indir. disc. (subj. I):	Er sagte, **ich verdiene** zu wenig Geld.
indir. disc. (subj. II):	Er sagte, **ich verdiente** zu wenig Geld.

Read the following passage and observe the way indirect discourse is expressed.

Mein Freund erzählte mir, ein Engländer, ein Franzose und ein Bayer hätten sich über die Unterschiede zwischen Schreibweise und Aussprache unterhalten.

Das sei sehr schwierig bei ihnen, habe der Brite erklärt. Sie schrieben zum Beispiel „Bir-ming-ham" und sprächen „Bör-ming-häm". Das sei kein Vergleich, habe der Franzose aufgetrumpft. Sie würden „Bor-de-aux" schreiben und „Bor-do" sagen. Das sei nichts, habe der Bayer erklärt. Sie würden „Wie meinen Sie bitte?" schreiben und sprächen „Ha?"

Check Your Comprehension

A. *Rewrite the following paragraph in the passive voice.*

Sie haben diesen Deutsch-Kurs für das erste Studienjahr beendet. Wir Autoren hoffen, daß Sie nicht nur Schweiß und Tränen vergossen haben. Man kann natürlich ein Grammatikbuch nicht mit einem Liebesroman oder einem Krimi vergleichen. Man muß manchmal etwas erklären, damit

Sie verstehen, was Sie in den Übungen tun. Grammatik lernt man am besten, wenn man sie ständig anwendet und wiederholt. Die deutsche Sprache kann man jedoch am besten lernen, wenn man sie spricht. Wir hoffen, daß Sie Ihr Deutsch-Studium im zweiten Jahr fortsetzen werden.

Bis dahin: „Auf Wiedersehen!"

B. *Rewrite the paragraph above in indirect discourse, first in the first-person singular and then in the first-person plural. Begin the paragraph with the opening phrase* **Die Autoren schreiben, ich (wir)** . . .

APPENDIX

English Equivalents of Conversations

Since conversational style tends to be highly idiomatic in every language, English translations of the German conversations must often deviate substantially from the original with respect to idiom structure. In cases where the difference between German and English is especially great, a more literal but less idiomatic translation is in brackets [ ]. In some instances, English conversational style requires the addition of a word or part of speech not found in the German original. These additions are placed in parentheses ( ). Affective exclamations cannot be translated literally and are merely rendered by their English near-equivalents.

Chapter 1:   (A Piece of) Information

JUDY	Hello, I'm looking for the "Institute of German Language and Literature."
MR. KELLER	Johannisstraße (number) one. It's right over there.—Are you from the United States [America]?
JUDY	Yes, I'm from Buffalo, New York. My name is Judy Miller.
MR. KELLER	And now you're studying here in Germany?
JUDY	Yes, I'm studying German and sociology.
MR. KELLER	That's interesting.
JUDY	By the way, I'm [just] looking for a book by Kafka. It's called *Amerika*. I hope it's here.
MR. KELLER	I'm not sure. The card catalogue is right over there. Good luck!
JUDY	Thank you for the information. Good-bye.
MR. KELLER	Good-bye, Miss Miller.

Chapter 2:   A Telephone Conversation

MONIKA	Hi [you], Jürgen, this [here] is Monika. I hope you aren't too busy [have a moment's time] right now.
JÜRGEN	Hm! Why?
MONIKA	Because we just got [now have] a stereo set with (a) tape recorder and record player. It's brand new.
JÜRGEN	Really? Man, that's great. (What do) you have, a Grundig stereo set?

MONIKA	No, I believe it's a [from] Sony. The sound is simply fantastic [I find the sound simply fantastic]. Do you perhaps have a record by Dave Brubeck?
JÜRGEN	Sorry, I don't have a record by Brubeck, but I do have a few jazz records— by Louis Armstrong, for instance, and. . . .
MONIKA	Super! By the way, do you know the record "Down by the River" by Neil Young?
JÜRGEN	No, is it (a) new (one)?
MONIKA	It's not new, but I think it's really good [I find the record really good].
JÜRGEN	Great! I'll be over right away [I'm coming immediately]. See you, Monika.
MONIKA	So long, Jürgen. Till later.

Chapter 3: A Bus Ride

Airport Berlin-Tempelhof. Robert is just arriving in West Berlin (after traveling) from Hanover. He picks up [takes] his baggage and leaves the hall. Outside the taxis are waiting. He asks a cab driver for information.

ROBERT	Excuse me, is there a bus [does a bus go] from here to Schöneberg?
CAB DRIVER	Well, come on. Get in. I'll take you there.
ROBERT	No thanks. You know, I'm a student. Unfortunately, I don't have enough money for a taxi.
CAB DRIVER	(That's) too bad.—Do you see the bus stop over there? Take line fifteen.

Robert sees a bus coming.

BUS DRIVER	Hurry up, step in, please. We're leaving right away. Step in and put your [the] luggage in the corner over there.
ROBERT	Are you leaving already? Are you going directly to Schöneberg?
BUS DRIVER	Nope, [you know,] we're heading for [driving to] the city center, to [where there is] the Europa-Center and the Kurfürstendamm.
ROBERT	Oops, this isn't line fifteen then? What am I going to do now?
BUS DRIVER	Change at Kaiser-Wilhelm-Straße. (Take) number eight.
ROBERT	I see. Then please (give me) a ticket to Schöneberg.
BUS DRIVER	(That will be) one forty, please.

The bus driver calls out the Kaiser-Wilhelm-Straße. Robert changes into bus (number) eight. The bus is jam packed [very full].

BUS DRIVER	Move on (to the rear). Move on (to the rear), please.
ROBERT	Schöneberg's City Hall, please. How far is that from here?
BUS DRIVER	Four stops. I'll call it out shortly.
ROBERT	Many thanks.

Chapter 4: The Student Room

Heinz is a student in Marburg. He's looking for a room. He goes to a rental agency and talks to [with] Miss Schell.

MISS SCHELL   Good morning. What can I do for you?

HEINZ   I'm a student here in Marburg and (I'm) looking for a room.

MISS SCHELL   What kind of room would you like? I mean, for how much?

HEINZ   For approximately 200 marks per month [monthly].

MISS SCHELL   One moment, please. How about [is it with] a room directly by the university? It costs 240 marks, with heating (included).

HEINZ   Hm. That's not particularly cheap. Does it have cooking facilities?

MISS SCHELL   Yes, I'm sure.

HEINZ   Does the room also have a shower or a bath?

MISS SCHELL   No, but (it does have) a sink.

HEINZ   And how about [is it with] the toilet?

MISS SCHELL   It's just [directly] across the hall [opposite the room].

HEINZ   And how far is it to the bus stop?

MISS SCHELL   Approximately five minutes on foot.

HEINZ   (That's) not bad! What's [how is] the address, please?

MISS SCHELL   Mrs. Becker, (number) five Lindenstraße, near the Hindenburgplatz.

HEINZ   Thank you. What's your fee [how much does it cost]?

MISS SCHELL   Eight marks. Please sign the form and give it to Mrs. Becker.

HEINZ   And where do I pay the eight marks?

MISS SCHELL   Go over there to the cashier's desk, please.

HEINZ   OK, many thanks. Good-bye.

Chapter 5: In Court

DISTRICT ATTORNEY   Mr. Steinhoff, will you please tell the court [us] how [that was with] the accident occurred.

DEFENDANT   Well, I went to [visited] a party at some friends' house.

D.A.   I see, you went to a party! Just what did you drink there?

DEFENDANT   We drank (were drinking) wine, beer, or orange juice.

D.A.   I see. And naturally you drank orange juice.

DEFENDANT   I believe (so), yes.

D.A.   How is that? You believe (so)? I don't understand you. The police stopped you on the way (home) and took a blood test. Did you really drink nothing but orange juice?

DEFENDANT   Maybe somebody mixed in some Vodka. I'm not sure.

D.A.	And that, of course, you didn't notice. Or have you already forgotten it? You damaged public [state] property, (you know).
DEFENDANT	Oh, you mean the tree? Yes, how in the world did that [really] happen? There was a Porsche coming from the right, and (it) passed me. Whereupon [and then] I quickly turned left.
D.A.	Mr. Steinhoff, the tree, however, was [standing] on the right.
DEFENDANT	Well, then I probably didn't see it because . . . .
D.A.	[Give me an] answer, please.
DEFENDANT	I don't know . . . .
D.A.	Then I'll give you the answer. The answer is clear: unfortunately you had too much orange juice in (your) blood!

Chapter 6: The Coffee Bar

Georg and Sibille had a date for nine o'clock in the morning. The meeting place was (to be) a coffee bar. Georg is [comes] fifteen minutes [too] late.

SIBILLE	There you are finally. Where (in the world) have you been?
GEORG	Hi, Sibille. I'm sorry. I meant [really wanted] to be on time. But, you know, I was supposed to buy [bring along] a few rolls, and then . . . .
SIBILLE	. . . and then you couldn't find a parking spot again. Right?
GEORG	Not quite. I found a parking meter right in front of the bakery, but I completely forgot to put [throw] in a nickel. And then came . . . .
SIBILLE	. . . a policeman, of course.—By the way, here's some [the] coffee for you. Don't let it get [become] cold. Cream?
GEORG	A little. Enough, thank you.—Well, a police car drove up [came] and stopped. A policeman got out and—what do you think?—(that) man was, in fact, just about to give me a ticket. Fortunately, however, I was just able to . . . .

Just at that moment, a student tried to pass Georg and pushed him by mistake.

STUDENT	Oh, pardon me. I didn't mean [really didn't want] to do that. [Has] anything happen[ed]?
GEORG	(Don't worry) it's not so bad. A little bit of coffee . . . .
SIBILLE	(It) doesn't matter. That sweater should have gone to the cleaner's a long time ago. It's really quite dirty.
GEORG	Perhaps we can take it right over there to the express dry-cleaner's? Would you like another cup of coffee?
SIBILLE	No thanks. Let's go to the cleaner's right away instead.

Chapter 7:   The Ski Vacation

Jens and Wilfried have (their) Christmas holidays and wish to take a skiing vacation. The question is, where? The central mountains in Germany (for instance, the Harz or the Black Forest) most often don't have enough snow during the Christmas season [vacation]. The Alps are better. But it's too far and too strenuous (to go there) by car. Therefore, instead of the Volkswagen they want to take a train.

JENS   Hi, Wilfried, you're back already. Were you successful in finding a few brochures for our [the] winter vacation?

WILFRIED   Yes, I was at a travel agency early this morning. You know, (the one) near the Kaufhof, just around the corner. They told me to [recommended that I] make reservations as quickly as possible. It's quite difficult to still get a room. Anyway, here are brochures from Touropa, Scharnow, Hummel, and Tigges.

JENS   I see (that) you've also brought a prospectus from Neckermann. Well, if that isn't enough for us . . . !

WILFRIED   Well, I brought everything—on account of the prices, you know. After all, we have to make comparisons.

JENS   Certainly—Tigges. Let's see!—Hm, Berchtesgaden—great! And here, Garmisch—not bad either! Just a moment—almost 400 marks for a two-week ski vacation? That's a lot of money.

WILFRIED   Yes, that is a lot! Say, is it really as expensive to take a vacation in Austria as it is in Germany?

JENS   Probably not. Let's see what Neckermann has to offer in Austria. —Here, for example. What do you think of the Arlberg Pass in Austria?

WILFRIED   For skiing, ideal! But how much does it cost?

JENS   Just a moment. Here two weeks for 320 marks. That's with shower, balcony, and three meals [board] a day.

WILFRIED   That's cheap. But wait a minute. Does that include the train fare?

JENS   Oh, yes. Even with a special train. The special trains of a travel agency are as good as the Intercity trains or the TEEs.

WILFRIED   Look here. The train travels from Hamburg through North Germany and the Ruhr to Cologne. From there it goes through the Rhine Valley and the Black Forest to Lake Constance.

JENS   And then (from there) you take the bus on to Arlberg. I know that route. I suggest we try to get a room at Arlberg. At any rate, I'd prefer a room with bath instead of a shower.

WILFRIED   Let's see what we can still get this late (in the season). I'm going to call Neckermann right now.

JENS   Let's hope it works.

Chapter 8: The City Map

The train from Frankfurt is on time. Fred opens the door and steps out of the train. He puts his [the] briefcase under his [the] arm and walks into the entrance hall of the railroad station. Next to the ticket counter he sees a policeman. Fred walks up to him and asks for some [an] information.

FRED Pardon me, how do I get from here to the university?

POLICEMAN To the university? Well, that I have to show you on the map of the city over there.

In front of the map of the city.

POLICEMAN You see, we're right here where the arrow is [at the arrow]. There's the central railroad station.

FRED Yes (I see). And now where is [does] the university [lie] (from here)?

POLICEMAN The university is up here by the Karlsplatz. Just a moment. Oh, yes, here (it is).

FRED That means first I have to cross this street. (Right?)

POLICEMAN Quite right. Then over there at the corner you come to Adenauer-Allee. From there you go straight ahead to Schützenstraße. That's two, no, three intersections from here.

FRED Adenauer-Allee is here; then—just a moment—Schützenstraße. OK, I've got it.

POLICEMAN Take Schützenstraße [up] to the municipal theater and then (go) left. From there (go) straight ahead [up] to the Karlsplatz.

FRED And you said there's the university?

POLICEMAN Yes, It's a new building. By foot, approximately fifteen minutes.

FRED Many thanks.

POLICEMAN You're very welcome.

Chapter 9: In the National Museum

CHARLIE What a collection! I must say, Herbert, your National Museum is really outstanding. I believe it can easily be compared [one can easily compare it] to our Museum of Modern Art. Don't you think so?

HERBERT Certainly! Our collection has, above all, many paintings from the romantic (period). In this respect it is indeed unique. But, of course, many works from the post-war period are equally important.

CHARLIE Yes, in this area your museum is famous the world over.

HERBERT	That's right. By the way, have you seen the paintings over there? They're all [paintings] by artists from America. Many I find very beautiful; others, however, (I find) less so [not so good]. But that is, of course, a matter of taste.
CHARLIE	Yes, I've seen several. It seems that the influence of the United States in the field of culture is really not limited [only] to Hollywood westerns and television detective stories!
HERBERT	Of course not. I believe this trend has been constantly increasing in the past few years.
CHARLIE	That's really interesting. Our influence on the European economy is steadily declining, but our influence in art and culture is continually rising. How is that possible?
HERBERT	Yes, that's really the way it looks. However, that kind of development had to come. Today Europe is no longer as dependent on the United States as (it was) only a few years ago. Let's assume, if America . . . .
CHARLIE	You know, I find this all very interesting. But didn't we come here [want] to see the exhibit?
HERBERT	You're right. I agree with you. Well then, back to culture!

Chapter 10:   At the Watchmaker's

WATCHMAKER	Hello, Mrs. Lenz. May I help you?
MRS. LENZ	Hello, Mr. Beuse. I'm afraid this new watch [here] is broken. Look it doesn't run anymore.
WATCHMAKER	Let me see. Yes, that's an expensive watch. "Made in Switzerland."
MRS. LENZ	Pardon? What did you say?
WATCHMAKER	I said, "Made in Switzerland." Look, here it says so.
MRS. LENZ	I see. Yes, that watch is from Switzerland.
WATCHMAKER	Didn't your husband buy this watch here a few months ago?
MRS. LENZ	Yes, exactly. But how can a new watch stop running? That never happened with my old watch.
WATCHMAKER	Don't worry, Mrs. Lenz. Modern watches are very well made. There isn't much that can go wrong with them. I'll open it up.
MRS. LENZ	Fortunately, this watch is still under warranty.
WATCHMAKER	How long have you had this watch now, Mrs. Lenz?
MRS. LENZ	Since last summer. That's about a year.
WATCHMAKER	Then we'll probably have to replace the old battery with a new one. That's all.
MRS. LENZ	So the watch isn't broken at all?
WATCHMAKER	Not at all. With electronic watches like this one, the battery needs to be replaced every one to two years. See, it [the watch] works again. That's twelve marks fifty.

MRS. LENZ   That was certainly simple. Thank you very much, Mr. Beuse. Good-bye.
WATCHMAKER   Good-bye, Mrs. Lenz.

Chapter 11:   In the Supermarket

MRS. HELMS   Say, Ernst, what do you think of green salad and fresh fruit for lunch today? You know, the doctor said . . . .

MR. HELMS   Yes, yes. Nothing fat, nothing sweet, nothing too spicy, no fried meat, and so on, and so on.

MRS. HELMS   That's right. But naturally you may have [eat] fresh yogurt or a boiled egg.

MR. HELMS   I know, I know.—Say, Ilse, didn't we want to invite the Meyers for fondue sometime? We promised it to them such a long time (ago).

MRS. HELMS   But Ernst, you know meat cooked in oil doesn't agree with you.

MR. HELMS   Of course. I don't mean [didn't think of] meat fondue but [of] a nice cheese fondue.

MRS. HELMS   I see. OK. Yes, that's different [something else]. How about inviting the Meyers for tomorrow night? So what do we need for fondue?

MR. HELMS   I think we need about one pound of Swiss cheese and a pound of Gruyère.

MRS. HELMS   And what kind of wine shall we have [does one take]? White?

MR. HELMS   White (wine), of course. It has to be a nice, dry white wine. I still have a good one in the cellar.

MRS. HELMS   Do you also have some kirsch at home?

MR. HELMS   Unfortunately, no, (I don't). But over there on the shelf are several bottles.

MRS. HELMS   Good. It doesn't have to be an expensive one. Do we need anything else?

MR. HELMS   How about fresh white bread?

MRS. HELMS   We still have some [deep] frozen white bread at home. That's just as good as fresh.

MR. HELMS   Wonderful. I can hardly wait until tomorrow night! At last, we'll have something tasty to eat again.

Chapter 12:   The Heat Wave

PETER   Today is certainly the hottest day of the year. I can't stand this heat any longer! It's even worse than last year.

ROLF   I don't know. I think we had [there were] even [some] warmer days last year than today.

PETER Well, perhaps it was really [in fact] a little hotter then than today. But that doesn't make the heat any more bearable.

ROLF I suggest that we stop studying [working] for the exam now. Do you know what the worst (thing) is?

PETER You mean that by tomorrow we (will) have forgotten everything?

ROLF Exactly. To hell with this stupid geometry! I just don't understand that Euclid. Do you get that stuff?

PETER Not much better than you (do). Come on, let's go to the swimming pool. It'll be cooler there.

ROLF Good idea. The question is only where (do we go)? Do we want to go to the Odenwald pool?

PETER Yes, that's fine with me. To be quite honest, I'd rather go there than to the Olympia pool. I think the water is cleanest there.

ROLF And, in addition, there are probably fewer people.

PETER That could be, but it's also certainly more expensive in the Odenwald pool.

ROLF Why? Didn't you say recently (that) it's cheaper there?

PETER Well, that was certainly true then. In the meantime, however, everything has become more expensive.

ROLF It's crazy. In winter we have to spend more money for heating, and in summer (we have to pay) more for cooler water. Everything is more expensive. Our inflation is really getting worse and worse.

Chapter 13: In City Hall

MR. SCHNEIDER Good morning. I would like to apply for a passport.

OFFICIAL Oh? Where would you like to travel (then)? Namely, for most European countries an ID card [personal identification] is sufficient.

MR. SCHNEIDER I know, but I want to drive [by car] through the GDR[1], and for that I'll probably need a passport.

OFFICIAL That's right, of course. Please fill out this application form.

MR. SCHNEIDER Thank you. Oh, now I don't have my ballpoint pen with me. May I borrow one from you [can you give me one]?

OFFICIAL Certainly, but I can also type it out (for you) now [fill out the application form now with the typewriter] since I don't have anything (else) to do at the moment.

MR. SCHNEIDER That's really very kind of you.

OFFICIAL Your surname and first name, please.

MR. SCHNEIDER Schneider, Helmut.

---

[1]German Democratic Republic (East Germany).

OFFICIAL	Zip code [post office number], place of residence, and street address?
MR. SCHNEIDER	Seven Stuttgart, (number) ten Bahnhofstraße.
OFFICIAL	Your place of birth, Mr. Schneider?
MR. SCHNEIDER	Oberammergau in Bavaria.
OFFICIAL	And your date of birth?
MR. SCHNEIDER	November 10, 1950.
OFFICIAL	Occupation?
MR. SCHNEIDER	Bank employee.
OFFICIAL	(Would you) please sign here. Thank you. Now, I still need your ID card and two passport pictures.
MR. SCHNEIDER	Here's my ID card. I didn't know [exactly] the regulations, and (so) I didn't know how many passport pictures are required. But, fortunately, I brought two along.
OFFICIAL	Fine. Then everything is in order. We'll mail the passport to you within the next few days.
MR. SCHNEIDER	Many thanks. Good-bye.
OFFICIAL	Good-bye, Mr. Schneider.

Chapter 14: The Menu

Peter and Helga are sitting in the restaurant Stuhlmacher and are studying the menu.

PETER	Look here, Helga—the menu. Hm! Specialty of the house, pork shank from the grill. Do you think that's [something] for us?
HELGA	Certainly not for me. Just remember that I can't eat that much. What I'm really hungry for right now is fish.
PETER	OK then. Although I know that you really do like [to eat] fish, I don't understand how you can renounce good grilled pork shank! Would you like duckling, perhaps?
HELGA	Oh no! Do you [really] know how many calories are in duckling? If you really want to know what I want, it's trout [If you ask me what I'm craving, then my answer is trout]. But I don't know if you can get fresh trout here.
PETER	Of course, you can. I know that [it] because I've eaten here several times [often]. But before I order I must know whether you would like blue trout or "the miller's wife's style."
HELGA	You mean boiled or fried.
PETER	Right! By the way, if you want to know what I want. I'd like a nice rump-steak with onions and tossed salad.

HELGA   Hm, not bad! OK, then, I'll take fried [the miller's wife's] trout. But, as you know, I also just love [to eat] rumpsteak. Will you let me taste a small piece of it?

PETER   But of course. If you like, you may gladly have a piece.

HELGA   Good. You know, I find it really quite cozy here.

PETER   So do I. I believe we can order now. Waiter, please bring us the wine list too.

Chapter 15:   In Front of the Camera Shop

Hans is showing his American friend Jerry, whom he met in the United States, through the business district [streets] of his native city. Jerry, who is traveling in [visiting] Germany for the first time, speaks German quite well.

JERRY   What really impresses me here is your store windows, which I find very attractive.

HANS   Yes, that's right. Most shops really decorate their windows very attractively, for which, however, one has to pay higher prices.

JERRY   Yes, they spend a lot of money on advertising. Hey, let's see how much they want [ask here] for those cameras [which stand] in the window over there.

The two friends cross the street [in order] to see how much the cameras cost. Suddenly a taxi comes around the corner. Its brakes screeching [with screeching brakes], it comes to a stop [stops] directly in front of them.

HANS   Look out!

JERRY   Man, that guy almost got us! Naturally (it's) a cab driver. A man who [whoever] drives that wildly must be mad. Or do they fight the population explosion hereabouts with cars?!

HANS   Well now, it's really not that bad.

JERRY   Ah! Here are the cameras. Man, the prices are simply astronomical. The same as at home. Over there in the corner is a Rolleiflex, which you can't get at home for less than three hundred dollars. And, there, look at all the Japanese cameras.

HANS   Yes, well, Japan's optical industry obviously dominates the world market. We can't keep up with them any longer.

JERRY   Why (do you say that)? [The firm] Leica, whose products practically everyone knows, is certainly as good as Nikon.

HANS   Oh, that reminds me [you remind me thereby] that I need another (roll of) color film.

JERRY   And I want to see if I can get Kodak film for my camera here.

Chapter 16: The Boss

Boss	Good morning, Miss Hansen.
Secretary	Good morning, Mr. Neumann. I'm glad you're back. How was your business trip?
Boss	Fine, thanks. A bit exhausting but otherwise quite successful. I hope you didn't overwork yourself during [while] the week [eight days] I was gone.
Secretary	By no means. I was just a bit upset that the delivery from Brinkmann & Co., which was promised (us) for May 23rd, hasn't arrived yet.
Boss	What? Brinkmann hasn't delivered the cases yet? What's the date today?
Secretary	It's May 30th already.
Boss	I'll give them a call right away. Give me their number, please. How many cases did we actually order?
Secretary	(We ordered) forty big ones and eighty-five small ones. Brinkmann's telephone number is area code 025034, and then 7071.
Boss	Thank you. I'll take care of it right away. Anything else of importance?
Secretary	Yes. The Brandt company wrote on May 26th. They want to know if we can deliver eighteen pieces of equipment, type LS 34, next week.
Boss	Delivery is probably no problem, but let me talk with my section manager first. Did you take down any other important deadlines?
Secretary	Yes, on Monday, June 6th, there will be a meeting at eleven o'clock. Mr. Krause has already excused himself because he is going on vacation on June 4th.
Boss	Good. I don't have time to read my mail right now. Oh, Miss Hansen, would you please make me a cup of coffee; (it makes) work go so much better.
Secretary	Oh yes. Your work! Coffee will be ready in three minutes.

Chapter 17: At the Service Station

Attendant	Good evening, may I help you?
Günter	Fill (it) up, please. Ten liters super and the rest regular [gas].
Attendant	Your gas tank is still locked. Could you give me the key, please.
Günter	Oh, of course. I always forget [that]. Here are the keys. This one opens [is for] the gas tank.
Attendant	Thanks. I see from your license plate that you're from Göttingen. Beautiful city. I lived there for five years.
Günter	Yes, it's easy to take [one can easily stand it there]. I'm (a student) at the university there.
Attendant	I see. What are you studying?

GÜNTER	Medicine. I'm in my seventh semester.
ATTENDANT	Well, we need physicians very badly. How's [it with] the oil?
GÜNTER	Yes, please check the oil too. These old VWs use up quite a lot. It's better, of course, with the new cars.
ATTENDANT	True. You need [it lacks] half a liter. What kind of oil do you use?
GÜNTER	Thirty weight, please. Oh, could you also check the tires. I think the right front tire is a little low [has too little air].
ATTENDANT	Sure. Anything else? [Do you have another wish?]
GÜNTER	No, thanks. That's all.
ATTENDANT	Would you like a receipt?
GÜNTER	No, thanks, (that's) not necessary. Well then, good-bye.
ATTENDANT	Good-bye! Have a nice trip. And say hello to Göttingen for me.

Chapter 18:   A New Year's Eve

It's shortly before midnight. Outside, you can already hear the bang of exploding firecrackers. Mr. and Mrs. Schröder are discussing their plans for the new year. Mr. Schröder carefully opens a bottle of champagne.

MRS. SCHRÖDER	Actually, I'm very happy that we're celebrating New Year's Eve all alone this time.
MR. SCHRÖDER	Yes, I've also had my fill of the usual New Year's Eve party with dancing [dance music] and fireworks. Till midnight we might just as well think about what we want to do [undertake in the] next year.
MRS. SCHRÖDER	One thing I can promise you: I will now finally start my diet and also be a little more active [engage] in sports.
MR. SCHRÖDER	Well, Luise, if you come to Garmisch with me at Easter and go skiing for two weeks [fourteen days], you probably won't have to be so strict with your diet. What do you think? How the two of us will lose weight on a ski vacation!
MRS. SCHRÖDER	I don't know if at my age I'll still go skiing, Rudi. But since we'll have an indoor swimming pool in our hotel, I'll go swimming while you're on the ski slopes.
MR. SCHRÖDER	Tell me, won't you go easy on [reduce] your smoking next year? [Meanwhile] I've completely given it up [weaned myself away from it]. For me it'll be the second year without smoking cigarettes.
MRS. SCHRÖDER	Truly admirable! (Ever) since the doctor told you that . . . . But you're right. I'll try to give it up too, although it certainly won't be easy.
MR. SCHRÖDER	Do you hear the church bells (ringing)? It's midnight. The new year has begun. Here, take your glass.

MRS. SCHRÖDER Well, then. Happy New Year! I hope all our wishes [will] come true.

MR. SCHRÖDER I hope so, too. Cheers, Luise! Come here to the window and look at the beautiful fireworks.

Chapter 19:   Students in Munich-Schwabing

ROLF Look, there it is already. I'm telling you, if you haven't seen Schwabing, you haven't seen Munich.

KATRIN You mean those figures there on the sidewalk?

ROLF Yes, but from here you can't see much [there isn't much to recognize] as yet. Let's go closer.

KATRIN Rolf, see there, the long-haired guy [one] over there has exhibited [at the long-haired one's (stand) there are exhibited] a lot of paintings. Do you think he painted them all by himself [they were all painted by him]?

ROLF Absolutely. Most of the people who display their handiwork here are studying at the famous Munich Academy of Art. Many (of them) sell the things they made [which were created by themselves].

KATRIN I must say I like the paintings on the sidewalk. The colors are really unique.

ROLF Yes, I like the colors, too, but otherwise the picture is a little too abstract for me.

KATRIN So, and? I find that with these abstract pictures our fantasy at least is stimulated a bit.

ROLF You're right, of course. Look here, what do you think of this silver jewelry?

KATRIN Very beautiful. Did the students make it too? [Has it also been made by the students themselves?]

ROLF But of course. Everything you see here [and which is offered] for sale has been created by the students themselves.

KATRIN Oh, look here (at) this necklace! Isn't it beautiful?

ROLF Yes, really. It would certainly go very well with your black sweater. You know what? I'll buy it for you if you invite me [I'm invited by you] tonight for a homemade pizza.

KATRIN Well, that we can talk about!—Thank you, Rolf, this necklace is really great. I'll wear it tonight when I serve you (my) homemade pizza.

Chapter 20:   In the Café

MRS. DAHL Ah, there you are, Luise. I'm sorry that I'm a quarter hour late [that I've come a quarter hour too late]. I could have been here long ago if I hadn't missed the streetcar.

Mrs. Carlsen	It [that] certainly doesn't matter, Gerda. Sit down and taste this delicious pastry. Coffee's coming right away; I've already ordered it.
Mrs. Dahl	[You know,] Luise, I was just at Hamann's—you (must) know [already], the furniture store near city hall—and I saw several marvelous pieces, really just [to] my taste. I would have loved to have taken them right with me. We definitely need an easy chair in the living room and [really] (some) new chairs for the dining table, too.
Mrs. Carlsen	Nowadays a person shouldn't hesitate too long since prices keep going up.
Mrs. Dahl	If I had only had the money I would have definitely bought the armchair right away. But you must know we have to think about such a purchase twice. If only my husband would finally get a raise again! With our income we almost can't afford anything anymore.
Mrs. Carlsen	Yes, if I had known that the cost of living would go up so much one day, I would [then] have certainly finished my education (to be) [as] a librarian, and things would be going better for us today.
Mrs. Dahl	I think sometimes too that now, when we still don't have any children, I should look for a job. Then we wouldn't need to live from hand to mouth.
Mrs. Carlsen	But tell me, Gerda, how would it be if we'd close this depressing topic so we could enjoy our coffee.
Mrs. Dahl	You're probably right. But next Monday I'll seriously begin looking for a job.

Chapter 21: The Police Inspector

There's hardly a more thrilling television program for the German detective fan[s] than the series "The Police Inspector," Friday evenings at 8:15 p.m. Here's a section (from that program).

Mr. Scholz comes home very late this evening. His wife welcomes him quite agitatedly.

Mrs. Scholz	Finally you're here, Herbert! It was terrible. A half hour ago a Mr. Keller, police inspector, was here. He said he was from the department of criminal investigation and had to ask you a few questions. It has to do with murder [murder is at stake].
Mr. Scholz	What? Murder? How come, who's been murdered? What do we have to do with that? What did the inspector want to know? What did you tell him?
Mrs. Scholz	The bell rang about 9:30. A man was standing at the door, who said he was Inspector Keller from the homicide squad. I said he should come in, that it certainly must be an error, and so on.

Mr. Scholz	Certainly.
Mrs. Scholz	Then he asked if my husband was at home. I said, no, you're on a business trip today and would be coming back [only] later.
Mr. Scholz	Good! Go on. What did he still want to know, this Inspector Keller?
Mrs. Scholz	He asked if I know a Maria Korff. I said, yes, she's [that's] my husband's secretary. Why did he ask about her, I wanted to know.
Mr. Scholz	And, what did he say?
Mrs. Scholz	Miss Korff was—oh, Herbert, it can't be true—was—was found dead in her apartment last evening. Murdered! Herbert, I can't believe that! Say something!
Mr. Scholz	Maria?—Dead?—Murdered? Did the Inspector ask where I was last night?
Mrs. Scholz	Yes, I told him you were bowling [you had gone to bowl] just like every Wednesday. He said, "How's that? Yesterday was Tuesday." He completely confused me [made me completely confused].
Mr. Scholz	Did he say anything else?
Mrs. Scholz	Well, I asked what you had to do with the whole thing. He certainly wouldn't suspect that you—Herbert! What's (the matter) with you? You're so nervous.
Mr. Scholz	Nothing. It's only the shock, yes, the shock. Poor Maria! Did the Inspector say that he has to speak with me?
Mrs. Scholz	Yes, it's urgent. You should call him when you're back. He's looking for a witness.
Mr. Scholz	Oh, Gerda, I just remembered, that I still have to visit a client. If the Inspector comes back again, tell him I've . . . .
Inspector Keller	(That's) not necessary anymore, Mr. Scholz. Hands up and don't move. I must unfortunately ask you to come along.

Principal Parts of Verbs

Strong Verbs

Infinitive	*Present*	*Past*	*Past Participle*
backen (to bake)	bäckt	backte (buk)	gebacken
befehlen (to command)	befiehlt	befahl	befohlen
beginnen (to begin)	beginnt	begann	begonnen

Infinitive	Present	Past	Past Participle
beißen (to bite)	beißt	biß	gebissen
bergen (to save)	birgt	barg	geborgen
bersten (to burst)	birst	barst	ist geborsten
beweisen (to prove)	beweist	bewies	bewiesen
biegen (to bend)	biegt	bog	gebogen
bieten (to offer)	bietet	bot	geboten
binden (to bind)	bindet	band	gebunden
bitten (to request)	bittet	bat	gebeten
blasen (to blow)	bläst	blies	geblasen
bleiben (to remain)	bleibt	blieb	ist geblieben
braten (to fry)	brät	briet	gebraten
brechen (to break)	bricht	brach	gebrochen
dringen (to penetrate)	dringt	drang	ist gedrungen
empfehlen (to recommend)	empfiehlt	empfahl	empfohlen
erschrecken (to frighten)	erschrickt	erschrak	ist erschrocken
essen (to eat)	ißt	aß	gegessen
fahren (to drive)	fährt	fuhr	ist gefahren
fallen (to fall)	fällt	fiel	ist gefallen
fangen (to catch)	fängt	fing	gefangen
fechten (to fight)	ficht	focht	gefochten
finden (to find)	findet	fand	gefunden
flechten (to twist)	flicht	flocht	geflochten
fliegen (to fly)	fliegt	flog	ist geflogen
fliehen (to flee)	flieht	floh	ist geflohen
fließen (to flow)	fließt	floß	ist geflossen
fressen (to eat)	frißt	fraß	gefressen
frieren (to freeze)	friert	fror	gefroren
gären (to ferment)	gärt	gor	gegoren
gebären (to give birth)	gebiert	gebar	geboren
geben (to give)	gibt	gab	gegeben
gedeihen (to thrive)	gedeiht	gedieh	ist gediehen
gehen (to walk)	geht	ging	ist gegangen
gelingen (to succeed)	gelingt	gelang	ist gelungen
gelten (to be worth)	gilt	galt	gegolten
genesen (to recover)	genest	genas	ist genesen
genießen (to enjoy)	genießt	genoß	genossen
geschehen (to occur)	geschieht	geschah	ist geschehen
gewinnen (to win, gain)	gewinnt	gewann	gewonnen

Infinitive	Present	Past	Past Participle
gießen (to pour)	gießt	goß	gegossen
gleichen (to resemble)	gleicht	glich	geglichen
gleiten (to glide)	gleitet	glitt	ist geglitten
glimmen (to smoulder)	glimmt	glomm	geglommen
graben (to dig)	gräbt	grub	gegraben
greifen (to seize)	greift	griff	gegriffen
halten (to hold)	hält	hielt	gehalten
hängen (to hang)	hängt	hing	gehangen
hauen (to spank)	haut	haute (hieb)	gehauen
heben (to lift)	hebt	hob	gehoben
heißen (to be called)	heißt	hieß	geheißen
helfen (to help)	hilft	half	geholfen
klingen (to sound)	klingt	klang	geklungen
kommen (to come)	kommt	kam	ist gekommen
kriechen (to crawl)	kriecht	kroch	ist gekrochen
laden (to load)	lädt	lud	geladen
lassen (to let)	läßt	ließ	gelassen
laufen (to run)	läuft	lief	ist gelaufen
leiden (to suffer)	leidet	litt	gelitten
leihen (to lend)	leiht	lieh	geliehen
lesen (to read)	liest	las	gelesen
liegen (to lie)	liegt	lag	gelegen
lügen (to tell a lie)	lügt	log	gelogen
meiden (to avoid)	meidet	mied	gemieden
messen (to measure)	mißt	maß	gemessen
mißlingen (to fail)	mißlingt	mißlang	ist mißlungen
nehmen (to take)	nimmt	nahm	genommen
pfeifen (to whistle)	pfeift	pfiff	gepfiffen
preisen (to praise)	preist	pries	gepriesen
raten (to advise; guess)	rät	riet	geraten
reiben (to rub)	reibt	rieb	gerieben
reißen (to tear)	reißt	riß	ist gerissen
reiten (to ride)	reitet	ritt	ist geritten
riechen (to smell)	riecht	roch	gerochen
ringen (to wrestle)	ringt	rang	gerungen
rufen (to call)	ruft	rief	gerufen
saufen (to drink)	säuft	soff	gesoffen
saugen (to suck)	saugt	sog	gesogen

Infinitive	Present	Past	Past Participle
schaffen (to create)	schafft	schuf	geschaffen
scheiden (to leave)	scheidet	schied	ist geschieden
scheinen (to seem; shine)	scheint	schien	geschienen
schelten (to scold)	schilt	schalt	gescholten
schieben (to push)	schiebt	schob	geschoben
schießen (to shoot)	schießt	schoß	geschossen
schlafen (to sleep)	schläft	schlief	geschlafen
schlagen (to beat)	schlägt	schlug	geschlagen
schleichen (to sneak)	schleicht	schlich	ist geschlichen
schließen (to close)	schließt	schloß	geschlossen
schlingen (to wind)	schlingt	schlang	geschlungen
schmeißen (to fling)	schmeißt	schmiß	geschmissen
schmelzen (to melt)	schmilzt	schmolz	ist geschmolzen
schneiden (to cut)	schneidet	schnitt	geschnitten
schreiben (to write)	schreibt	schrieb	geschrieben
schreien (to cry)	schreit	schrie	geschrien
schreiten (to stride)	schreitet	schritt	ist geschritten
schweigen (to be silent)	schweigt	schwieg	geschwiegen
schwellen (to swell)	schwillt	schwoll	ist geschwollen
schwimmen (to swim)	schwimmt	schwamm	ist geschwommen
schwinden (to disappear)	schwindet	schwand	ist geschwunden
schwingen (to swing)	schwingt	schwang	geschwungen
schwören (to swear)	schwört	schwur	geschworen
sehen (to see)	sieht	sah	gesehen
sein (to be)	ist	war	ist gewesen
singen (to sing)	singt	sang	gesungen
sinken (to sink)	sinkt	sank	ist gesunken
sinnen (to meditate)	sinnt	sann	gesonnen
sitzen (to sit)	sitzt	saß	gesessen
speien (to spit)	speit	spie	gespie(e)n
spinnen (to spin)	spinnt	spann	gesponnen
sprechen (to speak)	spricht	sprach	gesprochen
sprießen (to sprout)	sprießt	sproß	ist gesprossen
springen (to jump)	springt	sprang	ist gesprungen
stechen (to sting)	sticht	stach	gestochen
stehen (to stand)	steht	stand	gestanden
stehlen (to steal)	stiehlt	stahl	gestohlen
steigen (to climb)	steigt	stieg	ist gestiegen

Infinitive	Present	Past	Past Participle
sterben (to die)	stirbt	starb	ist gestorben
stinken (to stink)	stinkt	stank	gestunken
stoßen (to push)	stößt	stieß	gestoßen
streichen (to stroke; spread)	streicht	strich	gestrichen
streiten (to quarrel)	streitet	stritt	gestritten
tragen (to carry)	trägt	trug	getragen
treffen (to hit; meet)	trifft	traf	getroffen
treiben (to drive)	treibt	trieb	getrieben
treten (to step; kick)	tritt	trat	getreten
trinken (to drink)	trinkt	trank	getrunken
trügen (to deceive)	trügt	trog	getrogen
tun (to do)	tut	tat	getan
verbergen (to hide)	verbirgt	verbarg	verborgen
verderben (to spoil)	verdirbt	verdarb	verdorben
verdrießen (to annoy)	verdrießt	verdroß	verdrossen
vergessen (to forget)	vergißt	vergaß	vergessen
verlieren (to lose)	verliert	verlor	verloren
verschwinden (to disappear)	verschwindet	verschwand	ist verschwunden
verzeihen (to forgive)	verzeiht	verzieh	verziehen
wachsen (to grow)	wächst	wuchs	ist gewachsen
wägen (to weigh)	wägt	wog	gewogen
waschen (to wash)	wäscht	wusch	gewaschen
weichen (to evade)	weicht	wich	ist gewichen
weisen (to show)	weist	wies	gewiesen
werben (to advertise)	wirbt	warb	geworben
werden (to become)	wird	wurde	ist geworden
werfen (to throw)	wirft	warf	geworfen
wiegen (to weigh)	wiegt	wog	gewogen
winden (to wind)	windet	wand	gewunden
zeihen (to accuse)	zeiht	zieh	geziehen
zwingen (to compel)	zwingt	zwang	gezwungen

Irregular Weak Verbs and Modals

Infinitive	Present	Past	Past Participle
brennen (to burn)	brennt	brannte	gebrannt
bringen (to bring)	bringt	brachte	gebracht
denken (to think)	denkt	dachte	gedacht

Infinitive	Present	Past	Past Participle
dürfen (to be allowed)	darf	durfte	gedurft
haben (to have)	hat	hatte	gehabt
kennen (to know)	kennt	kannte	gekannt
können (to be able)	kann	konnte	gekonnt
mögen/möchten (to like, like to)	mag	mochte	gemocht
müssen (to have to)	muß	mußte	gemußt
nennen (to name)	nennt	nannte	genannt
rennen (to run)	rennt	rannte	ist gerannt
senden (to send)	sendet	sandte	gesandt
sollen (to ought to)	soll	sollte	gesollt
wenden (to turn)	wendet	wandte	gewandt
wissen (to know)	weiß	wußte	gewußt
wollen (to want)	will	wollte	gewollt

Common Units of Measurement

Measures and Weights

1 ounce = 28 grams
1 pint *or* 16 oz. = 0.47 liter
1 quart *or* 2 pts. = 0.95 liter
1 pound *or* 16 oz. = 0.45 kilogram
1 ton *or* 2,200 lbs. = 1,000 kilograms
1 hundredweight *or* 100 lbs. = 45 kilograms

1 inch = 2.5 centimeters
1 cubic inch = 16 cubic centimeters
1 foot *or* 12 inches = 0.3 meter
1 yard *or* 3 feet = 0.9 meter
1 mile = 1,609 meters *or* 1.6 kilometers
1 square mile = 2.6 square kilometers

Maße und Gewichte

¼ Liter = 8.45 ounces *or* 0.53 pint
½ Liter = 16.9 ounces *or* 1.06 pints
1 Liter = 2.1 pints *or* 1.06 quarts *or* 0.26 gallon

1 Gramm *or* 0.001 kg = 0.04 ounce
1 Pfund *or* 500 g *or* ½ Kilo = 1.1 pounds
1 Kilogramm (Kilo) *or* 1 000 g *or* 2 Pfd = 2.2 pounds
1 Zentner *or* 100 Pfd *or* 50 kg = 110 pounds *or* 1.1 hundredweight
1 Quintal *or* 200 Pfd *or* 100 kg = 220 pounds *or* 2.2 hundredweight
1 Tonne *or* 1 000 kg = 2,200 pounds *or* 1.1 tons

1 Millimeter = 0.04 inch
1 Zentimeter *or* 10 mm = 0.4 inch
1 Kubikzentimeter = 0.06 cubic inch
1 Meter *or* 100 cm = 39.5 inches *or* 3.3 feet *or* 1.1 yards
1 Kilometer *or* 1 000 m = 1,100 yards *or* 0.62 mile
1 Quadratmeter = 10.8 square feet *or* 1.2 square yards

$$C = \frac{10(F - 32)}{18} \qquad F = \frac{18C}{10} + 32$$

VERGLEICHS-THERMOMETER

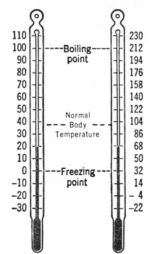

CENTIGRADE FAHRENHEIT

VOCABULARY

Nouns

The singular and plural of nouns are indicated, the genitive forms are not: **der Mann, ⁼er.**
Plurals of certain nouns do not exist or are rare in usage and are thus not listed: **der Schnee.**
Some nouns have special plural forms and do not merely add the standard endings: **das
Museum, –en = das Museum, die Museen.** To denote pronoun gender only, **das** in paren-
theses precedes names of countries: **(das) Afrika.** Nouns requiring a plural verb are indicated:
die Ferien (*pl.*). Nouns declined like adjectives are listed with both forms: **der Alte (ein
Alter), –n.**

Verbs

The principal parts of strong and irregular weak verbs are indicated; only the infinitives of weak
verbs are given: **wissen, weiß, wußte, gewußt; sagen.** Verbs that require the auxiliary **sein**
in the past participle are indicated: **rennen, rannte, ist gerannt.** Verbs requiring the dative
are indicated: **antworten** (*dat.*). Reflexive verbs that take the dative pronouns are indicated;
if there is no case indication, the pronouns are in the accusative: **sich notieren** (*dat.*); **sich
freuen.** Separable prefixes are denoted by a dot between the prefix and stem; the prefix is
indicated by a hyphen in the principal parts: **nach • denken, –dachte, –gedacht.** Participial
forms are not listed separately but by the infinitive unless they are used as independent adjectives: **lachen,** not **lachend,** *but* **ausgebucht,** not **aus • buchen.**

Adjectives–Adverbs

Only the adjectival meanings are given, except in certain instances where there is a difference
in adverbial meaning in English: **froh**   happy, glad; **gut**   good, (*adv.*) well. Irregular comparisons are not indicated. Adjectives followed by a hyphen cannot stand alone and must be
followed by an ending: **nächst-.**

Prepositions

The cases required of all prepositions, including those used with reflexive verbs, are indicated:
von (+ *dat.*); **sich freuen über** (+ *acc.*).

Abbreviations

The following abbreviations are used.

abbrev.	abbreviation	*indef.*	indefinite
acc.	accusative	*inf.*	infinitive
adv.	adverb	*interj.*	interjection
art.	article	*interrog.*	interrogative
coord.	coordinating	*pl.*	plural
conj.	conjunction	*pol.*	polite
dat.	dative	*poss.*	possessive
def.	definite	*prep.*	preposition
fam.	familiar	*sing.*	singular
gen.	genitive	*sub.*	subordinating
impers.	impersonal		

Parentheses in the English equivalents indicate words that have been added for a more
colloquial rendering or parts of the phrase that may or may not be included: **leid tun, tat, getan**
to be sorry (for); **das Prozent, –e** percent(age). Brackets indicate additional information for
more accurate comprehension: **ab • stellen**   to park [a car]. Expressions in italics indicate
editorial comment and are not part of the translation: **der Hausbesitzer, –**   house *or* property
owner; **der Audi, –s**   *German automobile.* A dash (———) indicates insertion of the original entry:
die Erfüllung, –en; in ——— gehen = in Erfüllung gehen.

DEUTSCH-ENGLISCH

A

ab · biegen, –bog, _ist_ –gebogen
to turn off

der **Abend, –e** evening;
morgen abend tomorrow
evening;
guten —— good evening;
heute abend this evening;
abends in the evening, nightly;
zu —— essen to have dinner

das **Abendessen, –** supper, dinner

das **Abendrot** sunset
aber (_coord. conj._) but; however, _indeed_
**ab · fahren, –fährt, –fuhr, _ist_
–gefahren** to depart, leave

die **Abfahrt, –en** departure

das **Abgas, –e** exhaust gas
**ab · geben, –gibt, –gab,
–gegeben** to give away, share

sich **ab · gewöhnen** (_dat._) to give up
[a habit]
abhängig von (+ _dat._)
dependent on

die **Abhebegeschwindigkeit, –en**
acceleration _or_ takeoff speed
ab · holen to pick up [someone],
fetch

das **Abitur, –s** _successful completion of
requirements for graduation
from secondary school_
**ab · nehmen, –nimmt, –nahm,
–genommen** to lose weight;
decrease
**ab · schließen, –schloß, _ist_
–geschlossen** to lock;
complete, conclude

der **Abschluß, ⸚sse** completion,
conclusion

sich **ab · schwächen** to decrease,
diminish
absolut absolute
ab · stellen to turn off; park
[a car], place
abstrakt abstract

die **Abteilung, –en** department,
section

der **Abteilungsleiter, –** department
manager
ab · wehren to prevent
ach oh, alas; **—— so** I see
acht eight
achten auf (+ _acc._) to watch
out for, pay attention to

der **Adel** nobility

die **Adresse, –n** address

(das) **Afrika** Africa
aha I see

die **Akademie, –n** academy

die **Aktentasche, –n** briefcase
aktiv active

der **Akzent, –e** accent

(das) **Alaska** Alaska

(das) **Albanien** Albania

der **Alkohol, –ika** alcohol
alle (_pl._) all

die **Allee, –n** avenue
allgemein general;
im allgemeinen in general
allein alone
allerdings however, in any case
allerhand quite a lot, quite a bit
als (_sub. conj._) when; than;
—— ob (_sub. conj._) as if;
—— wenn (_sub. conj._) as if
also well then; consequently, thus,
therefore
alt old

das **Alter** age

(das) **Amerika** America

der **Amerikaner, –** American
(citizen)
amerikanisch American
an (+ _dat._ or _acc._) at; on; to
an · bieten, –bot, –geboten
to offer
andere (_pl._) other(s); different
(ones)
ändern to change
anders different

die **Änderung, –en** change
an · erkennen, –erkannte, –erkannt
to recognize, acknowledge

der **Anfang, ⸚e** beginning
  an·fangen, –fängt, –fing,
    –gefangen to start, begin
  an·fertigen to make, produce
  an·feuern to incite, cheer up
  an·gehören (*dat.*) to belong to
der **Angeklagte** (ein **Angeklagter**), **–n**
  defendant
der **Angestellte** (ein **Angestellter**), **–n**
  employee
  an·greifen, –griff, –gegriffen
    to attack
die **Angst, ⸚e** fear; **keine —— haben**
  to have no fear, not to be afraid
  an·halten, –hält, –hielt, –gehalten
    to stop
  an·kommen, –kam, ist –gekommen
    to arrive
die **Ankunft** arrival
  an·nehmen, –nimmt, –nahm,
    –genommen to accept; assume
  an·regen to stimulate, excite
  an·rufen, –rief, –gerufen
    to telephone
  an·schalten to turn on,
    switch on
  an·schauen to take a look at;
    sich —— (*dat.*) to watch
  anschließend subsequently;
    including
  an·sehen, –sieht, –sah, –gesehen
    to take a look at; **sich ——** (*dat.*)
    to watch, inspect
der **Anspruch, ⸚e** demand, claim
  (an)statt (+ *gen.*) instead of
  an·steigen, –stieg, ist –gestiegen
    to rise, climb up, increase
  an·stellen to turn on
  an·stoßen, –stößt, –stieß,
    –gestoßen to give a push
  anstrengend strenuous, exacting
der **Anthropologe, –n** anthropologist
die **Anthropologin, –nen** (female)
  anthropologist
der **Antrag, ⸚e** application
das **Antragsformular, –e** application
  form
die **Antwort, –en** answer
  antworten (*dat.*) to answer, reply

  an·wenden to apply, use for
die **Anzeige, –n** advertisement
  an·ziehen, –zog, –gezogen
    to put on; **sich ——** to get
    dressed
der **Anzug, ⸚e** suit
  an·zünden to light
der **Apfel, ⸚** apple
die **Apfelsine, –n** orange
der **Appetit** appetite; **—— auf** (+ *acc.*)
  haben to be hungry for;
  guten —— eat hearty
der **April** April
(das) **Arabien** Arabia
die **Arbeit, –en** work, job
  arbeiten to work
der **Arbeiter, –** worker
die **Arbeiterin, –nen** (female) worker
der **Arbeitgeber, –** employer
der **Arbeitnehmer, –** employee
der **Architekt, –en** architect
der **Ärger** annoyance; anger
  ärgerlich angry
sich **ärgern** to be annoyed *or* upset;
  —— über (+ *acc.*) to be upset
  about
  arm poor
der **Arm, –e** arm
das **Aroma, –en** aroma, flavor
die **Art, –en** kind, sort [*species*];
  way [*manner*]
der **Artikel, –** article
der **Arzt, ⸚e** physician
das **Aspirin** (pl.) **–Tabletten** aspirin
  astronomisch astronomical
der **Atlantik** Atlantic Ocean
  atmen to breathe
die **Atmosphäre, –n** atmosphere
die **Attraktion, –en** attraction
  attraktiv attractive
  auch also, too; **—— wenn** (*sub.*
  conj.) even if
der **Audi, –s** *German automobile*
  auf (+ *dat.* or *acc.*) on; to
  auf·essen, –ißt, –aß, –gegessen
    to eat up, consume
  auf·fallen, –fällt, –fiel, ist
    –gefallen (*dat.*) to attract
    attention

auf·finden, –fand, –gefunden
to find, discover
auf·gehen, –ging, ist –gegangen
to rise; **auf und ab·gehen** to
walk up and down, pace
auf·hören to cease, stop, end
auf·kochen to bring to a boil
auf·passen to watch out,
be careful
aufregend exciting, stimulating
auf·schließen, –schloß,
–geschlossen to unlock
die **Aufschrift, –en** label, inscription
auf·stehen, –stand, ist
–gestanden to get up
auf·steigen, –stieg, ist
–gestiegen to rise
auf·treten, –tritt, –trat, ist
–getreten to occur
auf·trumpfen to boast
auf·wachen to wake up
auf·zeigen to point out
das **Auge, –n** eye; **aus den Augen**
verlieren to lose sight of
der **Augenblick, –e** moment;
einen —— just a moment
der **Augenzeuge, –n** eyewitness
der **August** August
aus (+ *dat.*) out of; from
die **Ausbildung, –en** training,
education
aus·fallen, –fällt, –fiel, ist
–gefallen to be cancelled
der **Ausflug, ⸚e** excursion
aus·füllen to fill out
das **Ausfüllen** filling out [of forms]
der **Ausgang, ⸚e** exit
aus·geben, –gibt, –gab,
–gegeben to spend (money)
ausgebucht sold out, full
ausgenommen (+ *acc.*) except
ausgezeichnet excellent
aus·halten, –hält, –hielt,
–gehalten to stand, endure
die **Auskunft, ⸚e** (piece of)
information
das **Ausland** foreign country(ies),
im —— abroad
aus·probieren to try out, test

aus·reiben, –rieb, –gerieben
to rub out
aus·rufen, –rief, –gerufen
to call out, announce
aus·ruhen to rest, relax
der **Ausschnitt, –e** section
aus·sehen, –sieht, –sah, –gesehen
to look like, appear;
gut —— to look good
außer (+ *dat.*) besides; except
außerdem moreover; besides that
außerhalb (+ *gen.*) outside of
die **Aussprache** pronunciation
aus·sprechen, –spricht, –sprach,
–gesprochen to pronounce
aus·steigen, –stieg, ist
–gestiegen to get out
aus·stellen to exhibit
die **Ausstellung, –en** exhibit
(das) **Australien** Australia
ausverkauft sold out
aus·ziehen, –zog, –gezogen
to take off; **sich ——** to get
undressed
das **Auto, –s** car, automobile
die **Autobahn, –en** freeway, highway
der **Autofahrer, –** (car) driver,
motorist
die **Autofahrerin, –nen** (female)
driver
die **Autofahrt, –en** car trip, drive
die **Autoindustrie, –n** automobile
industry
der **Automat, –en** vending machine
der **Autor, –en** author
die **Autovermietung, –en** car rental
(agency)

B

backen, bäckt, backte,
gebacken to bake
die **Bäckerei, –en** bakery
das **Bad, ⸚er** bath; bathroom;
(swimming) pool
die **Badehose, –n** bathing trunks
baden to bathe;
sich —— to take a bath
das **Badezimmer, –** bathroom

die **Bahn, –en** train; track
die **Bahnfahrt, –en** train trip
der **Bahnhof, ⸚e** railroad station
die **Bahnhofshalle, –n** entrance hall
    of a railroad station
bald soon
der **Balkon, –s** *or* **–e** balcony
der **Ball, ⸚e** ball
die **Bank, ⸚e** bench
die **Bank, –en** bank
der **Bankangestelle** (ein **Bankange-**
    stellter)**, –n** bank employee
das **Bankgeheimnis, –se** banking
    secret
der **Bankpräsident, –en** bank
    president
die **Bar, –s** bar
das **Bargeld** cash
der **Bart, ⸚e** beard
basta that's enough
die **Batterie, –n** battery
der **Bauer, –n** farmer
der **Baum, ⸚e** tree
der **Bayer, –n** Bavarian
(das) **Bayern** Bavaria
der **Beamte** (ein **Beamter**)**, –n**
    official; civil servant; clerk
beantragen to apply for
beantworten to answer
bedeuten to signify, mean
bedeutend significant, important
sich **beeilen** to hurry
beeindrucken to impress
beenden to end, finish
befehlen, befiehlt, befahl,
    befohlen (*dat.*) to command,
    order
sich **befinden, befand, befunden** to
    be located
begegnen (*dat.*) to meet
sich **begeistern für** (+ *acc.*) to
    enthuse, be excited about
der **Beginn** beginning
beginnen, begann,
    begonnen to begin
begrenzen to limit
begrüßen to greet; **sich ——** to
    greet each other
behandeln to treat, discuss

behaupten to assert, maintain
beherrschen to dominate
bei (+ *dat.*) with; near
beide (*pl.*) both, the two
beinahe almost
das **Beispiel, –e** example;
    zum —— for example
bekämpfen to fight (against)
bekannt well known, famous
der **Bekannte,** (ein **Bekannter**)**, –n**
    acquaintance
bekanntlich as is well known
sich **beklagen** to complain
bekommen, bekam, bekommen
    to get, receive
belegen to take (a course);
    enroll (in), register (for)
(das) **Belgien** Belgium
bellen to bark
die **Bemerkung, –en** remark, comment
benutzen *or* **benützen** to use
das **Benzin, –e** gasoline
beobachten to observe
beraten, berät, beriet, beraten
    to advise, counsel
bereisen to travel through
bereits already
der **Berg, –e** mountain
der **Bericht, –e** report; **nach einem**
    —— according to a report
berichten to report, inform
der **Beruf, –e** profession, occupation
berühmt famous
beschädigen to damage
beschließen, beschloß,
    beschlossen to decide
besehen, besieht, besah,
    besehen to examine, inspect
besetzt occupied
besitzen, besaß, besessen to own,
    possess
der **Besitzer, –** owner
besprechen, bespricht, besprach,
    besprochen to discuss
besser better; **—— als** better
    than
bestehen, bestand, bestanden
    aus (+ *dat.*) to consist of
bestellen to order

bestenfalls at best

bestimmt certainly, without doubt

die **Bestimmung, –en** regulation

der **Besuch, –e** visit; **zu** —— **kommen** to come for a visit

besuchen to visit

betrachten to look at; consider

beträchtlich considerable

das **Bett, –en** bed

betreffen, betrifft, betraf, betroffen to concern; **was das betrifft, . . .** as far as that is concerned

der **Beutel, –** bag

die **Bevölkerung** population

die **Bevölkerungsexplosion, –en** population explosion

bevor (*sub. conj.*) before

bevorzugen to prefer

bewegen to move

die **Bewegung, –en** motion, movement

bewohnen to live in; populate

bewundern to admire

bewundernswert admirable

bezahlen to pay

die **Bibliothekarin, –nen** (female) librarian

das **Bier, –e** beer

das **Bild, –er** picture

billig cheap, inexpensive

die **Biologie** biology

bis (+ *acc.*) until; (*sub. conj.*) "by," until; —— **zu** up to, as far as; —— **vor kurzem** until recently

bisher up to now

(ein) **bißchen** a little

bitte please; you're welcome; —— **sehr** you're very welcome; —— **schön?** may I help you? **wie** ——? what's that?, what did you say?

bitten, bat, gebeten um (+ *acc.*) to ask for, request

blättern in (+ *dat.*) to leaf *or* flip through

blau blue

bleiben, blieb, ist geblieben to remain, stay

blind blind

blöd stupid

blühen to bloom

die **Blume, –n** flower

das **Blümlein, –** small flower

das **Blut** blood

die **Blutprobe, –n** blood test

der **BMW, –s** *German automobile*

bohren to drill

braten, brät, briet, gebraten to fry

die **Bratwurst, ⸚e** fried sausage

brauchen to need, require

braun brown

brennen, brannte, gebrannt to burn

die **Bremse, –n** brake

der **Brief, –e** letter

die **Brieftasche, –n** wallet, billfold

der **Briefumschlag, ⸚e** envelope

die **Brille, –n** eyeglasses

bringen, brachte, gebracht to bring; take; fetch

der **Brite, –n** British citizen, Englishman

das **Brot, –e** bread

das **Brötchen, –** (bread) roll

die **Brücke, –n** bridge

der **Brunnen, –** well; fountain

das **Buch, ⸚er** book

buchen to book, make reservations

der **Buchstabe, –n** letter (of the alphabet)

der **Bulle, –n** bull

der **Bummel, –** stroll; **einen** —— **machen** to go for a stroll

das **Bundeshaus, ⸚er** Federal Building

die **Bundesrepublik Deutschland** Federal Republic of Germany (West Germany)

der **Bürgersteig, –e** sidewalk

der **Bus, –se** bus

der **Busfahrer, –** bus driver

die **Bus-Haltestelle, –n** bus stop

die **Butter** butter

C

das **Café, –s** café
die **Chance, –n** chance, opportunity
charmant charming
der **Chef, –s** boss
die **Chefin, –nen** (female) boss
der **Chefpilot, –en** chief pilot, captain
der **Chinese, –n** Chinese (citizen)
(das) **Chinesisch** Chinese (language)
der **Club, –s** club
der **Computer, –s** computer
der **Curry** curry
die **Currywurst, ⸚e** curry sausage

D

da (*adv.*) there, then; (*sub. conj.*)
since [*causal*], as; —— **unten**
down there
da drüben over there
dafür therefore; for that
damals at that time, then
die **Dame, –n** lady, woman
der **Damenbesuch, –e** woman's visit
damit (*sub. conj.*) so that
der **Dampfer, –** steamer, steamboat
die **Dampferfahrt, –en** steamer trip
(das) **Dänemark** Denmark
der **Dank** thanks, gratitude;
vielen —— many thanks
danke thank you
danken (*dat.*) to thank
dann then
daraufhin thereupon
darum therefore
daß (*sub. conj.*) that
das **Datum, –en** date
dauern to last
dazu for that purpose
die **DDR (Deutsche Demokratische
Republik)** German Democratic
Republic (East Germany)
dein (*poss.*) your
dekorieren to decorate
denken, dachte, gedacht to
think; —— **an** (+ *acc.*) to
think of, remember

denn (*coord. conj.*) for; (*interj.*); *because.*
for emphasis in questions; *actually*
(*adv.*) anyway
deprimierend depressing
der, die, das (*def. art.*) the, that
deutsch (*adj.*) German;
auf —— in German
(das) **Deutsch** German (language)
der **Deutsche (ein Deutscher), –n**
German (citizen)
(das) **Deutschland** Germany
die **Deutschstunde, –** German class
der **Dezember** December
die **Diät, –en** diet; **eine ——
machen** to go on a diet
dick fat, thick
der **Dieb, –e** thief
dienen (*dat.*) to serve
der **Dienstag, –e** Tuesday
dieser this, that
diesseits (+ *gen.*) on this side of
das **Ding, –e** thing; matter
direkt direct
die **Diskriminierung, –en**
discrimination
die **Diskussion, –en** discussion
diskutieren to discuss
doch (*coord. conj.*) after all, *yet, however,*
certainly; (*interj.*) for emphasis in
commands; (*adv.*) certainly, *really*
der **Dollar, –s** *unit of American currency*
der **Dom, –e** cathedral
die **Donau** Danube River
der **Donnerstag, –e** Thursday
das **Dorf, ⸚er** village
dort there
dorthin to that place
draußen outside
dreckig dirty
drei three
dreihundertzwanzig three
hundred twenty
dreimal three times
dreißig thirty
dreizehn thirteen
dringend urgent
drohen (*dat.*) to threaten
dumm stupid, dumb
dunkel dark

dunkelblau   dark blue

dünn   thin

durch (+ *acc.*)   through; by

durch·lassen, –läßt, –ließ, –gelassen   to let through

durch·lesen, –liest, –las, –gelesen   to read through

dürfen, darf, durfte, gedurft   to be allowed to

die **Dusche, –n**   shower

das **Dutzend, –e**   dozen

E

eben   now, just; even;   **gerade ——**   just now

ebenfalls   also, likewise

ebenso   just as

die **Ecke, –n**   corner

ehe (*sub. conj.*)   before

ehrlich   honest; **—— gesagt**   to be quite honest

das **Ei, –er**   egg

der **Eiffelturm**   Eiffel Tower

eigentlich   actually

das **Eigentum**   property

ein, eine, ein (*indef. art.*)   a

ein·atmen   to breathe in, inhale

ein·dringen, –drang, ist –gedrungen   to enter, penetrate; invade

eindrucksvoll   impressive

einfach   simple

ein·fallen, –fällt, –fiel, ist –gefallen (*dat., impers.*)   to occur to, come to mind

der **Einfluß, ̈sse**   influence

ein·führen   to introduce

der **Eingang, ̈e**   entrance

sich **einig sein, ist, war, ist gewesen** (*dat.*)   to agree

einige (*pl.*)   some, a few, several

der **Einkauf, ̈e**   purchase;   **Einkäufe machen**   to go shopping

ein·kaufen   to shop; **—— gehen**   to go shopping

das **Einkommen, –**   income

ein·laden, –lädt, –lud, –geladen   to invite

die **Einladung, –en**   invitation

ein·lösen   to cash, redeem

(ein)mal   once, ever; sometime

einmalig   unique

ein paar   a few, some

eins   one [numeral]

ein·schalten   to switch, turn on

ein·schlafen, –schläft, –schlief, ist –geschlafen   to fall asleep

ein·schließen, –schloß, –geschlossen   to include

die **Einschreibung, –en**   enrollment, registration

ein·steigen, –stieg, ist –gestiegen   to get into *or* onto

ein·treffen, –trifft, –traf, ist –getroffen   to arrive

der **Eintritt**   admission

ein·wandern   to immigrate

ein·wechseln   to exchange [money]

ein·werfen, –wirft, –warf, –geworfen   to drop *or* throw in

der **Einwohner, –**   inhabitant

einzeln   single, individual

das **Eis**   ice; ice cream

die **Eisenbarriere, –n**   iron barrier

der **Eiskaffee, –s**   coffee with ice cream

eiskalt   ice cold

elegant   elegant

elektronisch   electronic

elf   eleven

die **Eltern** (*pl.*)   parents

die **Emanzipation**   emancipation

emanzipieren   to emancipate

empfangen, empfängt, empfing, empfangen   to receive, welcome

empfehlen, empfiehlt, empfahl, empfohlen   to recommend

empirisch   empirical

das **Ende, –n**   end

enden   to end

endlich   finally

(das) **England**   England

der **Engländer, –**   Englishman

englisch (*adj.*)   English;   **auf ——**   in English

(das) **Englisch** English (language)

entdecken to discover

die **Entdeckung, –en** discovery

die **Ente, –n** duck

entfernen to remove, take away

die **Entfernung, –en** distance

entkommen, entkam, ist
entkommen (*dat.*) to escape

sich **entscheiden, entschied,**
entschieden to decide;
—— **für** (+ *acc.*) to decide on

sich **entschließen, entschloß,**
entschlossen to resolve, decide;
—— **für** (+ *acc.*) to decide on

sich **entschuldigen** to excuse oneself,
apologize

die **Entschuldigung, –en** pardon,
excuse; ——, **bitte** excuse me,
please

enttäuschen to disappoint

entweder either

entwickeln to develop

die **Entwicklung, –en** development

der **Erfolg, –e** success

erfolgreich successful

erfüllen to fulfill; **sich** —— to
come true, be fulfilled

die **Erfüllung, –en** fulfillment;
in —— **gehen** to come true,
be fulfilled

erhalten, erhält, erhielt,
erhalten to receive, get

erhitzen to heat up

erhöhen to raise

sich **erholen** to recover

erinnern an (+ *acc.*) to remind of;
sich —— **an** (+ *acc.*) to
remember

die **Erkältung, –en** cold

erkennen, erkannte, erkannt to
recognize, determine

erklären to explain; declare

die **Erklärung, –en** explanation;
declaration

sich **erkundigen nach** (+ *dat.*) to
inquire for *or* about

erlauben (*dat.*) to allow, permit

erleben to experience

ermorden to murder

ermüden, ist ermüdet to get tired

ernsthaft serious

ernten to harvest

erobern to conquer

erreichen to reach, accomplish

ersetzen to replace

erst- first

erst just, for the first time;
—— **einmal** first of all

erträglich bearable

erwarten to expect, await

erwidern to reply, retort

erwischen to catch, capture

erzählen to tell, relate

essen, ißt, aß, gegessen to eat

das **Essen, –** meal

das **Eßzimmer, –** dining room

der **Eßtisch, –e** dining table

der **Estrich, –e** (*Swiss*) attic

die **Etage, –n** floor

etwa about, approximately

etwas some, something

euer (*poss.*) your (*fam. pl.*)

die **Eurocheque-Karte, –n** European
traveler's check card

europäisch European

der **Euro-Scheck, –s** European
traveler's check

die **Ewigkeit** eternity

das **Examen, –ina** examination

die **Exkursion, –en** excursion

die **Expedition, –en** expedition

der **Experte, –n** expert

explodieren, ist explodiert to
explode

die **Explosion, –en** explosion

F

fabelhaft fabulous, wonderful

fahren, fährt, fuhr, ist *or* **hat**
gefahren to drive; go
(by vehicle)

die **Fahrkarte, –n** ticket

der **Fahrkartenschalter, –** ticket
counter

das **Fahrrad, ⁼er** bicycle

die **Fahrradtour, –en** bicycle trip

der **Fahrschein, –e** ticket

die **Fahrt, –en** trip, journey;
   gute —— have a good trip

der **Fall, ̈e** case; **auf keinen ——**
   by no means, under no circum-
   stances
   fallen, fällt, fiel, <u>ist</u> gefallen to fall
   falls (*sub. conj.*) in case, if
   falsch wrong, false

die **Familie, –n** family

die **Fantasie, –n** imagination, fantasy
   fantastisch fantastic

das **Farbband, ̈er** typewriter ribbon

der **Farbfilm, –e** color film
   fast almost
   faszinieren to fascinate
   faulenzen to be lazy

der **Februar** February
   fehlen (*dat.*) to lack; be absent;
     be missing *or* short
   feiern to celebrate

das **Fenster, –** window

die **Ferien** (*pl.*) vacation

das **Ferienhaus, ̈er** vacation home
   fern·sehen, –sieht, –sah, –gesehen
     to watch television

der **Fernseher, –** television set

der **Fernseh-Krimi, –s** TV mystery
   story

das **Fernsehprogramm, –e** TV
   program

die **Fernsehsendung, –en** TV show
   fertig ready, finished
   fett fat

das **Feuer, –** fire
   feuerfest fireproof
   feuerrot fire red

die **Feuerwehr** fire department

der **Feuerwehrwagen, –** fire truck

das **Feuerwerk** fireworks [*display*]

der **Feuerwerkskörper, –** rocket,
   fireworks [*explosive*]

der **Fiat, –s** *Italian automobile*

das **Fieber** fever; **das —— messen**
   to take (one's) temperature

die **Figur, –en** figure

der **Film, –e** film, movie

die **Filmanzeige, –n** movie
   advertisement

der **Filter, –** filter

finden, fand, gefunden to find

die **Firma, –en** company, firm

der **Fisch, –e** fish

die **Flamme, –n** flame

die **Flasche, –n** bottle

das **Fleisch** meat

der **Fleischer, –** butcher
   fliegen, flog, <u>ist</u> *or* hat geflogen
     to fly
   fluchen to curse

der **Flug, ̈e** flight

die **Fluggesellschaft, –en**
   airline company

der **Flughafen, ̈** airport

das **Flughafengebäude, –** airport
   terminal

der **Flugkapitän, –e** airline captain

die **Flugkarte, –n** flight ticket;
   air map

der **Flugkartenschalter, –** flight
   ticket counter

der **Flugplatz, ̈e** airport

das **Flugzeug, –e** airplane

der **Flugzeugentführer, –** [airplane]
   hijacker

die **Flugzeugentführung, –en**
   [airplane] hijacking
   folgen (*dat.*) to follow;
   im folgenden as follows; in
     the following (passage)

das **Fondue, –s** fondue

die **Forelle, –n** trout

das **Formular, –e** form (sheet)
   forschen to (do) research, explore

der **Forscher, –** researcher
   fort·setzen to continue

die **Fortsetzung, –en** continuation

das **Foto, –s** photograph

das **Fotogeschäft, –e** photography shop

die **Fotografie, –n** photography
   fotografieren to photograph,
     take pictures

die **Frage, –n** question;
   Fragen stellen to ask questions
   fragen to ask; **sich ——** to ask
     oneself

der **Franken, –** *unit of Swiss currency*

(das) **Frankreich** France

der **Franzose, –n** French citizen,
   Frenchman

französisch (*adj.*) French
(das) **Französisch** French (language)
die **Frau, –en** woman; Mrs.
das **Fräulein, –** young lady; Miss
der **Freitag, –e** Friday
fremd strange, foreign
sich **freuen** to be happy;
    —— **auf** (+ *acc.*) to look
    forward to; —— **über** (+ *acc.*)
    to be happy about
der **Freund, –e** friend
die **Freundin, –nen** (female) friend
freundlich kind, friendly
die **Friedenszeit, –en** peacetime
frieren, fror, gefroren to be cold,
    freeze
frisch fresh
froh happy, glad
früh early
der **Frühling, –e** spring
das **Frühstück** breakfast
frühstücken to have breakfast
sich **fühlen** to feel, perceive, experience
führen to lead, guide
der **Führerschein, –e** driver's license
fünf five
fünfzehn fifteen
fünfzig fifty
der **Funkturm, ̈e** radio tower
für (+ *acc.*) for
die **Furcht** fear
furchtbar terrible
fürchten to fear
sich **fürchten** to fear; —— **vor** (+ *dat.*)
    to be afraid of
der **Fuß, ̈e** foot; **zu** —— **gehen**
    to go by foot, walk
der **Fußball, ̈e** soccer (ball)
das **Fußballspiel, –e** soccer game
der **Fußballspieler, –** soccer player
der **Fußball-Star, –s** soccer star
der **Fußboden, ̈** floor

G

die **Gabel, –n** fork
der **Gangster, –** gangster
ganz quite; whole, complete;
    —— **recht** quite right

gar even; —— **nicht** not at all
die **Garage, –n** garage
die **Garantie, –n** guarantee, warranty
der **Garten, ̈** garden
der **Gast, ̈e** guest
der **Gastarbeiter, –** foreign worker
der **Gastprofessor, –en** guest professor
das **Gebäck** pastry
das **Gebäude, –** building
geben, gibt, gab, gegeben to
    give; **es gibt** (+ *acc.*) there is,
    there are
das **Gebiet, –e** area
die **Gebühr, –en** fee
die **Geburt, –en** birth
der **Geburtsort, –e** place of birth
der **Geburtstag, –e** birthday; date
    of birth
der **Gedanke, –n** thought, idea
die **Geduld** patience
gefallen, gefällt, gefiel, gefallen
    (*dat.*) to like, please, appreciate
gegen (+ *acc.*) against
gegenüber (+ *dat.*) opposite
die **Gehaltserhöhung, –en** salary
    increase, raise
gehen, ging, ist gegangen to go,
    walk; **zu Fuß** —— to go by
    foot; **nach Hause** —— to go
    home; **wie geht es Ihnen?**
    how are you?
die **Gehirnerschütterung, –en** brain
    concussion
gehören (*dat.*) to belong to
die **Geisteswissenschaft, –en**
    humanities
gelb yellow
das **Geld, –er** money
der **Geldbeutel, –** purse
die **Gelegenheit, –en** opportunity,
    chance
gelingen, gelang, ist gelungen
    (*dat., impers.*) to succeed in
das **Gemälde, –** painting
gemischt mixed
das **Gemüse** vegetable(s)
der **Gemüsestand, ̈e** vegetable stand
gemütlich cozy, comfortable,
    pleasant, genial

genau   exact, precise

genauso   in the same way;
   just as, the same as

genießen, genoß, genossen
   to enjoy

genug   enough; —— haben
   to have enough

genügen (*dat., impers.*)   to satisfy,
   be sufficient

die Geometrie   geometry

das Gepäck   luggage

gerade   just; straight;
   —— eben   just now

geradeaus   straight ahead

das Gerät, –e   equipment, tool,
   apparatus

das Gericht, –e   court; dish

gering   little, few

gern   gladly, with pleasure; *like to*
   etwas —— tun   to be happy to
   do something

das Geschäft, –e   store, shop; business

der Geschäftsmann (*pl.*, die
   Geschäftsleute)   businessman

die Geschäftsreise, –n   business trip

geschehen, geschieht, geschah, ist
   geschehen   to occur, happen

die Geschichte, –n   story

der Geschmack, ⸚e   taste; liking;
   nach —— sein   to be to
   (one's) taste

die Geschmacksache, –n   matter of taste

die Gesellschaft, –en   society

gesetzlich   legal

das Gespräch, –e   talk, conversation

die Gestalt, –en   figure

gestern   yesterday; —— abend
   last night

gesund   healthy

die Gesundheit   health

das Gewicht, –e   weight

gewiß   certain, definite

das Gewitter, –   thunderstorm

die Gewitterwolke, –n   thundercloud

gewöhnlich   usual

gewöhnt sein an (+ *acc.*)   to be
   used to

der Gin, –s   gin

die Gitarre, –n   guitar

das Glas, ⸚er   glass

glauben (*dat.*)   to believe, think

gleich   right away; later; same;
   bis ——   see you later, till then

die Glocke, –n   bell

das Glück   happiness; fortune; luck;
   viel ——   good luck; zum ——
   luckily; —— haben   to be lucky

glücken (*dat., impers.*)   to succeed,
   be lucky *or* fortunate enough

glücklicherweise   fortunately

glücklich   happy

die Glückszahl, –en   lucky number

das Grad, –e   degree [*temperature*]

der Grad, –e   degree [*academic*]

die Grammatik, –en   grammar

grau   grey

greifen, griff, gegriffen   to grasp;
   —— nach *or* zu (+ *dat.*)   to reach
   for

die Grenze, –n   border; limit

der Grieche, –n   Greek (citizen)

griechisch (*adj.*)   Greek

der Grill, –s   grill

grillen   to grill

die Grippe, –n   flu

der Groschen, –   = ten Pfennig (coin)

groß   great; big; large

die Größe, –n   size

grün   green

der Grund, ⸚e   reason; aus diesem
   ——   for this reason

gründlich   fundamental, thorough

die Gruppe, –n   group

der Gruß, ⸚e   greeting

grüßen   to greet

günstig   favorable

gut   good; (*adv.*) well

H

das Haar, –e   hair

haben, hat, hatte, gehabt   to
   have; own

halb   half

die Halle, –n   hall; room

das Hallenbad, ⸚er   indoor swimming
   pool

der **Hals,** ⸚e neck
die **Halskette, –n** necklace
die **Halsschmerzen** (*pl.*) sore throat
  halten, hält, hielt, gehalten
    to stop; hold; —— **für** (+ *acc.*)
    to think of, consider; —— **von**
    (+ *dat.*) to think about, have
    an opinion of
die **Haltestelle, –n** stop
die **Hand,** ⸚e hand
die **Handarbeit, –en** handicraft
das **Händedrücken** handshaking
das **Handgepäck** hand luggage
  handgeschrieben handwritten
die **Handgranate, –n** hand grenade
die **Handtasche, –n** purse
  hängen, hing, gehangen to hang
  hart hard; (*adv.*) heavily
  häufig frequent
der **Hauptbahnhof,** ⸚e central
    railroad station
die **Hauptstadt,** ⸚e capital city
das **Haus,** ⸚er house; **nach Hause**
    gehen to go home;
    zu Hause sein to be at home;
    nach Hause bringen to take
    home
der **Hausbesitzer, –** house *or* property
    owner
die **Hausbesitzerin, –nen** (female)
    house *or* property owner
das **Häuschen, –** small house
das **Häusermeer, –e** sea of houses
die **Hausordnung, –en** house rule
die **Hauswirtin, –nen** landlady
die **Heimatstadt,** ⸚e home town
  heim • suchen to afflict
der **Heimweg, –e** way home
  heiraten to marry, get married
  heiß hot
  heißen, hieß, geheißen to be
    called
  heiter clear, bright
das **Heizöl, –e** heating oil, fuel
die **Heizung, –en** heating (system)
  helfen, hilft, half, geholfen
    (*dat.*) to help, assist
  hell bright, light
  her [*direction toward the speaker*] here

heran • gehen, –ging, ist
  –gegangen to approach, go near
heran • kommen, –kam, ist
  –gekommen to approach,
  come near
herauf • kommen, –kam, ist
  –gekommen to come up
heraus • kommen, –kam, ist
  –gekommen to come out
herb dry
her • bringen, –brachte,
  –gebracht to bring
der **Herbst, –e** fall, autumn
herein • kommen, –kam, ist
  –gekommen to come in
herein • lassen, –läßt, –ließ,
  –gelassen to let in
her • kommen, –kam, ist
  –gekommen to come here
der **Herr, –en** man; gentleman; Mr.
die **Herrin, –nen** lady
herrlich magnificent
her • stellen to produce, make,
  originate
herunter • kommen, –kam, ist
  –gekommen to come down
das **Herz, –en** heart
herzlich cordial
heulen to howl, roar; cry
heute today; —— **abend**
  tonight, this evening;
  —— **morgen** this morning
heutzutage nowadays
hier here; —— **oben** up here
hin [*direction away from the*
  speaker] there
hinauf • gehen, –ging, ist
  –gegangen to go up
hinaus • gehen, –ging, ist
  –gegangen to walk out
hin • bringen, –brachte, –gebracht
  to take there
hinein • lassen, –läßt, –ließ,
  –gelassen to let in
hinein • mischen to mix in
hinein • tragen, –trägt, –trug,
  –getragen to carry in
hin • fahren, –fährt, –fuhr, –ist
  –gefahren to drive there

hin·fallen, –fällt, –fiel, ist –gefallen to fall down
hin·hängen to hang there
sich **hin·setzen** to sit down
die **Hinsicht, –en** regard, respect;
    in dieser —— in this respect
hin·stellen to place *or* put there
hinter (+ *dat.* or *acc.*) behind
hinunter·gehen, –ging, ist –gegangen to go down
hinunter·sehen, –sieht, –sah, –gesehen to look down
hinzu·geben, –gibt, –gab, –gegeben to add
die **Hitze** heat
die **Hitzewelle, –n** heat wave
hoch (hoh–) high
das **Hoch, –s** high pressure (area)
die **Hochschule, –n** university, college
die **Hochschulreform, –en** university reform
die **Höchsttemperatur, –en** maximum temperature
hoffen to hope
hoffentlich hopefully
die **Hoffnung, –en** hope
(das) **Holland** Holland
der **Holländer, –** Dutchman
holländisch (*adj.*) Dutch
der **Honig** honey
hören to hear, listen;
    —— über to hear about
der **Horizont, –e** horizon
die **Hose, –n** pants, trousers
das **Hotel, –s** hotel
hübsch pretty
der **Hund, –e** dog
hundert (one) hundred
der **Hunger** hunger; **—— haben** to be hungry
hungrig hungry
husten to cough
der **Hut, ⸚e** hat

I

ideal ideal
die **Idee, –n** idea

ihr *and* **Ihr** (*poss.*) her; their; your (*pol.*)
die **Illustrierte, –n** illustrated magazine
immer always; **—— wieder** again and again; **—— schlimmer** worse and worse
in (+ *dat.* or *acc.*) in; into
indem (*sub. conj.*) by + *progressive*
die **Industrie, –n** industry
das **Industriegebiet, –e** industrial area
die **Inflation, –en** inflation
die **Information, –en** information
informieren to inform
der **Inka, –s** Inca
die **Innenstadt, ⸚e** city center
innerhalb (+ *gen.*) inside of, within
die **Insel, –n** island
das **Institut, –e** institute
das **Instrument, –e** instrument
intelligent intelligent
interessant interesting
das **Interesse, –n** interest
sich **interessieren für** (+ *acc.*) to be interested in
inzwischen meanwhile, in the meantime
irgendein any(one)
irgendwelche any, some
irgendwo anywhere
(das) **Irland** Ireland
der **Irrtum, ⸚er** error
(das) **Italien** Italy

J

ja yes
die **Jacke, –n** jacket, coat
jagen to chase, pursue; drive fast
das **Jahr, –e** year; **seit einigen Jahren** for several years; **vor einigen Jahren** several years ago
das **Jahrhundert, –e** century
der **Januar** January
(das) **Japan** Japan
der **Japaner, –** Japanese citizen
japanisch (*adj.*) Japanese
die **Jazz-Platte, –n** jazz record

jeder each, every; (*pl.*) all
jedoch however
jemand someone; anybody
jener that
jenseits (+ *gen.*) on that side of
der **Jet, –s** jet plane
jetzt now
der *or* das **Joghurt, –s** yogurt
(das) **Jugoslawien** Yugoslavia
der **Juli** July
jung young
der **Junge, –n** boy
der **Juni** June
der *or* das **Juwel, –en** jewel

K

der **Kaffee** coffee
die **Kaffee-Bar, –s** coffee bar
der **Kalender, –** calendar
(das) **Kalifornien** California
kalifornisch (*adj.*) Californian
die **Kalorie, –n** calorie
die **Kamera, –s** camera
der **Kamerad, –en** comrade, fellow
der **Kamin, –e** fireplace
kämmen to comb;
    sich —— to comb [oneself]
der **Kampf, ⁼e** fight, battle
kämpfen to fight
der **Kandidat, –en** candidate
der **Kanzler, –** chancellor
kapieren to grasp, get (the idea)
kaputt broken, damaged,
    out of order
der **Karate-Schlag, ⁼e** karate chop
die **Karte, –n** card; ticket
die **Kartoffel, –n** potato
der **Käse** cheese
die **Kasse, –n** cashier's desk
der **Katalog, –e** card catalogue
die **Kathedrale, –n** cathedral
der **Kauf, ⁼e** purchase
kaufen to purchase, buy
kaum hardly
kegeln to bowl
kein no; not a; not any
keineswegs not at all, by no means

der **Keller, –** cellar, basement
kennen, kannte, gekannt to know,
    recognize, be acquainted with
kennen・lernen to meet, get to
    know
der **Kerl, –e** chap, guy
das **Kilo, –s** *abbrev.* for **Kilogramm**
das **Kilogramm, –e** kilo, kilogram
das **Kind, –er** child
das **Kindchen, –** small child
das **Kino, –s** movie theater
der **Kinobesuch, –e** visit to the
    movies
die **Kinokasse, –n** movie theater
    ticket counter
die **Kirche, –n** church
die **Kirchenglocke, –n** church bell
das **Kirschwasser** Kirsch
    [cherry liquor]
die **Kiste, –n** box, chest
der **Klang, ⁼e** sound
klappen (*impers.*) to work out,
    function
klar clear
die **Klasse, –n** class
die **Klassenkameradin, –nen**
    (female) classmate
das **Kleid, –er** dress
klein little, small
das **Kleingeld** cash, coins
klingeln to ring; **es klingelt**
    the doorbell rings
knallen to bang, crack
der **Knoblauch** garlic
das **Kochbuch, ⁼er** cookbook
kochen to cook; boil
die **Kochgelegenheit, –en** cooking
    facilities
der **Koffer, –** suitcase
der **Kollege, –n** colleague
das **Komma, –s** comma
kommen, kam, ist gekommen
    to come; **zu Besuch ——**
    to come for a visit
der **Kommissar, –e** police inspector,
    commissioner
der **Komponist, –en** composer
die **Kommunikation, –en**
    communication

die **Konferenz, –en** meeting,
  conference
konfus confused
der **König, –e** king
die **Konkurrenz** competition
der **Konkurrenzkampf, ̈e** competitive
  battle
können, kann, konnte, gekonnt
  to be able to, can
konstruieren to construct, build
die **Kontrolle, –n** control, inspection
das **Konzert, –e** concert
korrigieren to correct
kosten to cost
krank sick, ill
die **Krankheit, –en** sickness
die **Krawatte, –n** tie
die **Kreditkarte, –n** credit card
das **Kreditkartensystem, –e** credit
  card system
der **Kreis, –e** circle
die **Kreuzung, –en** intersection
der **Krieg, –e** war
der **Kriegsfall, ̈e** case of war
der **Krimi, –s** *abbrev.* for
  Kriminalroman
die **Kriminalpolizei** plainclothed
  criminal investigation police
der **Kriminalroman, –e** mystery novel,
  detective story
die **Krise, –n** crisis
(das) **Kuba** Cuba
die **Küche, –n** kitchen
der **Kuchen, –** cake
der **Kuckuck, –s** cuckoo; **zum ——**
  mit to hell with
der **Kugelschreiber, –** ballpoint pen
kühl chilly, cool
die **Kultur, –en** culture
das **Kulturmagazin, –e** culture
  magazine
sich **kümmern um** (+ *acc.*) to take
  care of
der **Kunde, –n** customer
die **Kunst, ̈e** art; fine arts
die **Kunst-Akademie, –n** academy of
  art
der **Künstler, –** artist

das **Kunstwerk, –e** piece of art
der **Kurs, –e** course
kurz short; (*adv.*) for a short time;
  vor kurzem a short time ago
kürzlich recently; shortly
der **Kuß, ̈sse** kiss
küssen to kiss
die **Küste, –n** coast
(das) **Kuweit** Kuwait

L

lachen to laugh
der **Laden, ̈** shop, store
die **Lampe, –n** lamp
das **Land, ̈er** country, land
die **Landebahn, –en** runway
landen ist *or* **hat gelandet** to land
die **Landeshauptstadt, ̈e** capital
  (of a country *or* state)
das **Landesmuseum, –en** national
  museum
die **Landeswährung, –en** national
  currency
die **Landschaft, –en** scenery, landscape
die **Landung, –en** landing
lang (*adj.*) long
lange for a long time
langhaarig long haired
langsam slow
der **Langschläfer, –** late riser
  [*lit.*, long sleeper]
längst long ago; for a long time
langweilig boring
lassen, läßt, ließ, gelassen
  to let, permit; **sich ——**
  to have *or* get (something) done;
  laß mal sehen let's see
laufen, läuft, lief, ist
  gelaufen to run
laut loud
leben to live, reside
das **Leben** life
die **Lebenskosten** (*pl.*) cost of living
lecker tasty, delicious
ledig single
legen to put, place, lay

der **Lehrer,** – teacher
die **Lehrerin, –nen** (female) teacher
leicht light; easy
leid tun, tat, getan (*dat.*) to be
sorry, feel sorry for
leider unfortunately; —— **nicht**
unfortunately not
leise quiet, soft
sich **leisten** (*dat.*) to afford
der **Leiter,** – head, manager, director
lernen to learn
lesen, liest, las, gelesen to read
der **Leser,** – reader
der **Leserbrief, –e** letter to the editor
letzt– last
leuchten to shine, beam
die **Leute** (*pl.*) people
das **Licht, –er** light
lieb dear
lieben to love
lieber rather, preferably
der **Liebesroman, –e** love story
liefern to deliver
die **Lieferung, –en** delivery
liegen, lag, gelegen to lie, be
situated
die **Limousine, –n** limousine
die **Linie, –n** line; figure
links left; **nach** —— to the left
der **Liter,** – liter
die **Literatur, –en** literature
die **Loge, –n** private box
der **Logenplatz, ⸗e** box seat
der **Lohn, ⸗e** wages, salary
sich **lohnen** (*impers.*) to be worthwhile
lösen to solve
los·fahren, –fährt, –fuhr, ist
–gefahren to depart, leave
los·gehen, –ging, ist –gegangen
to begin
der **Löwe, –n** lion
die **Luft, ⸗e** air
der **Luftpirat, –en** [airplane] hijacker
die **Lust, ⸗e** pleasure; desire;
—— **haben zu** (+ *inf.*) to
have a desire to; **keine** ——
haben zu (+ *inf.*) to have
no desire to

M

machen to make; **macht nichts**
it doesn't matter
das **Mädchen,** – girl
das **Magazin, –e** magazine
der **Magen, ⸗** stomach
der **Mai** May
mal sometime, once; ever;
jedes Mal every time;
zum erstenmal for the first
time; **laß** —— **sehen** let's see
once; **ein andermal** another time
malen to paint, draw
man someone; you, they; people
mancher many a; (*pl.*) some,
several
der **Mann, ⸗er** man
das **Mannequin, –s** model
die **Mannschaft, –en** team
der **Mantel, ⸗** (over)coat
die **Mark** *unit of German currency*
der **Markt, ⸗e** market
der **Martini, –s** martini
der **März** March
die **Maschine, –n** machine; carrier,
airplane
die **Masern** (*pl.*) measles
die **Medizin** medicine
das **Meer, –e** ocean, sea
mehr more; —— **als** more than
mehrere (*pl.*) several
mein (*poss.*) my
meinen to mean
die **Meinung, –en** opinion;
deiner —— **sein** to agree with
you
meist– most; **meistens** mostly; usually
die meisten most people
melancholisch melancholic, sad
die **Menge, –n** quantity; lot; crowd;
great number
der **Mensch, –en** man, human being;
von Menschen geschaffen
man-made
der **Mercedes,** – *German automobile*
merken to notice
messen, mißt, maß, gemessen
to measure

die **Metall-Industrie, –n** metal
    industry
der **Metallknopf, ⸚e** metal button
das **Meter, –** meter
die **Methode, –n** method
die **Miete, –n** rent
    mieten to rent
die **Milch** milk
    mild mild
der **Millionär, –e** millionaire
die **Minute, –n** minute
    mischen to mix, blend
    mit (+ *dat.*) with; by means of
    mit · bringen, –brachte, –gebracht
        to bring along
    mit · machen to participate in
    mit · nehmen, –nimmt, –nahm,
        –genommen to take along
der **Mittag, –e** noon; **zu** —— at
    noon; **mittags** (every) noon;
    zu —— **essen** to have lunch
das **Mittagessen, –** lunch
die **Mitte, –n** middle, center
das **Mittel, –** means
das **Mittelgebirge, –** central
    mountain range
das **Mittelmeer** Mediterranean Sea
die **Mitternacht** midnight
    mittler– medium, central
der **Mittwoch, –e** Wednesday
die **Möbel** (*pl.*) furniture
das **Möbelgeschäft, –e** furniture store
    möchten (*see* **mögen**) to like to
das **Modell, –e** model, pattern
    modern modern
    mögen, mag *or* **möchte, mochte,**
        gemocht to like, like to
    möglich possible; **soviel wie** ——
    as much as possible
    möglicherweise possibly
der **Moment, –e** moment; —— **mal**
    just a moment
der **Monat, –e** month
    monatlich monthly, per month
der **Mond, –e** moon
der **Montag, –e** Monday
der **Mord, –e** murder
die **Mordkommission, –en**
    homicide squad

der **Morgen, –** morning; **morgens** in
    the morning
    morgen tomorrow; **bis** —— until
    tomorrow; by tomorrow
das **Motiv, –e** motif, theme
    müde tired
das **Museum, –en** museum
das **Museumsviertel, –** museum
    district
die **Musik** music
    musizieren to make music,
    play an instrument
    müssen, muß, mußte, gemußt to
    have to, must

N

    na (*interj.*) well; —— **und?**
    so what?
    nach (+ *dat.*) after; to, toward;
    according to
    nachdem (*sub. conj.*) after
    nach · denken, –dachte, –gedacht
    to contemplate
die **Nachkriegszeit, –en** postwar
    period
der **Nachmittag, –e** afternoon;
    morgen nachmittag tomorrow
    afternoon; **nachmittags** in the
    afternoon
der **Nachname, –n** last name
die **Nachricht, –en** message;
    (*pl.*) news
    nächst– next, closest;
    nächste Woche next week
der **Nächste (ein Nächster), –n**
    the next one
die **Nacht, ⸚e** night
    nah(e) near, close
der **Name, –n** name
    nämlich namely; because
die **Nase, –n** nose
    naß wet
der **Nationalsport** national sport
    natürlich natural(ly), of course;
    unaffected(ly)
    neben (+ *dat.* or *acc.*) beside
    nehmen, nimmt, nahm,
    genommen to take

die **Neigung, –en** inclination; chance;
    eine —— zu a tendency to;
    a chance of
nein no
nennen, nannte, genannt
    to name, call
nervös nervous
nett nice, kind
neu new
der **Neubau, –ten** new building
(das) **Neuengland** New England
das **Neujahr** New Year's Day
neulich recently
neun nine
nicht not
nichts nothing; **—— als**
    nothing but
der **Niederschlag, ⸚e** precipitation
nieder · schlagen, –schlägt,
    –schlug, –geschlagen to knock
    down
nie(mals) never
niemand nobody
noch still, yet; **—— ein** another;
    —— einmal once again;
    —— nie never before
(das) **Norddeutschland** Northern
    Germany
nördlich (+ *gen.*) *or* **—— von**
    (+ *dat.*) northern, north of
der **Nordwesten** Northwest
normal normal, regular
das **Normalbenzin** regular gasoline
notieren to note; **sich ——** (*dat.*)
    to take down
nötig necessary
notwendig necessary
der **November** November
die **Nummer, –n** number
das **Nummernschild, –er** license plate
nun now; well; **—— ja** well then
nur only

O

ob (*sub. conj.*) whether
oben above, over; **hier ——** up
    here
der **Ober, –** waiter

ober– upper
obgleich (*sub. conj.*) although
das **Objekt, –e** object
obschon (*sub. conj.*) although
das **Obst** fruit
obwohl (*sub. conj.*) although
oder (*coord. conj.*) or
offen open, frank
offensichtlich obvious
die **Offensive, –n** offensive
öffnen to open
oft often
ohne (+ *acc.*) without
der **Oktober** October
das **Öl, –e** oil; fuel;
    dreißiger —— thirty weight oil
die **Oper, –n** opera
operieren to operate
optisch optical
die **Orange, –n** orange
der **Orangensaft, ⸚e** orange juice
das **Orchester, –** orchestra
die **Ordnung, –en** rule, regulation;
    in —— it's all right
der **Ort, –e** place; town
örtlich local
ost– east
(das) **Ostern** Easter
(das) **Österreich** Austria
österreichisch (*adj.*) Austrian
östlich (+ *gen.*) *or* **—— von** (+ *dat.*)
    east of; eastern

P

das **Paar, –e** pair; couple;
    ein paar a few
die **Pädagogik** pedagogy, education
das **Pamphlet, –e** pamphlet
das **Papier, –e** paper
der **Papierkrieg, –e** red tape
    [paper war]
der **Paprika** paprika [*spice*]
der **Park, –s** park
parken to park
das **Parkett, –s** front-row stall
der **Parkplatz, ⸚e** parking spot
die **Parkuhr, –en** parking meter
der **Partner, –** partner

die **Partnerin, –nen** (female) partner
die **Party, –ies** party
der **Paß, ⸚sse** passport; mountain pass
der **Passagier, –e** passenger
das **Paßbild, –er** passport picture
die **Paßbildgröße, –n** size of a
    passport picture
    passieren, <u>ist</u> passiert (*dat., impers.*)
    to happen, occur
die **Paßkontrolle, –n** passport
    inspection
der **Patient, –en** patient
    pausenlos incessant, without
    stopping
der **Personalausweis, –e** identification
    card
    pessimistisch pessimistic
der **Pfeffer** black pepper
    pfeifen, pfiff, gepfiffen to
    whistle
der **Pfeil, –e** arrow
(das) **Pfingsten** Pentecost, Whitsunday
    pflegen to take care of, nurse
das **Pfund, –e** pound
der **Philosoph, –en** philosopher
die **Physik** physics
die **Pille, –n** pill
der **Pilot, –en** pilot
die **Pizza, –s** pizza
das **Plakat, –e** poster
    planen to plan
die **Platte, –n** record
der **Plattenspieler, –** record player
der **Platz, ⸚e** place; seat
    plötzlich suddenly
(das) **Polen** Poland
die **Politik** politics
der **Politiker, –** politician
die **Polizei** police
der **Polizeiwagen, –** police car
der **Polizist, –en** policeman
der **Porsche, –s** *German automobile*
die **Post** mail; post office
die **Postkarte, –n** postcard
die **Postleitzahl, –en** post office
    number, zip code
der **Präsident, –en** president
der **Preis, –e** price; prize
    prima wonderful, great

die **Probe, –n** test
    probieren to test, try; taste
das **Problem, –e** problem
das **Produkt, –e** product
der **Professor, –en** professor
das **Programm, –e** program
der **Prospekt, –e** brochure
das **Prosit** toast; **prost** cheers
der **Protest, –e** protest
    protestieren to protest
die **Provinz, –en** province
das **Prozent, –e** percent(age)
    prüfen to test, examine, check
die **Prüfung, –en** test, examination;
    eine —— ab·legen to take an
    examination; eine ——
    bestehen to pass an examination
das **Publikum** audience
der **Pudding, –s** pudding
der **Pullover, –** sweater
der **Punkt, –e** point, dot; **um ——**
    zwölf Uhr at twelve o'clock
    sharp
    pünktlich on time, punctual

Q

    quälen to torture; torment; annoy
die **Qualität, –en** quality
der **Quatsch** nonsense, rubbish
    quietschen to squeak, screech
die **Quittung, –en** receipt

R

das **Rad, ⸚er** bicycle; wheel
das **Radio, –s** radio
die **Radtour, –en** bicycle trip
der **Rasen, –** lawn, grass
    raten, rät, riet, geraten to guess;
    (*dat.*) to advise
das **Rathaus, ⸚er** city hall
der **Ratskeller, –** cellar in city hall
    [*used as a restaurant*]
der **Rauch** smoke
    rauchen to smoke;
    Rauchen verboten no smoking

der **Raum,** ⸚e   room, space
reagieren   to react
das **Recht,** –e   right, law
recht   rather, fairly; **ganz** ——
quite right; —— **gut**   quite well;
einem —— **geben**   to agree
that a person is right;
—— **haben**   to be right
rechts   right, on the right hand;
nach ——   to the right
rechtzeitig   on time, at the right
time
reden   to talk
reduzieren   to reduce
die **Reform,** –en   reform
das **Regal,** –e   shelf
der **Regen,** –   rain
der **Regenmantel,** ⸚   raincoat
der **Regenschirm,** –e   umbrella
der **Regisseur,** –e   [theatrical]
director
regnen   to rain
reiben, rieb, gerieben   to grate;
grind; rub
reich   rich
reichen   to pass, reach
der **Reifen,** –   tire
die **Reihe,** –n   row, series, line
die **Reinigung,** –en   (dry)cleaner's
die **Reise,** –n   trip, journey; **eine**
—— **wert sein**   to be worth
a trip
das **Reisebüro,** –s   travel agency
die **Reisegesellschaft,** –en   travel
agency
reisen   to travel
der **Reisepaß,** ⸚sse   passport
der **Reisescheck,** –s   traveler's check
das **Reiseziel,** –e   destination
der **Reiter,** –   knight; rider
rennen, rannte, ist gerannt
to run
die **Rennstrecke,** –n   race track
die **Reparatur,** –en   repair
die **Reparaturkosten** (*pl.*)   repair
cost(s)
reparieren   to repair
der **Reporter,** –   reporter
reservieren   to make reservations

die **Residenz,** –en   residence
der **Rest,** –e   rest, leftover(s)
das **Restaurant,** –s   restaurant
das **Resultat,** –e   result
revidieren   to revise
der **Revolver,** –   revolver
das **Rezept,** –e   recipe; prescription
der **Rhein**   Rhine River
die **Rheinbrücke,** –n   bridge over
the Rhine
das **Rheintal**   Rhine valley
der **Rheinwein,** –e   Rhine wine
richtig   right, correct; proper
das **Riegelhaus,** ⸚er   half-timbered
house
der **Riese,** –n   giant
der **Rock,** ⸚e   skirt
roh   raw
rollen   to roll
der **Roman,** –e   novel
die **Romantik**   romanticism
der **Romantiker,** –   romanticist
romantisch   romantic
die **Rose,** –n   rose
das **Röslein,** –e   little rose
rot   red
der **Rucksack,** ⸚e   rucksack, bag
rufen, rief, gerufen   to call, shout
die **Ruhe**   rest; quiet
rühren   to stir
das **Ruhrgebiet**   Ruhr valley
das **Rumpsteak,** –s   rump steak
der **Rundfunksender,** –   radio station
rundlich   plump

S

die **Sache,** –n   matter, thing;
das ist meine ——   that's
my concern
der **Safe,** –s   safety deposit box
der **Saft,** ⸚e   juice
sagen   to say
die **Sahne**   cream, whipped cream
der **Salat,** –e   salad; lettuce;
gemischter ——   mixed salad
das **Salz,** –e   salt
die **Sammlung,** –en   collection
der **Samstag,** –e   Saturday

der **Satz,** ⁼e sentence
sauber clean
die **Sauna, –en** sauna
die **Schachtel, –n** box
schade too bad, unfortunate
schaden (*dat.*) to harm, damage
der **Schäferhund, –e** German
   Shepherd, sheepdog
schaffen, schuf, geschaffen
   to make, build, create;
   von Menschen geschaffen
   man-made
der **Schalter, –** switch; counter
scharf sharp; spicy
schauen to look
das **Schaufenster, –** shop window
der **Schaufensterbummel, –**
   window shopping stroll
der **Scheck, –s** check
scheußlich awful, abominable
schicken to send
schieben, schob, geschoben
   to push, shove, glide
schießen, schoß, geschossen
   to shoot
das **Schiff, –e** ship, boat
das **Schild, –er** sign
schlafen, schläft, schlief, geschlafen
   to sleep
das **Schlafzimmer, –** bedroom
schlank slim
schlecht bad
schließen, schloß, geschlossen
   to close, lock; conclude
schließlich finally, after all
schlimm bad; **nicht so ——** it's
   not so bad; **immer schlimmer**
   worse and worse
das **Schloß,** ⁼sser castle; lock
der **Schluß,** ⁼sse end; conclusion
der **Schlüssel, –** key
schmecken to taste;
   es schmeckt it tastes good
der **Schmuck** jewelry; decoration
der **Schnaps,** ⁼e *any hard liquor*
das **Schnäpschen, –** a little bit of
   Schnaps
die **Schnapsidee, –n** crazy idea
die **Schnecke, –n** snail

das **Schneckentempo** snail's pace
der **Schnee** snow
schneiden, schnitt, geschnitten
   to cut
schnell quick, fast
die **Schnell-Reinigung, –en** express
   drycleaning service
der **Schnupfen, –** head cold, sniffles
der **Schock, –s** shock
die **Schokolade, –n** chocolate
(adv.
Probably) **schon** already; **—— einmal**
   once before, ever; **—— wieder**
   already, once again
schön pretty, beautiful
die **Schönheit, –en** beauty
(das) **Schottland** Scotland
der **Schrank,** ⁼e cupboard; closet
schreiben, schrieb, geschrieben
   to write
die **Schreibmaschine, –n** typewriter
das **Schreibmaschinenpapier**
   typewriter paper
die **Schreibweise, –n** kind of writing;
   spelling
der **Schuh, –e** shoe
die **Schule, –n** school
die **Schülerin, –nen** (female) pupil
der **Schulkamerad, –en** fellow student
die **Schüssel, –n** bowl
die **Schwäche, –n** weakness; vice
schwarz black
die **Schweinshaxe, –n** pork shank
   or leg
der **Schweiß** perspiration
die **Schweiz** Switzerland
schwer difficult; heavy
die **Schwierigkeit, –en** difficulty,
   trouble
das **Schwimmbad,** ⁼er swimming pool
schwimmen, schwamm, ist
   geschwommen to swim
sechs six
der **See, –n** lake
die **See** sea, ocean
segeln to sail
sehen, sieht, sah, gesehen to see
sehr very; quite
sein, ist, war, ist gewesen to be
sein (*poss.*) his

seit (+ *dat.*) since; (*sub. conj.*)
  since, for [*temporal*]
seitdem (*sub. conj.*) since [*temporal*]
die **Sekretärin, –nen** (female)
  secretary
der **Sekt, –e** champagne
die **Sekunde, –n** second
selber (one)self
selbst (one)self; even
selbstgemacht homemade;
  made by hand
selten rare, seldom
das **Semester, –** semester
das **Seminar, –e** seminar, course
senden, sandte, gesandt to send
senden, sendete, gesendet
  to broadcast
der **September** September
die **Serie, –n** series
der **Service** service
servieren to serve
der **Sessel, –** armchair, easy chair
setzen to put, set; **sich ——** to sit
  down
die **Show, –s** show
sicher certain; safe
die **Sicherheit** security, safety
der **Sicherheitsbeamte, –n** security
  police (officer)
sieben seven
das **Silber** silver
der **Silvester(abend), –e** New Year's
  Eve
singen, sang, gesungen to sing
die **Sirene, –n** siren
sitzen, saß, gesessen to sit
der **Skandal, –e** scandal
skeptisch sceptical
der **Ski, –er** ski
das **Skigebiet, –e** ski area
der **Skihang, ⸚e** ski slope
das **Skilaufen** skiing
der **Skiurlaub, –e** ski vacation
so so, thus; I see; **—— ... wie**
  as ... as; **—— etwas** something
  like that
sobald (*sub. conj.*) as soon as
so daß (*sub. conj.*) so that
das **Sofa, –s** sofa

sofort right away, at once
sogar even
der **Sohn, ⸚e** son
solange (*sub. conj.*) as long as
solche (*pl.*) such
solch (ein) such (a)
sollen to be supposed to, shall
der **Sommer, –** summer
sondern (*coord. conj.*) but, on the
  contrary
der **Sonderzug, ⸚e** special train
der **Sonnabend, –e** Saturday
die **Sonne** sun
sonnig sunny
der **Sonntag, –e** Sunday
sooft (*sub. conj.*) as often as
sonst otherwise, else; **—— noch**
  etwas? anything else?
die **Sorge, –n** worry, grief; **keine ——**
  don't worry; **sich Sorgen machen**
  um to worry about
das **Souvenir, –s** souvenir
soviel as much, so much; **—— wie**
  möglich as much as possible
sowie (*adv.*) as well as; (*sub.*
  conj.) as soon as
die **Sowjetunion** Soviet Union
die **Soziologie** sociology
spät late; **zu —— kommen** to
  come too late
(das) **Spanien** Spain
der **Spanier, –** Spaniard
spanisch (*adj.*) Spanish
spannend exciting, tense, thrilling
sparen to save [something]
der **Spargel, –** asparagus
der **Spaß, ⸚e** fun, joke; **—— machen**
  to have fun; **viel —— haben**
  to have a good time
spät late; **wie —— ist es?**
  what time is it?; **zu —— kommen**
  to be (too) late
der **Spaziergang, ⸚e** walk;
  einen —— machen to take
  a walk
spazieren · gehen, –ging, ist
  –gegangen to walk
die **Speise, –n** meal, food
die **Speisekarte, –n** menu

der **Sperrsitz, –e** orchestra seat
die **Spezialität, –en** specialty
der **Spiegel, –** mirror
das **Spiel, –e** game, match
　spielen to play
die **Spielzeit, –en** time of playing;
　　sports season
das **Spital, ⸚er** (*Swiss*) hospital
der **Sport** sport(s); **aktiv —— treiben**
　　to be active in sports
das **Sportsmodell, –e** sports car
die **Sprache, –n** language
　sprachlich linguistic, oral
der **Sprachunterricht** language
　　teaching
　**sprechen, spricht, sprach, gespro-
　chen** to speak; —— **über** (+ *acc.*)
　　to speak about, discuss
　springen, sprang, <u>ist</u> gesprungen
　　to jump, leap
der **Staat, –en** state, nation
der **Staatsanwalt, ⸚e** district attorney
das **Staatseigentum** state property
das **Staatsexamen, –ina** state
　　examination [*for the equivalent
　　of an M.A. degree*]
　stabil solid, stable, steady
das **Stadion, –en** stadium
die **Stadt, ⸚e** city, town
das **Stadtbild, –er** character of a city
die **Stadtmitte, –n** city center
der **Stadtplan, ⸚e** city map
die **Stadtrundfahrt, –en** city
　　sightseeing tour
das **Stadttheater, –** city theater
das **Stadttor, –e** city gate
der **Stadtverkehr** city traffic
der **Stand, ⸚e** stand; position
　ständig always, constant,
　　regular, permanent
der **Star, –s** star
　stark strong
die **Stärke, –n** thickening agent;
　　strength, power
die **Startbahn, –en** runway
　statt (+ *gen.*) instead of
　statt · finden, –fand, –gefunden
　　to take place
die **Statue, –n** statue

das **Steak, –s** steak
　stehen, stand, gestanden to stand
　**stehen · bleiben, –blieb, <u>ist</u>
　–geblieben** to stop
　stehlen, stiehlt, stahl, gestohlen
　　to steal
der **Stein, –e** stone, rock
das **Steinchen, –** little stone
die **Stelle, –n** place, position
　stellen to put, place
die **Stellung, –en** position, job
　**sterben, stirbt, starb, <u>ist</u>
　gestorben** to die
die **Stereo-Anlage, –n** stereo set
die **Steuer, –n** tax
die **Stewardess, –en** stewardess
die **Stille** silence
　stimmen (*impers.*) to be right,
　　correct; agree
　stinken, stank, gestunken to
　　stink, smell foul
das **Stipendium, –en** stipend,
　　scholarship, grant
die **Stirn, –en** forehead, brow
　stoppen to stop
die **Story, –ies** story
das **Strafmandat, –e** ticket (for a
　　violation)
das **Sträßchen, –** little street
die **Straße, –n** street, road
die **Straßenbahn, –en** streetcar
die **Straßenbahnhaltestelle, –n**
　　streetcar stop
die **Strecke, –n** tract, area; route,
　　stretch
das **Streichholz, ⸚er** match
der **Streik, –s** strike
die **Struktur, –en** structure
das **Stück, –e** piece
der **Student, –en** student
das **Studentenparlament, –e** student
　　administration
die **Studentin, –nen** (female) student
das **Studienjahr, –e** year of study
der **Studienplatz, ⸚e** place to study
　studieren to study
das **Studio, –s** (broadcasting) studio
das **Studium, –ien** study
der **Stuhl, ⸚e** chair

die **Stunde, –n** hour

suchen to search, look for

der **Süden** south

südlich (+ *gen.*) *or* —— **von**
(+ *dat.*) south of, southern

die **Suppe, –n** soup

süß sweet

die **Süßigkeit, –en** sweet, candy

das **Symptom, –e** symptom

das **System, –e** system

T

die **Tablette, –n** pill, tablet

der **Tag, –e** day; **guten** —— hello;
jeden —— every day

der **Tageslauf, ⸚e** course of the day

täglich daily

der **Tank, –s** tank

tanken to fill up, refuel

die **Tankstelle, –n** gas station

der **Tankstellenbesitzer, –** gas
station owner

der **Tankwart, –e** gas station
attendant

tanzen to dance

das **Taschenmesser, –** pocket knife

die **Tasse, –n** cup

die **Tatsache, –n** fact; data

tatsächlich in fact, indeed, really

tauchen to dive, dip

der **Taucher, –** diver

das **Taxi, –s** cab, taxi

der **Taxifahrer, –** cab driver

die **Taxifahrerin, –nen** (female)
cab driver

der **Tee** tea

der **Teelöffel, –** teaspoon

**teil·nehmen, –nimmt, –nahm,
–genommen an** (+ *dat.*)
to participate in

das **Telefon, –e** telephone

das **Telefongespräch, –e** telephone
conversation

telefonieren to telephone

der **Teller, –** plate

die **Temperatur, –en** temperature;
die —— **liegt um** — **Grad** the
temperature is about — degrees

der **Teppich, –e** rug, carpet

der **Termin, –e** date

die **Terrasse, –n** terrace

teuer expensive

(das) **Texas** Texas

das **Theater, –** theater

das **Thema, –en** theme, subject, topic

tief deep

das **Tief, –s** low pressure (area)

tippen to type

der **Tisch, –e** table

das **Tischlein, –** small table

der **Titel, –** title

das **Titelbild, –er** front page picture;
title page

tja well

der **Toast, –e** toast

die **Tochter, ⸚** daughter

die **Toilette, –n** restroom, toilet

toll crazy, wild, great

die **Tomate, –n** tomato

das **Tonbandgerät, –e** tape recorder

das **Tor, –e** gate, goal; **ein** ——
schießen to score a goal

der **Torwart, –e** goalie

der **Tourist, –en** tourist

tragen, trägt, trug, getragen
to carry; wear

die **Tramschiene, –n** (*Swiss*) streetcar
track

die **Träne, –n** tear

der **Treffpunkt, –e** meeting place

treiben, trieb, getrieben to push,
force; impel; **aktiv Sport** ——
to be active in sports

der **Trend, –s** trend

die **Treppe, –n** stairs

trinken, trank, getrunken
to drink

trotz (+ *gen.*) in spite of

tschüß so long, later, bye-bye

tüchtig efficient, capable

tun, tut, tat, getan to do

der **Tunnel, –s** tunnel

die **Tür, –en** door

die **Türkei** Turkey

der **Typ, –en** type

die **Tschechoslowakei** Czechoslovakia

U

übel bad, evil; **nicht ——** not
  bad; **mir ist ——** I feel sick
  to my stomach
über (+ *dat.* or *acc.*) over;
  (+ *acc.*) across, about,
  concerning
überall everywhere
sich überarbeiten to overwork
  oneself
überholen to pass
sich überlegen (*dat.*) to think about
übermorgen day after tomorrow
überprüfen to examine, check
überqueren to cross
überraschen to surprise
die Überraschung, **–en** surprise
übersetzen to translate
überwiegend predominant
überzeugen to convince
üblich usual, general
übrigens by the way; moreover
die Übung, **–en** exercise
die Uhr, **–en** watch; clock;
  um wieviel —— (at) what time
der Uhrmacher, **–** watchmaker
um (+ *acc.*) around, at
der Umlaut, **–e** *vowel modification*
um · schalten to switch over
um · steigen, **–stieg,** ist **–gestiegen**
  to change [trains, buses, etc.]
die Umweltverschmutzung pollution
  [of the environment]
unabhängig von (+ *dat.*)
  independent of
unbedingt necessarily, absolute,
  without fail, by all means
und (*coord. conj.*) and
unerträglich unbearable
der Unfall, **–̈e** accident
unfreundlich unkind, unfriendly
ungeduldig impatient
ungefähr about, approximately
ungesund unhealthy
unglücklich unhappy; **—— sein**
  to be unhappy
die Universität, **–en** university
unmöglich impossible

unpopulär unpopular
unser (*poss.*) our
unsozial unsocial
unten down below, beneath;
  da —— down there
unter (+ *dat.* or *acc.*) under;
  among
unterdessen meanwhile
unter– lower
die Untergrundbahn, **–en** (*abbrev.*
  U-Bahn) subway
sich unterhalten, unterhält, unterhielt,
  unterhalten to discuss, talk;
  —— über (+ *acc.*) to talk about
die Unterhaltung, **–en** talk,
  conversation; **eine —— führen**
  to have a talk
der Unterricht instruction; lesson
der Unterschied, **–e** difference
unterschreiben, unterschrieb,
  unterschrieben to sign (by name)
die Unterschrift, **–en** signature
untersuchen to examine, check;
  investigate, inspect
die Untersuchung, **–en** test,
  examination; research
unterwegs on the way
der Urlaub vacation
die Urlaubsreise, **–n** vacation trip
die Ursache, **–n** reason, cause
die USA (*pl.*) USA, United States
utopisch utopian

V

die Vase, **–n** vase
der Vater, **–̈** father
die Verabredung, **–en** date,
  appointment
sich verabschieden (von + *dat.*)
  to say good-bye, take leave (from)
verändern to change, alter
verantwortlich responsible
verbieten, verbot, verboten
  to forbid; **Rauchen verboten**
  no smoking
verbinden, verband, verbunden
  to connect
verbrauchen to use, consume

verbreiten to spread, circulate
verbrennen, verbrannte,
   verbrannt to burn up
verbringen, verbrachte, verbracht
   to spend (time)
verdächtig suspicious
verdächtigen to suspect
die Verfolgung, –en pursuit
vergeblich in vain
vergessen, vergißt, vergaß,
   vergessen to forget
sich vergewissern to make sure
vergießen, vergoß, vergossen
   to pour out, shed
der Vergleich, –e comparison
vergleichen, verglich, verglichen
   to compare
verheiratet married
verhindern to prevent
verkaufen to sell;
   zum Verkauf for sale
der Verkehr traffic
verkehrt upside down; perverse
verlangen to demand, ask for
verlassen, verläßt, verließ,
   verlassen to leave (behind)
verletzen to hurt, harm; violate
sich verlieben to fall in love; —— in
   (+ acc.) to fall in love with
verlieren, verlor, verloren
   to lose; aus den Augen —— to
   lose sight of
der Verlobte, (ein Verlobter), –n
   fiancé
die Verlobte, –n fiancée
vermeiden, vermied, vermieden
   to avoid
die Vermietung, –en rent(ing)
vermissen to miss
das Vermittlungsbüro, –s rental agency
verpassen to miss, be late
sich verpflichten to oblige oneself
verrostet rusty
verrückt crazy, mad
verschieden different
das Versehen, – oversight; aus ——
   by mistake
versprechen, verspricht, versprach,
   versprochen to promise

der Verstand brains, intelligence
das Verständnis understanding;
   —— für etwas haben to
   understand or appreciate something
verstecken to hide
verstehen, verstand, verstanden
   to understand, comprehend;
   das versteht sich von selbst
   it goes without saying
verstören to trouble, agitate,
   irritate
versuchen to try
verteilen to distribute
vertragen, verträgt, vertrug,
   vertragen to digest, tolerate
vertrauen (dat.) to trust
verwöhnen to spoil
die Verzeihung pardon; ——, bitte
   pardon me, please
verzichten auf (+ acc.) to forgo,
   decline
viel much, (pl.) many; —— mehr
   much more
vielleicht perhaps
vier four
vierhundert four hundred
viertel fourth, quarter
das Viertel, – fourth, quarter
die Viertelstunde, –n quarter hour
vierzehn fourteen
vierzig forty
der Virus, –en virus
das Visum, –a visa
der Vogel, ⁀ bird
das Volkslied, –er folk song
der Volkswagen, – German automobile
voll full, packed; ——, bitte
   fill it up, please
völlig fully, quite, completely
das Vollkornbrot, –e whole wheat
   bread
die Vollpension, –en full board
von (+ dat.) by, from, of;
   —— mir aus that's fine with me;
   —— . . . nach from . . . to
vor (+ dat. or acc.) before, in
   front; (+ dat.) ago; —— allem
   especially, above all;
   bis —— kurzem until recently

die **Voralpen** (*pl.*) lower mountain range (north of the high alps in Switzerland)

vorbei · gehen, –ging, ist –gegangen to pass, go by

vor · bestellen to order in advance, make reservations

die **Vorbestellung, –en** advance order, reservations

der **Vorderreifen, –** front tire

der **Vorfall, ⁼e** incident

vorgestern day before yesterday

vor · kommen, –kam, ist –gekommen to occur

die **Vorlesung, –en** lecture

das **Vorlesungsverzeichnis, –se** course catalogue

der **Vormittag, –e** forenoon; **vormittags** in the forenoon

der **Vorname, –n** first name

sich **vor · nehmen, –nimmt, –nahm, –genommen** (*dat.*) to plan, intend; undertake

der **Vorsatz, ⁼e** intention, resolution

vor · schlagen, –schlägt, –schlug, –geschlagen to propose, suggest

vorsichtig careful, cautious

vor · stellen to introduce; **sich ——** to introduce oneself; **sich ——** (*dat.*) to imagine

der **Vorteil, –e** advantage

die **Vorwahl(nummer, –n)** area code

vor · zeigen, –zog, –gezogen to show

W

wachsen, wächst, wuchs, ist gewachsen to grow

die **Waffe, –n** weapon

der **Wagen, –** car, vehicle

wählen to elect; select, choose

während (+ *gen.*) during; (*sub. conj.*) while

wahr true

die **Wahrheit** truth

wahrscheinlich probably

die **Währung, –en** currency

der **Wald, ⁼er** forest

wandern to hike

wann when

warm warm

warnen to warn; **—— vor** (+ *dat.*) to warn of *or* about

die **Warnung, –en** warning

warten to wait; **—— auf** (+ *acc.*) to wait for

die **Wartezeit, –en** waiting time

das **Wartezimmer, –** waiting room

warum why

was (für ein) what (kind of a)

waschen, wäscht, wusch, gewaschen to wash; **sich ——** to wash oneself

die **Waschgelegenheit, –en** washing facilities; sink

das **Wasser, –** water

wechseln to (ex)change

die **Wechselstube, –n** currency exchange office

wecken to wake up

der **Weg, –e** way; **nach dem —— fragen** to ask directions

wegen (+ *gen.*) because of; due to

weg · legen to put aside

weg · stecken to put aside *or* away

weich soft

die **Weihnacht** *or* das **Weihnachten** Christmas

die **Weihnachtsferien** (*pl.*) Christmas vacation

weil (*sub. conj.*) because, since (causal)

der **Wein, –e** wine

die **Weinkarte, –n** wine list

weiß white

weit far, (*adv.*) widely

weiter further; **und so ——** and so on

weiter · fahren, –fährt, –fuhr, ist –gefahren to go on, drive on

weiter · gehen, –ging, ist –gegangen to go on, move on

weiter · reisen, ist weitergereist to travel on

welch (ein) what (a)

welcher which

die **Welt, –en** world

weltberühmt world famous

der **Weltmarkt**   world market

der **Weltmeister, –**   world champion

das **Weltmeisterschaftsspiel, –e**
    game for the world championship

die **Weltzeituhr, –en**   world clock
    [*showing the time in various cities
    of the world*]

wenden, wendete, gewendet
    to turn around

sich **wenden, wandte, gewandt an**
    (+ *acc.*)   to turn to

wenig (*adj.*)   little; **ein ——**
    several

wenige (*pl.*)   a few

wenn (*sub. conj.*)   if, when,
    whenever; **—— auch** (*sub. conj.*)
    even if

wer   who

die **Werbung**   advertising, publicity

werden, wird, wurde, <u>ist</u>
    geworden   to become

das **Werk, –e**   work

der **Wert, –e**   worth, value

wertvoll   valuable, precious

wesentlich   essential, substantial

west   west

der **Westen**   west [*direction*]

der **Western, –s**   Western (movie)

westlich (+ *gen.*) *or* **—— von**
    (+ *dat.*)   west of, western

das **Wetter**   weather

der **Wetterbericht, –e**   weather report

die **Wettervorhersage, –n**   weather
    forecast

wichtig   important

**widerstehen, widersteht,
    widerstand, widerstanden**
    (*dat.*)   to resist, oppose

wie (*sub. conj.*)   as, like; (*interrog.*)
    how; **—— bitte?**   how's that?
    what did you say?
        —— geht's?   how are you?

wieder   again; **immer ——**
    again and again; **nie ——**
    never again; **schon ——**   once
    again, already again

wiederholen   to repeat

das **Wiedersehen, –**   good-bye;
    reunion; **auf ——**   good-bye

wiegen, wog, gewogen   to weigh

das **Wiener Schnitzel, –**   veal cutlet

die **Wiese, –n**   meadow

wieso   why

wieviel   how much; (*pl.*) how
    many

wild   wild

der **Wille**   will, intention; **beim
    besten Willen**   with the best
    intentions

der **Wind, –e**   wind

winden, wand, gewunden
    to wind; **sich ——**   to meander

der **Winter, –**   winter

wirklich   really

die **Wirtschaft**   economy

die **Wirtschaftskrise, –n**   economic
    crisis

wissen, weiß, wußte, gewußt
    to know [a fact]

die **Wissenschaft, –en**   science;
    academic discipline

der **Wissenschaftler, –**   scientist;
    academician

der **Witz, –e**   joke, pun

wo   where

die **Woche, –n**   week

das **Wochenende, –n**   weekend

der **Wodka, –s**   Vodka

wofür   for what purpose

wohin   where (to)

wohl   probably; perhaps

wohnen   to live, reside

der **Wohnort, –e**   residence

die **Wohnung, –en**   apartment

das **Wohnviertel, –**   residential section

das **Wohnzimmer, –**   living room

wolkig   cloudy

wollen, will, wollte, gewollt
    to want to, intend to

das **Wort, ≃er**   word

wozu   what for, to what purpose

das **Wrack, –s**   wreck(age)

wunderbar   wonderful

sich **wundern**   to be amazed;
        —— über (+ *acc.*)   to be
    amazed at

wunderschön   wonderful, very
    beautiful

der **Wunsch,** ⸚e wish, desire
  wünschen to wish; **sich** ——
    (*dat.*) to desire
die **Wurst,** ⸚e sausage
  wütend furious

Z

die **Zahl, –en** number
  zählen to count
der **Zahn,** ⸚e tooth
der **Zahnarzt,** ⸚e dentist
  zehn ten
  zeigen to show, demonstrate,
    point out
die **Zeit, –en** time
die **Zeitschrift, –en** magazine
der **Zeitschriftenartikel, –**
    magazine article
die **Zeitung, –en** newspaper
der **Zeitungsstand,** ⸚e newspaper
    stand
das **Zelt, –e** tent
  zerstören to destroy
das **Zeug** stuff, thing
der **Zeuge, –n** witness
das **Ziel, –e** destination, goal
die **Zigarette, –n** cigarette
die **Zigarettenpackung, –en**
    cigarette pack(age)
die **Zigarre, –n** cigar
  ziemlich rather
das **Zimmer, –** room
  zögern to hesitate
der **Zoll,** ⸚e customs
der **Zollbeamte, –n** customs officer
die **Zollkontrolle, –n** customs
    inspection

  zu (+ *dat.*) to; (*adv.*) too; closed
die **Zubereitung, –en** preparation,
    cooking
der **Zucker** sugar
  zuerst at first
  zufrieden content, satisfied
der **Zug,** ⸚e train
  zu · greifen, –griff, –gegriffen
    to reach for
  zu · hören (*dat.*) to listen to
  zu · machen to close
  zu · nehmen, –nimmt, –nahm,
    –genommen to gain weight;
    increase
  zurück back
  zurück · fahren, –fährt, –fuhr, <u>ist</u>
    –gefahren to go back, return
  zurück · gehen, –ging, <u>ist</u>
    –gegangen to go back, return
  zurück · kommen, –kam, <u>ist</u>
    –gekommen to come back
  zurück · laufen, –läuft, –lief, <u>ist</u>
    –gelaufen to run back, go back
  zusammen together
der **Zuschauer, –** spectator
  zu · schicken (*dat.*) to send *or*
    mail to
  zu · sehen, –sieht, –sah, –gesehen
    to watch
  zu · steigen, –stieg, <u>ist</u>
    –gestiegen to get in, go on board
die **Zutaten** (*pl.*) ingredients
  zuviel too much
  zwanzig twenty
  zwei two
  zweihundert two hundred
die **Zwiebel, –n** onion
  zwischen (+ *dat.* or *acc.*) between
die **Zwischenlandung, –en** stopover
  zwölf twelve

ENGLISH-GERMAN

The English-German vocabulary lists only those English words or phrases required for translation of sentences from English to German or used as cues in certain exercises.

A

a ein, eine, ein

able, to be able können, kann, konnte, gekonnt

about ungefähr; über (+ *acc.*)

above über (+ *dat.* or *acc.*)

across über (+ *acc.*); —— **from** gegenüber (+ *dat.*)

after nach (+ *dat.*); (*sub. conj.*) nachdem

afternoon der Nachmittag, –e; **yesterday** —— gestern nachmittag

against gegen (+ *acc.*)

all alle; —— **the best** alles Gute

almost fast

although (*sub. conj.*) obgleich, obschon, obwohl

always immer

and (*coord. conj.*) und

architect der Architekt, –en

around um (+ *acc.*)

to **arrive** kommen, kam, ist gekommen; an · kommen, –kam, ist –gekommen

as if (*sub. conj.*) als ob; als wenn

to **ask** fragen; —— **about** fragen nach (+ *dat.*); **to** —— **each other** sich [*or* einander] fragen

as long as (*sub. conj.*) solange

as often as (*sub. conj.*) sooft

as . . . as so . . . wie

as soon as (*sub. conj.*) sobald, sowie

at an (+ *dat.*); bei (+ *dat.*)

away weg, fort

B

bad schlecht, schlimm

battle der Kampf, ⸚e

to **be** sein, ist, war, ist gewesen

because (*coord. conj.*) denn; (*sub. conj.*) da, weil

because of wegen (+ *gen.*)

beer das Bier, –e

before (*sub. conj.*) bevor, ehe; vor (+ *dat.* or *acc.*)

to **begin** beginnen; an · fangen, –fängt, –fing, –gefangen

beginning der Beginn; der Anfang, ⸚e

behind hinter (+ *dat.* or *acc.*)

beside neben (+ *dat.* or *acc.*)

to **believe** glauben (*dat.*)

to **belong to** gehören (*dat.*)

best das Beste; **all the** —— alles Gute

better besser

birthday der Geburtstag, –e

blind blind

bottle die Flasche, –n

to **build** bauen

business das Geschäft, –e

businessman der Geschäftsmann, *pl.* die Geschäftsleute

but (*coord. conj.*) aber; [*on the contrary*] sondern

butcher der Fleischer, –

to **buy** kaufen

by an (+ *dat.* or *acc.*); neben (+ *dat.* or *acc.*); von (+ *dat.*); (*sub. conj.*) indem

C

cab das Taxi, –s; —— **driver** der Taxifahrer, –

to **call** an · rufen, –rief, –gerufen; telefonieren

caller der Anrufer, –

camera die Kamera, –s

car   das Auto, –s; —— **rental
agency**   die Autovermietung, –en

card   die Karte, –n

to **cash**   ein·lösen

certainly   bestimmt, natürlich

cheese   der Käse

check   der Scheck, –s

child   das Kind, –er

Christmas   die Weihnacht *or* das
Weihnachten

clothes   die Kleidung

coffee   der Kaffee

cold   kalt

college   die Hochschule, –n; ——
reform   die Hochschulreform, –en

to **come**   kommen, kam, ist gekommen;
to —— **home**   nach Hause kommen

competition   die Konkurrenz

competitive battle   der
Konkurrenzkampf, ∸e

credit   der Kredit; —— **card**   die
Kreditkarte, –n; —— **card system**
das Kreditkartensystem, –e;
—— **system**   das Kreditsystem, –e

cup   die Tasse, –n

currency   die Währung, –en

to **cut**   schneiden, schnitt, geschnitten

D

day   der Tag, –e; **some** ——   eines
Tages; **twice a** ——   zweimal am
Tag

to **decide**   entscheiden, entschied,
entschieden; sich entschließen,
entschloß, entschlossen; **to** —— **on**
sich entscheiden für (+ *acc.*); sich
entschließen für (+ *acc.*)

discoverer   der Entdecker, –

district attorney   der Staatsanwalt, ∸e

diver   der Taucher, –

to **do**   tun, tat, getan

to **dress**   sich an·ziehen, –zog,
–gezogen

to **drink**   trinken, trank, getrunken

driver   der Fahrer, –

duck   die Ente, –n

during   während (+ *gen.*)

Dutchman   der Holländer, –

E

each   jeder, jede, jedes

Easter   (das) Ostern

to **eat**   essen, ißt, aß, gegessen

Europe   (das) Europa

even if   (*sub. conj.*) auch wenn

every   jeder, jede, jedes;
—— **day**   jeden Tag;
—— **weekend**   jedes Wochenende

everything   alles

excellent   ausgezeichnet

expensive   teuer

explorer   der Forscher, –

F

fall   der Herbst, –e

famous   berühmt

fat   dick

father   der Vater, ∸

finder   der Finder, –

fish   der Fisch, –e

flower   die Blume, –n

for   für (+ *acc.*); (*coord. conj.*) denn;
—— **which**   wofür

fresh   frisch

friend   der Freund, –e; (*female*)
die Freundin, –nen

from   aus (+ *dat.*); von (+ *dat.*)

to **fry**   braten, brät, briet, gebraten

fruit   das Obst

G

gas   das Benzin, –e; —— **station**
die Tankstelle, –n; —— **station
owner**   der Tankstellenbesitzer, –

German   (*adj.*) deutsch; (*noun*) der
Deutsche (ein Deutscher), –n

Germany   (das) Deutschland

to **get**   [*become*] werden, wird, wurde,
geworden; [*receive*] bekommen,
bekam, bekommen

to **get together**   zusammen·kommen,
–kam, ist –gekommen

to **get up** auf · stehen, –stand, ist
   –gestanden
   girl das Mädchen, –
to **give** geben, gibt, gab, gegeben (*dat.*)
to **go** gehen, geht, ging, ist gegangen;
   to —— home nach Hause gehen;
   to —— to work an die Arbeit
   gehen; arbeiten gehen
   good gut; **—— luck** viel Glück;
   —— bye auf Wiedersehen
   great wunderbar
   green grün

H

   hair das Haar, –e
   happy glücklich; **to be —— about**
   sich freuen über (+ *acc.*)
to **have** haben, hat, hatte, gehabt
to **have to** müssen, muß, mußte,
   gemußt
to **have something done** sich lassen,
   läßt, ließ, gelassen (*dat.*, + *inf.*)
   he er; **—— who** wer
   healthy gesund
to **hear** hören
   hello guten Tag
   her sie, ihr
   here hier
   herself sich, sie selbst
   him ihn, ihm
   himself sich, er selbst
   his sein
   home das Haus, ⸚er, **to come ——**
   nach Hause kommen; **to go ——**
   nach Hause gehen
   hospital das Krankenhaus, ⸚er
   how (*interrog. conj.*) wie

I

   I ich
   if (*sub. conj.*) wenn; **—— only**
   (*sub. conj.*) wenn . . . nur
to **imagine** sich vor · stellen (*dat.*)
   important wichtig
   in in (+ *dat.* or *acc.*)
   in case (*sub. conj.*) falls
   in front of vor (+ *dat.* or *acc.*)

   in order to um . . . zu
   in spite of trotz (+ *gen.*)
   inflation die Inflation, –en
   instead of statt, anstatt (+ *gen.*)
   intelligent intelligent
to **intend to** wollen
   interesting interessant
   into in (+ *acc.*)
to **introduce (someone)** vor · stellen;
   to —— oneself sich vor · stellen
   inventor der Erfinder, –
   it er, sie, es
   its sein, ihr

J

   juice der Saft, ⸚e

K

to **know (a fact)** wissen, weiß,
   wußte, gewußt; **to —— (someone)**
   kennen, kannte, gekannt; **to ——**
   (how to do something) können, kann,
   konnte, gekonnt

L

   last letzt-; **—— night** gestern abend
   later später; **see you ——** bis gleich
to **learn** lernen
to **leave** weg · gehen, –ging, ist
   –gegangen; **to —— by plane**
   ab · fliegen, –flog, ist –geflogen
   letter der Brief, –e
   less weniger
   like (*sub. conj.*) wie
to **like to** mögen/möchten, mag/möchte,
   mochte, gemocht; gern tun, tat,
   getan; **to —— most of all**
   am liebsten tun, tat, getan
   Lincoln der Lincoln, –s
   little klein; **a ——** ein wenig
to **look at** an · sehen, sieht, –sah,
   –gesehen; **to —— each other**
   sich an · sehen
   long lang; **so ——** bis gleich;
   tschüß; **for a —— time** lange
   (a) lot of viel

luck das Glück; **to be lucky**
Glück haben
luggage das Gepäck

M

man der Mann, ⸚er; der Mensch, –en
many viele
to **marry** heiraten
me mich, mir
meat das Fleisch
Mercedes der Mercedes, –
milk die Milch
Monday der Montag, –e;
on Mondays montags
money das Geld, –er
more mehr, lieber;
—— **than** mehr als
morning der Morgen, –;
this —— heute morgen
most meist-; —— **of all** am
meisten, am liebsten
my mein
myself mich, mir; ich selbst

N

name der Name, –n;
to be named heißen, hieß,
geheißen
nation die Nation, –en; das Land, ⸚er
national currency die
Landeswährung, –en
New Year's Day das Neujahr
New Year's Eve der
Silvester(abend, –e)
night die Nacht, ⸚e

O

oil das Öl, –e
old alt
Oldsmobile der Oldsmobile, –s
on auf (+ *dat.* or *acc.*), an (+ *dat.*
or *acc.*); —— **account of** wegen
(+ *gen.*)
one [*person*] man; einer, eine,
eines; [*number*] eins

only nur
opposition die Opposition, –en
or (*coord. conj.*) oder
orange die Orange, –en;
die Apfelsine, –n; —— **juice**
der Orangensaft, ⸚e
to **order** bestellen
our unser
ourselves uns; selbst
out aus (+ *dat.*)
outside of außer (+ *dat.*)
over über (+ *dat.* or *acc.*);
—— **there** da drüben
own eigen
owner der Besitzer, –

P

to **paint** malen
painting das Gemälde, –
paper das Papier, –e
pardon die Verzeihung;
—— **me** Verzeihung, bitte
parents die Eltern (*pl.*)
passport der Paß, ⸚sse;
—— **picture** das Paßbild –er;
—— **picture size** die
Paßbildgröße, –n
to **pay, be worthwhile** (*impers.*)
sich lohnen; **it doesn't pay**
es lohnt sich nicht
Pentecost (das) Pfingsten
permit erlauben (*dat.*); **to be per-
mitted to** dürfen, darf, durfte,
gedurft
picture das Bild, –er; das Gemälde, –
to **play** spielen
please bitte
to **possess** besitzen, besaß, besessen
to **prefer to** lieber tun, tat, getan
pudding der Pudding, –s
pupil (*fem.*) die Schülerin, –nen
purse der Geldbeutel, –
to **put on** an · ziehen, –zog, –gezogen

Q

quite ziemlich; ganz

R

to **read**   lesen, liest, las, gelesen
really   wirklich, eigentlich
to **recommend**   empfehlen, empfiehlt,
   empfahl, empfohlen
reform   die Reform, –en
to **remain**   bleiben, blieb, ist geblieben
to **remember**   sich erinnern an (+ *acc.*)
rental   die Vermietung, –en
to **repair**   reparieren
restaurant   das Restaurant, –s
right away   gleich, sofort

S

salad   der Salat, –e
to **say**   sagen
scientist   der Wissenschaftler, –
to **see**   sehen, sieht, sah, gesehen;
   —— **you later**   bis gleich
semester   das Semester, –
to **send**   schicken, senden
she   sie
to **shop**   einkaufen; Einkäufe machen
since   (*sub. conj.*) [*temporal*] seit;
   [*causal*] da, weil; (*as prep.*, + *dat.*)
   seitdem
to **sit down**   sich hin · setzen
size   die Größe, –n
to **sleep**   schlafen, schläft, schlief,
   geschlafen
small   klein
so   so; —— **long**   tschüß; bis gleich;
   auf Wiedersehen
some   etwas; —— **day**   eines Tages
something   etwas
so that   (*sub. conj.*) damit, so daß
Spaniard   der Spanier, –
to **speak**   sprechen, spricht, sprach,
   gesprochen
to **spend** (**money**)   aus · geben, –gibt,
   –gab, –gegeben
spicy   scharf
spring   der Frühling, –e; **in** ——
   im Frühling
station   die Haltestelle, –n
street   die Straße, –n

streetcar   die Straßenbahn, –en;
   —— **stop**   die
   Straßenbahnhaltestelle, –n
student   der Student, –en
stuff   das Zeug
such (**a**)   solch (ein)
suppose, to be supposed to   sollen
sure   gewiß
sweet   süß
to **swim**   schwimmen, schwamm, ist
   geschwommen
system   das System, –e

T

to **take**   nehmen, nimmt, nahm, genommen; **to** —— **off**   aus · ziehen,
   –zog, –gezogen; **to** —— **a walk**
   spazieren · gehen, –ging, –gegangen
to **talk**   sprechen, reden; —— **about**
   sprechen über (+ *acc.*); reden über
   (+ *acc.*)
to **tell**   sagen, erzählen
than   als
to **thank**   danken (*dat.*);
   thank you   danke;
   thank you very much   vielen Dank
that   jener, jene, jenes; der, die
   das; (*sub. conj.*) daß
the   (*def. art.*) der, die, das
their   ihr
them   sie, ihnen
themselves   sich; sie selbst
then   dann
there   da, dort
these   diese
they   sie
thing   das Ding, –e; die Sache, –n;
   das Zeug
to **think**   denken, dachte, gedacht;
   glauben (*dat.*)
this   dieser, diese, dieses
through   durch (+ *acc.*)
time   die Zeit, –en;
   more ——   mehr Zeit;
   what —— **is it?**   wieviel Uhr ist es?
to   zu (+ *dat.*); an (+ *acc.*);
   auf (+ *acc.*)

together zusammen

to **travel** reisen, ist gereist

traveler der Reisende (ein Reisender), –n

traveler's check der Reisescheck, –s

trip die Reise, –n

trout die Forelle, –n

twice zweimal

two zwei; **the ——** die beiden

typewriter die Schreibmaschine, –n; **—— paper** das Schreibmaschinenpapier

U

under unter (+ *dat.* or *acc.*)

to **undress** sich aus · ziehen, –zog, –gezogen

unhappy unglücklich; **to be ——** unglücklich sein

unique einmalig

until (*sub. conj.*) bis (*as prep.*, + *acc.*)

up to bis zu (+ *dat.*)

us uns

USA die USA; (das) Amerika

V

vacation der Urlaub; **—— trip** die Urlaubsreise, –n

very sehr

W

to **wait** warten; **—— for** warten auf (+ *acc.*)

walk der Spaziergang, ⁼e

to **walk** gehen, ging, ist gegangen; zu Fuß gehen; **to take a ——** spazieren · gehen

wallet der Geldbeutel, –

to **want to** möchten, mochte, gemocht; wollen, will, wollte, gewollt

warm warm

to **wash** waschen, wusch, gewaschen; **to —— oneself** sich waschen

to **watch** sich an · sehen, –sieht, –sah, –gesehen (*dat.*); sich an · schauen (*dat.*)

we wir

weather das Wetter

week die Woche, –n

weekend das Wochenende, –n

well gut

what (a) welch (ein)

what(ever) was

what kind of (a) was für (ein)

when (*sub. conj.*) wenn, als; (*interrog.*) wann

whenever (*sub. conj.*) wenn auch, wenn immer

whether (*sub. conj.*) ob

which der, die, das; was

while (*sub. conj.*) während (*as prep.*, + *gen.*)

white weiß

Whitsunday (das) Pfingsten

who(ever) wer

whom wen, wem

whose wessen

wine der Wein, –e

to **wish** wünschen

to **wish to** wollen; möchten

with mit (+ *dat.*); bei (+ *dat.*)

without ohne (+ *acc.*)

woman die Frau, –en

work die Arbeit, –en

worker der Arbeiter, –; (*fem.*) die Arbeiterin, –nen

world famous weltberühmt

worse schlimmer

to **write** schreiben, schrieb, geschrieben

Y

yesterday gestern; **—— afternoon** gestern nachmittag

yet noch

you (*fam. sing.*) du, dich, dir; (*fam. pl.*) ihr, euch; (*pol.*) Sie, Ihnen

your (*fam. sing.*) dein; (*fam. pl.*) euer; (*pol.*) Ihr

you're welcome bitte

yourself (*fam. sing.*) dich, dir; selbst; (*fam. pl.*) euch, selbst; (*pol.*) sich, selbst

Index

ILLUSTRATION CREDITS

Edith Reichmann, Monkmeyer Press Photo Service, New York: pp. 2, 14, 118, 141, 154, 194, 235
    bottom, 290, 318, 328, 343, 356, 358, 369, 398, 407, 424
Carolyn Watson, Monkmeyer: p. 15
Courtesy Liberaler Hochschulverband, Münster: p. 19
Courtesy German Information Center, New York: pp. 24, 26, 42, 56, 78, 91, 102, 104, 119, 140,
    167, 226, 244, 254, 260, 342, 413, 418, 428
Joseph Roter: pp. 30–32, 46/47, 142/143, 149, 185, 189, 301, 303/304
Sybil Shelton, Monkmeyer: p. 34
Courtesy Haus Neuerburg GmbH, Köln: p. 38
Inge Poschmann: pp. 53, 135
Photo Jan Lukas: pp. 60, 146
Michal Heron, Monkmeyer: p. 62
Wolf Gewehr: pp. 67, 70, 114, 132, 151, 163, 181, 196, 239, 279, 280, 284, 302, 306, 314, 319, 329
Foto Krautwasser, Stuttgart: p. 73
Courtesy Isolde Merker: pp. 96/97
Courtesy Westfälische Provinzial-Feuersozietät, Münster: p. 100
Hannoversche Allgemeine Zeitung *and* Peter Leger: p. 111
Courtesy Austrian National Tourist Office, New York: pp. 122, 206, 220, 386
Courtesy Fremdenverkehrsverband München-Oberbayern e.V.: pp. 130/131
Courtesy Dr. Tigges-Fahrten, Wuppertal (Orts- u. Hotelbeschreibungen aus den Reiseprospekten):
    p. 139
Fritz Henle, Monkmeyer: p. 172
Courtesy Swiss National Tourist Office, New York: pp. 177, 179, 186, 201, 216, 266, 336
Courtesy Großversandhaus Quelle Gustav Schickedanz KG, Fürth/Bayern: p. 185
Courtesy Kurfürsten-Warenversand GmbH, 5 Köln 60, Niehler Gürtel 102: p. 202
DIE ZEIT, Hamburg: p. 209, 341
Artisan Photographers, Inc.: p. 232
Courtesy Hermann Schroedel Verlag KG, Hannover (taken from SPRACHE UND SPRECHEN
    5): p. 235 top
Courtesy W. Bertelsmann Verlag KG, Bielefeld: pp. 236/237
Courtesy Westfälische Wilhelms-Universität, Münster (Formular der Westfälischen Wilhelms-
    Universität für Anträge ausländischer und staatenloser Bewerber auf Zulassung zum Studium
    für nicht zulassungsbeschränkte Fachrichtungen): pp. 242/243
Courtesy Restaurant Stuhlmacher: p. 255
Hoffmann und Campe Verlag, Hamburg (Matthaeus Merian „München" aus DIE SCHÖNSTEN
    STÄDTE BAYERNS c Hoffmann und Campe Verlag, Hamburg, 1964): p. 289
Courtesy Verlag Aschendorff, Münster (entnommen aus der im Verlag Aschendorff in Münster
    erscheinenden Tageszeitung „Westfälische Nachrichten", Ausgabe Freitag, 10. Mai 1974):
    p. 312
Courtesy Department of German, University of Southern California (taken from REPORT ON
    THE FIRST GERMAN SEMESTER, p. 92): p. 333
Courtesy ALTMANN, Institut für wissenschaftliche Partnerwahl, Hamburg: p. 334
Courtesy Brauerei Isenbeck AG, Hamm (taken from BÄDERMAGAZIN DEUTSCHLAND Nr.
    13, 1973): p. 340
Courtesy Deutscher Sportbund, Frankfurt am Main: p. 348
Courtesy BILD, Verlagsleitung, Hamburg *and* Deutscher Wetterdienst, Hamburg: p. 351
Courtesy Gregorio de la Gala: p. 365
Deutsche Fotothek, Dresden: p. 374
Klaus Pause, Pollingen/Obb.: p. 390
Eastfoto, New York: pp. 392/393
Courtesy Roy Blumenthal International Associates, Inc., New York: p. 402
Courtesy interRent, Hamburg: p. 421

Layout by Renate Hiller

Color photographs by Jan Lukas pp. i, ii, iii, iv, x, xi, xvi; Austrian National Tourist Office, p. ix

Cover design by William Yenne

NÖRDLICHES

Barentssee

EISMEER

GRÖNLAND
(dän.)

Nordkap

○ Murmansk

*Weißes
Meer*

○ Archangelsk

○ Reykjavik   ISLAND

A T L A N T I S C H E R   O Z E A N

S O W J E T U N I O N

○ Bergen

Russische S.F.S.R.

Wolga

Oslo ○

○ Leningrad

Helsinki ○

○ Moskau

○ Stockholm

Estnische
S.S.R.

Schottland
GROSS-

Nordirland ○

○ Göteborg

Lettische
S.S.R.

Glasgow ○

NORDSEE

DÄNEMARK

Riga ○

BRITANNIEN

○ Kopenhagen

Litauische
S.S.R.

○ Dublin
IRLAND

England

Wales

○ Birmingham

London ○

Der Kanal

NIEDERLANDE

Amsterdam ○

Hamburg ○

Berlin ○

R.S.F.S.R.

Minsk ○

Weißrussische
S.S.R.

Warschau ○

Kiew ○

P O L E N

Brüssel ○
BELGIEN

DEUTSCHLAND

Bonn ○

Ukrainische S.S.R.

Krakau ○

○ Frankfurt

Rhein

Prag ○

LUXEMBURG

TSCHECHOSLOWAKEI

Odessa ○

Paris ○

München ○

Moldauische
S.S.R.

Wien ○

Budapest ○

Cluj ○

Loire

Bern ○
SCHWEIZ

ÖSTERREICH

UNGARN

RUMÄNIEN

FRANKREICH

Lyon ○

Zagreb ○

Bukarest ○

Turin ○ Mailand ○

Po

Belgrad ○

Donau

*Schwarzes
Meer*

Bordeaux ○

Golf von Biscaya

Marseille ○

I T A L I E N

J U G O S L A W I E N

BULGARIEN

Sofia ○

TÜRKEI

Bilbao ○

ANDORRA

Adriatisches Meer

Tirana ○
ALBANIEN

PORTUGAL

Madrid ○

Barcelona ○

Korsika

Rom ○

Neapel ○

GRIECHENLAND

Lissabon ○

Tajo

SPANIEN

Valencia ○

Balearen

Sardinien

Athen ○

Sevilla ○

Palermo ○ Sizilien

Kreta

Gibraltar
(br.)

M I T T E L L Ä N D I S C H E S

○ Rabat
MAROKKO

Oran ○

Algier ○

Tunis ○

MALTA

M E E R

TUNESIEN

Bengasi ○

A L G E R I E N

Tripolis ○

L I B Y E N

A F R I K A

EUROPA

KEGELPROJEKTION

MEILEN

0   100   200   300   400

KILOMETER

0   100   200   300   400

Staatshauptstädte .... ○

Staatsgrenzen ....

Provinzgrenzen ....

Kanäle ....

ATLAS

Deutschland · Österreich · Schweiz

® Copyright HAMMOND INCORPORATED,
Maplewood, N.J. Printed in U.S.A.

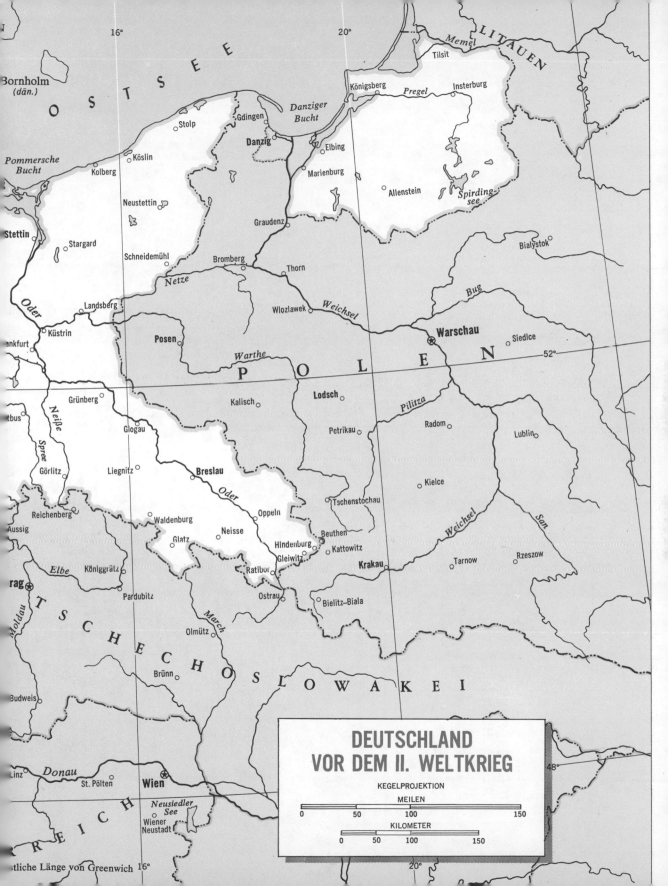

DEUTSCHLAND
VOR DEM II. WELTKRIEG

KEGELPROJEKTION

MEILEN

0   50   100   150

KILOMETER

0   50   100   150

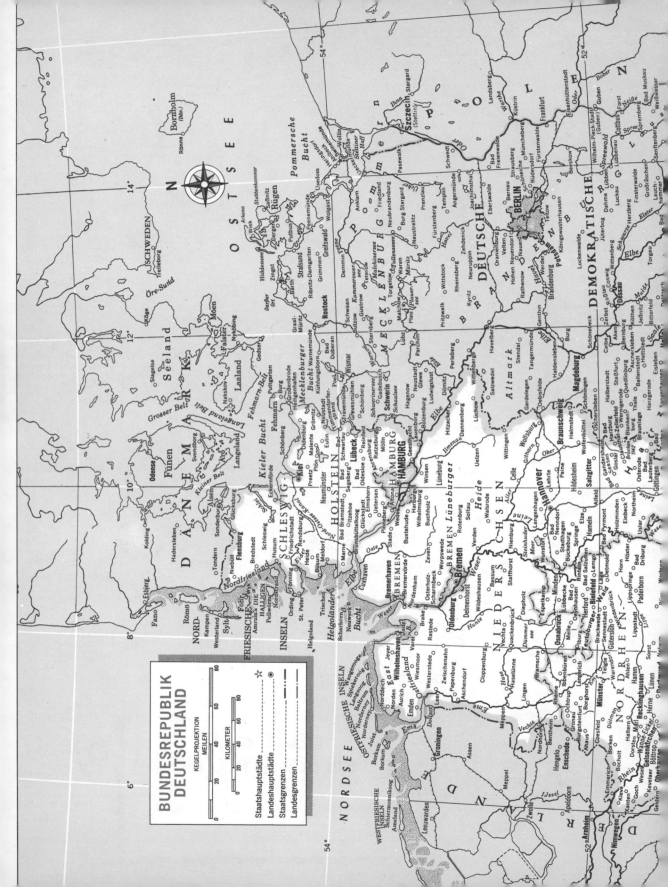

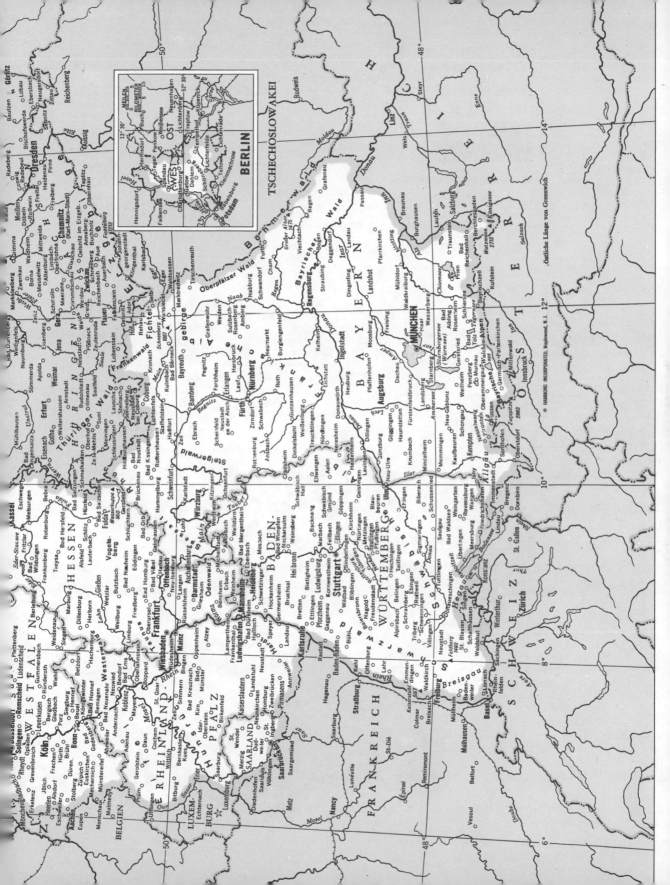

DEUTSCHLAND
Topographie

MEILEN
0 20 40 60 80
KILOMETER
0 20 40 60 80

Gebirge Hochland Tiefland Depression Wasser

Höhen in Meter

SCHWEDEN

DÄNEMARK

OSTSEE

Bornholm
(dän.)

Fehmarn

Rügen

Mecklenburger
Bucht

Pommersche
Bucht

NORDSEE

Nordfriesische In.

Helgoland

Nord-Ostsee
Kanal

Müritz

Ostfriesische In.

Hamburg

Elbe

Norddeutsches Tiefland

NIEDERLANDE

Bremen

Ems

Aller

Havel

Berlin

Oder

P
O
L
E
N

Mittelland

Hannover

Kanal

Weser

Spree

52°   52°

Rhein

Brocken
1142

Elbe

Ruhr

Harz

Saale

Leipzig

Neiße

Düsseldorf

Schiefergebirge

Fulda

Köln

Bonn

Lahn

Thüringer Wald

Erzgebirge

BELGIEN

Rheinisches

Eifel

Taunus

Werra

Rhön

Frankfurt

TSCHECHOSLOWAKEI

Main

LUXEM-
BURG

Mosel

Hunsrück

Nürnberg

Fränkische Alb

Böhmerwald

Saar

FRANKREICH

Stuttgart

Schwarzwald

Neckar

Schwäbische Alb

Donau

Alpenvorland

Isar

Donau

München

Inn

48°   48°

Rhein

Feldberg
1493

Bodensee

Iller

Lech

Chiemsee

A   l   p   e   n

Zugspitze
2963

SCHWEIZ

LIECHTEN-
STEIN

ÖSTERREICH

© Copyright HAMMOND INCORPORATED

8°   12°

Östliche Länge von Greenwich

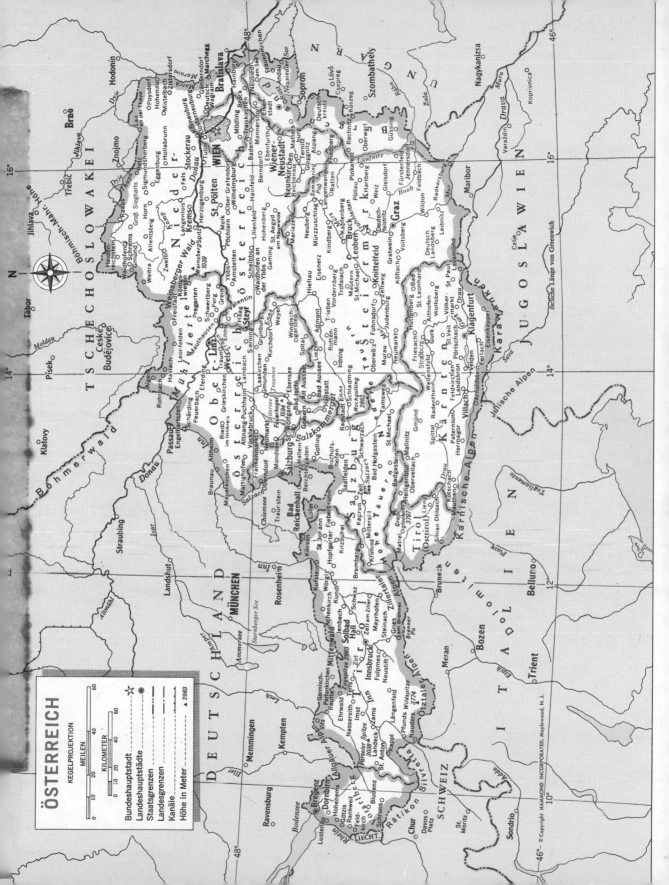

ÖSTERREICH

KEGELPROJEKTION

MEILEN

KILOMETER

Bundeshauptstadt	✶
Landeshauptstädte	◉
Staatsgrenzen	....
Landesgrenzen	._._._._
Kanäle	_____
Höhe in Meter	▲ 2963

© Copyright HAMMOND INCORPORATED, Maplewood, N.J.

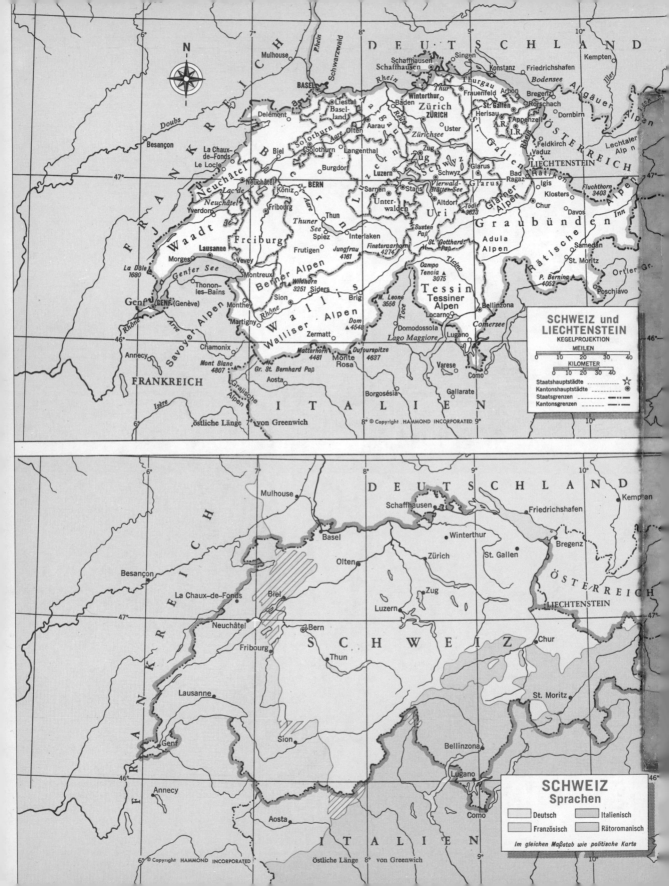

SCHWEIZ und LIECHTENSTEIN

KEGELPROJEKTION

MEILEN

0   10   20   30   40

KILOMETER

0   10   20   30   40

Staatshauptstädte .... ☆
Kantonshauptstädte .... ⊛
Staatsgrenzen .... ▄▄▄▄
Kantonsgrenzen .... ▄▄▄▄

SCHWEIZ
Sprachen

Deutsch	Italienisch
Französisch	Rätoromanisch

Im gleichen Maßstab wie politische Karte